EXPLORING BRITAIN'S
CHURCHES
& CHAPELS
INSPIRATIONAL JOURNEYS OF DISCOVERY

Commissioning Editor: Paul Mitchell
Internal repro: Sarah Montgomery
Cartography provided by the Mapping Services Department of AA Publishing
Colour separation by AA Digital Department
Production: Stephanie Allen

Produced by AA Publishing
© Copyright AA Media Limited 2011

Design and editorial by Creative Plus Publishing Limited
www.creative-plus.co.uk

With thanks to
Compilers: Mic Cady, Julia Brittain, Sue Joiner

For the National Churches Trust: Project coordinator: Charlotte Walshe
For Creative Plus Publishing Ltd
Publishing director: Beth Johnson   Editorial manager: Annette Love
Picture research: Claire Coakley   Design manager: Gary Webb
Designers: Suzie Bacon, Kirsty Poole   Editor: Corrine Ochiltree
Proof reader: Dawn Bates   Research: Jane Tranter
Indexer: Marie Lorimer

With special thanks to the estate of G Southwell
for photographic contributions.

ISBN: 978-0-7495-7074-3 (T) and 978-0-7495-7119-1 (SS)

Published by AA Publishing (a trading name of AA Media Limited, whose registered office is Fanum House,
Basing View, Basingstoke RG21 4EA; registered number 06112600).

Contains Ordnance Survey data © Crown copyright and database right 2011.

A04145

Printed in Dubai by Oriental Press

theAA.com/shop

Opposite page: *Memorial to Lord and Lady Milton, Milton Abbey, Dorset.*

EXPLORING BRITAIN'S
CHURCHES
& CHAPELS
INSPIRATIONAL JOURNEYS OF DISCOVERY

CONTENTS

*This page: All Saints, Ladbroke, Warwickshire (top);
St Nicholas, Newbury, Berkshire (below).*
Opposite page: *St Peter-on-the-Wall, Bradwell-on-Sea,
Essex (left); Hexham Abbey, Tyne and Wear (right).*

VISITING THE CHURCHES

The information supplied to the compilers of this book has come as much as possible from contributors who live near, or know, the churches and chapels. Included in each entry are directions to help the visitor: sometimes a church is in the centre of a town or village and, by its nature, easy to find. At other times it may be tucked away. In all cases the editors have endeavoured to give helpful advice as well as postcodes for people who have satellite navigation systems.

The contributors have given information on churches that are, to the best of their knowledge, open during the day. However, it is recommended that visitors check church websites – most are found easily on the internet – and phone ahead where possible to check that opening times have not changed. When searching on the web, check that the website is of the correct dedication: most towns have more than one church. Some useful websites are listed on page 252.

ABOUT THE NATIONAL CHURCHES TRUST

Britain's churches, chapels and meeting houses are an integral element of the nation's heritage and landscape. An unparalleled mix of history, architecture, art and spirituality, they form the centrepiece of thousands of towns and villages across the country. More than two-fifths of Christian places of worship in the UK are listed as of historic or architectural significance. Together they are an accessible and remarkable repository of heritage and art.

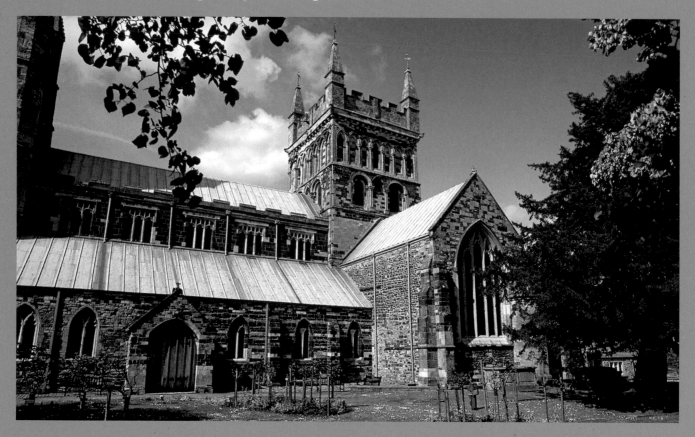

The National Churches Trust and its predecessor the Historic Churches Preservation Trust have, for almost 60 years, sought to help keep these important buildings alive. Independent of government and church authorities, the Trust provides support, advice and information to those caring for these buildings. This includes grants for building restoration and modernisation, support for local volunteer networks, and encouragement for these buildings to be open and of use to the wider community.

In delivering this support, the National Churches Trust works closely with the network of County Churches Trusts, which cover the majority of England. These charities, which are almost entirely dependent on volunteers, work to assist churches in their area through fundraising and grant-giving.

This book is a tribute to the knowledge and expertise of these Trusts and the buildings and tours they have selected. The Scottish Churches Architectural Heritage Trust, Scotland's Churches Scheme, the Heritage of London Trust

and the Friends of City Churches have similarly shared their knowledge of churches in Scotland and London. Furthermore, a selection of historic churches that have been closed to regular worship has also been included and those organisations that care for them – the Churches Conservation Trust (CCT), the Friends of Friendless Churches (FoFC) and the Historic Chapels Trust (HCT) – have contributed some of the best examples of these buildings.

This book brings together some of the finest of Britain's churches and chapels, explains why they are exceptional, what to look for and where to find them. The effort to protect and preserve these precious assets continues. Details for contacting the organisations involved can be found on page 252. Please visit **www.nationalchurchestrust.org** for more information about our work.

This page: Wimborne Minster, Dorset.

FOREWORD BY DAVID DIMBLEBY

If we have no sense of the past our sense of the present is diminished. Of the many gateways to our past the churches and chapels of Britain offer the most profound insights. Grand houses and castles may be more impressive but the simple parish church usually outdates them all.

I live in a Sussex hamlet right under the Downs. There are some traces of old houses, but nothing earlier than the 16th century. Our church, on the other hand, dates back to the mid-13th century and probably before that. Our first rector, Gervase, was worshipping here in 1226.

The church was described by Sir John Betjeman as 'ancient and rustic'. The entrance is along a short path, with banks of primroses on either side in spring, through a Victorian porch and down steps into a simple nave. It is cool, musty and a little damp. The white of the walls is broken only by the stone surrounds of the windows. On high days there are flowers on the windowsills and the altar. There are rows of seats at the back of the church but in front of them superior box pews, each with its own door. They date from the 18th century and still belong, as of right, to the grander houses in the hamlet. Undemocratic it may be but our church observes this tradition along with others. No Bible is read here except the King James Bible and no Matins or Holy Communion allowed except if it comes from the Book of Common Prayer. Woe betide a visiting priest who strays.

On Sundays there are usually 10 or 12 worshippers, friends who drink coffee together after the service is over and exchange a little light gossip. At any other time it is a tranquil place to pause and rest. I sometimes go in at the end of a walk across the Downs, along a chalk path through the woods until ahead of me I see the low wooden belfry, which seems to squat on the strong flint and stone walls of the church itself. Inside calm descends. The busy world really is hushed. I wander about transported through time by the tiny tomb of a child squeezed in sideways just by the chancel, and the two flamboyant memorials to a family long gone. They have left their mark with brilliantly coloured coats of arms and an inscription on one which reads like the perfect example of Christian virtue: 'She was one of the best of wives. Her devotion was constant and regular, her charity extensive, her conversation courteous and obliging. Godliness was her employment and heaven is her reward.'

Maybe this inscription was not entirely deserved but it gives an insight into the aspirations of a different era and a different way of thinking. I pause and reflect on what life must have been like then, in the 17th century, when this monument was erected, and all the centuries before, of the great host of people who have stood in this place and prayed and hoped for some sign of salvation or some respite from their cares and their pain. That is what is so thrilling about our churches and chapels – that they allow us, encourage us, to think back, to lose for a moment our obsession with our times and our troubles and put them in a wider context.

This book with more than 870 places chosen by those who love them, will help us explore our history, see many fine buildings and discover their secrets. Here they are waiting for you. Enjoy them.

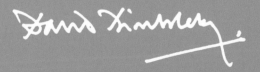

CHURCH HISTORY

Taken together, Britain's churches and chapels constitute one of the finest freely accessible collections of art and architecture in the world. With the earliest examples dating from the 7th century, they document more than a thousand years of styles, fashions, ways of worship and changing tastes in art and design.

Nowhere else in the world can you walk into a building that might contain a Saxon sculpture, a 13th-century brass memorial, 15th-century arches, 18th-century box pews, 19th-century stained glass designed by a famous pre-Raphaelite painter, and lovingly crafted kneelers made by today's parishioners.

Some of these buildings and their contents are among the greatest works of art anywhere and from any time. But among these astonishing riches there are always objects that remind us that churches and chapels were built and used by ordinary people, and that ordinary people often have thoughts other than holy. Humour and strangeness are often met in churches – perhaps in a carved misericord depicting a drunkard, or a couple at each other's throats on a carved bench-end.

Every aspect of human life is reflected somewhere, somehow, in our churches and chapels. Not surprising, since until very recently church and chapel were the focus of all aspects of life for most people: from birth to death; in sickness and in health; in good times and in the worst of times; in war and in peace.

These unique treasure houses are to be found throughout Britain, often seemingly forgotten, and often in settings that are quintessentially British. Indeed, one of the greatest pleasures of visiting such places can be the setting. Whether it dominates the high street of a bustling market town, is tucked by a hill on the outskirts of a sleepy village, or stands quite alone in a remote field, a church or chapel defines and refines the landscape it stands in. Indeed, if you want to discover a Britain that is often still astonishingly and wonderfully unspoiled, you could do worse than use this book as your guide.

This introduction gives a brief overview of the periods of church building and their characteristics; visiting a church or chapel can be a fantastic visual journey through the ages. Turn to pages 250–1 for a glossary of specialist terms found in this guide, plus diagrams of church layouts.

USING THIS BOOK

There are more than 45,000 churches and chapels in Britain. It would be impossible to include all of them in a book of this kind and it would not reflect our intentions, which are to guide the visitor to some of the best and most memorable Christian places of worship.

One of John Betjeman's rules for including a church in his book *Pocket Guide to English Parish Churches* is that it should be 'worth bicycling twelve miles against the wind to see'. We have not set the bar quite so high, or as physically demanding perhaps, but the idea is the same – the building and/or its contents as well as its setting have to be something genuinely special.

The tours
One of the unique aspects of this book is that the buildings are grouped together in such a way that you can plan a whole day – or two – of exploring, centred on one particularly outstanding key church. In this way, churches and chapels that are perhaps of themselves more modest are included so as to make a more complete tour of the area. The most outstanding or key building in the area is given prominence, as shown by its presence on the area map, followed by the other churches and chapels in the tour.

The selection
The buildings have been chosen primarily by local experts, basing their choices on their knowledge of the area, and these on-the-ground experts have provided as much information as possible from which the book has been compiled. Very often there are other churches in the area that by pure reason of space we cannot include; the best of these are featured in the 'Also in the area' panels at the end of a tour, with a handy indication of their merits.

Opening times
Generally, the churches and chapels in this book are open to all and at all reasonable times. If buildings are open at special times, we have noted this under 'Where'; see page 252 for some websites you can use to check before you visit. Practice changes, perhaps due to updated insurance demands or a new incumbent.

This page: *St Winnow, Cornwall. Like so many churches it is a beautiful building in a wonderful setting, and is packed with fascinating treasures. In St Winnow's case these include a superb collection of medieval bench-ends, stained glass from about 1500, and a lovingly restored rood screen.*

THE EARLIEST BRITISH CHURCHES

It was in the years after 312, when the Roman Empire adopted Christianity, that the earliest Christian buildings in Britain were built. Though no church of that time survives in Britain (such buildings have, however, been excavated here), the basic 'basilica' design formed the core of most subsequent churches.

Pre-Saxon churches

Basilicas were the aisled public halls or law courts that were a central feature of all Roman towns. Basilica-type churches were entered through a western porch, or narthex, which led to an open space, the nave, which was lit by high clerestory windows. At the eastern end, separated from the nave by an arch or triple arch, was an apse, or sanctuary, which contained the altar. The nave might have had side aisles, or transepts (each transept being called a porticus by the Romans). See page 250 for diagrams of typical church designs.

After the Roman legions left Britain in 410 such buildings gradually fell into disuse and the next generation of churches was built by missionaries. The followers of Saint Augustine landed on the Eastern coasts in the late 400s and built their wooden churches very much on the basilica model.

Followers of the 'Celtic' Church landed on the Western coasts and built much simpler wooden chapels consisting of one tiny room, called a cell. This room was where the missionary or priest prepared the mysteries of the communion. The congregation gathered outside this room to join in the service, and eventually built its own room – a nave – adjoining the cell, which became the chancel of the church. There was no seating, and sermons were rare.

None of these earliest post-Roman wooden churches survives, but the church of St Andrew at Greensted in Essex, has wooden walls that may date back to the 800s or 900s, making it the earliest still-standing wooden church in Europe.

The Synod of Whitby in 664 brought together the Roman, or Augustinian, Church and the Celtic Church, creating one English Church, and bringing a unified way of thinking about worship and church layouts to Saxon architecture.

Saxon churches

It is not uncommon to find Saxon, or partially Saxon, stone churches in England. Many churches that show few outward signs of Saxon work rest on Saxon foundations; many have concealed Saxon elements.

Examples of complete or nearly complete Saxon churches include Brixworth in Northamptonshire, built in the late 7th century and with many distinctive Saxon features including round-headed arches made with re-used Roman bricks.

Also in Northamptonshire is All Saints' Church, Earl's Barton, whose Saxon tower is the quintessence of Saxon architecture and decoration, with 'long-and-short' masonry at the corners, and long masonry 'pilaster' strips and patterns, all for decorative rather than structural effect. Earls Barton tower also has a classic round-headed Saxon two-light window with stubby supports called balusters. Another distinctive Saxon feature is windows with triangular heads, as can be seen at the church of St John the Baptist at Barnack, near Stamford, Cambridgeshire.

Saxon sculpture

There are few examples of complete Saxon and Celtic sculpture and internal ornament left, but enough remain to show that pre-Norman church art was highly sophisticated, assured and beautiful. It is distinguished from Norman carving by its fluid lines and classical feel, directly inspired by North African and Mediterranean art.

Outstanding is the cross shaft outside Bewcastle Church in Cumbria (below). Dating from the late 7th century, this is completely covered in intricate carvings that include animals, birds, plants, abstract designs and biblical figures. It is one of the great masterpieces of European art.

The centrepiece of many Saxon churches was a depiction of Jesus's Crucifixion, called a rood. Often this was made of wood, and none of these survive, but some were made in stone. Although all have been deliberately defaced (people were afraid of their power), there are still remarkable surviving fragments of some of these, such as at Romsey Abbey in Hampshire.

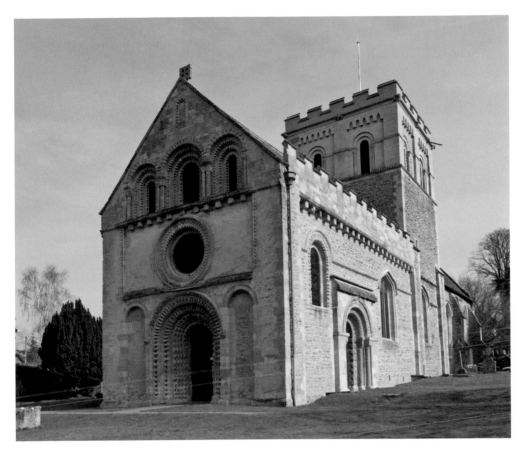

Round towers

There are more than 180 round church towers in England. Of those that remain, the vast majority are in Suffolk and Norfolk, such as that at Haddiscoe, Norfolk (*below*), with a few outliers including two in Berkshire. Experts differ as to the origins and dates of round towers, but some were certainly built in Saxon times. More are now thought to be early Norman.

Most are built of flint, and this seems the most convincing reason that they are round, as square flint structures are difficult to build without workable stone at the corners. Such stone was expensive because it had to be brought into the area, so round towers were easier and cheaper to build. They often escaped later rebuilding or changes because many are in small, remote villages that could not afford more ambitious towers.

A number of experts continue to believe that at least some of the round towers were built for defensive purposes, and cite the traces of doorways at first floor level where a ladder could be pulled up once the villagers were safely inside. Also, many round towers are built near to the sea or close to rivers – just the kind of places that would have been prone to a sudden waterborne attack by Viking raiders.

Norman churches

The Norman Conquest of 1066 changed the face and future of Britain. For churches, it often meant partial or wholesale rebuilding, as Norman architectural ideas, usually termed Romanesque, differed from Saxon ideals. The Normans preferred the basilica plan for their buildings, and often made much more substantial buildings than had the Saxons. The strength and solidity of much Norman church architecture accounts for the survival of so much of it – in later centuries whole churches might be rebuilt but the Norman doorways and arches were often retained, even if moved to a different part of the building.

Distinctive features of Norman architecture include rounded arches with recessed borders, often decorated with zig-zags, chevrons or beakheads (which look exactly as they sound). In some cases this decoration is extraordinarily ornate, as at Kilpeck in Herefordshire. Here, elsewhere in the county and across the country, the sculptors have taken their inspiration from Viking, Spanish and even Moorish motifs, resulting in a profusion of pattern and imagery. A feature of many Norman doorways is a tympanum carved in the space between the door lintel and the arch above it. Tympanums often depict biblical scenes, which sometimes incorporate vividly imagined mythical creatures.

Frequently, Norman church architecture is massive and without decoration, as in the many round pillars and piers still found in parish churches in England. Norman windows were small to begin with, but they advanced on Saxon architecture by having narrow mullions or uprights rather than the large balusters.

Opposite page: Altar in the Saxon church of St Laurence, Bradford-on-Avon, Wiltshire (left). *This page:* The Norman church at Iffley shows the solidity of the architecture (above); Kilpeck, tympanum, showing mythical creatures surrounding the arch (left).

GOTHIC ARCHITECTURE

In the last half of the 12th century there was a transition from the Romanesque style to the Gothic style that was to dominate British church architecture for several hundred years.

Early Gothic churches

This change began with the introduction of pointed arches. Far from being a mere decorative device, pointed arches are structurally much stronger than rounded arches, and enabled bigger, bolder churches to be built. The development of vaulting, happening at the same time, meant that roofs could be built of stone rather than of leak- and fire-prone wood or thatch. Stone roofs could be much less acutely pitched.

Windows became larger, and this encouraged the introduction of glass and stained glass; the stained glass often appearing in the form of brightly coloured medallions. Lancet windows, often in groups of three, are a distinctive feature of this Early Gothic or Early English style. Stonework became more elegant, with the appearance of complex mouldings and intricately carved piers and capitals.

Overall, the insides of churches became lighter and brighter, with sunlight from enlarged windows illuminating the wall paintings that were so popular throughout the 12th and 13th centuries. There were more ceremonies and ceremonial occasions happening in churches, resulting in the enlargement of many east ends, often to accommodate new altars to favoured saints and martyrs. Painted and sculpted screens of stone or wood separated the east end from the nave, which was often the scene of secular gatherings.

Outside, larger windows were very obvious, as were the buttresses and flying buttresses that supported vaulted roofs and thinner walls.

High Gothic churches

The period in church architecture that is traditionally known as Decorated developed seamlessly from the Early Gothic style and lasted for about a hundred years, from the middle of the 13th century until the 1370s.

The term 'Decorated' accurately and succinctly sums up the look and feel of the style: rich, intricate and elaborate detailing appeared everywhere, perhaps especially in windows and in complex vaulting. Window designs became ever more full of variety,

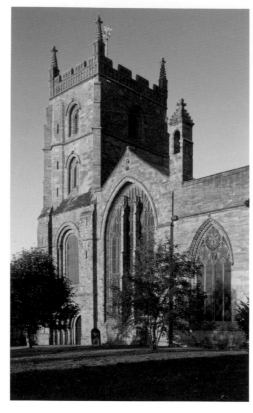

developing from circular, trefoil and interlaced lancet shapes into complex and filigree patterns that culminated in 'reticulated' windows, where repeated fluid patterns of interweaving stonework create an impression almost of stone flames.

A change in church activities during this period meant that more sermons were preached, resulting in the introduction of pulpits – at first very simple – from which the Word of God could be declaimed. Sermons meant longer services and this led to the introduction of seating in some churches. At first these were simple stone ledges along the walls, only later intruding into the open spaces of the nave.

Perpendicular style

This last great period of Gothic architecture, unique to Britain and lasting from the last third of the 14th century until the 1530s, includes what many consider the best of church building in Britain. As with the Decorated style, the term Perpendicular perfectly summarises aspects of this great age of construction.

Porches

For many parishioners the most directly important part of the church was the porch. Originally often built to provide protection against draughts penetrating inside the church, porches took on a life of their own, becoming the setting for marriages, legal dealings and much else besides. Later, small rooms were often built above the porches, as at Berkswell in Warwickshire (*below*), sometimes as lodging for a priest, or as school rooms or meeting rooms for the people of the parish.

This page: *St Peter and St Paul, Leominster, Herefordshire, showing the High Gothic south aisle window (centre); elaborately carved foliage on the pillars at Southwell Minster, Nottinghamshire (above).*

In fact the style had begun to emerge in the late 1340s, otherwise a cataclysmic era in British history: the plagues of that time, allied with repeated periods of atrocious weather, cut a swathe through the population, with perhaps as many as a third left dead. Entire villages were deserted and some towns left almost empty. Yet by the 15th century, England had recovered to become one of the most prosperous nations in Europe, with a wealth largely built upon the riches derived from the wool industry and advances in agriculture generally.

The 'wool' churches found across the country are a reflection of this wealth, and a burgeoning of creativity and building of churches as the merchants of the area put their money into outward and visible signs of their piety. In such churches you will find astonishing riches, from the great light-enabling windows down to details such as carvings on bench-ends, and from extraordinary and ever more elaborate fan vaulting to wooden roofs that incorporated the finest structural carpentry. There is also decoration in the form of such things as life-sized angels with wings outstretched.

Some churches were rebuilt, while others had new floors, towers, porches, chapels, rood lofts and screens, seating, monuments, sculpture and glowing stained glass. These churches must have

Vaults, ribs and fans

Originally, the ribs of vaulted ceilings were purely functional – their role being to support the ceiling. But by the 14th century ribs had taken on a decorative life of their own, with numerous longer ribs creating star-shapes, and shorter ribs – called lierne ribs – sub-dividing the star-shapes into yet more complex patterns. At the intersections of the ribs were placed decorative bosses, often carved and brightly painted.

In the early 15th century the uniquely English decoration called fan vaulting appeared, first at Gloucester Cathedral and then in many other churches and cathedrals (as in Sherborne Abbey, Dorset, *right*). At first the fans grew upwards and outwards, rather like symmetrical stone trees, but eventually fan vaults included astonishing drooping stone cones, hanging from the ceilings like delicate, hallucinatory stalactites.

been extraordinary to enter: celebrations of God in light, colour, carving and paint.

But changes in forms of service, the ways in which people thought about their relationship with God, and broader changes in society, as well as Henry VIII's Reformation, saw much of that glory swept away over the next two centuries.

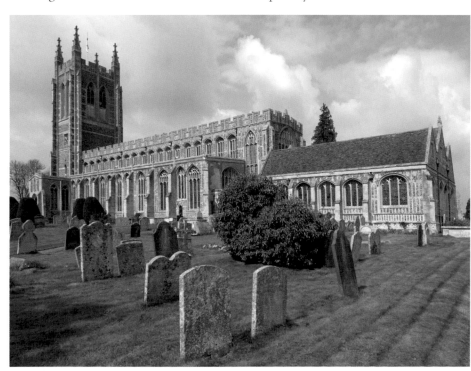

This page: A carving of St Catherine on the Spring Chapel Screen, Lavenham (above); exterior of Long Melford, a Perpendicular-style 'wool' church (left).

TUDOR AND JACOBEAN TIMES

It is difficult not to blame Henry VIII for the destruction in England's churches that began in 1536 and continued right the way through until the Commonwealth years in the 17th century. But although Henry formalised the deep changes going on in society with his Reformation, many scholars think that the end of the 15th century had in fact already seen the culmination of the great age of church building.

Tudor and Jacobean

The deep changes that Henry put in motion when he split with Rome had a profound and often catastrophic effect on church buildings. After 1534 virtually no churches were built for 100 years, although the day-to-day impact in most parishes was not noticeable at first.

The Dissolution of the Monasteries in 1536–9 resulted in the demolition of most monastic places of worship, the loss of many collegiate chapels and the alteration of some parish churches. In 1538 shrines were dismantled and relics destroyed; in 1547 all imagery on walls and in windows was forbidden; in 1550 stone altars were replaced with wooden tables.

Much of this was in line with generally accepted new thinking in religious practice, but what went with it was wanton and pointless destruction on a huge scale. To add further insult to further injury, during the reign of Edward VI (1547–53) all church treasures (gold, silver, plate and precious objects of all sorts) were confiscated, the riches gained being shared among Edward and his friends at court.

Commonwealth years

Even amid all the political change and religious destruction, much survived until the Puritans had their way from 1649–60, after the Civil Wars. It was then that much of the medieval glass that had graced and enriched churches was smashed.

The Restoration

Charles II coming to the throne in 1660 after Cromwell's death was a kind of symbolic marker that the dramatic upheavals in the Church and society of the previous 200 years were nearing an end. By then society was very different and the Old (Catholic) Church was a distant memory for most people. In the 17th century more pulpits, pews and lecterns had begun to appear in churches, outward signs of

significant changes in the way that churches were thought of and used, with preaching and sermons increasingly important. The church architecture of that time is usually modest and unassuming, with the most showy new items often tombs, monuments and fittings. And secular-seeming imagery – such as pineapples and the peculiar silly, chubby, winged creatures called putti – rather than the straightforward religious ones appear in churches more and more. Monuments increasingly seem to celebrate man rather than God. All these are very clear signs of a very different world from the medieval one.

This page: The Grinling Gibbons font cover in All Hallows by the Tower, City of London, is an example of the ornate fittings that were increasingly added to churches after the restoration of the monarchy in 1660 (above).

Wren Churches

The Great Fire of London began on 2 September 1666 and by the time the flames died down 87 medieval churches had been destroyed. It was immediately decided to rebuild 51 of them and the architect chosen to mastermind the rebuilding was Christopher Wren, then 34 years old. Remarkably, within 10 years most were complete, or nearly so, although several remained without towers until necessary money could be found.

On difficult sites and with little money, Wren created an astonishing variety of churches, often combining Gothic styles with Baroque and Renaissance ideas. His towers were designed so that each one would be a distinctive and unique landmark on the London skyline, such as St Bride's, Fleet Street (*below*).

The Wren churches – of which 23 still remain – opened the way for architects such as Nicholas Hawksmoor, James Gibbs and Thomas Archer to build churches that looked very different from those that had gone before.

Pulpits

The earliest surviving pulpits date from the 15th century and are often octagonal, frequently painted and sometimes carved. Some are raised up on slim, elegant wooden stems. The best carved examples can be found in Somerset and Devon.

Some of these early pulpits have 'testers' or sounding boards – carved wooden canopies above the lectern designed to amplify the preacher's voice, as in the pulpit in St Mary's, Avington, Hampshire (*below*).

Pulpits reached their heyday in the 18th century when they were the main focus of church worship. Such pulpits may be two- or even three-deckers, with a seat for the parish clerk, a reading pew and, above them, the pulpit. Some churches still preserve, although few use, the hour glass that the preacher used to time his sermons.

This page: *A classic Georgian exterior in brick at St Mary Magdalene, Willen, Buckinghamshire (top right); interior of St Mary Magdalene, Croome D'Abitot, Worcestershire, flooded with light from the large windows filled with clear glass (right).*

THE HANOVERIAN AND GEORGIAN PERIODS

The late 17th and early 18th centuries saw a return to church building, albeit on a much smaller scale than in the 15th century. Existing churches were changed and adapted, most often with the addition of elaborate pulpits, but also with box pews and galleries the order of the day. Often this was to fit in more worshippers, especially in the burgeoning towns and cities.

New churches in the Georgian period were frequently built of brick, taking their overall design from classical ideas, rather than medieval and Gothic, as these were considered to be uncouth if not downright barbarous. The insides were laid out as 'preaching boxes', the emphasis being on the pulpit and the preacher. Many are filled with light – clear glass and white-painted walls making it easier for the preacher to see all that was going on, and nowhere for the devil to hide.

A return to a form of Gothic happened towards the end of the 18th century with the building of 'Gothick' churches. In these churches natural light is reinforced by the lightness of the building materials – internally, plaster and wood replace stone as the materials of choice.

Monuments became increasingly common in churches, some of them coming to dominate the interiors. At the same time, churchyard monuments flourished, as did the much more modest, though often more appealing, slate headstones.

But by the end of the 18th century there was something visibly amiss with many churches – decay and ruin were becoming more and more common. This reflected a loss of direction and a moral lassitude within the established Church. At the same time Nonconformist churches and chapels began to appear; simple, bright and new in comparison to the old churches, many of which were cluttered, dark and dismal.

VICTORIAN TIMES

Huge changes in society happened throughout the 19th century. Hundreds of thousands left the countryside, moved into the towns and cities and began to worship in new chapels rather than old churches.

The result of this movement of population was a crisis for many rural medieval churches, and the Victorians came to the rescue. However, much was swept away that should not have been, irreplaceable treasures were discarded through ignorance or the pressures of fashion. Cheap, mass-produced items – pots, lamps, tiles, benches – replaced medieval objects that were doubtless tired, but genuine.

Some Victorians wanted churches to look more 'medieval' and 'holy', which meant dark; so in came gloomy, frequently poor, stained glass that still disfigures many churches. Out went the box pews and the galleries; in came the

big, overpowering organ. Many Victorians had an idea of what they thought the medieval churches had been like, not what they had actually been like. They wanted to reinvigorate the Church and its churches, and it is undoubtedly true that without them hundreds of medieval churches would have fallen into ruin.

In the new towns and cities Classical-looking 'Commissioners' churches were built from 1820 onwards with the help of government funds to provide worshipping space for urban dwellers. And in the countryside hundreds of new churches were built in the Gothic style. This great wave of building means that very many of our churches today are Victorian, or so much rebuilt as to be essentially Victorian.

This page: The Congregational chapel at Saltaire, West Yorkshire, completed in 1859 with its remarkable circular tower (top right); Victorian pulpit at All Saints Margaret Street, London, in medieval style (centre right); Brompton Oratory, London, built in 1880–4 (below right).

Lecterns

The purpose of a lectern is to hold the Bible opened flat for reading aloud. The earliest date from the 14th century and look rather like small desks; some are wooden and some brass. More immediately appealing are eagle lecterns, also made either of wood or brass. Some 40 medieval brass eagles survive (*below*, from Clare, Suffolk) and about 20 wooden ones. But there are hundreds of later eagle lecterns. The eagle was believed to be able to fly the highest of all birds and so be the nearest to heaven.

CHURCHES TODAY

World War II saw the destruction of hundreds of churches in towns and cities through enemy bombing. Since then the threat has been internal, a loss of congregations that has left many churches all but empty on Sundays. In the countryside especially, some churches now have very few parishioners to frequent them.

However, the arrival of strong community and evangelical congregations has revived many previously flagging urban churches. An astonishing number of country churches are well-loved and well-kept, as this book shows again and again, increasingly by secular 'Friends' organisations. Most of these are open to all at reasonable times. A few new churches are being built. They may look very different to the tiny primitive buildings that the missionaries built over 1,000 years ago, but they show very clearly that churches still have a role to play in our so-called secular world.

This page: Chatsworth Baptist Church, West Norwood, South London, a fine example of 1960s design (above top); Holy Cross Church, Gleadless Valley, Sheffield (above centre); St Mary's, Wellingborough, Northamptonshire, the masterpiece of 20th-century architect Sir Ninian Comper; the interior is said to 'literally bring you to your knees' (above and left), see website before visiting.

THE WEST COUNTRY

The spectacular landscape and ancient history of this western corner of Britain has created a truly diverse treasure trove of churches and chapels, with the breathtaking spires of Somerset being considered by some as the crowning glory of the West Country.

In the far west, Cornwall feels quite different to the rolling hills of Devon and Somerset. Once over the Tamar and in Cornwall you are in a different land, one in which many people spoke only Cornish until the 17th century.

Here, the principal building material is granite, grey in the rain but twinkling in the sunshine. The churches often hunch themselves into valleys and hillsides, sheltering from the storms that drive in from the Atlantic. On the coasts, many of the churches have prominent towers, to act as guides for shipping. Some of the churches feel like ships themselves inside, especially with rain lashing against the windows.

Devon is altogether greener and gentler, and was always a wealthier county than Cornwall, with churches that reflect that wealth. Some, like Ottery St Mary, are cathedral-like in scale and fittings. Others, like those on the north coast, have some of the rugged qualities of the Cornish churches. In many there are wonderful rood screens and bench-ends.

Somerset has some of the finest churches in England, many of them paid for by men who had become fabulously rich in the medieval wool trade. And it is the soaring towers of Somerset churches that proclaim that wealth most loudly of all.

Dorset is gentle and very content to receive visitors who do not want to venture further west. Dorset's churches reflect that gentleness, but often have unexpected and dramatic features within, like the almost unbelievably splendid roof at Bere Regis.

Wiltshire is dominated by Salisbury Plain and by the downs that stretch north and south. It has towns and villages that seem to see the 21st century as a brash upstart, and its churches are often timeless, whether grand, like Edington, or still in Georgian times, like Old Dilton.

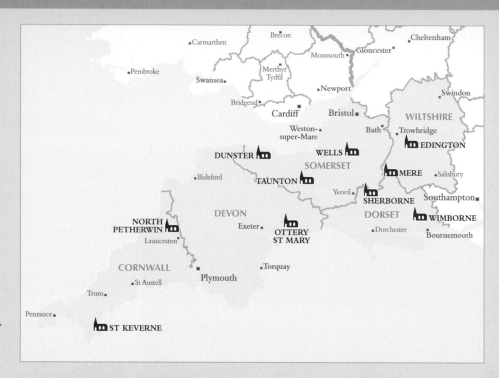

This page: St Nicholas, Moreton, is a lovely example of a Georgian Gothic church.

THE FAR WEST OF CORNWALL

Like Wales and Brittany, this westernmost part of England is firmly rooted in Celtic traditions. Wild and remote, and always influenced by the sea, this is where Celtic saints came to found churches or to seek prayerful isolation. The churches here reflect that history: the names are often Celtic, and there are ancient Celtic stone crosses in many of the churchyards.

Gwinear St Winnear

Why visit: *Many ancient features*
Where: *In Churchtown, TR27 5JZ*

St Winnear's battlemented granite tower with its square stair turret can be accurately dated to 1441, when a bequest was made to build it. There was an earlier, Norman church on this site, fragments of which were found when the church was restored in 1879. Some of the decorated stones were reset in the tower and porch.

Inside there is much of interest, including the base of the rood screen, with detailed carved symbols of Christ's Passion. Parts of what were presumably the bench-ends of the church have been re-used in the pulpit, lectern and kneeling desk. The granite font is rather odd; its base is Norman but the rest dates from 1727. Close by is part of a Celtic cross with a figure of Christ on it that may date back to the 9th century.

St Keverne St Keverne

Why visit: *Interesting architectural details; many shipwreck memorials*
Where: *In centre of village, north end of High Street, TR12 6NE*

This is one of Cornwall's largest and architecturally most intriguing churches. It retains an open feel partly because the pews were removed altogether at one time and when replaced in the 1970s wide alleyways were left, as they would have been in medieval times, to allow for processions to pass easily.

Much of the church dates from the 15th century, but the remarkable multi-coloured pillars are 13th-century. They are not made of local stone and may have come from Brittany. Parts of the church

were rebuilt after the spire was struck by lightning in 1770. Most unusually the church has three rood stairs (only one was needed). This may be because the relative positions of the nave and chancel shifted over time. The 15th-century font has angels at the corners, and is unusual in having prominent letters carved into it: AM for Ave Maria and IHS for Jesus. St Keverne's bench-ends have been restored, but are still full of interest, with many symbols of Jesus's Crucifixion.

The tower and spire are very prominent, and are still a daymark for sailors; offshore are the rocks called the Manacles, a notorious shipping hazard. Many sailors have come to grief in these waters over the centuries, as the number of memorials in the church and the churchyard attests.

St Hilary St Hilary

Why visit: *Ancient tower; gripping history*
Where: *At St Hilary Churchtown, reached off the B3280, beyond St Hilary school, TR20 9DQ*

A fire and deliberate vandalism have marred the history of this handsome church. It is dedicated to a 4th-century French bishop, and it is just possible that the first church on this site was built then. The shape of the churchyard suggests that it may have originally been a Roman fort, guarding the tin mines that attracted traders to Cornwall for over 2,000 years.

Two stones here confirm the ancient lineage: one is a Roman milestone, from

306; the other is a memorial to 'Not son of Not'. It dates from the 6th or 7th century, and is proof of Christianity here at that time.

The church was almost entirely destroyed by fire on Good Friday 1853. Only the tower with its broach spire, a shipping landmark for both Mount's Bay and St Ives Bay, survived. The church was rebuilt in 1854 by architect William White of Truro, who retained as much as he could from the old church.

In the 1920s the church was decorated and embellished by artists of the Newlyn School, who were friends of the then vicar, a prominent Anglo-Catholic. In 1932 vandals masquerading as Protestant law enforcers attacked the church and caused much damage. The churchyard is full of elaborate and impressive tombs.

St Just in Penwith
St Just

Why visit: *Ancient stones; wall paintings*
Where: *High Street, TR19 7EZ*

Built of large blocks of worked granite, St Just's church is entered through a handsome battlemented porch. It dates from the 14th to 16th centuries.

There are many exciting features to be found in the church. The oldest is a memorial stone dating from the 5th or 6th century inscribed 'Silus lies here'. Then there is a Saxon cross shaft re-used as a lintel. The church was restored in 1866, when six wall paintings were discovered. Two remain: one of St George and the Dragon, the other a 'Warning to Sabbath Breakers'. There are two medieval crosses in the churchyard, one with a Crucifixion.

Mawgan in Meneage
St Mawgan

Why visit: *Memorials to local families*
Where: *Gear Hill, TR12 6AD*

St Mawgan, who may have founded the church here in about 700, appears as a statue on the church tower, which also has carved shields of arms on it. One of these is of the Carminow family, and inside the church are two worn 14th-century effigies thought to be of Sir Roger de Carminow and his wife Johana.

Another family whose shields appear on the tower is the Vyvyans. They had a private pew in what is now the north transept and their funeral helms and tombs are in the church.

The church dates from the 16th century, with a later north aisle, and has a wide variety of Gothic window types. It also still has much of its original wagon roof, complete with bosses and angels.

Opposite page: The nave of St Keverne's church, with its multi-coloured pillars (left); St Winnear (right).
This page: The intersecting arches in St Hilary's church allow light to enter the church in unusual ways (left); nave and transept at Mawgan in Meneage (centre); Sancreed's church, with one of its ancient crosses close to the porch (right).

Sancreed St Credan

Why visit: *Ancient crosses; rood screen; paintings*
Where: *Opposite Glebe Farm, TR20 8QS*

In the churchyard here are two very early full-length crosses, both with crucifixions carved into them. They may date from the 10th century and are outstanding examples of their kind. There are three more cross-heads in the churchyard.

The pretty granite church dates from the 15th century, and still has the base of its rood screen. This has its original paint, and includes pictures of a spotted goat, a jester, a triple-headed king (perhaps representing the Trinity), birds and other beasts. The 15th-century font has shield-bearing angels at the corners, and there are 16th-century bench-ends.

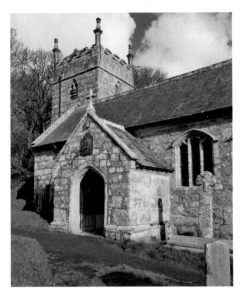

ALSO IN THE AREA

Breage St Breaca
Why visit: *Wall paintings*

Madron St Maddern
Why visit: *Setting; fixtures and furnishings*

Mullion St Mellanus
Why visit: *Bench-ends*

St Buryan St Buryan
Why visit: *Rood screen*

AROUND THE NORTH OF CORNWALL

Several of the churches in this group have extensive records that document their histories, with details that bring the past to life. In the churches themselves there is a remarkable range of features, including Norman fonts, medieval wall paintings and benches, and bench-ends.

North Petherwin
St Paternus

Why visit: *Well-documented history*
Where: *Hellescott Road, PL15 8LR*

This is a very large and splendid church for a small rural community. The village was originally in Devon, though it lies west of the Tamar and has always been part of the archdeaconry of Cornwall.

Round columns with scalloped capitals dating from about 1200 in the north aisle show the Norman origins of the church. Unusually for Cornwall, the church has a clerestory, dating from the 14th century. When the north chapel was added in 1518–24 its large windows and much taller monolith granite piers negated the need for a clerestory as so much more light was let in by the new building style.

The piers of the south aisle are made of two distinct types of granite. The building accounts of 1506–11 show that the whiter granite came from a quarry at Hingston Down near Kit Hill in south-east Cornwall, while the browner granite comes from Roughtor on Bodmin Moor, closer to North Petherwin and therefore cheaper to transport. The records also show that in 1507 the parishioners of North Petherwin had paid to open their own quarry on the moor, a glimpse into the world of the 16th century. In fact the parish went on to obtain granite from yet another quarry on the moor after the south aisle was built.

A further insight into the past is provided by the fact that the names of the three Bretons who carved the rood screen are known; they were Peter Papyas, John Oliver and William Oliver. They did the work between 1518 and 1524 and were paid 24 shillings a foot. As well as the base of their screen, the church preserves a Norman font, wagon roofs with decorated wall plates, and 17th-century communion rails, now used as a tower screen.

Egloskerry
St Petrock and St Keri

Why visit: *Norman details; 16th-century effigy*
Where: *At T-junction, PL15 8RU*

Despite over-rigorous restoration in Victorian times, this village church has regained much charm after recent restoration programmes.

Notable features to look out for include a tympanum over the north door with a serpent carved on it, and another, originally from over the south door and now inside the church, with a Lamb of God carving. There is a simple Norman font, and an unusual and rare Norman pillar piscina.

There is an alabaster tomb probably of Edward Hastings, Lord of Penheale, dating from 1510. It is interesting because he is shown in civilian clothes, not the military attire that was the norm. Another unusual survivor is a section of early 17th-century stained glass.

Laneast
St Sidwell and St Gulvat

Why visit: *Medieval benches; rood screen; stained glass*
Where: *Off the A935, PL15 8PN*

Set at the head of a wooded valley, Laneast church has an almost complete and very well-preserved set of medieval benches and bench-ends, a well-preserved rood screen, and a prayer desk from the beginning of the 16th century.

The stained glass is also medieval and includes part of a Crucifixion in the east window and St Christopher in the south chancel. The font is Norman. In the church is a memorial to astronomer John Couch Adams, who discovered the planet Neptune in 1846.

Poughill St Olaf

Why visit: *Wall paintings; 16th-century woodwork*
Where: *Off Poughill Road, EX23 9EP*

The churchwarden's records for this church are particularly detailed and enable precise dates to be given to many features in the church. For example, work was done on the rood loft and rood screen in the 1530s, including the construction of stairs.

The church has two wall paintings of St Christopher. The records reveal that in the 1520s the church had at least five guilds, including one to St Christopher, and one to St Olaf (a Scandinavian saint). There are excellent bench-ends here, as well as a medieval south door and roof bosses dating from the 1530s.

Poundstock St Winwaloe

Why visit: *Wall paintings; 16th-century guild house*
Where: *West of the A39, off Vicarage Lane, EX23 0AX*

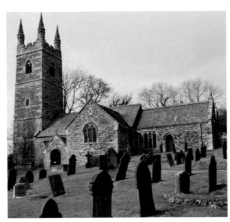

St Winwaloe's is set in a wooded hollow and has features from many ages, including a Norman font, a 16th-century chest and an early 17th-century pulpit.

On the north wall are wall paintings, one a graphic and bloody 'Warning to Sabbath Breakers' showing various tools adding to Christ's suffering (the message was 'Don't work on Sundays'), and the other of the Seven Deadly Sins. There are also fragments of other wall paintings.

Parts of the rood screen survive, as does a symbol of St Luke in a panel of medieval stained glass.

Close to the church is a rare survivor: a guild house, dating from the 1500s. These were once common near churches and were where parish feasts were held, ale was brewed and cakes were baked. Most of these were demolished or turned to other uses when feasting and beer-drinking on church property became socially and morally unacceptable.

Tremaine St Winwalo

Why visit: *Setting; wagon roof and Norman font*
Where: *North-west of the hamlet of Tremaine, PL15 8SA*

Set on its own among trees, Tremaine's little church is peaceful and rugged.

It has Norman details that include a tympanum and window, both on the north side of the church, and, inside, a Norman font with a round bowl and cable moulding. The wagon roof and its bosses date from the early 16th century. The unusual steps cut into the thickness of the north wall led to the rood loft.

Opposite page: *Norman – on the left – and later work at North Petherwin (left); Egloskerry (right).*
This page: *Rows of medieval benches at Laneast (top left); Poughill (below left); Poundstock (centre); the 16th-century wagon roof at Tremaine (above).*

ALSO IN THE AREA

Kilkhampton St James
Why visit: *Benches and bench-ends*

Launcells St Swithin
Why visit: *Setting; Georgian fittings; bench-ends*

EAST DEVON TREASURES

This is the Devon of quiet rolling countryside, where, away from the main roads, the 21st century seems mercifully distant. It is also a countryside of excellent though scattered churches, each with its own character, but each also having a 'Devon' feel. Features in common in several of them are beautiful and unspoiled rood screens showing Devon church art and craftsmanship at its best.

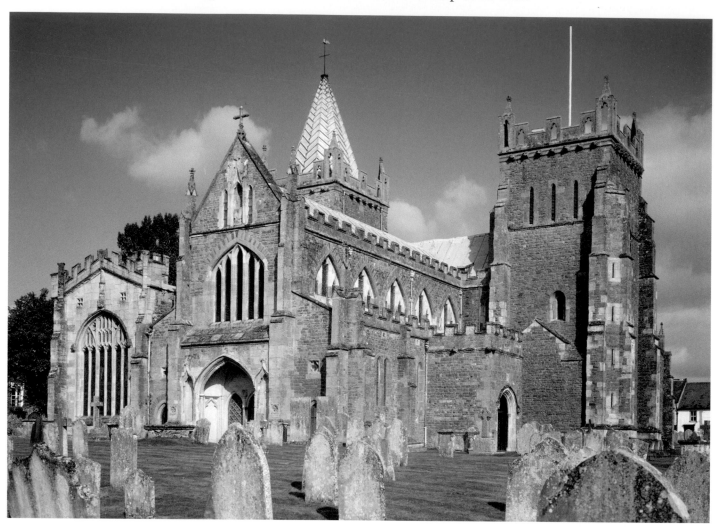

Ottery St Mary St Mary

Why visit: *Cathedral-like splendour*
Where: *The College, near the library, EX11 1DJ*

This is far and away the grandest church in east Devon, and one of England's outstanding parish churches.

The site on which it stands had been part of a manor belonging to Rouen Cathedral in Normandy since the 11th century. In 1335 it was bought by Bishop Grandisson of Exeter, who almost entirely rebuilt the church that had stood here, using Exeter Cathedral as a model for much of the architecture. Even

though it stands on a churchyard mound in the centre of the little town, the church does not overpower it. This is partly because the churchyard is large and the church is set away from the immediate buildings, and partly because the church is rather low. It has two towers, as does Exeter Cathedral.

Inside, the church is full of riches, but opinion is divided on the colour scheme that was adopted for much of the building in 1977. Some think the colours inappropriate; others that they bring an echo of medieval vibrancy to the church.

Bishop Grandisson's work can be seen everywhere, and the bishop himself can be seen depicted on one of the bosses in

the Lady Chapel. The bosses in the church are outstanding, depicting a huge range of subjects and all worth looking at.

The Dorset Aisle was added to the church in about 1520. It has superb fan vaulting with extraordinary pendants. The arcade capitals here are also remarkable, taking many shapes and forms.

Monuments include those of Sir Otho Grandisson (brother of the Bishop) and his wife, from 1359, shown under ornate canopies covered with shields. There is a remarkable clock with a brightly painted wooden face from Grandisson's time in the church, and a wooden eagle lectern of the same date that is one of only a very few of its kind in England.

Crediton Holy Cross

Why visit: *Impressive town church*
Where: *Church Lane, off East Street, EX17 2AH*

Built of red sandstone, this is one of the finest town churches in Devon. It has an illustrious history, having been the site of a minster established in 739, and later a cathedral until 1050, when the See was moved to Exeter. After that it became a collegiate institution and remained so until the Dissolution, at which time the parish bought the church for £200.

Essentially it is a 12th-century cruciform building that was extensively remodelled in the 14th and 15th centuries. It has a magnificent clerestory, a rarity in Devon churches. Among features of interest are a number of monuments, including that of Sir John Sully and his wife of 1387; Sir William Periam of 1604; and John Tuckfield of 1630. The latter is particularly impressive, with black columns and a life-sized seated figure of his wife, Elizabeth.

Cullompton St Andrew

Why visit: *Wonderful roof and outstanding screen*
Where: *In Church Street, off Cullompton's main street, EX15 1JU*

St Andrew's is all of a piece, built of red sandstone in the 15th and 16th centuries. Its tower is handsome, with stepped buttresses rising to a battlemented parapet, and stone figures and a prominent clock on the west side.

The interior of the church is dominated by an extraordinary wooden barrel-vaulted roof, which stretches the entire length of the building. It is painted in blues, crimsons and golds, which bring out the intricate patterns of the timbers as they intersect. As wonderful, and as colourful, is the original wooden screen that spans the width of the church.

As if all this were not enough, the church has chapels and aisles containing superb craftsmanship. The Lane Aisle has exuberant fan vaulting and stonework, while the Moore Chapel may be more restrained but is also beautiful. There are figures and carvings everywhere in the

church, and one truly unique item: a Golgotha. This consists of two huge, dark masses of oak, carved with skulls, bones and rocks. It would once have formed the base of the Crucifixion that stood above the rood screen. It is the only one of its kind to survive.

Kentisbeare St Mary

Why visit: *Rood screen; 17th-century gallery*
Where: *On the junction of Priest Hill and Fore Street, EX15 2AD*

The chequered tower of St Mary's is striking and unlike any other in Devon. It is built from red sandstone and white Beer stone and dates from the 14th century. Most of the rest of the church dates from a century or so later.

The interior contains much of interest. At the west end is a handsome gallery dated 1632, while stretching across the nave and south aisle is a rood screen that is one of the best of its kind in Devon. It carries the arms of John Whiting, a merchant venturer who built the south aisle and who is buried there. He died in 1529 and is buried here with his wife, Anne. Also buried here is Mary Wotton, great-aunt to Lady Jane Grey.

Plymtree
St John the Baptist

Why visit: *Rood screen*
Where: *Opposite junction of Green End Lane, EX15 2JU*

Most of the exterior of St John's dates from the 14th and 15th centuries. It is a handsome church but it is the internal fittings that make it so interesting. Of these, the rood screen is the highlight. It was probably made in the 1470s and has a fan-vaulted top. The figures on the panels retain much of their original colour and include St Catherine, St John the Baptist and the Adoration of the Magi. In total there are 34 painted panels.

The church also has wagon roofs, excellent bench-ends, 17th-century altar rails and an 18th-century font.

Tiverton St Peter

Why visit: *Reminders of wealth from wool*
Where: *St Peter Street, by the river, EX16 6RP*

The tall, red sandstone tower of St Peter's is an outstanding part of Tiverton's townscape. It is a large church dating from the 15th century, with a south porch and south chapel added in 1517 by John Greenway, whose riches came from the wool trade. There are reminders of the source of his wealth everywhere on the southern part, with carvings of woolpacks, ships, figures and horses.

The memorial to Greenway and his wife Alice is inside the church, in the aisle that he built.

Opposite page: *The grandeur of Ottery St Mary.*
This page: *Cullompton's colourful screen.*

ALSO IN THE AREA

Honiton St Michael
Why visit: *Memorials; view from churchyard*

Branscombe St Winifred
Why visit: *Norman church packed with interest*

FROM EXMOOR TO THE SEA

The tumbled landscapes of north-west Somerset, where the Quantocks, the Brendon Hills and Exmoor plunge to the Bristol Channel, are the setting for several remarkable churches. In a county well known for fine churches, these are among the less-visited gems: some parts of this area feel remote indeed. Dunster, by contrast, is no stranger to visitors, while Hartland, farther west, feels different again, its North Devon parish as exposed to the Atlantic as anywhere in the West Country.

Culbone St Beuno

Why visit: *Tiny, ancient church; an enchanting coastal setting.*
Where: *Some 3 miles west of Porlock along the coast path, or a 1.5-mile walk from the nearest parking area (narrow lane leading north off the A39), TA24 8PQ*

With its unusual dedication to a 6th-century saint from North Wales, this is usually considered to be the smallest church in England. It is set in a wooded combe.

A two-light Romanesque window, cut from a single block of stone, recalls the Saxon and Norman origins of the simple two-cell church. The porch and the little 19th-century spire are among later additions, which also include a medieval rood screen, a 17th-century squire's pew, and a 20th-century reredos by the Arts and Crafts architect Charles Voysey.

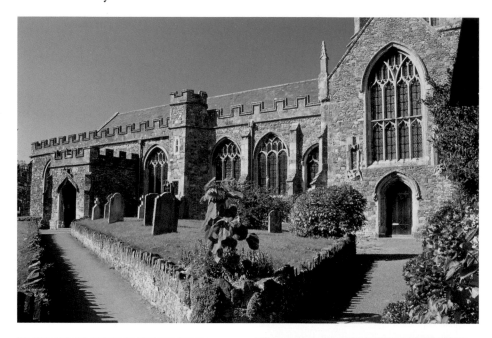

Dunster St George

Why visit: *A historic parish and priory church; a very long 15th-century rood screen*
Where: *Tucked away on the north side of Dunster's narrow main street (Church Street), TA24 6RY*

An uneasy truce between priory and parish characterised the early history of this church, which served both communities: the townsfolk used the west end, while the monks worshipped at a separate high altar at the east end. An agreement of 1357 set out the responsibilities of each congregation, and the building continued as two churches in one until 1539, when both the priory and its mother priory at Bath were dissolved by Henry VIII.

The most notable feature inside is the astonishing screen, dating from 1498. Take time to look closely at the exquisite carving. Spanning the entire width of the building, the screen was constructed

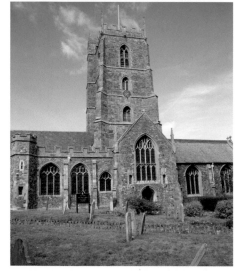

mid-way down the 'town' part of the church, to separate the parish nave from its choir and sanctuary. The chancel, with its lancet windows, was rebuilt by the monks in the 13th century, and the priory is also recalled, outside the north transept, by a lovely memorial garden on the former site of its cloister.

Hartland St Nectan

Why visit: *Dramatic location; landmark tower; impressive rood screen*
Where: *At Stoke, between Hartland village and Hartland Quay on the west coast, EX39 6DU*

Here one of the tallest towers in Devon, emphasised by its long, rather low church, has been a landmark for sailors for nearly 600 years. The interior is quite a surprise: both more spacious and more lavishly fitted than you might expect. The 11-bay rood screen, as wide as the church, has incredibly elaborate carving on its cornice, and ribs with intricate bosses just below. At one time, it had seating and an organ on top.

Other features to look out for include a decoratively carved font from an earlier church of 1170, and quite a collection of interesting monuments. They include a very ornate Perpendicular tomb chest from nearby Hartland Abbey and an unusual plaque of 1610 to Anne Abbott. Two modern slate tablets commemorate Sir Allen Lane, founder of Penguin Books, who died in 1970, and his publisher uncle, John Lane, founder of The Bodley Head.

Selworthy All Saints

Why visit: *A landmark church with spectacular interior; distant views over Exmoor*
Where: *On the minor road through the village of Selworthy, off the A39 between Minehead and Porlock, TA24 8TR*

The gleaming limewashed walls of this imposing church overlooking Exmoor give a foretaste of the wonderfully light and spacious-feeling interior, with its slender white pillars and soaring wagon roofs. The south aisle, from 1538, is a masterpiece with splendid Perpendicular window tracery in the local style. The upper floor of the unusual two-storey porch incorporates an interior balcony from where the lords of the manor could watch the proceedings, theatre-style: this was an early 19th-century conversion by the Acland family of nearby Holnicote. Two family members are commemorated by plaques at the west end.

Stogumber St Mary

Why visit: *An intriguing church to explore; exuberant work from several periods, both inside and out*
Where: *Up a narrow lane in the centre of Stogumber village, south of the A358 between Minehead and Taunton, TA4 3TA*

St Mary's tall, sturdy-looking 14th-century tower is one of the oldest features of this church, which incorporates a mix of differing styles. One Victorian vicar, a devotee of William Morris, redecorated the chancel with colourful Arts and Crafts work. Prominent between it and the separate 15th-century Sydenham Chapel is a huge classical tomb – that of Sir George Sydenham, who died in 1597 and whose daughter married Sir Francis Drake.

Stogursey St Andrew

Why visit: *A church with an interesting history; some fine Norman features*
Where: *In Stogursey village, north of the A39 between Bridgwater and Watchet, Church Street, TA5 1RG*

This is a priory church, presented soon after 1100 to the Benedictine Abbey of Lonlay, near Falaise in Normandy, but then reclaimed by Henry V. It was later given to Eton College by Henry VI.

The building's Norman legacy includes the west door and the rounded arches at the crossing, with their lavishly carved pier capitals dating from the late 11th century. The nave was rebuilt around 1500 and a Victorian restoration was responsible for much of the decorative work, and for the tower's delicate parapet. There are 14th- and 15th-century tombs of William and John de Verney. Among the 16th-century bench-ends, look for one with a spoonbill – a bird once common on the flooded Somerset Levels but no longer found in Britain.

Tawstock St Peter

Why visit: *A remote but rather grand church; wonderful monuments and fittings*
Where: *Down a lane leading east out of Tawstock village, EX31 3HY*

Deep Devon lanes lead to the out-of-the-way spot from where this early 14th-century cruciform church looks out over the Taw Valley to Codden Hill beyond. The earls of Bath owned the park in which the church stands, and it is for their magnificent 16th- and 17th-century family monuments that many visitors come here.

The collection includes one of the best Jacobean monuments in the country: an alabaster tomb of William Bourchier, the 3rd earl, who died in 1623. Wearing a crimson robe over his armour, and an earl's coronet, he lies beside his wife Elizabeth, with family crests at their feet, plus kneeling children and a baby below. Also nearby is a rare early wooden effigy of a lady, which is believed to date from the 15th century.

The Jacobean panelled family pew is another remarkable feature, enclosed with pillars and a canopy rather like a four-poster bed. Don't miss the beautifully carved screen in the chancel, and another in the south aisle.

Opposite page: Views of Dunster, south front (top) and tower (below).
This page: *Selworthy (left); a Norman arch at Stogursey (centre).*

ALSO IN THE AREA

Chittlehampton St Hieritha
Why visit: *Outstanding tower*

Molland St Mary
Why visit: *Georgian fittings including a three-decker pulpit*

Parracombe St Petrock CCT
Why visit: *Georgian box pews; unusual chancel screen with scriptural texts*

Swimbridge St James
Why visit: *Medieval furnishings including a rood screen*

THE CENTRE OF SOMERSET

The towers of Somerset's churches are world famous, and this group of churches includes some of the best. There is much else to see and enjoy, from mysterious Norman carvings at Stoke sub Hamdon to modest Quaker architecture at Long Sutton, and including stone characters called hunky-punks on several of the churches.

Taunton St Mary Magdalene

Why visit: *Tower*
Where: *Centre of Taunton, east end of Hammet Street, TA1 1SA*

St Mary's has the most celebrated of all Somerset's famous towers. It is the tallest, the grandest, and the most ornate. When seen from Hammet Street – which is the right place to view it – it is a marvel of stonework rising through four stages to a crown of turrets, pinnacles, battlements and tracery that is more light and air than solid stone.

It looks just as it did when completed in 1514. But the tower is not quite what it seems, because it was rebuilt from the ground up in 1862 by Sir George Gilbert Scott, when it was in danger of collapse. Sir George recreated the tower exactly as it had been, and re-installed the original statues in the rebuilt niches.

The rest of the church is genuinely as it was in the early 16th century, incorporating work from earlier centuries. On the south porch, dated 1508, are niches with carvings, the central one showing the Crucifixion.

The interior of the church is light and airy, and full of angels. They are on the nave piers, on the capitals of the tower

arch, and, most of all, on the roof of the nave, where they stand out all the more as they are gilded. The tie beam roof is typical of Somerset roofs of this kind.

Much of the church is painted, and there are Victorian statues and stained glass, a legacy of the Reverend Dr James Cottle, who came here in 1840. The stained glass tells the story of such glass through the 19th and early 20th centuries, with work by the famous glassmakers Clayton and Bell. From 1902 there is a memorial to the Somerset and Dorset Light Infantry. Figures in the glass range from King Alfred to Albert, the Prince Consort.

Brympton St Andrew

Why visit: *Setting; peaceful interior*
Where: *From the centre of Brympton, Old Road then Brympton Avenue, BA22 8TD*

Church, manor house and overall setting combine here to make a memorable scene. There was also once a medieval village, but that has disappeared.

The church does not have a tower but a strange oblong bell turret on a stone stalk, which does not detract from the overall charm of the building. The church was built in the 14th and 15th centuries by the lord of the manor, and is conveniently set next door to his house. Because there is no longer a village here it feels rather like a private chapel.

Inside, there is a stone screen with detailing that includes a Green Man. Dominating part of the church is a monument to the Sydenham family, who once owned the house. It dates from 1626. In the north chapel are yet more tombs and memorials plus medieval windows to see.

Curry Rivel St Andrew

Why visit: *Beautiful windows; interior full of interest*
Where: *Church Road, north side of village green, which is north of A377, TA10 0HQ*

The church tower is a landmark for a long way around, and was rebuilt in 1861 to the original medieval designs. It is in blue lias stone, rather than the Ham stone from which the rest of the church is built.

The entrance to the church is a handsome two-storey porch, on either side of which are windows with superb tracery. The church has a battlemented roofline on which are carvings including people playing instruments such as

fiddles, bagpipes and horns. The inside of the church is full of interest, the oldest part being the 13th-century north chapel, which has a tomb thought to be of Sabrina de Lorty, the chapel's founder. Behind railings, and under a semi-circular canopy, are the effigies of Marmaduke Jennings and his son Robert, dating from the early 17th century. Carved woodwork from the 15th and 16th centuries includes bench-ends, two screens and the roof of the north aisle.

Ilminster St Mary

Why visit: *Wadham Chapel*
Where: *In the centre of Ilminster, Barton Court, TA19 0DU*

There has been a church on this site since at least 762, but the present building dates from the second half of the 15th century. There were restorations and rebuilds in 1825 and again in 1882. These changed the internal arrangements, firstly to put galleries up, then to take them down.

The church interior remains tall, light and airy, in no small part due to the clerestory windows.

The pride of Ilminster is the Wadham Chapel, which on the outside is a masterpiece of Perpendicular architecture. Inside are monuments to the Wadham family. There is a 15th-century table tomb to Sir William Wadham and his mother, and a 17th-century tomb chest and wall monument to Nicholas Wadham and his wife Dorothy, the founders of Wadham College, Oxford. Both tombs have magnificent brasses.

Isle Abbotts
St Mary the Virgin

Why visit: *Tower with original sculpture and hunky-punks*
Where: *Abbotts Way, TA3 6RJ*

Like so many Somerset churches, Isle Abbotts has a splendid tower, and this one is especially graceful, built of Ham stone between 1510 and 1520, with three distinct stages. Very often in such towers the niches that originally held statues are empty, but here ten remain, and they are very fine examples of early 16th-century sculpture. They include figures of the Virgin Mary, the risen Christ and saints. Beneath the traceried battlements at the top of the tower are eight hunky-punks, the carved stone figures that are such a speciality of Somerset churches.

Inside, the nave and chancel have barrel-vaulted roofs, while the north aisle has an almost flat panelled roof. In the 14th-century chancel are an elaborate piscina, surrounded by carved panels, and a sedilia formed of three tub-like stone seats. The Norman font is covered in strange carvings, one of which looks like an upside-down sea creature, with legs.

Opposite page: Taunton's nave roof with gilded angels (top), and details of the tower.
This page: *Brympton (left); Curry Rivel (centre); Isle Abbotts (above).*

Long Sutton
Friends' Meeting House

Why visit: *Unchanged Quaker meeting place; original Georgian features*
Where: *Northern edge of Long Sutton village, junction of A3728 and B3165, Langport Road, TA10 9NE*

Built in 1717, this is one of the finest Quaker meeting houses in the country. It still retains many of its Georgian features, including a gallery that was originally for women, and a symbolic meeting house lantern. The windows are particularly fascinating because they still have their original glazing bars and blown glass.

Nearby are 17th-century cottages that were the original meeting house and were later used as a Quaker school.

Martock All Saints

Why visit: *Remarkable roof*
Where: *Church Street, TA12 6JL*

All Saints is built entirely from the local Ham stone, quarried not far away. It is a handsome town church with a history stretching back to at least as early as the 12th century, as some of its architectural details show. But it is the magnificent nave roof that makes the church so renowned. It was constructed of oak in 1513 and is of the tie-beam style that is so often found in churches in this area, but the craftsmen excelled themselves here. It has been calculated that there are over 700 individual wooden panels in the roof, each with a different pattern. On the cross-beams are angels with outstretched wings.

Below the roof and between the clerestory windows are carved niches, each one different, and with painted apostles dating from the 17th century on the back walls.

Stoke sub Hamdon
St Mary the Virgin

Why visit: *Outstanding Norman and later church*
Where: *Stoke sub Hamdon village is off the A303; the church is a mile east of the village, beneath the Iron Age ramparts of Ham Hill, on East Stoke, TA14 6UF*

St Mary's is built of the local, golden Ham stone, and has features from the 12th century to the 20th. There are two doors into the nave; the main one has over it a Norman tympanum with carvings that include birds in a tree, the Lamb of God, and a centaur firing a bow at a lion. There are further interesting carvings on the outside of the church, including a serpent-like dragon being slain, geometrical shapes and gargoyles.

The interior is full of interest, including the imposing Norman chancel arch with its three orders of billet, zig-zag and lozenge shapes. The font is 12th-century, while the pulpit and communion rails are from the 17th century. The very large reredos is 20th-century.

Westonzoyland
The Blessed Virgin Mary

Why visit: *Tower; nave roof*
Where: *Church Lane, TA7 0EP*

The splendid tower can be seen for miles across the flat landscape that surrounds it. Built in the 15th century, it has four stages, the lowest is plain apart from a large west window. The topmost stage is the most ornate and culminates in battlements with delicate Somerset tracery. The south porch, south transept and south aisle are also battlemented.

Inside, the church is tall, light and airy, and has a superb tie-beam roof. Winged angels catch the eye first, but the whole roof is full of wonderful carpentry. The south aisle roof is just as good. The screen is modern, but re-uses fragments of the original. Some of the bench-ends are 15th century, as is the font and some of the glass in the chancel. All were gifts from the church's founder, Richard Bere, Abbot of Glastonbury.

This page: The Friends' Meeting House, Long Sutton (top left); angel at Martock (top centre); Norman symbolism seen at Stoke sub Hamdon (below centre).

ALSO IN THE AREA

Long Sutton Holy Trinity
Why visit: *Restored screen; tie-beam roof*

Muchelney
St Peter and St Paul
Why visit: *17th-century painted roof with voluptuous angels*

Taunton St James
Why visit: *Tower; carved font*

Taunton St John
Why visit: *19th-century Anglo-Catholic by Sir George Gilbert Scott*

TOWERS OF SOMERSET AND THE MENDIPS

Church towers are among the special sights of Somerset: tall, elegant and usually built in the 15th and 16th centuries, in the style known as Perpendicular. Many were funded by the proceeds of a thriving wool industry and built using the various fine local limestones. The design of some of the finest and loftiest Somerset towers was influenced by the cathedral and abbey of Wells and Glastonbury, two of the towns at the heart of this group of churches.

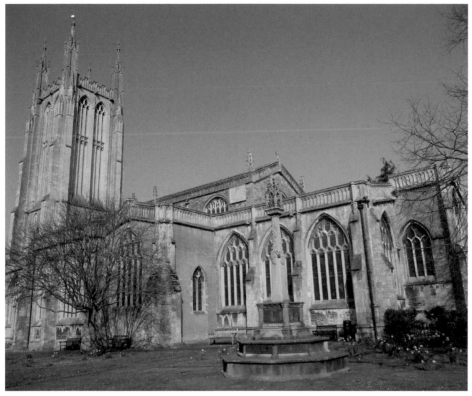

Wells St Cuthbert

Why visit: *One of England's largest and grandest parish churches*
Where: *To the west of Wells city centre, St Cuthbert Street, BA5 2AW*

Its tall, splendid 15th-century west tower is surely the main reason why this striking parish church – the largest in Somerset – is often mistaken for Wells Cathedral.

Large Perpendicular windows, including a clerestory, fill the huge interior with light. This works to dazzling effect, particularly highlighting the extravagantly decorated 16th-century tie-beam roof of the nave, which bristles with brightly painted carved angels, shields and rosettes. It was repainted in 1963, but in colours believed to be close to those of the original scheme.

A new church here, replacing an even earlier foundation, was begun in the early 13th century – around the same time as the building of the cathedral. Thereafter, for some 300 years, the race was on to make this building taller and better, as though in competition with its illustrious neighbour. Until 1561 St Cuthbert's even had two towers, the second one at the crossing; it must have been a severe blow, both to the structure and to local pride, when this collapsed.

A happier event was the Victorian rediscovery of two stone reredoses, one in each transept. They had been severely damaged and then covered with plaster at the time of the Reformation. One of them, a rare representation in stonework of a Tree of Jesse, can be confidently dated to 1470 – the contract with its maker still exists. Furnishings and fittings to look out for include the wooden pulpit of 1636, with carved depictions of stories from the Old Testament, and some fine Victorian work that includes the choir stalls and a splendid eagle lectern.

This page: St Cuthbert's, Wells, is a masterpiece both inside and out, with a soaring tower and a nave roof with carpentry picked out in bright colours.

Axbridge
St John the Baptist

Why visit: *Elegant church in a charming townscape*
Where: *The Square, BS26 2BW*

A long flight of steps leading up to it from the town square gives great presence to this distinguished-looking limestone building, the walls of which are topped with a parapet of intricately pierced stonework. The light interior, with its high ceilings and large windows with clear glass, owes much to a more than usually sensitive late-Victorian restoration of a mainly 15th-century building. The remarkable blue-and-white ceiling of the nave was painstakingly created in decorative plasterwork by a local craftsman in 1636, for the sum of 10 guineas.

Brent Knoll St Michael

Why visit: *Ancient and unusual site; interesting bench-ends*
Where: *On the upper edge of Brent Knoll village, Church Lane, TA9 4DG*

Set on the lower slopes of the isolated hill from which it takes its name, Brent Knoll church stands on an ancient Christian site. Though most of the present building is 14th- and 15th-century, there is a Norman column in the north aisle. The Norman zig-zag moulding over the south door was replicated by a much later

craftsman in the decorative woodwork on the Jacobean pulpit. The church is known for its 15th-century bench-ends, most famously a series of three that portray a tale of vengeance involving a cleric – possibly the then Abbot of Glastonbury. He is depicted as a fox in ecclesiastical robes with crozier and mitre.

Cameley St James CCT

Why visit: *Unrestored interior*
Where: *In a hamlet on a lane leading west off the A37 at Temple Cloud, Cameley Road, BS39 5AH*

This unspoilt rural gem is a complete contrast to the grand churches of Somerset. The tower, tall for the size of the church, is handsomely built in Mendip stone in the Somerset style, but the rest of the church is made of much more rustic-looking blue Lias stone.

The interior is the real surprise: a haphazard but somehow harmonious mix with something from every era: medieval bench-ends, Georgian furnishings and galleries, as well as some fragmentary wall paintings spanning around 500 years – all set within a simple medieval building.

Chewton Mendip
St Mary Magdalene

Why visit: *The tower, spectacular both close up and from a distance*
Where: *In Church Lane, off the A39 to Wells, BA3 4SW*

The tower alone is reason enough to visit this church, a distinctive landmark high in the Mendips. It is one of the tallest Somerset towers and one of the

finest, and its date of 1541 also makes it one of the last to be built before the Reformation. The church to which it was added is much older – look for Norman work in the north door and in the east wall of the nave and chancel arch. People in trouble could use the 'frith stool' or sanctuary seat, built into the wall under a window on the north side of the chancel. It entitled them to claim the protection of the church.

Glastonbury
St John the Baptist

Why visit: *Setting; tower and spacious interior with some interesting details*
Where: *Halfway along the High Street, BA6 9DR*

A fine, tall tower helps this church to hold its own among its more famous neighbours, Glastonbury Tor and the abbey ruins. Ancient Christianity and King Arthur are in Glastonbury's blood: this church stands on a Saxon site – the first church on record dates from 1175.

A 'new' church is recorded in 1428–9, and the 'new' tower (the second tallest in Somerset) followed after the original began to shed its pinnacles in the 1460s. The roof, with its clerestory and angel busts, is a little later. Pieces of medieval glass from the original east window are re-used in the chancel, and St George's Chapel has a screen made from 15th-century oak fragments.

Mells St Andrew

Why visit: *Elegant exterior and tower; Arts and Crafts memorials and other works*
Where: *At the end of New Street, near the Talbot Inn, BA11 3PW*

The patronage of the family from the adjacent manor linked this 15th-century church with some famous names from the Edwardian and late Victorian arts world. There are works here by Burne-Jones, Eric Gill, William Nicholson, Sir Alfred Munnings and Sir Edwin Lutyens, and the World War I poet Siegfried Sassoon is buried in the churchyard.

With its magnificent Somerset tower and fan-vaulted south porch, the church itself is more than worthy of these

connections and of the lovely village in which it stands – and which also has a Lutyens war memorial.

Shepton Mallet
St Peter and St Paul

Why visit: *Panelled roof above the nave*
Where: *In the town centre on Peter Street, BA4 5BW*

Topped by the stump of a spire that was never built, the tower of Shepton Mallet church dates from around 1380 – much earlier than most of the renowned Somerset towers. The church's crowning glory is inside, high above the narrow nave. An amazing oak wagon vault consists of 350 separate panels, each with a different design and separated by superb

bosses. Carved angels along each side complete this masterpiece, which dates from the late 15th century.

Stratton-on-the-Fosse
Downside Abbey

Why visit: *Huge and imposing 20th-century Gothic revival church*
Where: *In Stratton-on-the-Fosse on the A367, BA3 4RH*

It is perhaps not surprising that the Abbey Church of St Gregory the Great recalls a great French cathedral, for the Benedictine community that settled at Downside in 1814 had its origins in northern France. The great Roman Catholic church that was eventually built has work by eminent British architects including Sir Giles Gilbert Scott (nave and tower) and Sir Ninian Comper (great east window and Lady Chapel furniture). The church serves not only the monastic community but also the adjacent Roman Catholic boarding school.

Opposite page: Plasterwork ceiling at St John's, Axbridge (left); biblical text at Cameley (centre).
This page: St Andrew, Mells (top left); nave roof at St Peter and St Paul, Shepton Mallet (left); Downside Abbey (above).

Wedmore St Mary

Why visit: *Imposing and historically interesting church; fascinating carvings on the exterior*
Where: *On Church Street (B3139), BS28 4AA*

With its commanding central tower and elevated position, this cruciform church presides over its village very much like a small cathedral.

It is mostly a 15th-century rebuilding of a much earlier church. There may have been a Saxon church here: it is known that Wedmore was part of an estate belonging to the Saxon kings of Wessex, and King Alfred had a house nearby. Inside, the church is spacious and airy, with slender pillars and high ceilings in the side aisles. The congregation was large: a 1547 record tells of 1,000 communicants at one service. Take time to look at the detailing on the church's exterior, which includes many gargoyles.

St Mary's porch has two rooms, one above the other, probably used by priests at one time. The porch shelters a beautiful re-used 13th-century doorway, and also a door that has 13th-century hinges and the initials, marked out in nail heads, of the church wardens who had the door remade in 1677.

ALSO IN THE AREA

Bath Bath Abbey
Why visit: *Huge late Perpendicular church; west front*

Bruton St Mary
Why visit: *Two towers: one fine Perpendicular, the other smaller and earlier*

Croscombe St Mary
Why visit: *Jacobean woodwork including rood screen*

Evercreech St Peter
Why visit: *Perpendicular tower; 19th-century gargoyles*

Frome St John
Why visit: *Pleasing setting; Anglo-Catholic furnishings and artworks*

THE HEART OF DORSET

Sherborne Abbey is undoubtedly the star of this group of churches, but each of the others has something special, including Laurence Whistler's unique windows at Moreton, the amazing 15th-century roof at Bere Regis, and Puddletown's set of 17th-century furnishings.

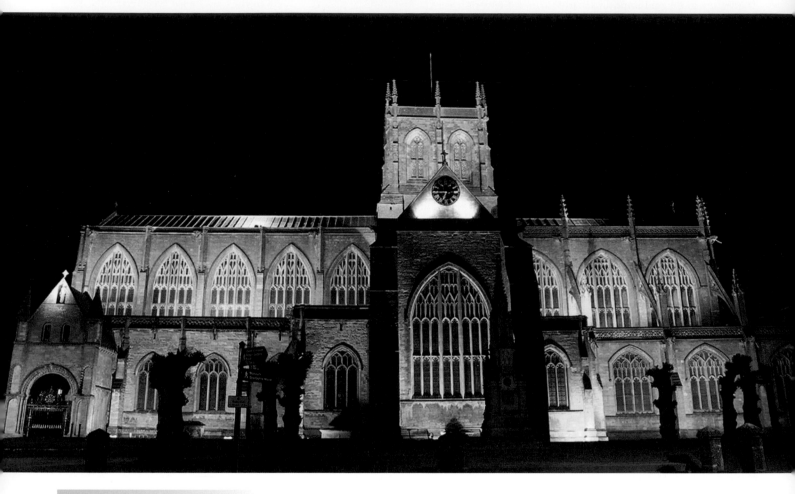

Sherborne
Sherborne Abbey

Why visit: *Superb abbey church; outstanding fan vaulting*
Where: *Centre of Sherborne, DT9 3LQ*

The great golden Ham-stone bulk of Sherborne Abbey presides benignly over its little medieval town. Founded in 705 as a Benedictine monastery, the church served as the cathedral of the western part of the area of Wessex and was dedicated to St Mary the Virgin. It was rebuilt in the 10th century and again in the 12th (by which time the see had been removed to Salisbury). The Norman crossing and much other work survives.

During the Dissolution in 1539 it was sold to the townspeople and became their parish church.

A century earlier, in 1437, the townspeople had fallen out so badly with the monks of the abbey that they burned much of the church down. They had to pay for the rebuilding, so they ended up owning a building they had already largely paid for.

Parts of the abbey were used by Sherborne School until as late as the 20th century. At one time the headmaster's house also included the 13th-century Lady Chapel.

The abbey's great glory springs from two building campaigns of the 15th century. These gave the church most of its present character, including the breathtaking fan vaults, the first ever attempted on this scale, and some of the best to be seen anywhere in the country. The vaulting is all the more effective because it achieves its greatness by

delicacy and lightness. Integral to the vaulting are many bosses with foliated, heraldic or naturalistic designs. There are corbels with scenes from 15th-century life as well as other images.

There are many treasures in the church including the heaviest peal of eight bells in the world (the tenor, Great Tom, was the gift of Cardinal Wolsey), a lovely engraved glass reredos by Laurence Whistler in the Lady Chapel, and a late 20th-century west window by John

Hayward. There are also fascinating misericords on the seats of the choir stalls, including one with a lively carving of a wife beating her husband, as well as a number of tombs. The south transept is home to a grand and imposing marble monument to John Digby, Earl of Bristol, who is flanked by his two wives. It was made by John Nost in 1698.

Opposite page: Sherborne Abbey illuminated at night (top); a misericord of a man being beaten by his wife (below).
This page: The fan-vaulted ceiling (right); the grand monument to John Digby, and delicately engraved glass reredos in the Lady Chapel (below).

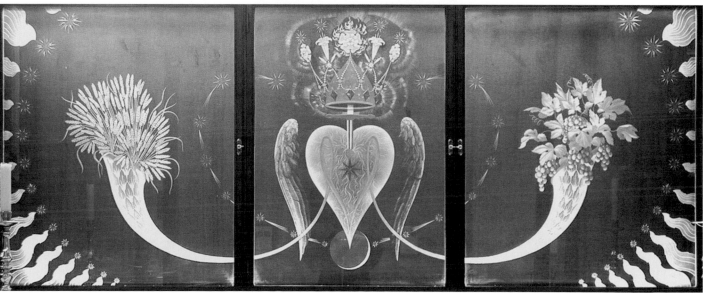

Bere Regis
St John the Baptist

Why visit: *Wonderful 15th-century roof*
Where: *Behind West Street at the end of Church Lane, BH20 7HQ*

Tucked away in a quiet part of the village, St John's church is handsome from the outside, being built of stone and flint, but it is the inside that makes this church the gem of this part of Dorset.

It is the astonishing timber roof of about 1475 that draws the eye: brightly painted beams span the nave, and protruding from them are 12 life-sized figures. Between and among these are painted faces and bosses, including a face believed to be that of Cardinal Morton; the roof was his gift to the church.

Buckland Newton
Holy Rood

Why visit: *15th-century details*
Where: *On a lane west of Buckland Newton village, west of the B3143, DT2 7BX*

Set away from its village, Buckland's church looks unappealing at first because the outside is rendered. But inside it is a fine church with an Early English chancel and 15th-century nave. Above the south doorway is a small Norman sculpture of a seated Christ and inside is a slate relief. The latter is a much earlier addition. At the entrance to the tower is a screen with delicate linenfold carving.

Cerne Abbas St Mary

Why visit: *Medieval woodwork; 17th-century texts*
Where: *Abbey Street, DT2 7JQ*

St Mary's was built by the nearby abbey (of which the gatehouse remains at the top of the village street). Largely 15th-century in appearance, including an elegant tower, the church was originally built in the 1300s. Above the west door is a stone carving of Mary and the infant Jesus. In the nave are elegant painted biblical texts, originally painted in 1679. There is a 15th-century rood screen, and the elaborate wooden pulpit with its tester dates from 1640.

Carved into the chalk hillside above the church is the world-famous Cerne Abbas Giant, which may be prehistoric, or, as some local legends say, may have been carved by a monk as a joke against a disgraced senior cleric.

Hilton All Saints

Why visit: *Rescued treasures from Milton Abbey*
Where: *North of Milton Abbey, entry via Church Row, DT11 0DG*

The church looks down through its quiet rural village towards Milton Abbey. It is predominantly 15th-century, though the porch is earlier, now being clasped by the south aisle. The windows of the north aisle were acquired at the Dissolution from the abbey cloisters and moved bodily up the hill, complete with their delightful corbels. In the church are two

beautiful panels of early 16th-century paintings showing the Apostles. These also came from Milton Abbey.

Milton Abbey

Why visit: *Majestic building*
Where: *West of Blandford Forum, north of Milton Abbas, King Edwards Drive, DT11 0BZ*

The abbey is beautifully set in a bowl of the Dorset hills, next to a great 18th-century mansion by the architect Sir William Chambers, which replaced the monastic buildings, except for the abbot's spectacular great hall.

A huge Norman church that originally stood here was completely destroyed by a fire in 1309 and the present chancel, of the late 1330s, is built on the grandest scale, though in the style of the very early 14th century. The transepts and tower followed in succeeding years but the nave was never built. In 1539, at the Dissolution of the Monasteries, the abbey became the parish church for a small town that grew up around the church.

When the estate was sold to William Damer in 1752, who later became Lord Milton, he began the mansion we see today, and also had the little town demolished so as not to spoil his view. The house is now a public school and the abbey its chapel.

Despite so many changes of fortune, the abbey is outstanding and contains many treasures. These include stone vaulted roofs, a superb medieval reredos and the poignant 18th-century marble monument to Lord and Lady Milton.

Moreton St Nicholas

Why visit: *Georgian Gothic church with outstanding 20th-century glass*
Where: *In Moreton village, off the B3390; west of Bovington Camp, DT2 8RH*

Standing proud on a prominent mound, Moreton's church is a neat and immaculate example of Georgian church architecture. It was built in 1776 and is an unusual shape, almost square, with a large semi-circular apse. The south side is

particularly graceful, with an ogee-headed doorway under the tower.

The inside is flooded with light from the large windows. These have outstanding engraved glass by the artist Sir Laurence Whistler, installed in the 1950s after the church was restored following bomb damage in 1940.

T.E. Lawrence (Lawrence of Arabia), who died in 1935, is buried in the separate cemetery down the lane.

Over Compton
St Michael

Why visit: *Setting; statue of Robert Goodden*
Where: *On Compton Road, extending east of Over Compton, DT9 4QU*

The church stands beside Over Compton House, home of the Goodden family. There are several monuments to the family in the church, the most notable being that of Robert Goodden, who died

in 1828. It is made of white marble and is life-sized, with the Squire and his clothes beautifully observed in an informal pose.

The church has a lot more to see, including a three-decker Jacobean pulpit.

Puddletown St Mary's

Why visit: *18th-century fittings; medieval tomb*
Where: *The Square, DT2 8SN*

St Mary's is big and handsome and one of the most interesting churches in the West Country. It dates mainly from the 15th century, including the carved wooden roof in the nave that is one of the most arresting features of the building.

The church has a marvellous and almost complete set of box pews, gallery, three-decker pulpit and other fittings from 1635. There is a Norman font, and there are 17th-century texts on the walls.

The Athelhampton chapel has fine tombs of the Martyn family of nearby Athelhampton. The early 16th-century tomb and effigy of Sir William Martyn is memorable for the small monkey at his feet, which has uncannily human fingers.

Trent St Andrew

Why visit: *Spire; interior rich in interest*
Where: *In Trent village between Manor House and Church Farm, DT9 4SL*

Set in a pretty, rambling village, with an early 16th-century priests' house next door, St Andrew's is a very attractive church, and has one of only three medieval spires to be found in Dorset.

Its 14th- and 15th-century interior is packed with interest, including a 15th-century font and cover, 16th-century bench-ends, and a 17th-century Flemish

carved pulpit. But pride of place is taken by the superb 16th-century screen, which is one of the best in Dorset.

Yetminster St Andrew's

Why visit: *Carvings and furnishings*
Where: *South-east of Yeovil, off the A37, Church Street, DT9 6LG*

The church has a 13th-century chancel but the rest of the church – nave, aisles, tower and porch – is unusually the product of one building campaign, of about 1470, and is fashionably embattled.

Of that period inside the church are several small sculptures, including a fox being hung by geese, the remains of much painted decoration in the roof, and several benches, some with poppyheads.

Opposite page: Apostle in the roof at Bere Regis (left); Cerne Abbas (centre); Milton memorial, Milton Abbey (right).
This page: Moreton (left); effigy at Puddletown (centre); Trent (above).

ALSO IN THE AREA

Melbury Bubb St Mary
Why visit: *Remarkable font*

Whitcombe CCT
Why visit: *Lovely church with wall painting of St Christopher*

Winterborne Came
St Peter CCT
Why visit: *Atmospheric church among trees*

Nether Cerne All Saints CCT
Why visit: *Idyllic setting*

EAST DORSET

Wimborne's fascinating minster makes a grand focus for the churches of this part of Dorset. Many of the churches in the area are tucked away in quiet countryside, but they are well worth seeking out, often for their unspoiled interiors.

Wimborne Minster

Why visit: *One of the most interesting churches in Dorset*
Where: *High Street, BH21 1HT*

This large and exciting church, dedicated to St Cuthburga, was founded in 705. A nunnery here was dissolved in the 11th century and a college of canons served the parish until the Dissolution. There is a small fragment of Saxon work but today the grand late Norman nave and central lantern tower are succeeded by a raised chancel of the following century, with its famous 12th-century Moses corbel and an east window of three elegant lancets.

The tall west tower was added in the late 15th century, as was a nave clerestory and timbered roof and, later still, completely inappropriate but rather charming battlements on the tower. The stone used for the church is of several different kinds and colours, giving it a mottled appearance.

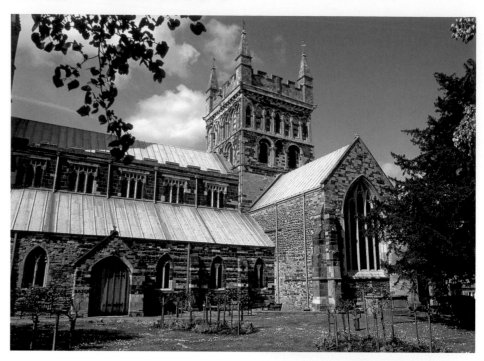

Monuments appear in profusion inside the church and include an unusual one to 17th-century lawyer Anthony Ettricke, who committed the Duke of Monmouth to the Tower. He was such an awkward man that he announced that he would not be buried in the church or out of it – so his tomb was set half in and half out of the south wall of the Chapel of the Holy Trinity.

Nearby are the dignified effigies of John and Margaret de Beaufort, grandparents of Henry VII. They are holding hands. In St George's Chapel is the tomb and effigy of Sir Edmund Uvedale, who died in 1606. He is in armour, lying on his side and propping himself up on his elbow. He has two left feet, the result of the right one having been broken off in an accident and being replaced with a copy of his left foot by mistake. Next to Sir Edmund is a wooden Saxon chest made from a solid lump of oak in about 900.

An astronomical clock dating from about 1320 shows the sun and the moon going round the earth. On the first floor of the south transept there is a chained library from 1686, with many ancient books. Under the west tower is a memorial tablet to Isaac Gulliver, a well-known smuggler who was also twice church warden.

Blandford Forum
St Peter and St Paul

Why visit: *Important 18th-century church*
Where: *Church Lane, DT11 7AD;*
usually open 9.30am–12 noon

The town of Blandford, church and all, was burned down in 1739, and the highly cultivated local builder architects, the Bastard brothers, rebuilt it in the finest contemporary style.

Now in sad disrepair, the church is one of the best examples of mid-18th-century work in the country, still with most of its contemporary pews and a grand organ of 1796 in the west gallery. The highly sympathetic chancel was added by a local builder in 1896 – he mounted the Georgian apse on rollers and ran the whole thing to the east!

Chalbury All Saints

Why visit: *Georgian fittings*
Where: *North of Wimborne Minster, on lanes east of the B3078, BH21 7EY*

Tiny and remote, the whitewashed church at Chalbury dates back as far as the 12th century but contains a full 18th-century set of perfectly preserved furnishings, including a three-decker pulpit, squire's pew and box pews. Opposite the squire's pew is a row of seats for servants, while some of the enclosed pews were reserved for different farms in the area. The nave is separated from the chancel by a delightful arch supported on slender wooden pillars.

Tarrant Rushton St Mary

Why visit: *Lamb of God lintel*
Where: *At the end of a lane north of the hamlet, past the mill, DT11 8SQ*

Perhaps the prettiest of the series of churches in the Tarrant valley, St Mary's is a largely 14th-century church with a feeling of great antiquity. It is notable for the remarkable carved 12th-century lintel over the door depicting the Lamb of God flanked by enigmatic figures. In the chancel are two large jars called acoustic pots, which were used to make the services more audible in the body of the church. There are also three fantastically shaped squints, or hagioscopes.

Wimborne St Giles
St Giles

Why visit: *Superb restoration by Sir Ninian Comper*
Where: *Butts Close, BH21 5LZ*

St Giles' church stands beside a picturesque almshouse and near to the great house of the Ashley Coopers, Earls of Shaftesbury. It is externally 18th-century but reached its present internal form in 1910 when, after a fire, it was fitted out entirely by Sir Ninian Comper with a reredos, screen, glass, furniture, gallery, organ case, font cover and all – a perfect Comper church.

The church has grand Ashley memorials including a magnificent tomb of 1627 of Sir Anthony, a Rysbrack bust of the 1st Earl and a grand Scheemakers standing wall monument for the 3rd Earl.

Every window has the Comper signature of a strawberry leaf, but they are not always easy to find.

Winterborne Tomson
St Andrew CCT

Why visit: *Delightful tiny church with box pews*
Where: *Next to a farmyard off lanes just to the north of the A31, east of Bere Regis, DT11 9HA*

Tiny and neat, Winterborne Tomson's church is a quintessential Norman chapel, complete with an apse at the east end. It has no tower, just the smallest possible bellcote.

Inside the church is charm itself, with silvery oak box pews, a pulpit and rudimentary screen. The wagon roof also has pale oak beams. The church was rescued by architect A.R. Powys and restored in memory of Thomas Hardy. The restoration money came from the sale of one of Hardy's manuscripts.

Opposite page: The 12th-century Moses corbel in Wimborne Minster (left); its central tower (top right); the nave of the church (centre right); the unusual astronomical clock (below right).
***This page:** St Peter and St Paul, Blandford Forum (left); squint at Tarrant Rushton (centre); delightful and tiny St Andrew's, Winterborne Tomson (above).*

ALSO IN THE AREA

Canford Magna
Why visit: *Naval memorials*

Poole St James
Why visit: *Georgian woodwork*

Tarrant Crawford
St Mary the Virgin CCT
Why visit: *14th-century wall paintings*

WALL PAINTINGS AND SCULPTURE

Medieval churches were full of art. In some, almost every available surface was covered in paintings; the same church may have had a carved and painted screen, a life-size rood or Crucifixion, and possibly rich vestments for the priest as well as gold and silver vessels for the taking of the Communion.

Wall paintings

The earliest wall paintings date from the beginning of the 12th century, a time when very many churches were bright with paintings. The scenes depicted were biblical stories, biblical characters, symbolic images, or legends with a clear moral message. Where pictures could not fit, then patterns were used, and the traces of such painted decoration can often still be made out on pillars, arches and around the church windows.

The pictures told the Bible's stories in visual terms for congregations who could not read. Many look unsophisticated to our eyes, but in most the message or image is quite clear, which was the point of them. Some are masterpieces in their own right, and show the love and mastery of line which marks out so much British art.

Some of the oldest wall paintings are at Kempley, Gloucestershire, dating back to perhaps as early as the 1130s, and the most complete set of their age in England. Virtually the whole of the chancel is covered in them. Many are frescoes, painted directly on to wet plaster. They show Christ in Majesty, Angels, the Evangelists and much more.

'Doom' paintings were favourites for many artists. In these, the Last Judgement is depicted, often with imaginatively horrible scenes showing sinners about to endure the eternal torments of hell. Doom paintings were most often placed on and around the chancel arch – a large space, and one that directly confronted the congregation. In Salisbury, the Church of St Thomas has just such a Doom in that position; it was re-touched in the 19th century but almost certainly retains the content and impact it had when painted in the late 15th century.

Even more graphic in its depictions of the fate awaiting sinners is the 'Ladder of Souls' painting at Chaldon in Surrey. Here, the 13th-century artist has let his imagination run riot, with the lower part of the painting showing devils dealing with those guilty of each of the Seven Deadly Sins. The upper part of the picture shows souls being weighed on one side and Christ defeating Satan on the other. The parts of the painting are linked by a picture of a ladder, the upper part of which reaches up to heaven.

Individual saints were often shown in wall paintings, one of the most popular being St Christopher carrying the child

Screens and roods

The most arresting elements in medieval churches other than the wall paintings were screens and their associated roods, or Crucifixions. Made of wood or stone, these separated the nave from the chancel. Most were elaborately carved and painted. The rood itself consisted of Jesus on the cross, flanked by Mary and St John the Evangelist. All the roods were removed during the Reformation and none now survive. But there are still many screens – especially wooden ones – to be seen, and they often remain the highlight of the church.

The best areas for screens are East Anglia and the West Country. In East Anglia among the most celebrated are at Ranworth (*below*) and Attleborough, both in Norfolk. They are 15th-century and stretch across the width of their churches. In Devon, exceptionally beautiful screens can be seen at Kentisbeare and Hartland.

Jesus. These pictures often face the main entrance to the church, as at Whitcombe in Dorset.

During the Reformation many wall paintings were whitewashed over, replaced with painted texts from the Bible, themselves often remarkable works of art. When the Arts and Crafts movement became influential in the

19th century, visual art returned to church with a flourish, with artists such as Edward Burne-Jones creating a new language for religious art based on traditions going back nearly 1,000 years.

Sculpture

Huge amounts of sculpture, especially imagery of, or connected with, the Virgin Mary was destroyed or defaced during the Reformation, when 'popery' came to be feared and loathed. But you can still see sculpture of all sorts from all periods, such as the Saxon flying angel at St Michael's Church, Winterbourne Steepleton in Dorset, or the breathtaking array of Norman sculpture at Kilpeck, Herefordshire, including a holy water stoup with carved hands clasped round it.

Easter sepulchres, where they survive, are often richly carved, as at All Saints, Hawton in Nottinghamshire, where the 14th-century sculptor has included superb sleeping soldiers guarding the tomb of Jesus. Wooden sculpture ranges from a medieval angel at St James's, Louth in Lincolnshire, to the early 18th-century 'Poor Man of Pinhoe' who stands on a box on which is inscribed 'Remember Ye Poor'.

Opposite page: Extraordinarily complete wall paintings at Kempley, Gloucestershire.
This page: Doom painting over the chancel arch at St Thomas, Salisbury, Wiltshire.

Church art today

Modern art often seems to work best in modern settings, as at St Laurence Church, Catford, London. Here, a huge polished steel circlet surrounds a glass cross. But the most interesting churches are often the ones with objects and art from many different ages, and it is perhaps a missed opportunity that there is so little contemporary art in old churches. It can work: All Saints, Tudeley, Kent, has stained glass windows designed by artist Marc Chagall. The first one was installed in 1967 and was so successful that Chagall windows were commissioned for the entire church, the last ones being installed in 1985.

THE EDGE OF SALISBURY PLAIN

This small area of west Wiltshire holds quite a concentration of the stonemason's art in a handful of villages that had access to limestone (much of Wiltshire is on unworkable chalk). Edington's 14th-century church heralded the beginning of Perpendicular architecture in the area, and by the following century prosperous clothiers were providing the funds for the new style to find exuberant expression in carved stonework of almost every kind: soaring vaulting, slender pinnacles, delicate window tracery and gruesome gargoyles.

Edington Priory Church

Why visit: *Cathedral-like village church structurally largely unchanged since the 14th century*
Where: *In Edington village, off the B3098, Monastery Road, BA13 4QJ*

With its unusual dedication to St Mary, St Katharine and All Saints, Edington's battlemented church is of a size and splendour out of all proportion to the quiet little village in which it stands. Its history explains all: it was founded as a monastic church in 1351 by a local man who attained national importance both in the Church and as a royal administrator. William of Edington had become Bishop of Winchester in 1346 and was planning a new nave and west front for the city's great cathedral, so he was no stranger to grand churches. The other priory buildings have disappeared, but the church is as fine as ever. It is a wonderful setting for the sacred music of the Edington Festival. This has taken place every August for more than 50 years and hosts cathedral choirs and other distinguished performers.

The date of this beautifully proportioned cruciform church is remarkable: it was built very shortly after the Black Death – a time when church building had suffered along with many other aspects of community life. A second unusual fact is that the church, completed within a mere 10 years, encapsulates the change from the Decorated to the Perpendicular style, incorporating features from both. Compare the styles of the windows and stonework in different parts of the church and note the distinctions.

The structure is basically unaltered since it was built, and there is even some original 14th-century glass remaining, but the interior had a 17th-century re-fit when the pink-and-white plaster ceilings of the nave and crossing were installed, along with some fine woodwork including the pulpit, font cover and communion rails.

These improvements were probably funded by the Lewis family, who lived in what then remained of the priory. The 17th-century monument in the chancel is to Sir Edward Lewis (who died in 1630) and his wife, Lady Anne Beauchamp.

This page: *Edington Priory (top left); the monument to Sir Edward Lewis and Lady Anne Beauchamp (far left). Cherub detail on the ceiling of the Lewis tomb (left).*
Opposite page: *Sharington monument at Lacock (left); Old Dilton (top centre); one of the many carvings at Steeple Ashton (centre, below) and soaring nave (right).*

Great Chalfield
All Saints

Why visit: *Historic church in an unforgettable setting*
Where: *In the hamlet of Great Chalfield, between Melksham and Bradford-on-Avon, SN12 8NJ*

A medieval manor house complete with a moat (now in the care of the National Trust) shares an idyllic location with this little church, which is recorded as early as 1349. The nave was built around then, though there was a chapel here before that, and the font may well date from that time. The church has a great sense of continuity, with family chapels from the 15th and 18th centuries, a three-decker pulpit of around 1680, and a modern stained glass window by local artist Andrew Taylor, depicting the parable of the sower. The spired bellcote contains a single bell, which was cast in 1622.

Lacock St Cyriac

Why visit: *Gargoyles; decorated bosses*
Where: *Off to the east of the main street, Church Street, SN15 2LB*

The village of Lacock is indelibly linked with pioneering photographer, William Henry Fox Talbot, whose family home was Lacock Abbey. The mainly 15th-century parish church, with its unusual dedication and lavish detailing, is worth a visit for its decorative vaulting, gargoyles, bosses and the fine 16th-century tomb of William Sharington, Fox Talbot's ancestor.

Old Dilton
Blessed Virgin Mary CCT

Why visit: *Rural setting; unspoilt Georgian interior*
Where: *South-east of Dilton Marsh, off the A350, BA13 4DB*

Grassy slopes and a wooded lane frame this little rural church whose community mostly deserted it some 300 years ago with the decline of the wool industry – though regular services took place here until a new church was built at nearby Dilton Marsh in 1844. The 18th-century interior has survived intact: an airy space full of unpretentious charm, with box pews, a three-decker pulpit and a gallery that served as a schoolroom (complete with fireplace). The churchyard and exterior are equally unspoilt, all overlooked by a little stone spire rising above a bellcote.

Steeple Ashton St Mary

Why visit: *Lavish collection of 15th-century carvings, both inside and out*
Where: *North of village centre, just off the main street, Church Street, BA14 6EW*

This village church of 1500 has such an amazing array of roof pinnacles that it is known locally as the Cathedral of Avon Vale. It must have looked even more splendid before it lost its spire in the late 17th century, after it was twice struck by lightning. The interior is just as impressive, with light pouring in through the huge Perpendicular windows of the clerestory, and elegant vaulting, in both wood and stone, of which any cathedral could be proud. Take time to look closely at the vast array of carvings, both figurative and decorative, that seem to pop up wherever you look.

ALSO IN THE AREA

Keevil St Leonard
Why visit: *Interesting monuments and important screen*

Trowbridge St James
Why visit: *Large Perpendicular church with angel ceiling and stained glass*

Westbury All Saints
Why visit: *Large 15th-century cruciform church with a notable peal of eight bells*

SOUTH WILTSHIRE

The A303 trunk road to the West Country cuts straight through this part of Wiltshire, but only a few minutes from the road there are peaceful towns and villages in wonderfully unspoilt countryside. The churches in this area are often surprisingly grand; Mere and Tisbury being the prime examples. There are much smaller, more modest but still very worthwhile churches, such as at Stourton, on the remarkable National Trust Stourhead Estate.

Mere
St Michael the Archangel

Why visit: *Setting; pews; monuments; screen*
Where: *In Church Street, off Salisbury Street and beyond the library, BA12 6DS*

These days Mere is a quiet little town, bypassed by the ever-thundering A303 to the north. The church and its yard are tucked away in an even quieter part of town, surrounded by pretty cottages. The churchyard is spacious, dotted with tombs and with 12 yew trees tightly clipped into skittle shapes. These are known as the 12 Apostles.

The church itself is exceptionally interesting, both inside and out. The 15th-century tower looks down on a building from the 13th, 14th and 15th centuries. It is usually approached from the north, but the south side is intriguing. There is a military-looking porch and the Bettesthorne Chapel, with its parapet pierced by keyhole-shaped openings that reinforce the castle look.

Inside, the church still has its pews dating from 1640, and a restored medieval screen that has a Crucifixion flanked by figures of the Virgin Mary and St John. The handsome font, with shield and quatrefoil patterns, is 15th-century with a later base.

The Bettesthorne Chapel is a highlight, with 14th- and 15th-century tombs and brasses, and some medieval glass in the windows. In the chancel the choir stalls are Victorian but have retained 10 of the original medieval misericords from the 14th and 16th centuries. Much of the stained glass is also Victorian, but some of it is of a high quality, by Henry Holiday and the well-known firm of Clayton and Bell. There are traces of wall paintings on the south wall.

Donhead St Mary
St Mary

Why visit: *Imposing village church; features from almost every period of its history*
Where: *Near the centre of Donhead St Mary, Church Hill, SP7 9DJ*

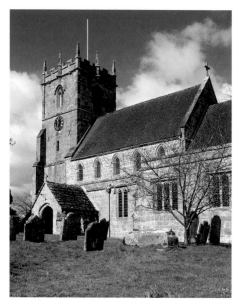

Tucked away on opposite sides of the Nadder valley, the Donhead parishes – St Mary and St Andrew – once made up an estate that belonged to Shaftesbury Abbey. In the 11th century the land was divided into two parishes, each with its own church. It is thought that St Mary's was the first to be founded. The deep tub font with arch and pillar moulding dates from the 12th century, while much of the present building is 13th-century, including the lancet windows of the nave clerestory. Later additions include 15th-century work such as the tower. The roof and other features, including much of the glass, date from a 19th-century restoration.

East Knoyle St Mary

Why visit: *Links with Sir Christopher Wren; chancel plasterwork*
Where: *Hindon Road, SP3 6AE*

This village is known for its connection with Sir Christopher Wren, who was born in a cottage here in 1632. His father (also called Christopher) was rector of the 13th-century church, and would have been familiar with the battlemented tower that dates from about 1450. Dr Wren commissioned the ornate pictorial plasterwork in the chancel, only to have it used as evidence against him at his trial during the Civil War; the Puritans considering it idolatrous. He lost his living but the plasterwork has survived. Recent additions to the church include a 20th-century window by architect and artist Sir Ninian Comper, and a window that commemorates the millennium.

Maiden Bradley
All Saints

Why visit: *17th-century fittings*
Where: *Church Street (B3092), BA12 7HA*

Although fragments of Saxon stonework have been found here, the earliest documented evidence of a church on this site is from 1102, and the earliest parts of the present church date from the 1170s. Much of the church, however, dates from the 14th century. As with so many churches, a great deal of restoration work was done in the 19th century.

The church is entered through its original 14th-century oak door, still with its hinges and iron studs. The handsome font with four supporting pillars is made of Purbeck marble and dates from about 1200. The pulpit, the front of the priests' stalls and the pews in the centre of the nave are late 17th-century.

Stourton St Peter

Why visit: *A part of the Stourhead landscape; Stourton and Hoare family monuments*
Where: *Beside a minor road opposite the pedestrian entrance to Stourhead garden, High Street, BA12 6QE*

This pleasing little medieval church is much visited, standing as it does in a key position overlooking the 18th-century picturesque landscape of Stourhead – now a popular National Trust estate. The monuments are a popular attraction, including those of the Stourton family, who had been established here for many generations before Henry Hoare I (1677–1725). When he bought the property in 1717, he set about replacing the medieval house to create the Stourhead that we know today. His son, also Henry (1705–85), developed the remarkable landscaped grounds. There are monuments to both men, and to other Hoare family members. The church has kept parts of its 14th-century work, though there was a Victorian reconstruction, during which it acquired another aisle, a vestry and a clock.

Opposite page: The tower of St Michael's, Mere (top left), and a detail of the medieval glass in the Bettesthorne Chapel (below left); Donhead St Mary (right).
This page: 17th-century pews at Maiden Bradley (left); monument to Henry Hoare I in Stourton church (centre); Tisbury (right).

Tisbury
St John the Baptist

Why visit: *Large and historic church*
Where: *In Church Street, off High Street, at the south end of Tisbury, SP3 6AZ*

It is possible that there has been a church on this site since Saxon times, as it is known that there was an abbey in Tisbury in the 7th century. Between 1180 and 1200 an impressive Norman church was built here, and parts of this remain in today's church. The chancel was rebuilt at the end of the 13th century, and the nave was rebuilt in 1450. In the 1700s the spire was struck by lightning twice. The second time, in 1762, the spire collapsed, destroying parts of the church. Restorations were carried out in the 1850s at the instigation of the vicar, F.E. Huchinson.

There are excellent roofs in the church, and the pulpit and some of the pews are from the 1600s. Members of the Arundell family of nearby Wardour Castle are buried in the chancel, including Lady Blanche, who defended the castle against Parliamentary forces for nine days in 1643. She had 25 men compared to the Parliamentary force of 1,300.

ALSO IN THE AREA

Berwick St Leonard
St Leonard CCT
Why visit: *12th-century church; 17th-century monuments*

Fisherton Delamere
St Nicholas CCT
Why visit: *Flint and stone church with a 20th-century screen*

SOUTHERN ENGLAND

It is still possible in southern England to escape from bustling towns and busy roads and enjoy beautiful countryside that provides remarkably quiet and rural locations for many of its churches. The influences of Norman and Saxon incomers can be seen in many of them.

Hampshire is a county of contrasts: chalklands in the north and centre, and clay and gravel in the south-west, much of it covered by the New Forest. Hampshire's churches are modest for the most part, often built of local materials, with brick and flint much in evidence. Many of them have somehow escaped the tentacles of development, even those in the shadow of large towns.

Berkshire is even more prey to the demands for development, but its western downs and their chalk-stream valleys are unspoiled, and probably more prosperous now than during the 14th–17th centuries' wool trade. As with Hampshire, many churches are unassuming and built of local materials.

Until medieval times and beyond, Surrey was very thinly populated, as the poor soils and dense forests discouraged large-scale settlement. But it does have stone of various sorts suitable for building, so its – for the most part – modest churches often have charm enhanced by being built of a pleasing mix of materials, including wood, which was plentiful.

Sussex (West and East) shares, with Surrey, the Weald, a huge area that was still thickly forested at the end of the Middle Ages. The iron industry brought wealth, and some is reflected in Sussex churches. The chalklands, including those at the coast, were easier to travel through and cultivate, and the Sussex coast was often where visitors (and invaders) from Europe landed, including, most famously the Normans, who began their conquest here. All of those factors and influences can be seen in Sussex's varied churches.

Kent, like Sussex, was also historically influenced by incomers, including the Romans, and, later the Normans. Kent's churches reflect that history, including the finest Norman work at Barfrestone and Patrixbourne, as well as the very different Romney Marsh churches.

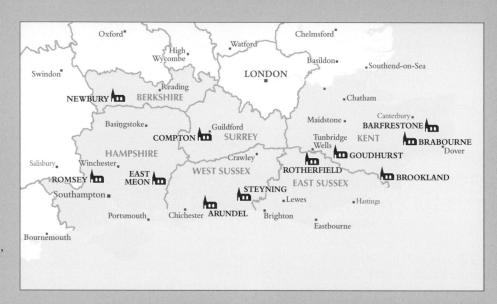

Opposite page: *St Mary and St Blaise, the ancient priory church in Boxgrove, between Chichester and Arundel, is a wonderful mix of styles dating from the 12th century and later.*

AROUND THE NEW FOREST

West Hampshire's most imposing church is Romsey Abbey, an important Norman building that protects unique Saxon sculpture. To the south of Romsey is the New Forest and here, as well as on the forest's western edges, is a cluster of churches that range from Saxon at Breamore, to High Victorian at Lyndhurst, to delightful country churches at East Wellow, Ellingham and Minstead.

Romsey Abbey of St Mary and St Ethelflaeda

Why visit: *Superb Norman architecture; two Saxon roods*
Where: *In the centre of Romsey, on Church Lane, SO51 8EN*

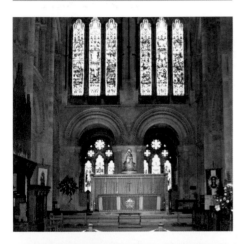

Founded in 907, the abbey was at first a nunnery then, from 974, a Benedictine Abbey of nuns. It escaped demolition at the Dissolution of the Monasteries because four Guardians petitioned Henry VIII for it to be saved, ultimately paying £100 so that it could belong to the townspeople of Romsey.

Although a parish church, the abbey feels like a small cathedral; this is primarily because of the unity and scale of the Norman architecture. The nave consists of massive Norman piers supporting three storeys, built between 1120 and 1250. The transepts, crossing and chancel all have the same unified Norman look and feel. Contributing to the cathedral-like atmosphere are chapels in both transepts and at the east end of the chancel. In these are monuments and treasures of many kinds, including, in the Chapel of St Nicholas, the simple grave

of Earl Mountbatten of Burma, whose family home, Broadlands, is on the outskirts of the town.

St Ethelflaeda's Chapel commemorates the abbey's 10th-century Abbess, Ethelflaeda, daughter of King Edward the Elder, who founded the abbey. An ancient tomb here is of an abbess and includes a carving of her crozier. Next door, in St Anne's Chapel, is one of Romsey's greatest treasures – a Saxon rood showing the Crucifixion of Jesus. Made in about 960, it shows Christ on the Cross surrounded by angels, the Virgin Mary and St John, and with two Roman soldiers at Christ's feet. Like all such sculpture, it had its details carefully chiselled off by religious zealots during the Reformation. Outside the abbey is another priceless rood, dating from a little later, this time showing Christ with arms outstretched in welcome and with the hand of God above his head in blessing.

Back inside the abbey, fragments of the earliest phase of building, from the 900s, can be seen on the south side of the north transept. Nearby in St Lawrence's Chapel is a 16th-century painted reredos, while St George's Chapel has floor tiles that are 700 years old. Throughout the abbey there are many richly carved and decorated corbels and capitals.

The abbey has a modest tower surmounted by a wooden belfry that was built in 1624.

Breamore St Mary

Why visit: *Saxon architecture and lettering*
Where: *North of Breamore village, next to Breamore House, SP6 2DF*

Breamore is one of the most famous and important Saxon churches in England, notable for its many Saxon details, but especially for the Saxon inscription carved into the arch of the south porticus. Translated, the inscription reads: 'Here the Covenant becomes manifest'. Other important Saxon details include a rood with later wall paintings, along with exterior masonry with typical Saxon long-and-short work and pilaster strips re-using Roman materials. The church is in a peaceful setting.

East Wellow St Margaret

Why visit: *Rural setting; burial place of Florence Nightingale*
Where: *Just off Broad Woods Lane, SO51 6DR*

Flint walls, a low, steeply pitched roof and a 15th-century wooden porch give the outside of St Margaret's a quiet rural charm. The largely 13th-century interior has an important collection of wall paintings from that time, including a figure of St Christopher carrying the infant Jesus. To his right is a figure of St Margaret of Antioch, martyred because she refused to become part of a harem.

Many people come to East Wellow church to visit the grave of Florence Nightingale, who was buried here with great ceremony on 20 August 1910 and with almost the entire village in attendance. She lies in the family grave, even though her own wish had been to give her body to medical research.

Ellingham St Mary

Why visit: *Ancient and welcoming church with outstanding 15th-century screen*
Where: *In Ellingham, at end of a cul-de-sac lane off Ellingham Drove, BH24 3PJ*

Although largely stone-built, St Mary's is entered through a charming early 18th-century brick porch, with a large blue and gold sundial. Inside, the church has a 15th-century barrel roof and screen, above which is a plaster tympanum on which are painted the Creed, the Ten Commandments and the Lord's Prayer. The pulpit is Jacobean.

Lyndhurst
St Michael and All Angels

Why visit: *Outstanding Pre-Raphaelite decorations*
Where: *In the centre of Lyndhurst, on Church Lane, SO43 7BD*

This Victorian church was built between 1858 and 1869 to the designs of William White, who may have been inspired by Gothic ideas, but who created a building that is idiosyncratic and personal.

The exterior of red brick with yellow detailing is dominated by a large spire-topped tower. But it is the interior that makes this church so special. Here, the idiosyncratic architecture works especially well, with exposed brick in reds, yellow and white being used to great effect, particularly in the arches. In the nave roof are life-sized wooden angels.

Many of the greatest names in Victorian arts and crafts have works in the church: there is stained glass designed by William Morris (some consider this to be his finest work in glass), Edward Burne-Jones, and by the renowned firm of Clayton and Bell. Capping it all is a remarkable picture by Frederick, Lord Leighton of the story of the Wise and Foolish Virgins.

Outside is the grave of Alice Hargreaves, better known by her maiden name of Alice Liddell, who inspired Lewis Carroll to write the *Alice* stories. She was born in 1852 and died aged 82 on 16 November 1934.

Minstead All Saints

Why visit: *Beguiling unrestored New Forest church*
Where: *On lane south of Minstead village, opposite junction with Congleton Close, SO43 7EX*

The forest crowds up to the churchyard here, and yews and oaks overhang the lychgate. From the outside, the little church looks rather like a cottage with extensions added willy-nilly. The informal feel is reinforced inside with an enchanting jumble of seats, private pews and galleries dating from the 17th and 18th centuries.

All Saints probably looks as many rural churches did before Victorian restorations tidied them up; its remote rural setting helped it to escape such attentions. So the private pews remained, some with fireplaces and furnishings. The tomb of Sir Arthur Conan Doyle, the creator of Sherlock Holmes, is in the churchyard.

Opposite page: Romsey Abbey exterior (top) and interior (below).
This page: The Nightingale family memorial at East Wellow; Florence is remembered simply as 'FN' (left); Lyndhurst tower (centre); Minstead (above).

ALSO IN THE AREA

Damerham St George
Why visit: *Rural setting; castle-like exterior; light-filled interior*

Fordingbridge St Mary
Why visit: *Friendly town church with historic details*

Hale St Mary
Why visit: *Rural setting; stern Baroque exterior*

SOUTH-EAST HAMPSHIRE

Many of the churches in this cluster are in the Meon Valley and are associated with St Wilfrid, who came here in the mid-7th century to convert the pagan Meonwara tribe. So it is perhaps not surprising that some of the churches have Saxon origins, and several are still substantially Saxon. Today, south-east Hampshire is dominated by Portsmouth and its ever-expanding suburbs and road network, but all the churches described here are in rural or village settings.

Corhampton

Why visit: *Tiny Saxon church*
Where: *Just off the A32 in Corhampton hamlet; use signed car park, SO32 3ND*

This tiny church, perched on top of a round mound that may be prehistoric, is almost entirely Saxon. There is Saxon detailing to be seen on the outside in the form of pilaster strips, long-and-short work, and the Saxon doorways. Inside, there is a Saxon chancel arch, and interesting medieval wall paintings.

The east end of the church collapsed in 1842 as a result of a road widening scheme, and was carelessly repaired in red brick. Like South Boarhunt, at the other end of the Meon valley, Corhampton church has a huge and ancient yew tree overshadowing it.

Droxford
St Mary and All Saints

Why visit: *Many ancient features*
Where: *Off the main street (A32), SO32 3PA*

What a visitor first sees of Droxford's church is the imposing square flint tower and its stair turret, both dating from the 16th century. The rest of the church is also built of flint, but mainly from the 12th and 13th centuries, inside and out. Both the north and south doors are Norman, with typical zig-zag ornamenting around them.

A good deal of repair work was done in Georgian times, including the insertion of the little dormer windows that add charm to the roof.

Inside, the church is full of interest, from the massive 12th-century pillars to the neat box pews, each with a little door.

East Meon All Saints

Why visit: *An outstanding Norman church with one of the country's most famous fonts*
Where: *The Hyde, GU32 1NJ*

This is by far the grandest church in the Meon valley, largely built by the Normans in the period from 1080 to 1150. It stands high above the village, and the tall broach spire above the massive Norman stone tower is visible for miles.

The church is entered through an imposing Norman south door, and the interior is dominated by the massive Norman arches of the crossing. Elsewhere there is Early English work from the 13th century, with windows from the 14th and 15th centuries. In the late 19th century the church was heavily restored, with further restoration in the early 20th century by Sir Ninian Comper.

East Meon's greatest treasure is the font of black Tournai marble, one of only seven such in England, four of which are in Hampshire. Dating from about 1150, it was made in Tournai in Flanders, and was probably a gift to the church from the Bishop of Winchester, Henry of Blois.

Idsworth St Hubert

Why visit: *Idyllic church; rural setting*
Where: *On lanes north-east of Finchdean; south-east of Chalton, PO8 0BE*

This lovely little church has everything going for it on the outside: a superb setting in the middle of fields under huge skies, appealing red-tiled roofs, glittering flint walls, and an idiosyncratic boarded bell-turret.

Inside, it is better still. The church escaped Victorian restoration entirely, but was brilliantly rescued and repaired by architect Harry Goodhart-Rendel in 1912. He renovated the box pews, Jacobean pulpit and much more, and revealed the Norman and later origins of the church. The delicate plasterwork in the chancel roof is his. In the chancel is a splendid plaque celebrating Thomas Padwick and Thomas Smith, earlier repairers of the church in the late 18th and early 19th centuries.

Also in the chancel is the greatest treasure, a wall painting of about 1330. In two parts, the lower part shows scenes from the life of St John the Baptist, while the upper may represent scenes from the life of St Hubert, or be a re-telling of legends surrounding the early life of St John – experts differ in their opinion.

South Boarhunt
St Nicholas

Why visit: *Remarkable Saxon survivor*
Where: *Boarhunt Road, in the tiny hamlet of South Boarhunt, PO17 6HP*

This Saxon church has changed very little since it was built sometime before 1066. There were repairs and restorations in the 18th and 19th centuries, but these have not changed the Saxon feel. Externally, the most exciting Saxon feature is the window (now blocked on the inside) on the north side, towards the east end. It may have been the only window in the original church. Inside, the dominant feature is the Saxon chancel arch. Most of the fittings – pews, pulpit, gallery – date from the restoration of 1853, although they feel earlier. There is excellent and intricate flintwork called galletting on the west front.

Southwick St James

Why visit: *Perfect village church packed with interest*
Where: *High Street, PO17 6EF*

This beautifully cared-for church was largely rebuilt in 1566, and then remained virtually unchanged until the Georgian period. The west gallery with its barley-twist wooden columns, the upholstered box pews, nicely done up in blue with red carpets, the three-decker pulpit (also furnished in reds and blues), and the reredos with its Baroque painting all date from that time.

Warblington
St Thomas a Becket

Why visit: *Rural, coastal ancient building*
Where: *Off Church Lane, a small lane off the A27 south of Emsworth, PO9 2TU*

This is a real refuge from the hurly-burly of south-east Hampshire's roaring trunk roads and endless suburbs.

Parts of the original Saxon church can be made out in the tower, and there is much of interest both inside and outside. The north porch with its massive 14th-century timbers is especially attractive. There are two early 19th-century grave watchers' huts in the churchyard among the ancient yews.

Warnford Our Lady

Why visit: *Rural setting; fascinating interior; splendid 17th-century tomb*
Where: *In Warnford Park, via footpath from A32, SO32 3LA*

Dating mainly from the 1190s, Warnford church has an earlier tower and Saxon roots. The first church on the site may have been built by St Wilfrid in the 680s. Of the many highlights, outstanding are the 17th-century wooden altar table, the chancel screen (with a 20th-century rood) and tower screen, both of about 1634, a row of wooden medieval seats, and an early 12th-century font.

Clamouring for attention, and a real surprise in such a setting, are the Neale monuments on either side of the altar. That on the south side is the most spectacular and has life-sized figures of Sir Thomas Neale (died 1621) and his two wives, and smaller figures of nine (of 10) children. At the east end of the churchyard, accessible by gate, are ruins of a rare 13th-century house, built by the St John family. By the 16th century it was reduced to being a barn, and in the 18th century was turned into a scenic ruin.

You can only reach the church by footpath; cars should be parked in Warnford.

Opposite: Norman splendour at East Meon (left); east end of Droxford (right). *This page:* Southwick's church and churchyard (top centre); the 13th-century nave at Warblington (below centre).

ALSO IN THE AREA

Fareham Holy Trinity
Why visit: *Airy, welcoming interior; innovative Victorian structure*

Meonstoke St Andrew
Why visit: *Pleasant and well-loved 13th-century village church*

Portchester St Mary
Why visit: *Grand Norman church*

Titchfield St Peter
Why visit: *Rich and complex history; extraordinary Wriothesley Monument*

IN WEST BERKSHIRE

All the churches in this group are on or near the River Lambourn, which rises on the downs close to the horse-racing centre of Lambourn and flows east along a gentle valley dotted with attractive villages to reach Newbury. The churches at either end of the valley – at Lambourn and Newbury – are splendid buildings, but in between there are much more modest churches, including the little gem at East Shefford. Two of the handful of round towers outside East Anglia can be seen in the valley.

Newbury St Nicholas

Why visit: *Outstanding 'wool church' from the 1500s*
Where: *Junction of West Mills and Bartholomew Street, RG14 5HG*

It may seem odd to us, in the 21st century, that it was not at all unusual for wealthy medieval people to spend some of their own fortunes on such buildings as churches. This is the case with Newbury's large and lavish parish church, built between 1509 and 1533 in the Perpendicular style.

The donor was John Smallwood (also known as Jack O'Newbury and John of Winchcombe), a fabulously rich merchant who made his money in the woollen cloth trade. John, who is buried in the church, did not see it finished, as he died in 1519, but his initials, 'JS', can be seen on the roof bosses and elsewhere in the church. His son inherited his father's wealth and lived to see the church completed. During the Civil War of the 1640s, Parliamentary troops took the church over and used it as a stable, prison and hospital. As well as despoiling it in that way, they also destroyed much that they considered to be 'popish'.

The church was restored in late Victorian times, and the stained glass that makes the church so gloomy was installed after the restoration.

Among the interesting things inside is a fine Jacobean pulpit dated 1607. The reredos was made by Sir Ninian Comper in the 20th century.

East Garston All Saints

Why visit: *Painted woodwork*
Where: *Just north of East Garston, off Station Road, RG17 7HH*

Tucked away in a wooded corner on the edge of East Garston, All Saints is a pretty and well cared-for church. It dates from the 12th century, with some 14th-century additions, and it was extensively restored in 1876.

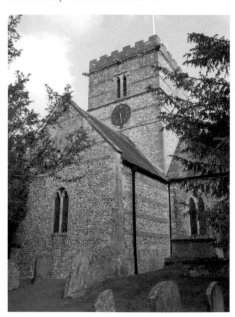

The church has a painted timber ceiling, and is especially notable for work by Victorian artist Nathaniel Westlake. He was best known for his stained glass, but at East Garston he also painted the reredos, and, in the nave, a Tree of Jesse.

This page: *The nave and chancel of St Nicholas, Newbury (centre); St Nicholas from the Kennet and Avon Canal (left); East Garston (above).*

East Shefford
St Thomas CCT

Why visit: *Tiny idyllic church in a meadow*
Where: *Off the Newbury Road, just east of Great Shefford, RG17 7EF*

There is no road access to this beguiling little church and there is no authorised parking nearby. It is approached along footpaths, but it is well worth the effort.

Its setting is lovely: in a lush meadow close to the River Lambourn and with a background of gentle Berkshire countryside. The church itself is tiny and attractive, with a bellcote at the west end.

Inside, there are remains of wall paintings from as early as the 12th century, as well as biblical texts painted after the Reformation. The most striking monument in the church is that to Sir Thomas and Lady Beatrice Fettiplace, made in about 1450, with their full-sized effigies. Another Fettiplace monument, from 1524, is set into the north wall of the chancel.

Lambourn
St Michael and All Angels

Why visit: *Handsome Norman church with chapels and monuments*
Where: *Parsonage Lane, in the centre of Lambourn, RG17 8PA*

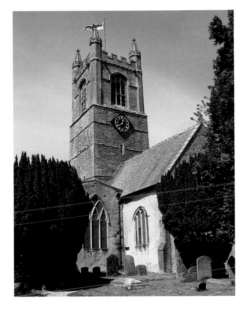

Lambourn's large and imposing church dates from about 1180, although there may well have been a church here even before the time of King Alfred. Later work includes the upper stages of the tower, from the 16th century, and chapels added at about the same time.

In St Katherine's Chapel is a mid-16th-century tomb of Sir Thomas Essex and his wife; their effigies are accompanied by a dolphin and a winged horse. German stained glass from the 16th century can also be seen here. In Holy Trinity Chapel is the tomb of John Estbury, who died in 1508. Very unusually, the brass on the tomb top retains some of its original coloured enamel. Also in Holy Trinity Chapel is an arch with hunting scenes carved on it.

Memorials in the church include a number to members of the Garrard family, spanning more than 400 years.

This page: Wall painting (top left), and Fettiplace monument (below left), both at East Shefford; the lower part of Lambourn's tower is 12th-century, the upper part 16th-century (centre); two of Wickham's bizarre elephants, inspired by a visit to a Paris exhibition (right).

Wickham St Swithins

Why visit: *Saxon tower; Victorian idiosyncrasy in the north aisle*
Where: *On Church Hill, just off the B4000, RG20 8HD*

Prepare yourself for surprises when you go into this church. From the outside nothing looks untoward, except that the tower is clearly Saxon, and the whole of the rest of the building is obviously very much later.

In fact, the body of the church was built in the 1840s by architect Benjamin Ferrey. It has a nave and north aisle, both with very high, dark roofs. And it is in the dimness of these roofs that the surprises lurk: there are carved angels in the nave, and eight enormous elephant heads in the aisle. They are here because the man paying for the new church, William Nicholson, saw four papier mâché elephant heads at an exhibition in Paris, thought they would look good in the church, and had four more specially made to go with them. The decor in the rest of the church is exuberant, but it's the elephants that stay in the memory.

ALSO IN THE AREA

Boxford St Andrew
Why visit: *15th-century, with Saxon remains*

Great Shefford St Mary
Why visit: *The oldest of Berkshire's two round towers*

Welford St Gregory
Why visit: *The other round tower in Berkshire*

AROUND ARUNDEL

The part of Sussex around Arundel and Chichester, between the South Downs and the sea, has a legacy of foreign influences that have shaped Britain's story. The Romans established a great palace at Fishbourne, beside a sheltered creek near Chichester. King Harold sailed from Bosham to meet William of Normandy. The great monastic tradition of Normandy was introduced to England here, and Caen stone arrived from France to build some of our cathedrals. This rich past is reflected in the area's enormously varied churches.

Arundel St Nicholas

Why visit: *Complex history; unusual semi-enclosed stone pulpit*
Where: *London Road, BN18 9AT; parish office open Tue–Fri*

As part of Arundel's striking hilltop townscape, the parish church is eclipsed by more flamboyant buildings that are visible for miles around: notably the huge 'Victorianised' castle and the Roman Catholic cathedral. However, the Church of St Nicholas has an interesting and unique history.

Built in 1380, when Arundel was already well established as a busy international port and market town, its main church served two communities. Like many town churches, it was both a monastic and a parish building: here, the nave belonged to the town and the chancel to a college of priests. This worked until 1544, but when Henry VIII swept away the monasteries, the east end of the church became the property of the Fitzalan family of Arundel Castle.

St Nicholas's has, in effect, been two separate places of worship ever since: one Roman Catholic, the other Anglican.

The former chancel, which was completely walled off for many years, can now at least be seen through a wrought-iron grille. Known as the Fitzalan Chapel, it is the grandest part of the church, with Perpendicular windows and a collection of elaborate monuments of the Fitzalan family, Earls of Arundel, and their heirs, the Dukes of Norfolk. The chapel can normally be reached only from the castle.

The nave is largely unaltered from its 1380 building. From around the same time are the octagonal font, made of Sussex marble, and faded wall paintings, in the north aisle, depicting the seven deadly sins and the seven works of mercy. The unusually elaborate canopied stone pulpit in the centre aisle, thought to be slightly later in date, was designed by one of the architects of Canterbury Cathedral.

Outside, it is worth walking round to the west end of the church to see the fine Perpendicular west window and the attractive porch below. Both are part of a planned restoration programme to make a grand entrance to the church.

Birdham St James

Why visit: *Unusual tower of 1545*
Where: *In Church Lane, Birdham, PO20 7SP*

Huge buttresses and a massive stair-turret flank the 16th-century tower of this tucked-away village church south-west of Chichester, the cathedral of which is depicted, with Jesus and St James in a boat, in the modern stained glass of the east window. A mix of ancient and modern is characteristic of the church, with the 14th-century work of the nave and chancel arch sitting alongside the results of Victorian and later restorations, and some modern furnishings. A very old, incredibly twisted yew tree stands in the churchyard.

This page: The 15th-century cadaver tomb of the 14th Earl of Arundel (left), and the east end (centre) of St Nicholas's, Arundel. The church has been divided in two since the 16th century – the nave is Anglican, the chancel is Roman Catholic.

Bosham Holy Trinity

Why visit: *Ancient church in a delightful waterside village*
Where: *High Street, overlooking Bosham harbour, PO18 8LY*

Clearly annotated 'Bosham ecclesia', this venerable old church, with its great Saxon chancel arch, is depicted on the Bayeux Tapestry. Its history goes back considerably further: it stands on the site of a Roman basilica, and a Roman arch is still in place beneath the Saxon one. The lower part of the tower is also Saxon. It is topped with a distinctive shingled broach spire. The east window is remarkable for its fine group of stepped lancets with five lights – Early English windows usually have only three.

Boxgrove
St Mary and St Blaise

Why visit: *Outstanding 12th- and 13th-century priory church with exquisite 16th-century decorative work*
Where: *In the middle of Boxgrove village at the end of Church Lane, PO18 0ED*

This amazing building is the surviving part of a Benedictine priory that was established here early in the 12th century as an offshoot of the great Norman abbey of Lessay in France. The priory church is a splendid and harmonious blend of Romanesque and Gothic.

A later embellishment is the wonderful 16th-century ceiling depicting flowers and foliage surrounding family crests.

They are those of Thomas West, the 9th Lord de la Warr, who commissioned the paintings, and his wife Elizabeth. The couple are also remembered in the magnificently ornamented de la Warr chantry chapel built in 1532 – only a few years before Boxgrove Priory was dissolved by Henry VIII.

Chichester
Chapel of St John CCT

Why visit: *Rare example of a Georgian proprietary chapel*
Where: *St John's Street, Chichester, PO19 1UR*

This octagonal building of 1813 is properly titled the Proprietary Chapel of St John the Evangelist. Proprietary chapels solved a problem in towns where burgeoning populations had outgrown the parish churches, and were built to allow more people to attend services. They were funded by issuing shares and had no part in parish life, so could not hold weddings or baptisms. Well-to-do churchgoers would pay for their pews,

and free seating for the poor was often a statutory requirement.

St John's has many features typical of Georgian churches, and most of these are unchanged, though the downstairs pews (for the poor) were renewed by a Victorian benefactor. The pews in the gallery were for the proprietors: the cost of renting or buying a pew varied according to its size and position. Long sermons were the order of the day, so a conspicuous and extraordinary three-decker pulpit is the chapel's main focus, with a simple altar tucked away behind it. The four wall panels above the altar carry biblical texts rather than pictures, and the windows have plain glass panes.

Climping St Mary

Why visit: *Unusual and delightful early medieval church*
Where: *Church Lane, Climping, BN17 5RB*

The coastal parish of Climping (also spelled Clymping), just west of the River Arun, has a remarkably sturdy-looking church that is said to have begun life as a Norman watchtower. An exuberant Romanesque doorway and narrow windows with zig-zag carving would have made the tower an outstanding building in its own right, but around 1220, some 50 years after it was completed, it was joined by an Early

This page: Holy Trinity, Bosham (left); Boxgrove (top, centre) and its 16th-century painted ceiling (below centre); the early 19th-century octagonal Chapel of St John the Evangelist in Chichester (above).

English church, with a steeply pitched roof and simple, slender lancet windows. The resulting composite early medieval building is a delight.

Lyminster
St Mary Magdalene

Why visit: *Historic church; a wealth of Saxon and Norman work*
Where: *Just west of the A284 leading north out of Littlehampton, BN17 7QJ*

King Alfred is recorded as having bequeathed Lyminster to his nephew in 901. It was the site of a Benedictine nunnery, and the flint church we see today has Saxon origins as the present walls go back to about 1040. The Saxon church served both parish and nuns, who worshipped separately: parishioners in the nave and nuns in the chancel, divided by a wooden partition. Even the roof of the nave is thought to be Norman, and other 12th-century features include the font and the west door.

Selsey St Peter

Why visit: *A Victorian rebuilding with an intriguing past*
Where: *St Peter's Crescent, on the west side of the main road into Selsey village, PO20 0NP*

Selsey was an island when the Christian missionary St Wilfrid landed there in the 6th century. The monastery he founded was an important Christian centre until Chichester Cathedral was built a few miles to the north, some 500 years later.

The early history of Christianity around Selsey is hazy, partly because coastal erosion has changed the shape of this low-lying promontory over the years. Church Norton, north-east of Selsey village on the edge of Pagham Harbour, was the site of a medieval church, but by the 19th century this was not the population centre and a new church was needed. In 1865, the architect J.P. St Aubyn undertook a project that entailed moving the entire nave of the old church, and this became St Peter's: hence the 12th- and 13th-century arcades. The font is also Norman. The chancel remains where it was, and is now known as St Wilfrid's Chapel (CCT).

Sidlesham
St Mary Our Lady

Why visit: *Large Early English church near Pagham Harbour*
Where: *In Church Lane, Sidlesham, PO20 7RE*

St Mary's is a large church for its village, but imagine a time when this coastal parish and nearby Pagham Harbour were busy with maritime trade, and it is easy to see why this should have been so.

There was a church on the site in Saxon times. The present one dates from the early 13th century but is a lighter and airier building than most churches of its day. The battlemented tower and the minstrels' gallery are 15th-century. The church's interior would have been painted, and fragments of pigment can still be seen on the stonework. Look, too, for the 'mass dial', cut into a stone outside the south door to indicate service times.

Yapton St Mary

Why visit: *A pleasingly unspoilt country church*
Where: *On the corner of Church Road and Church Lane, BN18 0EH*

Yapton's charming and distinctive church has changed surprisingly little since it was completed around 1220. The tiled roof sweeping down to low eaves is typical of Sussex, and the late medieval west porch, its great timbers infilled with local flints, is a delightful example of vernacular detailing. The sturdy Norman tower is just as attractive, with its pyramidal shingled cap. It has a slight lean. Inside, don't miss the very early, tub-shaped limestone font carved with Maltese crosses and chevron patterning.

This page: Nave and chancel at St Mary, Climping (left); St Mary Our Lady, Sidlesham (centre); St Mary, Yapton (above).

ALSO IN THE AREA

Felpham St Mary
Why visit: *Mentioned in Domesday Book. Norman nave, 13th-century aisles*

East Lavant St Mary
Why visit: *Norman nave with 17th-century tower*

North Stoke
St Mary the Virgin CCT
Why visit: *Virtually unchanged medieval church*

Tortington
St Mary Magdalene CCT
Why visit: *Tiny rustic church with Norman doorway*

THE ADUR VALLEY

Sussex is full of historic villages, and the area around the River Adur has plenty of fine churches to visit. Until the 15th century the river was navigable for some miles inland, and after the Norman Conquest its lower reaches became an important shipping route, with a castle at Bramber to guard it. Like the Arun, to the west, the Adur has many early churches quite close to it, with a wealth of splendidly carved Norman arches that have escaped later 'improvements'.

Steyning
St Andrew and St Cuthman

Why visit: *Impressive mainly Norman church; carved arches and capitals*
Where: *In Vicarage Lane, on the northern edge of the town centre, BN44 3YL; parish office open week-day mornings*

Steyning is now some five miles inland, but it was once busy with seagoing vessels, which moored in an inlet known as St Cuthman's Port. St Cuthman was an 8th-century Saxon saint who settled here, and founded the first church. Over the centuries he became special to Steyning: his name was added to the dedication of the church as recently as 2009.

A modern sculpture of him was made to commemorate the millennium: he is looking across the road at his church. He is also depicted in several stained glass windows in the church: in one as a shepherd, in another as a builder, and in a third wheeling his invalid mother many miles to Steyning in a handcart – a colourful and extraordinary episode in the story of his life.

St Andrew and St Cuthman's has 12th-century craftsmanship that is remarkably fine, even in a county where much good Norman work has survived. Begun around 1080, the original church was cruciform, and nearly twice the size of the present building. It had transepts and a much longer chancel than the present 19th-century one, as well as two extra bays at the west end of the nave, where the 16th-century flint chequerwork tower now stands.

With its high roof, crossing tower and clerestory, it must have been an awesome building indeed. The earliest part that remains is that which now forms the chancel arch, immensely high and with decoratively carved capitals. The surviving bays of the nave arcade, built around 1170–80, have truly exuberant carving on most of the arches and capitals, each one different, with no shortage of the customary zig-zags and scallops as well as many less conventional motifs and designs that repay a really close look.

Amberley St Michael

Why visit: *Norman chancel arch; Early English chancel*
Where: *Church Street, towards the western end of Amberley village, BN18 9NF*

Overlooking the wetland nature reserve of Amberley Wild Brooks, St Michael's is itself overlooked by the scarp slope of the South Downs. Next to it is Amberley

This page: Fine Norman stonework at Steyning (left); St Michael, Amberley (above).

Castle, a 14th-century bishops' residence (now a hotel), all in a quintessentially pretty downland village. The interior of the church lives up to its lovely setting. A splendid Norman chancel arch, with scalloped capitals and chevron carving as at Steyning, frames a simple Early English east window of three lancets, dating from about 1230. Soon after this, the tower was begun. The south doorway, with delightful foliage carvings spilling from the capitals, followed in about 1300. Incredibly, the fragments of wall paintings of the Crucifixion, on the south side of the chancel arch, have survived from about the same period.

Bramber St Nicholas

Why visit: *Largely Norman church; an interesting setting and history*
Where: *East of the A283 and just south of Bramber Castle, BN44 3WE*

St Nicholas shares a chalk hilltop with the ruins of the castle; both were built soon after the Norman Conquest by William de Braose, a close associate of William the Conqueror. Originally a cruciform monastic church or chapel for the castle, it became a parish church in the 13th century.

The nave, with its unmistakably Norman south doorway, and the crossing (now the chancel) have survived from the original church. The chancel arch has Norman carvings on the capitals. The tower dates from a substantial 18th-century renovation programme commissioned by the vicar of the time, Thomas Green, who died in 1789 and is commemorated, with his wife and daughter, in one of the monuments in the church.

Cowfold St Peter

Why visit: *Village setting; sandstone tower; early windows in chancel*
Where: *The Street, just off the A272 in the centre of Cowfold, RH13 8DN*

Although Cowfold church stands near a very busy road junction, the churchyard has something of the character of a village green because of the array of cottages that overlook it – including Margaret Cottages, once the parish workhouse. The oldest part of the church, dating from the 13th century, is the chancel; its north-facing lancet windows still have some medieval stained glass.

The sturdily battlemented tower, of Wealden sandstone, is 15th-century, as are the timber porch, the octagonal font and an outstanding, very large brass commemorating Thomas Nelond of Lewes priory, who died in 1433 – though this is not normally on public view.

Cuckfield Holy Trinity

Why visit: *Victorian interior*
Where: *Church Street, on the southern edge of Cuckfield village, RH17 5JZ*

Looking across to the South Downs from its breezy hill, this church in the historic Wealden village of Cuckfield witnessed the comings and goings of travellers taking the old road from London to Brighton for many centuries.

Cuckfield's importance and prosperity ensured that the church was well looked after: it has additions and improvements from almost every period since it was built in the 13th century. The foundations of a 12th-century church on the site have

been found beneath the nave floor. Much of the special character of the interior is due to 19th-century workmanship – but this was no heavy-handed restoration, such as is seen in many churches. The medieval nave arcades and 15th-century wagon roof still provide the spacious-feeling framework, but the exuberant painted ceiling, all flowers and leaves, is Victorian, as are the colourful carved angels, and the screen, pulpit and stained glass. The slender wooden broach spire that topped the 13th-century tower caught fire in 1980 but was rebuilt to the same design, though with a steel frame.

Shipley St Mary

Why visit: *Norman structure; attractive setting with interesting 20th-century associations*
Where: *Church Close, between the A24 and A272 south-west of Horsham, RH13 8PJ*

St Mary's stands in water meadows beside the young River Adur, close to the white windmill made famous as the fictional home of Jonathan Creek of TV fame. This 19th-century smock-mill belonged to the poet Hilaire Belloc for nearly 50 years until his death in 1953.

Another famous name connected with Shipley church is that of the composer John Ireland, who died in 1962 and is buried in the churchyard. Here he is commemorated by a slate memorial in the church.

This page: Norman interior at Bramber (left); Cowfold (centre); 17th-century Caryll monument at Shipley (above).

The building, of the mid-12th century, has largely retained its original form, including a sturdy tower supported on Norman arches. The rather stern appearance of the church may reflect the fact that it was built for the Knights Templar. Later embellishments include an alabaster monument of 1616 to Sir Thomas Caryll and his family, and 19th- and early 20th-century stained glass. A detail in one of the south windows shows Shipley Windmill with its original brown tiled cap.

Sompting St Mary

Why visit: *Uniquely shaped, early tower*
Where: *Just north of the A27, north-east of Worthing, off Church Lane, BN15 0AZ*

Travellers unfamiliar with the A27 near Worthing could be forgiven for suddenly imagining themselves in the Rhine Valley when the extraordinary tower of this ancient church comes into view. Its date has recently become a matter of debate. A church here is certainly mentioned in the Domesday Book, and today's church still has fragments of 11th- and 12th-century carved stonework, but the tower – for many years believed to be Saxon – may be later, or may well have been built in two stages at different times. However, even conservative estimates put the earliest part at something approaching 1,000 years old.

The shape of the tower, with four gables supporting four steeply sloping lozenge-shaped roof elevations in a

design known as a Rhenish helm, is not found elsewhere in Britain but is familiar in northern Europe. Additions and alterations to the church were made after it was taken over first by the Knights Templar in 1154 and then the Knights Hospitaller in 1306. Unfortunately, much more recent developments have severed the church from its village (now almost part of Worthing), on the other side of the busy dual carriageway.

Warminghurst
Holy Sepulchre CCT

Why visit: *Unspoilt, remote-feeling medieval church; 18th-century interior*
Where: *A mile north-west of Ashington, along Church Park Lane, RH20 3AW*

It is as though this little 13th-century country church had been left forgotten by time – and perhaps sometimes left unloved – for many years, after it was given a Georgian refit. Fortunately the Churches Conservation Trust cares for it now, and the 18th-century fittings make it clear that someone cared for it then, too: box pews, three-decker pulpit, a font and several monuments all date from that period. The dignified panelled timber screen creates a rather special effect when sunlight pours through its three arches. Queen Anne's coat of arms, at the top, was probably repainted and possibly embellished by a Victorian craftsman.

This page: Sompting's unique Rhenish helm (left); the Georgian interior of Holy Sepulchre, Warminghurst (above).

West Grinstead St George

Why visit: *Country church with Norman origins and work from various periods*
Where: *On the south-west edge of the hamlet of West Grinstead, off the B2135 north-west of Partridge Green, RH13 8LR*

Barely half a mile from the busy A24, West Grinstead church stands in a pleasantly rural setting on the edge of the Weald, with its 13th-century tower and shingled broach spire overlooking the River Adur. Victorian-rendered walls belie a building with a history that dates back to the 11th century.

It has served generations of local landowners, many of whom have contributed to the improvement and embellishment of their church through the ages. Some are commemorated by a collection of mainly 18th-century monuments. Their descendants sat in the 19th-century pews here, which were allocated by name to the farmsteads where they lived: some names on the pews, such as Hobshorts and Brighthams, still appear on the Ordnance Survey map.

ALSO IN THE AREA

Bolney St Mary Magdalene
Why visit: *11th- and 12th-century church with Victorian additions*

Henfield St Peter
Why visit: *Medieval church heavily restored in the 1870s*

Parham St Peter
Why visit: *Estate church in lovely setting in Parham Park; its village was removed in the 19th century*

Storrington St Mary
Why visit: *Mainly 13th-century church with later rebuilding*

Thakeham St Mary
Why visit: *Mostly medieval church, with 15th-century porch and font*

West Chiltington St Mary
Why visit: *Interesting features from many periods; medieval wall paintings*

THE HIGH WEALD

With its steep slopes and dense woodland, the High Weald of Sussex remained untamed for longer than the county's coastal plain and chalk downs. Wealden towns and villages prospered and grew from Tudor times, mainly with the development of the iron industry. Later, the advent of railways and commuting brought a different kind of wealth as London's elite moved south. As usual, social and economic changes like these influenced the development of churches and other buildings.

Rotherfield St Denys

Why visit: *Historic church packed with interesting features from many centuries*
Where: *Church Road, south of the B2100 as it enters Rotherfield from the west, TN6 3LG*

This historic hilltop village in the High Weald lies close to the source of the Rother, the Sussex river from which it takes its name. Rotherfield was an important hub of the Wealden iron industry, which flourished here for nearly 500 years until the Industrial Revolution, bringing prosperity that accounts for many of its handsome old houses.

The large sandstone church has a very long story and is full of interest, with

features from almost every period. The ancient yew tree in the churchyard is said to pre-date the 8th-century wooden church that once stood here. The north-east corner of the present building incorporates the first stone church, of 1060, with some of its distinctive Saxon masonry still visible on the outside.

Later it became the Nevill Chapel: the Nevill family were lords of the manor of Rotherfield from 1450, and their coat of arms appears on one of the roof bosses and also on the elaborately carved oak font cover, made in 1533. The octagonal late Norman font was recovered from a nearby farm in the late 19th century after being lost for many years.

From the 17th century Rotherfield has a fine pulpit (1632), with a delicately

carved tester above, and from the 18th century some remaining box pews. The pre-Raphaelite east window of 1878, illustrating the *Te Deum*, is by Sir Edward Burne-Jones and William Morris.

St Denys is also noted for its wall paintings, especially a 15th-century Doom painting above the chancel arch. There are fragments of other medieval paintings elsewhere in the church.

The 15th-century battlemented tower houses a peal of eight bells plus a carillon so that chimes can be played by a single ringer, using all eight. The tower is topped by a slender spire, clad with chestnut shingles. This had to be rebuilt after the devastating storm of October 1987. Its new steel framework was lowered in sections from a helicopter. Timbers from the original spire were given a new lease of life: a local craftsman made them into a cross and an altar table, both now in the church.

The original dedication of the church was to St Dionysius, a 3rd-century bishop of Paris also known as St Denys or Denis. A statue of him carrying his mitred head in his hands still stands outside the city's cathedral, Notre-Dame. The story of his martyrdom is that after he was beheaded, he picked up his head and continued preaching as he walked to Montmartre.

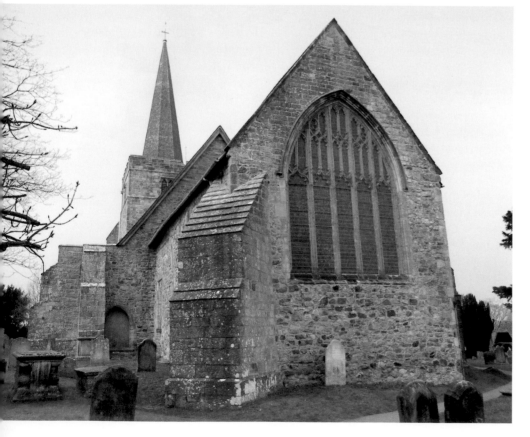

This page: *The exterior of the chancel at Rotherfield, with its rebuilt spire in the background (left); chancel interior (above).*

Coleman's Hatch
Holy Trinity

Why visit: *Gothic Revival church*
Where: *On the B2110 in Coleman's Hatch, TN7 4HN*

Holy Trinity was built shortly before World War I. It is 14th-century Gothic in style, with a sandstone tower topped by an elegant spire. The architects were A. W. Blomfield & Sons, a distinguished family practice associated with many Victorian and Edwardian churches, schools and other public buildings.

Eridge Green Holy Trinity

Why visit: *An attractive 19th-century church with later alterations and fittings*
Where: *At Eridge Green, on the A26, TN3 9DX*

The building of this little 19th-century church, with its miniature tower overlooking the busy A26, marked the founding of a new parish here in 1853. Despite its comparatively short history, it has undergone several changes and additions, from the large east window of 1893 to the family pew at the west end, built in the 1950s for the Marquesses of Abergavenny of nearby Eridge Park.

Ticehurst St Mary

Why visit: *Medieval glass, and 16th-century oak font cover*
Where: *Near the centre of Ticehurst village, to the south of the main street, TN5 7AB*

Records from the 12th century mention a church at Ticehurst, but the present building is thought to have been built by Sir William de Etchingham after completing nearby Etchingham church in the 1370s. Apart from a prize-winning extension of 2010, the basic structure dates almost completely from the 14th century.

The extraordinarily large west window has kept its original Decorated tracery. The window in the north wall of the chancel has original glass depicting a Doom, or the Last Judgement, with some people being boiled in a cauldron while others are in a cart pushed by devils. The coat of arms above – that of the Etchingham family – also appears on a roof boss. Don't miss the wonderful font cover, with its intricately carved oak panels and opening doors.

Wadhurst
St Peter and St Paul

Why visit: *A large, light, historic church of Norman origin; cast-iron tomb slabs inside*
Where: *In the centre of Wadhurst, TN5 6AA*

More than 30 cast-iron memorials are set into the floor of this medieval church. This remarkable collection is a vivid reminder of the importance of the iron industry in Wadhurst, which was one of the last places to produce traditional Sussex iron before the new technology of the Industrial Revolution took over.

The tomb slabs date from the 17th and 18th centuries. Several of them carry the name of the principal local family of ironmasters: Barham. John Barham, who died in 1723, and his wife Lucy, are commemorated by a large marble wall memorial in the chancel.

With its Norman tower and its 13th-century arcades, Wadhurst church had already taken its present form by the 14th century, when the shingled broach spire (now slightly crooked) was added to the tower. The 15th-century south porch, with a priest's room (called a parvise) above, was the only major later addition.

Withyham
St Michael and All Angels

Why visit: *Sackville family monuments*
Where: *Just south of the main road through Withyham, TN7 4BA*

High up on the northern fringes of Ashdown Forest, Withyham church is a pleasing jumble of red-tiled roofs that shelter weathered sandstone walls. The 14th-century church was wrecked in 1663 by a lightning strike of such force that the bells melted. An almost complete rebuilding followed, incorporating what remained of the old church.

Outstanding are the monuments to several generations of the Sackville family. Their family seat had been nearby Buckhurst Park long before Elizabeth I granted her cousin, Thomas Sackville, the vast house and park at Knole, a few miles to the north. In contrast to the dramatic statuary of her ancestors, a simple plaque commemorates the gardener and poet Vita Sackville-West, of Sissinghurst fame, who died in 1962. Her ashes rest in the family vault, in an inkpot.

This page: Sackville monument in Withyham church (above).

ALSO IN THE AREA

Etchingham
The Assumption of Blessed Mary and St Nicholas
Why visit: *Grand 14th-century church built by Sir William de Etchingham*

Brightling St Thomas a Becket
Why visit: *Mainly 13th-century church, best known for the tomb of eccentric local squire 'Mad Jack' Fuller. He died in 1833 and reputedly sits upright, holding a bottle of wine, beneath a huge stone pyramid in the churchyard*

Burwash St Bartholomew
Why visit: *Early Norman tower with later medieval arcades; cast-iron tomb slabs; connections with Rudyard Kipling*

Mayfield St Dunstan
Why visit: *Early church, rebuilt after a fire in 1389 and with some interesting 17th-century fittings*

TOWERS AND SPIRES

Church towers and spires are iconic symbols of the British landscape. Even in remote and wild places you are rarely more than a few miles from one. They watch over towns and villages, act as waymarks on coastlines, and are guides in moorland. So they have practical uses, but most of all they are expressions in stone of the pride and beliefs of the parishes that built them.

Saxon and Norman towers

Towers such as those at Barton-on-Humber, Lincolnshire, and Earls Barton, Northamptonshire, show the classic distinguishing features of Saxon towers: pilaster strips imitating wooden decoration, 'long-and-short' stonework, and both round-headed and triangular-headed windows. One of the earliest is at Monkwearmouth, Durham. Their sturdy, strong, appearance has led many to think they were built for defence. Some are more than 1,000 years old, including that at Sompting, Sussex, surmounted by a stubby pyramidal spire that is unique in Britain. At Barnack, Northamptonshire, is a Saxon tower with some superb decorative work, surmounted by a broach spire that may be one of the earliest in England, dating from about 1200.

Norman towers are often massive, straightforward and practical. A good example is that at Old Shoreham, Sussex, while nearby New Shoreham has the truly impressive Norman church that superseded it when Old Shoreham's harbour silted up. Its great tower has quintessential Norman window openings.

In Britain the largest Norman tower is at Tewkesbury Abbey, Gloucestershire. It is gigantic – perhaps the biggest in Europe – but has arcading and other detailing that give it a lightness and grace. There are visible traces on the abbey tower of an earlier and higher roofline for the body of the building. This is often seen and usually indicates that new

architectural ideas and improved building techniques, including the addition of guttering and drainage, meant lower rooflines could be introduced.

Gothic towers and spires

Superb combinations of tower and spire were built in the Early English and Decorated periods. Raunds in Northamptonshire is an excellent example, with four distinct lower stages – one of which has unusual W-shaped mouldings. Above these rise the spire with little spire-lights becoming smaller as they go up. St Wulfram's, Grantham,

This page: The massive 12th-century Norman tower at Tewkesbury Abbey is the largest of its kind in Britain (above).

Lincolnshire, mixes Early English and Decorated to create a wonderful tower and spire. Shottesbrooke, Berkshire, and Ashbourne, Derbyshire, both have soaring spires dating from the second half of the 14th century.

St Botolph's, Boston, Lincolnshire, universally known as the Boston Stump, has one of the tallest towers in England, and is consequently one of the most well-known anywhere. It is topped with

Timbered towers

Towers built of timber have a timeless charm that is hard to resist. They were usually built in areas where the most readily available building material was wood. Often, the timber framing inside the tower is gigantic. Such towers are difficult to date, but many are probably from the 14th to 16th centuries. Examples are at Pirton (*right*) and Dormston, which are both in Worcestershire, and at Melverley, Shropshire, and Brookland, Kent.

a decorated octagonal lantern, one of the few of its kind left. The tower was built between 1450 and 1520 and is a landmark for miles around.

For many, the best combination of tower and spire is at Louth, Lincolnshire.

Somerset towers

Spires began to be less popular in the last Gothic period, the Perpendicular, but the towers built then are among the finest in England. Somerset has the most spectacular collection of such towers anywhere. The most elaborate is St Mary Magdalene, Taunton, which dates from 1514. Others in Somerset include Bruton, Evercreech, Huish Episcopi, Ilminster, Westonzoyland and Leigh-on-Mendip. Taken together, they make the ultimate concentration of such buildings anywhere in the world. Wealth from wool enabled these astonishing creations to be erected.

Later towers

In comparison to those built in the Gothic periods, many towers of the 17th

Church bells

Church towers are built principally to house bells and a surprising number still hold a medieval bell. It is uncommon to be able to see the bells in any tower, but in Britain they are hung on wheels to enable ringers to ring in a particular way to make the classic sound of English bells. Some churches may have one or two bells only; peals of six or eight are common whereas 10 or 12 are generally found in major churches, or in a wealthy parish. The best counties for old bells are Devon, Somerset, Norfolk and Suffolk.

and 18th centuries are restrained and sedate, but Sir Christopher Wren's London churches, built in the years after the Great Fire of 1666, are marvels, both individually and as a group. The architects that he worked with and who came after him, such as Nicholas Hawksmoor, created completely distinct churches and towers. Examples of Hawksmoor's work in London are: St Anne, Limehouse, with a diagonally placed lantern; St George, Bloomsbury, with a bizarre stepped top on which cavort a lion and a unicorn; St Mary Woolnoth, which has severe classical orders and columns that loom forbiddingly over the streets around it.

A return to Gothic ideas came in the Victorian period, with the Gothic Revival. The most inspired architects of that time created towers that are as audacious as any from earlier periods. For example William Butterfield's All Saints, Marylebone, London, has a tower with a polychromatic colour scheme.

Architects of the Arts and Crafts movement (1850–1915) melded styles from all ages to create often very beautiful structures. One of the most beguiling is at Brockhampton-by-Ross, Herefordshire, where architect William Lethaby built two towers – one central, square and stone, the other a timbered bell tower – linked by a thatched nave. It is a church like no other.

This page: *The steeple at St Nicholas, Trellech, Gwent, is a rarity in Wales. It was rebuilt in the 18th century.*

ROMNEY MARSH AND RYE

Romney Marsh is a very special kind of landscape, claimed from the sea from Roman times onwards, sometimes lost back to the sea through storms and flooding, and frequently scoured by gales. Its churches stand like sentinels over the marshy landscapes, some of them remote and isolated, some in hamlets, and some in the Marsh towns. Each is different, and each has something to offer. Although not part of Romney Marsh, Rye and Winchelsea are included here as they are very close, and their histories have also been shaped by the sea.

Brookland St Augustine

Why visit: *Extraordinary detached bell tower; charming church with very rare 12th-century lead font*
Where: *High Street, TN29 9QR*

St Augustine's is well known for its remarkable detached bell tower; its size and shape is unlike any other in Britain. When it was built in the 12th century its huge timbers were exposed, but in the 15th century the entire structure was covered in wooden cladding in three layers one on top of the other (like stacked cups) much increasing the height of the structure.

The church itself reveals why the tower was never intended to be attached to it: the nave arcades are at a tipsy angle, and were supported by internal buttresses as the church was built, showing that the builders were contending with unstable foundations from the start. Attaching a heavy tower to the body of the church would have made it even more unstable.

The church is entered through a disarmingly rural porch, complete with stable doors, to the right of which is a miniature clock tower with tiny battlements. Inside, it is open, spacious and full of light. The nave has old seating, some of it still on the wooden platforms that raised the pews above the floor to keep damp and cold at bay. The box pews are the highest on the Marsh.

The church contains many individual items of interest such as fragments of medieval glass, a 13th-century wall painting, and memorials, but it is the lead font that is Brookland's special treasure. Made in the 1100s, it is one of only 30 such fonts in Britain. On it are two sets of scenes, one depicting the labours of the month – such as scything, pruning, threshing and hunting – and the other set showing the signs of the zodiac. It is beautiful as well as very rare.

Burmarsh All Saints

Why visit: *Norman doorway*
Where: *In Burmarsh hamlet, off Beach Road, TN29 0JJ*

Still Norman in feel despite Victorian restoration in 1876, Burmarsh church is entered through a Norman doorway over which is carved a face that looks anything but friendly. The doorway and guardian monster are protected by a 16th-century porch.

Inside there is a screen erected in 1923 to two Burmarsh men killed in World War I. On the floor of the church is a medieval bell, removed from the tower because it was cracked.

Dymchurch
St Peter and St Paul

Why visit: *Uncluttered little church with Norman features*
Where: *Hythe Road, TN29 0LD*

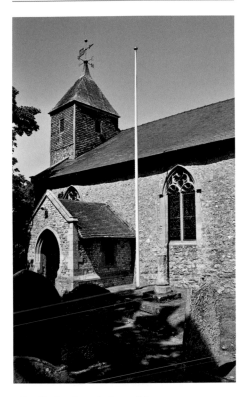

This little church has a Norman core, but was altered and extended in the 13th century. It was dramatically changed in the 1820s when the original Norman tower was replaced with the present rather insignificant one and when the north wall was removed in order to make the nave bigger. This work was undertaken to enlarge the church for a growing population. The simple Norman chancel arch with its zig-zag decoration is still in place.

East Guldeford St Mary

Why visit: *Medieval and Victorian angels*
Where: *In East Guldeford, reached along a footpath from the A259, TN31 7PA*

All of the other Romney Marsh churches are in Kent, but this one is in East Sussex, and it is one of the latest, built in 1505 on land reclaimed from the sea. It is a low, brick-built building with substantial brick buttresses and a squat tower.

The inside of the church is very simple, with box pews lining the nave. Much of the interest is at the east end, where large angels were painted on the chancel walls in the 19th century. They echo the stone angel corbels in the chancel that survived destruction after the Reformation.

Ivychurch St George

Why visit: *Big, light-filled church*
Where: *Oasthouse Field, TN29 0AZ*

Long, low and with a battlemented and buttressed tower, St George's is built on a grand scale, and was perhaps always larger than its rural agricultural population ever actually needed.

It was rebuilt almost from scratch in the mid-14th century, with nave, chancel, and with north and south aisles the whole length of the church. Inside it is light, airy and spacious, with two elegant lines of arches. In the chancel are handsome 15th-century stalls, of a kind most often seen in cathedrals rather than parish churches. On the walls are original, oval text boards. The church was damaged by bombing in World War II but was subsequently fully restored.

Lydd All Saints

Why visit: *Imposing 'Cathedral of the Marshes'*
Where: *Church Road, in the centre of Lydd, TN29 9DU; open weekdays in term time, and in August*

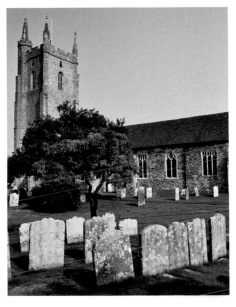

Almost of cathedral size, and called the 'Cathedral of the Marshes', Lydd's church was built in the 13th century when the town was at the height of its prosperity. It incorporates masonry from long before that, in the form of the remains of a 4th- or 5th-century Roman basilica.

The tall and imposing tower, a landmark for this part of the Marsh, was built between 1442 and 1446 by Thomas Stanley, a senior mason at Canterbury Cathedral.

In the church are a number of medieval brasses, an effigy of a 14th-century knight and a rare, double, piscina.

During World War II a bomb destroyed the east end of the church, but it was completely restored, including the three lancet windows, which now have bright stained glass designed by Leonard Walker.

Opposite page: The chancel at Brookland (left), and its remarkable 12th-century lead font (right).
This page: *Dymchurch, exterior (top left) and Norman chancel arch (below left); the 15th-century tower of St George, Ivychurch (centre); Lydd's tower (above) was also built in the 15th century, under the supervision of a master mason from Canterbury Cathedral.*

New Romney St Nicholas

Why visit: *Norman and later church that survived a terrifying storm*
Where: *Church Lane, TN28 8EU*

In 1287 a catastrophic storm smashed its way across the Romney Marshes, causing incalculable damage and smothering New Romney in tons of sand, gravel and silt. The little town never recovered, and the deluge of material explains why the west door of St Nicholas's church is far below present-day ground level. The east end was rebuilt later in the early 14th century, possibly as a result of damage from the storm.

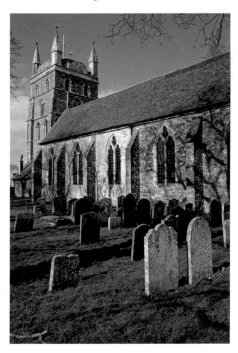

The church as it is today still has its large tower, with lower stages that are very clearly Norman. The upper stages are later, as they have slightly pointed arches, and mark the transition from the Norman style to Early English.

When the east end of the church was rebuilt in the 14th century its chancel and two flanking chapels were built to have a harmonious façade. Each of the three parts has windows in the Reticulated style with flowing tracery.

There are wonderful architectural details inside, much of it saved in 1880 by the Society for the Protection of Ancient Buildings, which persuaded the vicar to stop the 'restoration' that he had begun. It was the society's first notable campaign.

Old Romney St Clement

Why visit: *Setting and exterior; box pews and other fittings inside*
Where: *Off the A259, TN29 0HP*

John Betjeman described this church as 'tumbledown' in the 1960s, but he also made it clear that he liked it. It has been rescued with help from the Romney Marsh Historic Churches Trust, and as with all the churches under its wing, St Clement's today is cared for, and still retains its charm and history.

The lovely rural setting helps, as does the church's friendly jumble of red-tiled roofs, buttresses, mixed building materials in the walls, and rustic broach spire that crowns the tower.

The core of the church dates from the 12th century, with additions in the 13th and 14th centuries. Inside is an excellent collection of post-Reformation fittings, including 17th-century commandment boards behind the altar, a gallery and

18th-century box pews. The pews and gallery are painted pink, a legacy from the film *Dr Syn*, filmed here in the 1960s and starring Patrick McGoohan.

Playden St Michael

Why visit: *Shingled spire; screens and other fittings*
Where: *Rectory Lane, off the A268, opposite the Care Centre, TN31 7PH*

West of the River Rother, St Michael's spire is a landmark from across the Romney Marshes. It has 12th-century arcades and two screens, the one in the north aisle with elaborate carving. A 17th-century belfry ladder is preserved, and set into the floor is a memorial to a 16th-century Flemish brewer, with pictures of the barrels of his trade.

Rye St Mary

Why visit: *Lovely church in historic setting*
Where: *In Rye, East Sussex, set back off Church Square, TN31 7HF*

Set in the heart of Rye, surrounded by narrow streets lined with picturesque houses, St Mary's is a natural magnet for visitors to the ancient Cinque port.

This page: *New Romney (left); Old Romney chancel (top centre), and pink pews (below centre); the quarter boys and their clock at St Mary's, Rye (above).*

66

It is most celebrated for its quarter boys; cherubs on the outside of the church who strike the quarter hours. They are a later addition to a clock mechanism that was made in 1560. The boys themselves are modern replicas of the original 18th-century figures, which had become weathered. The original boys are now inside the church, where the huge pendulum of the clock can be seen.

The church was restored by the Victorians, but much of the original Norman and later fabric can be seen. A happy legacy of the 19th century is the stained glass in the window of the north aisle, designed by Edward Burne-Jones.

St Mary in the Marsh

Why visit: *Pretty marshland church*
Where: *In the hamlet of St Mary in the Marsh, off St Mary's Road, TN29 0DG*

Set in a part of the marshes that remains largely agricultural, St Mary's was originally built in the first half of the 12th century. The chancel, nave and tower proved to be too small for the growing population in the next century, so it was enlarged. The porch was added in the 15th century.

There is a 13th-century font near the south door, and the church has an 18th-century pulpit and early 19th-century box pews. In the churchyard is a simple memorial to Edith Nesbit, author of *The Railway Children* and other children's books.

Snargate St Dunstan

Why visit: *Marshland church with interesting features*
Where: *Off Snargate Lane (B2080), TN29 9RX*

Like so many Romney Marsh churches this one seems far bigger than any population at any time could have justified. In medieval times, however, this was a rich and very busy landscape. The church was originally built in the 12th century, and grew as the population of the area increased.

The church has interesting roof bosses, an early 16th-century wall painting of a ship, and a lead plaque commemorating roof repairs done in 1780 by 'T Apps, carpenter, and all his jolly men'. Snargate is one of the many Romney Marsh villages associated with smuggling. Some of the tales were set down as stories and poems in the *Ingoldsby Legends*, supposedly written by Thomas Ingoldsby. In fact they were written by Richard Barham, vicar of Snargate in the 1820s.

Snave St Augustine

Why visit: *Marshland church saved by the Romney Marsh Historic Churches Trust*
Where: *In Snave hamlet, just off the A2070, TN26 2QJ*

This little church was declared redundant in 1983, but was saved by the Romney Marsh Historic Churches Trust, which now maintains it. Like other Marsh churches, its once rural setting is marred by the encroachment of modern buildings. The church has an unusual internal arrangement, with a Lady Chapel almost as prominent as the chancel. Above the entrance to the Lady Chapel is a royal arms of 1735.

Winchelsea St Thomas

Why visit: *Evocative remains of a once grand church; superb 14th-century tombs*
Where: *St Thomas Street, TN36 4EB*

In 1288, after the old town was destroyed by the sea, Winchelsea was built as a new, planned, town.

The church was given a large and prestigious plot within a very spacious churchyard. Quite what it looked like when complete we don't know, as the town was devastated in French raids several times in the 14th century, suffered terribly in the plagues of the same century, and then fell into further decay when the harbour silted up. What remains of St Thomas's today is the chancel, rebuilt tower and an intriguing jumble of ruins.

The chancel is superb, and contains some of the finest tombs in England, hinting at what the church may have been like when it was complete. The architecture is from about 1300, while the five tombs date from a little later. They are memorials to members of the Alard family, who had founded chantry chapels here. The magnificent effigies lie beneath sumptuous carved canopies.

This page: St Mary in the Marsh and its churchyard, which has a memorial to Edith Nesbit (left); St Augustine, Snave, renowned for its spring displays of daffodils (centre).

ALSO IN THE AREA

Brenzett St Eanswith
Why visit: *Ancient church with interesting fixtures and fittings.*
Locked – key at Church House

Fairfield St Thomas a Becket
Why visit: *Supremely atmospheric Marsh church reached over fields.*
Locked – key at nearby farmhouse

Newchurch
St Peter and St Paul
Why visit: *Large church with 15th-century font. Locked – keyholder lives nearby*

THE KENTISH WEALD

Here, around the eastern end of the Weald, many towns and villages retain their traditional buildings of local materials: timber-framing, weatherboarding and clay tiles are what give them their special character. Sandstone from the High Weald – sometimes with an ochre tinge because of its iron content – was used for many of the churches, such as Goudhurst. These were often built, enlarged or embellished on the proceeds from the iron and wool industries, based on local raw materials that brought employment and wealth to their parishes.

Goudhurst St Mary

Why visit: *Unusual 17th-century tower; excellent monuments*
Where: *Church Road, TN17 1AL*

One of a number of Wealden settlements ending in '-hurst' (meaning a wooded hill), Goudhurst has a curious church tower that will not easily be forgotten. Broad for its height, and in a style that seems part Gothic, part classical and part Georgian, it sounds unprepossessing but is in fact remarkably handsome. Its date, too, is unusual: 1638–40, when it replaced an earlier tower that was struck by lightning. There is an unusual three-light window above the west door looks down to Gouldhurst's High Street.

Inside the church, take time to look at the monuments to several generations of the Culpeper family of nearby Bedgebury. There is a fine and fascinating assortment including a 15th-century brass, 16th-century painted wooden effigies of Sir Alexander Culpeper and his wife, and a Jacobean wall memorial in marble and alabaster. There are also some later monuments, to the Campion family.

There was reputedly a smugglers' tunnel from Goudhurst church to the adjacent Star & Eagle inn, and a violent episode in the church's history was the Battle of Goudhurst, on 20 April 1747. On one side were members of the brutal Hawkhurst Gang: smugglers notorious throughout the south-east of England for their ruthlessness. On the other was Goudhurst's band of militia, set up to control the increasing problem: smuggling became rife in the Weald after the demise of the iron industry left hundreds of men unemployed. Three of the smugglers were killed in the confrontation at Goudhurst church, and the following year many of the rest of the gang were arrested, tried and hanged.

Cranbrook St Dunstan

Why visit: *Impressive late-medieval church in an important and attractive little town*
Where: *In the middle of Cranbrook, at the eastern end of the High Street, TN17 3HA*

The old market town of Cranbrook shares with Tenterden the claim to be the capital of the Kentish Weald. The splendidly lofty Union Windmill of 1814 (still working) probably eclipses the church as Cranbrook's most famous landmark, though the church has been known as the 'Cathedral of the Weald'.

It is dedicated to St Dunstan, an influential 10th-century archbishop of Canterbury, and is indeed a large and imposing building. It is Perpendicular in style and recalls the 15th-century clothiers and Flemish weavers who helped turn Cranbrook into a successful and wealthy town. An unusual feature of the church is an 18th-century baptismal font designed for total immersion.

This page: Grand 16th-century Culpeper monument in St Mary's Goudhurst (top left), and its early 17th-century tower (below left); the nave at Cranbrook (above).

Mereworth St Lawrence

Why visit: *An entirely 18th-century church in the classical tradition*
Where: *West of the A228 in Mereworth, on Tonbridge Road, ME18 5LU*

The old church at Mereworth was found to spoil the view of John Fane, 7th Earl of Westmorland, from his splendid new Palladian house – so he demolished it (he had already done away with the old castle and the village) and built a new classical church, and a new village, nearby.

Completed around 1746, the church certainly catches the eye with its slender baroque spire and semicircular portico. Some may consider the interior overpowering for rural Kent, with its Doric columns, a painted barrel-vault and decorative cornices, plus a liberal helping of trompe-l'oeil work and some rather hectic stained glass. Memorials that were preserved from the previous church include brasses and marble effigies.

Speldhurst St Mary

Why visit: *Pre-Raphaelite stained glass*
Where: *North-west of Tunbridge Wells, on Speldhurst Hill, TN3 0NL*

Though very close to Tunbridge Wells, Speldhurst has a pleasing village-like feel and the Victorian Gothic church fits in well. It is known, first and foremost, for its fine series of Victorian stained glass windows – much of it made in the workshops of Morris & Co after the church was rebuilt in the 1870s, with the designs done by Burne-Jones, Dante Gabriel Rossetti, Ford Madox Brown and other key members of the Pre-Raphaelite movement. It is hard not to marvel at this glass: St Mary holding a Madonna lily (a key Pre-Raphaelite motif); the four evangelists; a roundel depicting Christ in Glory surrounded by angels in gold, red and white. Angels are everywhere, many of them playing musical instruments. The rich, subtle colours in the windows are remarkable: St Nicholas in robes of green and red; Pope Gregory in intricately worked gold; more angels with delicately executed wings in pink and white, and foliage in many shades of green.

Tenterden St Mildred

Why visit: *Perpendicular tower (an unusual style for Kent)*
Where: *Set back from the High Street, off Church Street, TN30 6AR*

Since 1461, the broad street of this busy little town – and much of the countryside around – has looked up to the elegant pinnacled tower of St Mildred's. At its base is the grand entrance to the church, and also a very large Perpendicular window. Parts of the church date back to the 12th century, but Victorian restoration work changed the feel of the church's interior.

The 15th-century font remains, and the delightful 17th-century monument to Mr and Mrs Herbert Whitfield recalls the trade that brought prosperity to Tenterden and other Wealden towns: he was a local ironfounder.

This page: Baroque ostentation at Mereworth (left); the 15th-century tower at St Mildred, Tenterden (above).

Tudeley All Saints

Why visit: *Complete set of stained glass windows by Marc Chagall*
Where: *Just off Five Oak Green Road, TN11 0NS*

This tucked-away church, rebuilt in the 18th century, is internationally known for its astonishing set of windows by the 20th-century Russian-born artist Marc Chagall, better known for his paintings and for his dramatic cathedral glass in France – where he spent most of his adult life – and at Chichester.

Inside Tudeley church, a plain floor and walls ensure that all attention is on the wonderful colours of Chagall's windows: blues and purples on the north side, with yellows and oranges taking the full impact of the sun on the south. The east window makes the biggest impact: installed in 1967 to commemorate a young woman who drowned in a sailing accident in 1963. The remaining windows were completed in 1985, just before the artist's death at the age of 97, making this the only church in England with a complete set of Chagall windows.

ALSO IN THE AREA

Capel St Thomas a Becket
Why visit: *Small Norman church with 13th-century wall paintings; crown-post roof*

East Peckham St Michael CCT
Why visit: *Church of Norman origin; spectacular hilltop setting; weathervane*

Horsmonden St Margaret
Why visit: *Handsome 14th-century church of Wealden sandstone (about 2 miles south of Horsmonden village)*

Penshurst St John the Baptist
Why visit: *15th-century sandstone church restored by Sir Gilbert Scott; monuments; Becket window from 1970*

Woodchurch All Saints
Why visit: *Large 13th-century church with rare double hagioscope, Bethersden marble and east window by Kempe*

CENTRAL KENT

Kent has always been a predominantly rural county, and one of the county's pleasures is exploring quiet, off-the-beaten-track villages and hamlets and their churches. In this cluster of churches, you will find three – Badlesmere, Elmstead and Hastingleigh – that feel very remote from the rush and hurry of the modern world. The others are in villages and little towns that are a delight to visit for themselves.

Brabourne
St Mary the Blessed Virgin

Why visit: *Fine chancel with Norman glass; many monuments*
Where: *Off The Street, TN25 5LR*

A church has existed on this site since Saxon times, but the oldest part of the present building dates from 1144. Looking from the outside, the structure consists of a squat western tower, a nave with a 13th-century south aisle, a chancel, and a south chapel built by Sir William Scott in the 15th century. The tower began to collapse in about 1700 so the upper stages were taken down and a huge buttress was constructed to strengthen the original 12th-century stonework.

There are many important features inside, the most special of which is the easternmost window on the north wall of the chancel. This is the only window in Britain that is complete with Norman glass in its original setting. This window is just as it was in the 12th century, the pattern of the leadwork corresponding in character with the string-course beneath.

In the chancel is what is almost certainly a heart shrine, built for the heart of John Balliol, founder of Balliol College, Oxford and father of John Balliol le Scot, King of Scotland. John Balliol died in 1269 and his widow had his heart preserved. She carried it with her in a casket of silver and ivory and it was buried with her in Scotland. Their son later brought the heart to Brabourne after his defeat by Edward I. Eighteen generations of the Scott family, descended from Balliol, are buried in the church.

Badlesmere St Leonard

Why visit: *Church crammed with interest*
Where: *East of the A251 on Dayton Road, north of Leaveland and Badlesemere, ME13 0NL*

Tucked away down a quiet lane next to a farm, 13th-century St Leonard's is tiny and does not look promising at first as it is rendered on the outside. The inside, however, is beautifully cared for and full of interest. It is crammed with box pews and other old furnishings, including the Victorian oil lamps that John Betjeman admired in the 1960s. There are also medieval bench-ends, a royal arms of George I and modern stained glass.

Brook St Mary

Why visit: *Norman church with remarkable 13th-century wall paintings*
Where: *The Street, TN25 5PF*

Setting so often creates the initial atmosphere for a church, and here the mixture of an informal path over a little bridge into a churchyard full of trees and shrubs is the perfect introduction to the military-looking Norman tower. In fact the tower, probably built in the closing years of the 11th century, is later than the rest of this delightful church, which is one of the earliest complete Norman churches in the country, perhaps dating from the 1080s.

Its complex ownership, essentially meaning that it belonged to Canterbury Cathedral rather than being a simple parish church, explains why it has survived so unaltered. The architecture of the interior is very plain and simple, built

This page: Brabourne's truncated tower, with massive buttresses to shore it up.

for strength and solidity rather than show. But the insides were enhanced with wall paintings in the 13th century, and these are some of the best in Kent, indeed they rank with the best in England.

Those in the chancel are the most outstanding, and are what remains of a scheme of roundels that once covered a large area. They contain scenes from the life of Christ, and other stories that enlarge on the Bible stories. Their colours have changed and faded with the passing of the centuries: what are now blacks were once bright red, for example.

There are other paintings in the nave, not so well preserved, including one of St Christopher. There is also a wall painting in what was a private chapel in the tower, but this is only open by prior appointment.

Charing St Peter and St Paul

Why visit: *Impressive interior*
Where: *Pett Lane, off the High Street, at the end of Market Place, TN27 0LP*

Charing is a pretty village, and Market Place is lined with old buildings of flint and brick, including the ruins of an archbishop's palace. The church is handsome, with a buttressed and battlemented tower, and dates originally from the late 1400s. It was partly destroyed by fire a century later, and the replacement roofs are clearly dated 1592 and 1620. The interior is impressive, with a mixture of old and modern fittings.

Elmstead St James the Great

Why visit: *Setting; Honywood memorials*
Where: *In Elmstead hamlet, TN25 5JL*

The hamlet of Elmstead is little more than a group of farms clustered round a church on the North Downs. The exterior view of the east end of the church is of three flint-built gables. Beyond is the unusual and distinctive west tower, capped by a belfry and stubby spire.

The church has Norman origins, probably being built in the 1090s. Many additions to the Norman church were built in the ensuing centuries. The aisles in the late 1100s, part of the tower in the 12th century, the extended chancel in the 13th century, the north and south chapels in the early 14th century and so on through the ages, culminating in major restoration in the 19th century. The present church is an attractive, peaceful mixture of styles with many monuments, most of which are memorials to the Honywood family.

Hastingleigh St Mary the Virgin

Why visit: *Delightful church in a very rural setting*
Where: *South-east of Hastingleigh village, on a lane reached by travelling south of the village then turning east, TN25 5HU*

This beautifully simple building is in a valley about a mile from Hastingleigh village. There may have been a church here in the 6th century, but the present building is largely Norman and Early English. The lychgate was made in 1993 by local craftsmen to commemorate 700 years of worship. The north wall of the church is the oldest part and probably

contains Saxon workmanship. Inside, looking from the Norman nave, the excellent 15th-century rood screen stands out and, beyond that, the exceptionally long and light chancel with a floor level unusually lower than that of the nave.

Wye St Gregory and St Martin

Why visit: *A handsome town church with an eventful history*
Where: *Churchfield Way, TN25 5ES*

There has been a church here, dedicated to St Gregory, since early Saxon times. It was rebuilt around 1290, then, in the 15th century, Archbishop John Kempe, who was born in Wye, restored and enlarged the church when he founded a college for priests here. It was a cruciform church complete with tower and spire. In 1572 a lightning strike damaged the spire and for more than 100 years the tower remained insecure. It fell in 1686, destroying the chancel and east end of the church. After temporary repairs, the chancel was rebuilt during the reign of Queen Anne, so the church now has a medieval nave and a Stuart chancel. The tower was rebuilt on the side of the chancel in 1706 to complete the patchwork effect.

Inside, the church is spacious and full of light. Near the west door is a model showing the original church before the catastrophes of 1572 and 1686.

This page: Looking through the chancel arch to the wall paintings at Brook (top left); Charing's tower (below left).

ALSO IN THE AREA

Chilham St Mary
Why visit: *Large and handsome church in very attractive small town*

Westwell St Mary
Why visit: *13th-century church with parts of its Jesse window still in place*

Boughton Aluph All Saints
Why visit: *Light-filled 13th- and 14th-century church*

EAST KENT

Outstanding Norman decoration at Barfrestone and Patrixbourne is the highlight of this group of churches in east Kent. But the other churches here have much to offer, from further superb Norman work at St Clement's in Sandwich, to rural charm at Littlebourne and 17th-century extravagance – a grandiose monument at Wingham.

Ickham
St John the Evangelist

Why visit: *Pretty setting; two 14th-century tombs*
Where: *The Street, CT3 1QW*

Barfrestone St Nicholas

Why visit: *Norman decorative stonework of the highest quality*
Where: *Off Pie Factory Road, CT15 7JQ*

This is Kent's finest Norman church, and has some of the best Norman decorative stonework in Britain.

It was clearly an important building, since although the lower half of the church is made of flint, the entire upper half and the doorways – which is where the decorative stonework can be found – is built of Caen stone, exported at considerable expense from Normandy.

It's best to do a thorough exploration of the outside of the church before going inside. The main door is on the south side, and has wonderful carved decorations with Christ at the centre surrounded by complex carvings with dozens of tiny individual characters, including, on the outside part of the frieze, knights, ladies and tradespeople. Farther in are animals both real and imaginary; some seem to be clothed, and some seem as big as the humans next to

them. Farther along the wall is a blocked priest's door, also with elaborate decorative work, and close to that is a niche with re-assembled fragments that include the tail of an enormous fish.

Above all of this extraordinary work is a line of corbels, each one carved – some with human faces, some with monsters.

The east end of the church has a magnificent and very unusual wheel window above arcading and corbels, with niches on either side of the window, in one of which is a mounted rider. The wheel window is surrounded by complex carving, and the spokes of the wheel are being swallowed by faces with huge teeth, bulging eyes and foliage for hair.

The interior looks, at first sight, to be altogether more restrained and formal, especially with the arrangement of a chancel arch flanked by blank arches that once contained altars. But it soon becomes clear that there is almost as much carving to wonder at inside. Whether real or imaginary, each carving had significance and meaning.

The church has no tower, but it has a bell, hung from a yew tree, connected to the church by an ingenious rope system.

With a handsome broach spire and walls of flint, stone and brick, St John's is set in a large and attractive churchyard. Dating from Norman times, and with 13th- and 14th-century additions, the church has a chancel that is considerably higher than its nave. The two transepts have complementary monuments: in the south transept is the tomb of Thomas da Baa dating from 1339, while in the north is that of William Heghtesbury, from 1372. There is also an ancient iron-bound chest, which contained vestments in the 14th century.

Littlebourne
St Vincent of Saragossa

Why visit: *Quiet and historic church with splendid nearby barn*
Where: *Church Road, CT3 1UA*

Set in a large and leafy churchyard, this attractive flint-built church dates from the 13th century, thought to be founded by the monks of St Augustine's Abbey in Canterbury who may have used Littlebourne as a vineyard. Next to the church is an enormous thatched barn dating from about 1340, which may have been their grange. It is now sometimes used for exhibitions.

This page: *Contrasting flint and Caen stone at St Nicholas, Barfrestone (top left); lancets in the chancel at Ickham (above).*

The square tower has a shingled spire. Inside, it is tranquil and uncluttered, and there is a clear difference between the pillars of the south and north aisle. The north aisle collapsed in the early 18th century, and was rebuilt with thin pillars and round-headed arches. The chancel is much taller than the narrow nave.

A faded wall painting of St Christopher is surrounded by paintings of ships, a reminder that the sea is only a few miles away, and that until the 1500s it was much closer to Littlebourne in the shape of a sea channel called the Wantsum that made Thanet, just to the north, an island.

Patrixbourne St Mary

Why visit: *Brilliant decorative Norman stonework, close in look and feel to that at Barfrestone*
Where: *Patrixbourne Road, CT4 5BP*

Like Barfrestone, only a few miles to the south east, Patrixbourne has an important Norman church. And the two churches have so much in common, including wheel windows and two highly decorated south doors, that it seems likely they shared the same builder. As at Barfrestone, Patrixbourne's decorated stonework is Caen stone from Normandy, and Patrixbourne church was given to a priory in Rouen in 1200.

The south door here is particularly fine, with Christ in Majesty in the tympanum surrounded by a dazzling array of carved patterns, foliage, animals, birds, people, and creatures of the apocalypse. The wheel window is at the east end, and as at Barfrestone, the spokes of the wheel are being eaten away by monstrous creatures.

Inside, the main attraction is the stained glass. Depicting different subjects, the panels include 16th- and 17th-century Swiss glass, with people in Swiss costumes and alpine landscapes. There are also grisaille scenes of the life of Christ, as well as figures of saints and secular scenes including characters such as Pyramus and Thisbe, familiar to us from Shakespeare's *A Midsummer Night's Dream*.

Sandwich St Clement

Why visit: *Impressive Norman church full of interest*
Where: *Church Street, CT13 9EH*

Set in one of Kent's prettiest little towns, St Clement's stands next to the ramparts of what was a Cinque port until the river silted up and left the town stranded. The church has a substantial Norman tower with three tiers of blind arcading topped by castellations. The pillars that support the rounded arches have curiously carved capitals with various ornaments of scrolls, foliage and grotesque figures.

The body of the church is square and the aisles are wide, creating a spacious feeling emphasised by the large organ that divides the south side of the church in two. In St Margaret's Chapel there is a complete medieval tiled floor, and the Chapel of St George contains a statue of St John taken from Lincoln Cathedral by Puritans in the 17th century. The roof of the nave has a series of angel heads with wings and decorated bosses against the oak rafters. The octagonal heraldic font has on one of its faces the arms of ancient Sandwich, and on the south face, the arms of Archdeacon Robert Hallum, who it is believed gave the font to the church in 1406.

Wingham St Mary

Why visit: *Large church with timber pillars; overwhelming Oxenden monument*
Where: *Off the A257, CT3 1BB*

In the late 1200s the Archbishop of Canterbury established a college here for a master and six canons (priests), which accounts for the large size of this church, and also for the timber-framed houses opposite, which were where the master and his canons lived.

Rebuilding became necessary in the 16th century, but by then money was short (said to be because the funds raised for the rebuilding were embezzled by the person entrusted with the money). Only the south aisle was rebuilt, and even that was done on a tight budget, as timber was used for the pillars rather than the usual (but pricey) stone.

In the south transept and completely dominating all around it is the bizarre Oxenden monument. Dating from 1682, it consists of a huge obelisk decorated with tumbling fruit and flowers, at the foot of which are four chubby putti, one holding a helmet.

Look out for the other monuments including one to Sir Thomas Palmer of 1624 showing him in Jacobean armour. There are early 14th-century misericords in the church, including one depicting a Green Man. The stone reredos in the chancel is 15th-century and came from France. It was given as a gift to the church in the 1930s.

This page: The interior of St Vincent of Saragossa, Littlebourne showing the thin pillars of the north aisle.

ALSO IN THE AREA

Knowlton St Clement CCT
Why visit: *Pretty medieval church with marble, stained glass and carved wood; set in the grounds of a manor house*

Sandwich St Peter CCT
Why visit: *Medieval church with excellent monuments; still rings the 8pm curfew bell*

Sandwich St Mary CCT
Why visit: *Norman and later church with wooden columns*

Waldershare All Saints CCT
Why visit: *Norman church on the North Downs with an over-the-top 18th-century monument looking rather like a giant wedding cake*

IN SURREY VILLAGES

The churches of Surrey tend not to shout about their riches, and many are positively modest about their histories and treasures. Many of us will find them all the more attractive for that reason. The churches in this cluster are often still fundamentally as they were when they were built, sometimes Norman, sometimes later. Some contain great art, such as the brasses at Stoke D'Abernon; some are home to work of great individuality, such as the Drummond Chapel at Albury. Each is special in its own way.

Compton St Nicholas, and Watts Cemetery Chapel

Why visit: *Unique sanctuary; bizarre memorial chapel*
Where: *The Street (B3000), GU3 1EG*

Its pre-Norman tower alone would make this church special, but what makes it both unique and mysterious is its two-storey sanctuary. This dates from the end of the Norman period and consists of a lower sanctuary with a rib-vaulted ceiling, above which is the upper sanctuary. Separating the upper sanctuary from the rest of the church is a wooden rail carved from a single block of wood dating from about 1180. That makes it the oldest wooden decorative timber-work in the country.

There is much else of interest to see in the church, including a font of about 1160, medieval patterned wall paintings, a 17th-century pulpit, and monuments ranging in date from the 14th to the 18th century. In the east window is a stained glass panel of the Virgin and Child from the early 13th century.

In the new churchyard, east of the church, is the extraordinary Watts Cemetery Chapel. This was consecrated by the Bishop of Winchester in 1898 but not finally finished until 1904. It was created by Mary Watts as a memorial to her husband, George, a celebrated Victorian artist. The outside is bright red brick, the inside a dizzying mass of colour, pattern and painted figures that almost defies description. Aldous Huxley is buried in the chapel grounds.

This page: St Nicholas, Compton (top left), and the extraordinary red-brick Watts Chapel nearby (below left); the 'Old Church' at Albury (right).

Albury
St Peter and St Paul CCT

Why visit: *Norman tower; sumptuous Victorian chapel*
Where: *In Albury Park, between Albury and Shere, GU5 9BB*

Worship eventually stopped at this ancient church in the 1840s. This followed a long period during which two owners of the estate, by a mixture of unscrupulous legal tactics and harassment, obliged the occupants of the village to move to the nearby hamlet of Weston.

A subsequent owner, Henry Drummond, was the person who actually closed the church, after having built a large chapel (known as the Catholic Apostolic Church) close by for a religious sect he supported. He also built a brand new church for the people of Weston. The village was renamed Albury.

The 'Old Church', as it is known, has a Saxon core, on which was built a Norman church. The Norman tower preserves a small Saxon window and Saxon stonework. The eccentric looking dome on top of the tower was added in the early 19th century. Apart from the tower, most of the church dates from the 13th and 14th centuries, with the addition of a handsome north porch in the 15th or 16th century.

Dominant within the church is the Drummond Chapel, created by Augustus Pugin, one of the most original and inspired architects of the first half of the 19th century, for Henry Drummond. The chapel is a dazzling display of colour and decoration, from the stained glass to the floor tiles, and from the painted ceiling to the sculpture and painting on the walls.

Dunsfold
St Mary and All Saints

Why visit: *Remarkable surviving 13th- and 14th-century features*
Where: *Off Church Road, west of Dunsfold village, GU8 4LT*

Author, artist and founder of the Arts and Crafts movement, William Morris called this 'the most beautiful country church in all England'. One of the things that would have attracted him to the church is that, apart from the dumpy 15th-century timber-framed tower and spire, it was virtually all built between 1270 and 1290 and has remained largely unchanged.

There are some remarkable surviving features from medieval times at Dunsfold. Perhaps uniquely the church still has several of the drainage sluice holes at the base of the walls, which let water out when the church floor was washed. Two of these are still oak lined, and have chained wooden plugs that were used to keep out draughts and rodents. Inside there are equally remarkable survivors: what may be the oldest church seating in England. These ancient pews date from between 1409 and 1441.

The church has some remains of 13th-century stained glass and traces of medieval wall paintings. The font is also 13th-century.

Pyrford St Nicholas

Why visit: *Little-changed Norman church*
Where: *Off Church Hill, south of Pyrford village, GU22 8XH*

Pyrford's church retains the shape it had when first built in Norman times, apart from the addition of a bell-turret and north porch in Tudor times, and a vestry in the 19th century. Its immensely thick walls were built without foundations, which accounts for the addition of stone buttresses in later centuries.

Inside, there are 15th-century pews, a pulpit dated 1628, and tantalising fragments of wall painting that may date back to the building of the church in about 1140.

Shere St James

Why visit: *Handsome church built of many different materials*
Where: *Church Lane, off the Square, GU5 9HG*

Viewed from the south, St James's shows many details of its long history: the little south porch of wood and brick sheltering a Norman doorway and 13th-century door; the south aisle, part of the original building of about 1190; the Bray Chancel at the east end dating from the 13th century; and at the west end, the external stairway leading to the gallery, dating from 1748. The materials used to build the walls of the church are fascinatingly diverse: re-used Roman tiles, flint, clunch, local stone of various sorts, Caen stone from Normandy, and Tudor brick.

The inside of the church has a great deal of interest, including a massive oak chest from about 1200 and a font of about the same age, 15th- and 16th-century brasses in the chancel, and a tiny statuette of the Madonna and Child, dating from about 1300.

This page: 15th-century tower at Dunsfold (top left); Norman doorway at Shere, with typical zig-zag patterning (above).

Stoke D'Abernon St Mary

Why visit: *Early brasses and other monuments; strange 17th-century pulpit*
Where: *Just south of Stoke D'Abernon, off the A245 at Parkside School, KT11 3PX; open most weekend afternoons*

From the outside St Mary's looks pleasant but undistinguished, like thousands of churches the Victorians 'restored'. The church did have substantial Saxon elements until 1866, and some can still be seen inside. It is the features inside that draw visitors to the church.

St Mary's is famous for having two of the oldest and finest brasses in the country. Until recently one of them was thought to be *the* oldest, but that has proved not to be the case. Nonetheless, they are remarkable. Both are to Sir John D'Abernon – father and son. The earlier dates from 1327 and shows Sir John full-sized (he was a very large man) in chainmail and holding a spear. His son is in plate armour; his brass dates from about 1340. There are five other brasses nearby. Also in the church are memorials to the Vincent family, brightly painted Jacobean tombs with life-sized figures.

In front of the chancel is a lavishly decorated wooden pulpit from 1620, at the foot of which are monstrous creatures. Close by are an hour glass and lectern from the same period.

ALSO IN THE AREA

Alfold St Nicholas
Why visit: *Timber belfry, Norman font, 17th-century pulpit*

East Clandon
St Thomas of Canterbury
Why visit: *Quiet village church dating back to Norman times*

Hascombe St Peter
Why visit: *Exemplary High Victorian architecture*

Witley All Saints
Why visit: *13th-century, restored and enlarged by Sir Aston Webb in 1899*

LONDON

Unlike parish churches standing proud in village or rural settings, many of London's churches are well-kept secrets, hidden in unfamiliar places. This makes their discovery all the more exciting. The City churches are ordered by their dedications, not by place name.

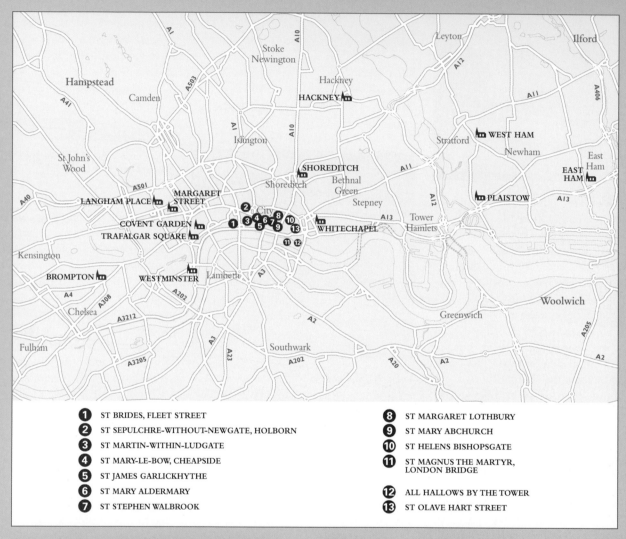

1. ST BRIDES, FLEET STREET
2. ST SEPULCHRE-WITHOUT-NEWGATE, HOLBORN
3. ST MARTIN-WITHIN-LUDGATE
4. ST MARY-LE-BOW, CHEAPSIDE
5. ST JAMES GARLICKHYTHE
6. ST MARY ALDERMARY
7. ST STEPHEN WALBROOK
8. ST MARGARET LOTHBURY
9. ST MARY ABCHURCH
10. ST HELENS BISHOPSGATE
11. ST MAGNUS THE MARTYR, LONDON BRIDGE
12. ALL HALLOWS BY THE TOWER
13. ST OLAVE HART STREET

This page: St Helen's, Bishopsgate, with its unusual double façade hinting at the twin naves inside.
Opposite page: St Magnus the Martyr, London Bridge.

The famous City churches of Christopher Wren are often tucked up side streets or winding little alleyways and are hinted at only by the soaring steeples that tantalise the determined explorer. Ususally built in the Neoclassical style over medieval or earlier foundations, together they are a unified expression of faith, not only in Christianity but also in London's ability to rise out of the ashes of the Great Fire. In contrast, the churches of the East End enjoy more varied settings and inspiration. Some were originally places of worship for immigrants in poor neighbourhoods, while others grew up from sleepy 'rural' churches and are still tranquil oases in the bustle of a huge conurbation. On the other hand, what characterises the churches of the West End from Covent Garden to Brompton, is the sheer exuberance that arises out of new ideas, newly opened land and new-found wealth. Their rich construction and decoration still has the power to surprise and delight.

CITY OF LONDON CHURCHES

The story of the City churches is one of loss and regeneration, from the inevitable slow crumbling of the early medieval structures through the cataclysmic events of the Great Fire of 1666 and the enemy bombing of World War II. But, above all, it is the story of one man, Sir Christopher Wren, whose energy and creative vision wrought London's skyline from the ashes below. Although they are the lion's share of those included here, not all City churches are Wren's. Yet it was he who set the standard for the graceful spires that rise up unexpectedly from narrow streets and lanes, and cluster like exclamation marks around the huge dome of St Paul's Cathedral.

St Stephen **Walbrook**

Why visit: *Wren's masterpiece dome*
Where: *39 Walbrook next to the Mansion House, EC4N 8BN (Tube: Bank or Monument)*

Nothing prepares you, as you climb the 13 steps up to St Stephen's, for the majestic space within. Because it was never intended to stand alone, the exterior is roughly finished. But inside the dome is Wren's finest, based on his original design for St Paul's.

By the 18th century, the building was world-famous, the Italian sculptor-architect Antonio Canova declaring, 'We have nothing to touch it in Rome.' And the architectural historian Nikolaus Pevsner lists it as one of the 10 most important buildings in all of England. Wren lived at no. 15 Walbrook and took

special care in rebuilding this, his parish church, between 1672 and 1679, after the previous 15th-century church was destroyed in the Great Fire. The steeple was added in 1713–7, but the large domed vestibule – the first to be built in England – is integral to his original vision, inspired perhaps by the domed churches he had seen in France.

Unlike St Paul's, which is fashioned in heavy masonry, the dome of St Stephen's rests on elaborate carpentry frames so that it requires much smaller supports, giving an unparalleled feeling of lightness and brightness, uninterrupted by galleries. The spiritual effect depends not on decorative richness but on pure geometry and soaring space.

In Victorian times, the windows were filled with stained glass, which was destroyed in World War II. This has mostly been replaced with clear glass as higher surrounding buildings have robbed the church of much of its light. (Otherwise, the church sustained only slight damage in the war.) In 1888, the box pews were removed and the paving stones were replaced by mosaic, which unfortunately contradicts Wren's statement that this is a Neoclassical not a Gothic church.

According to the precepts of the day, the pulpit is more impressive than the altar, which in Wren's time, therefore, missed out on using the space beneath the dome. Now, however, Henry Moore's controversial massive white polished-stone altar, installed in 1987, stands proudly in the centre of this wonderful church, under the glorious dome.

This page: *The dome of St Stephen's, rising above Henry Moore's stone altar.*

All Hallows **by the Tower**

Why visit: *Oldest church in the City of London*
Where: *Byward Street, next to the Tower of London, EC3R 5AS (Tube: Tower Hill)*

The Saxon Abbey of Barking was built in 675 on the site of a Roman building, traces of which can be seen in its Crypt Museum. The church boasts a 7th-century wall from the original abbey, and the outer walls are 15th-century. All Hallows is the only London church with existing Anglo-Saxon fabric, visible in the Undercroft Chapel where the altar is thought to come from the Templar Church of Richard I in the Holy Land.

Among its treasured possessions are 17 memorial brasses, mainly in the sanctuary and the Lady Chapel. There is a prized baptismal font cover carved in 1682 by Grinling Gibbons (at a cost of £12), and also on display are the church registers, which record the baptism of William Penn, the founder of Pennsylvania.

Partially rebuilt in the 17th century, the church escaped serious harm in the Great Fire, which was observed by Samuel Pepys from its tower. Not so lucky in World War II, it suffered severe bomb damage but was subsequently beautifully restored. The main interior is entirely post-war, a masterly interpretation of the late Gothic style.

St Bride **Fleet Street**

Why visit: *Wren's most famous spire*
Where: *Just off Fleet Street by Ludgate Circus, EC4Y 8AU (Tube: St Paul's)*

Built by Wren in 1671–8 over medieval crypts, this church contains thousands of human remains and a display of other archaeological artefacts tracing 2,000 years of London history. Standing 69m (226ft) high, this is Wren's tallest church after St Paul's. It is noted for its tiered spire – four octagonal stages capped with an obelisk, a ball and vane – said to have been copied by a local baker, William Rich, for a wedding cake design now popular the world over; the wedding dress of his bride is displayed in the crypt. The parish was a centre for the development of early printing and

became the spiritual home of the English newspaper industry for 500 years, with plaques commemorating well-known Fleet Street journalists. The interior of the church was destroyed by bombing in World War II. It was restored in the 1950s in a classical style that differs from a typical galleried Wren church.

St Helen **Bishopsgate**

Why visit: *Collection of pre-Great Fire artefacts*
Where: *Just off Bishopsgate, in Great St Helen's, EC3A 6AT (Tube: Liverpool Street, Bank, Monument or Aldgate)*

The present church contains a fragment of a 13th-century nuns' choir that was constructed alongside a pre-existing parish church, which explains its unusual shape: there are two parallel naves, with a line of arches and a screen separating the two original structures. This configuration was disrupted after 1992, when an IRA bomb shattered all the glass windows and destroyed the east window of the nuns' choir. The current

Evangelical ministry of the church set up ranks of chairs facing the pulpit in the middle of the south wall, with a (to some) uncomfortable result that disturbs the impact of the best set of pre-Fire monuments of a London parish church.

The London volume of *Buildings of England* series lamented, 'the [1993–5] restoration shows no sense of a creative dialogue between past and present… The loss to the viewer's perception of the unique early history of the church is also grave.' However, the architect Quinlan Terry took the opportunity to restore the floor to its original medieval level and to install a new gallery along the full width of the west end.

St James **Garlickhythe**

Why visit: *The 12m (40ft) ceiling – the highest in the City*
Where: *Garlick Hill, at the junction of Cannon Street and Queen Victoria Street, EC4V 2AF (Tube: Mansion House)*

This church's name refers to its position on the Thames, 'hythe' being a Saxon word for jetty, where the medieval herbal medicine garlic was unloaded and traded. It was also the London starting point for pilgrims to Santiago de Compostela in northern Spain.

The current building is Wren's replacement (1676–82) of its medieval predecessor. The white Portland stone exterior is deceptively simple, but the steeple is one of the City's most beautiful. It has a belfry storey with louvre windows, a pierced parapet with urns, and a spire with a three-stage lantern and diagonally projecting columns.

Damage was caused in World War II when a massive bomb fell on the church but did not explode. Restoration erased Victorian 'improvements' to the interior, which is now near perfect. The splendidly carved lion and unicorn armorial supporters are notable, while the quality of light admitted through the clear glass clerestories gives the church its popular nickname, Wren's Lantern.

***This page:** St Bride's restored Neoclassical interior (top centre); the bell-turret of St Helen's, Bishopsgate, which sits above the parallel naves (below centre).*

St Magnus the Martyr
London Bridge

Why visit: *The most magnificent Anglo-Catholic interior of any City church*
Where: *Lower Thames Street, London Bridge, EC3R 6DN (Tube: Monument)*

The original church, founded in the early 12th century, was one of the first buildings to be destroyed by the Great Fire as it stood just 300m (1,000ft) from Pudding Lane. Its rebuilding was taken over by Wren in 1671 and mostly completed by 1684.

That building had nine bays incorporating a tower at the west end but, between 1762 and 1768, the two westernmost bays were demolished to allow for a widened pedestrian route through the base of the tower on to old London Bridge; the tower's lowest storey became and still is a porch.

There have been many changes to the building since 1684. Finally, in 1924, the spacious, severe interior was restored in a neo-Baroque style to reflect its Anglo-Catholic congregation. The high altar is backed by a two-storey reredos and flanked by two side chapels. On the north wall is a Russian icon, while in the south aisle stands a statue of St Magnus, holding a model of the church.

St Magnus also contains an extraordinary 4m- (13ft-) long scale model of old London Bridge, with which it has been so intimately connected throughout the years.

St Margaret **Lothbury**

Why visit: *Fine 17th-century woodwork, some from other demolished Wren churches*
Where: *Lothbury, behind the Bank of England, EC2R 7HH (Tube: Bank)*

First mentioned in 1185 and rebuilt in 1441, the current church by Wren was completed in 1692; the tower by Robert Hooke was finished in 1700. Among the wealth of fine Wren-era woodwork made for St Margaret's are the high altar reredos, the pulpit and the baptismal font.

Pieces brought here in the 19th century from other Wren churches then being demolished include the magnificent choir screen (1683–4) from All Hallows the Great, one of only two such screens to have survived; the tester above the pulpit is from the same church. The finely carved font and the reredos in the south chapel (both thought to be by Grinling Gibbons) were brought here from St Olave Jewry. Colourful paintings of Moses and Aaron on either side of the high altar are from St Christopher-le-Stocks. The church miraculously escaped serious damage in World War II.

St Martin-within-Ludgate
Ludgate

Why visit: *Superb 17th-century woodwork and other interesting furnishings*
Where: *Ludgate Hill, EC4M 7DE (Tube: St Paul's)*

The most striking feature of St Martin's exterior is its tall sharp leaded spire, which when seen from the lower part of Fleet Street, is a deliberate foil to the massive rounded dome of St Paul's Cathedral beyond. No doubt Wren planned this dramatic effect when he reconstructed the previous medieval church, destroyed by the Great Fire, between 1677 and 1684. Notable woodwork includes the original reredos, communion table, communion rails and pulpit. There are also breadshelves, on which wealthier worshippers would place bread for the poor of the parish to collect. The font under the organ gallery is inscribed with a Greek palindrome: NIYON ANOMHMA MH MONAN OYIN ('cleanse my sin not only

my face'). The carved oak double churchwarden's chair is a curiosity, and the large central brass chandelier, still with real candles, was brought from St Vincent Cathedral in the West Indies in 1777. The building sustained the least damage of all City churches during World War II.

St Mary **Abchurch**

Why visit: *Least altered, and beautiful (though smallest) of Wren's London churches*
Where: *In a cobbled yard in Abchurch Lane off Cannon Street, EC4N 7BA (Tube: Monument or Cannon Street)*

When Wren rebuilt this 12th-century church in 1681–6, he employed some of the greatest craftsmen of his age. Grinling Gibbons carved the huge limewood reredos, the only piece in the City certainly documented as being by him. A bomb blast in World War II shattered it into 2,000 pieces but it was carefully restored to the original state between 1948 and 1953 when the pieces were meticulously reassembled.

William Snow, a parishioner, painted the breathtaking wide and shallow dome in 1708. The dome, which cannot be seen externally, is supported on eight arches above four plain brick walls, making the interior seem spacious and light. The woodwork in the interior is the best surviving complete set, with the pulpit and tester, doorcases and west gallery being particularly fine.

This page: *The neo-Baroque chancel of St Magnus, replacing Wren's more severe original (left); St Martin's spiky leaded spire (above).*

St Mary **Aldermary**

Why visit: *Magnificent fan-vaulted ceiling in the only surviving Wren church built in the Gothic style*
Where: *Watling Street at Bow Lane, EC4M 9BW (Tube: Mansion House)*

This is thought to be the oldest church in the City dedicated to the Virgin Mary. The medieval building was replaced by one in the Gothic style in 1510 but was then destroyed in the Great Fire.

Reconstruction was carried out under the supervision of the Wren office, though there is no evidence that Wren himself had much of a hand in it – the parishioners were much attached to the Gothic style, for which Wren had no enthusiasm. The work was completed in 1682 and is now regarded as one of the two most important 17th-century Gothic churches in England.

The fan vaulting is particularly spectacular and makes St Mary's a joy to experience. Much of the interior furnishings reflect the heavy Victorian refurbishment in 1876, though the stained glass windows date mainly from the early 1950s, replacing the Victorian windows, which were shattered by World War II air raids.

St Mary-le-Bow **Cheapside**

Why visit: *Its famous bells*
Where: *Cheapside, EC2V 6AU (Tube: Mansion House or St Paul's)*

This is perhaps the best known City church because of references to its bells: a true Cockney is said to be born within

the sound of them, they are supposed to have called Dick Whittington to return to the City, and they rang out when Charles I was beheaded in the London in 1649, as immortalised in the nursery rhyme *Oranges and Lemons*.

The church dates from Norman times, when it was known as St Marie de Arcubus (or le Bow) because of the bow arches of stone in its crypt. Wren continued the arch theme in his new design when, from 1670 to 1675, it was one of the first churches he rebuilt after the Great Fire. Its huge steeple is a square tower 72m (235ft) tall, topped by a dragon-shaped golden weathervane. Wren's church was almost completely destroyed above ground by bombing in World War II, and the bells were sent crashing to the ground.

The church was completely rebuilt in 1956–64, with only the tower and lofty spire remaining of Wren's work. The modern church is attractive and bright; a statue of Captain John Smith, the founder of Virginia and a former parishioner, stands in the churchyard.

St Olave **Hart Street**

Why visit: *The smallest medieval church remaining in the City*
Where: *Hart Street, EC3R 7NB (Tube: Tower Hill or Monument)*

Some of the original fabric of this church built in 1270 remains, including the crypt. The usual entrance is from Hart Street, with the floor well below street level. The aisles and tower date from the mid-15th century. On the south side of the church there is an atmospheric churchyard and the visitor will find this is the best viewing point to see the exterior of the building.

This was the parish church of Samuel Pepys; he is buried here and a memorial bust of his wife gazes towards the former Navy Office gallery where he once sat. St Olave's largely escaped the Great Fire thanks to Pepys and William Penn Sr (father of the founder of Pennsylvania), who created firebreaks around it. Although the church was gutted by firebombs in 1941, it was restored in 1951–4, successfully retaining an atmosphere both intimate and antique.

St Sepulchre-without-Newgate **Holborn**

Why visit: *Its musical associations*
Where: *Holborn Viaduct at Giltspur Street, EC1A 9DE, opposite the Old Bailey (Tube: St Paul's)*

There has been a church on this site since Saxon times, but the present building dates from 1450. It was gutted by the Great Fire, which left only the walls and tower standing. The parish set about rebuilding it in 1667–71 – without reference to Wren – based on the burnt-out shell. There have been frequent alterations over the years, and much of the remaining 17th-century interior disappeared in drastic re-ordering between 1873 and 1880. It is the largest parish church in the City, a wide, roomy space with a coffered ceiling.

Known as the National Musicians Church, it has a chapel dedicated to St Cecilia containing Sir Henry Wood's ashes and stained glass windows commemorating the singer Dame Nellie Melba and the composer Walter Carroll. The church is also home to the Loos Cross, brought from the World War I battlefield where 100 officers and men from the City of London Rifles lost their lives in 1915.

This page: *High above St Mary's is its spectacular fan-vaulted ceiling (left); colourful stained glass window at St Sepulchre-without-Newgate (above).*

LONDON'S EAST END

The churches of the East End are nothing if not varied – and very surprising. While many jostle for space in inner-city neighbourhoods, others are practically bucolic: St Mary Magdalene, East Ham, stands at the edge of a huge nature reserve, and St John-at-Hackney is set in large attractive gardens. These six churches may range in age from 100 to 1,000 years old, but they all have rich historical associations. Together, they are a testimony to changing times, and an unchanging devotion to the spiritual needs of their local communities.

All dignity is restored, however, at the south front of the church, even though it has lost its crowning features: the clock, the bell turret and a large weathervane in the shape of St George and the Dragon. The interior retains remarkable and mostly original furnishings, including a complete set of box pews. Deep galleries standing on eight Tuscan timber columns still loom overhead around three sides of the building. This is a simple Protestant layout; there is no central aisle – and no wasted space.

As if to herald the supreme importance of the sermon, the magnificent high central double-decker pulpit stands behind a railed altar and is flanked by two carved timber commandment boards in German. In a prominent position at this end hangs the coat-of-arms of George III, showing the mark of loyalty normally adopted by Anglican churches.

During the Nazi period, St George's Pastor, Julius Rieger, set up a relief centre for Jewish refugees from Germany, who were provided with references to travel to England. The leading theologian and anti-Nazi activist Dietrich Bonhoeffer was also associated with the work of St George's when Bonhoeffer was pastor at the nearby St Paul's church from 1933 to 1935.

From 1763 until 1996, St George's was a place of Lutheran worship; now it is the headquarters of the Historic Chapels Trust and is used for organ recitals.

This page: The handsome exterior and galleried interior of St George's (left), with its original box pews (below).

Whitechapel St George's German Lutheran Church

Why visit: *The oldest-surviving German church in Britain*
Where: *55 Alie Street, E1 8EB (Tube: Aldgate or Aldgate East); open by appointment only Mon–Fri, 9am–5pm (tel 020 7421 0533)*

St George's has changed little since 1763, when it was established in the immigrant neighbourhood of Whitechapel by German refugees seeking religious asylum in London and working mainly in the sugar trade. The church is handsome and majestic yet sober, with its dark burnished wood offset by pristine white walls and small stained glass windows.

In its original architecture and construction, the church is not evidently German. Nor was the manner of its worship. Its first pastor, Dr Gustav Anton Wachsel, fanned controversy by conducting services in English, discharging the German choir in favour of 'violins, trumpets, bassoons and kettledrums' and supposedly assaulting the organ bellows blower.

East Ham
St Mary Magdalene

Why visit: *Its peaceful 'rural' setting, deceptively near a busy main road*
Where: *Norman Road at High Street South, E6 3BA, off the A13*

This parish church is the oldest Norman church in London still in weekly use. It stands in solemn grandeur in a 9½-acre churchyard, now managed as a nature reserve. The main body of the church was built about 1130 in the Romanesque style, but the tower dates mainly from the 16th century. There is a fine doorway between the tower and nave.

In the chancel, the blind arcading of Norman arches is of special interest, as are the 12th-century Cistercian wall paintings. These were covered over many years ago with limewash to preserve them, leaving some small 'windows' to show what lies beneath. The limewash is now being carefully scraped away.

Hackney
St John-at-Hackney

Why visit: *Vast classical-style building set in attractive gardens*
Where: *Lower Clapton Road, E5 0PD (Tube: Bethnal Green)*

Built in 1792 on a Greek cross plan, this huge structure stands on the site of the old church of St Augustine, dating back to 1275. That medieval church was demolished in 1798 – except for its tower, which was left intact to hold the bells as funds did not run to building a tower on the new church until 1816.

The original St Augustine Tower remains standing to this day in the church gardens, which also contain some

impressive headstones and monuments. After a fire in 1955 destroyed some of the interior, the church acquired altar hangings designed for the coronation of Queen Elizabeth II.

Plaistow
Memorial Community Church

Why visit: *Interesting remnant of an East End social project begun in the 1920s*
Where: *395 Barking Road, E13 8AL*

The Memorial Baptist Church building was opened in 1922 to house the church – then known as West Ham Central Mission – and its welfare work. Its imposing Byzantine façade, with two great towers, possibly followed a minor trend in church building started by Westminster Cathedral. The congregation at the time envisioned 'a great cathedral church towering above the mean streets of West Ham' and dedicated it to local men who were killed in World War I. The names of 169 of them are cast into the 10 memorial chime bells in the east tower.

Shoreditch St Leonard

Why visit: *Its glorious, soaring Palladian style, and theatrical associations*
Where: *Shoreditch High Street, E1 6JN (Tube: Old Street or Liverpool Street)*

St Leonard's is the first 'Actors' Church', as England's first purpose-built theatre was nearby, and several important Elizabethan theatre folk, including James and Richard Burbage, are buried in the medieval crypt. The current building

dates from about 1740 and was built in the new classical Palladian style, which caused a scandal at the time. It boasts a magnificent 59m (192ft) steeple, modelled on Wren's St Mary-le-Bow, and a giant four-column Tuscan portico.

Original 18th-century fixtures also remain, including the font, pulpit, communion table, clock, organ case, breadshelves and Commandment boards. The parish stocks and whipping post stand in the porch.

West Ham All Saints

Why visit: *Its traditional status as the 'Cathedral of the East End'*
Where: *7 Church Street, Stratford, E15 3HU (Tube: Plaistow)*

The parish church of West Ham was established in 1135 and rebuilt in Early English style in the reign of Henry II (1154–89), when its Norman walls were pierced with arches and round pillars, and the north and south aisles added. The 23m (74ft) tower is early 15th century, the north chapel is built in Tudor brick, and the pews are 18th-century – being stripped of their dark paint in the 1970s.

During the Victorian restoration the reredos, designed by Sir George Gilbert Scott (architect of the Albert Memorial) was installed in the sanctuary.

This page: The ancient Norman façade of St Mary Magdalene (left); St John-at-Hackney, surrounded by its lovely gardens (centre); the dramatic Tuscan portico of the Actors' Church, St Leonard (above).

FROM COVENT GARDEN WEST

The cultural and physical wealth of London's West End has endowed its churches with unimaginable riches. They in turn reflect the life of the nation: from medieval St Margaret's at the heart of Westminster Square to Inigo Jones's 17th-century marvel of civic planning, St Paul's, Covent Garden; from St Martin-in-the-Fields and All Souls, Langham Place – both reflecting Britain's sovereign might – to the Victorian high seriousness of the Brompton Oratory and All Saints, Margaret Street. The capital has hundreds of inspiring churches, but these are six of the very best.

Margaret Street All Saints

Why visit: *A marvellous expression of Gothic Revival and Anglo-Catholic faith*
Where: *7 Margaret Street, W1W 8JG (Tube: Oxford Circus)*

Tucked behind busy Oxford Street lies this gem of High Victorian Gothic architecture, designed by William Butterfield and completed in 1859. Historian Roy Strong describes it as 'a world vibrant with glorious imagery: friezes of saints in ceramic, an abundance of mosaic in alabaster and marble, patterns in brick and tile covering every surface, painted images and guttering candles and, above all, the haunting cavernous chancel

and sanctuary…' The design grew out of the mid-19th-century desire to return the Church to the splendour of the Middle Ages.

This style of architecture chimes neatly with its current Anglo-Catholic style of worship that includes ritual, a traditional liturgy, choir and organ music, embellished vestments and incense. All this makes for a heady mix that fairly overwhelms the senses.

Approached through a secluded courtyard, the church and its buildings are constructed in a bold chequered brick pattern, topped by a tower and spire that looms over the crowded street. To the left is the old Choir School, attended by Laurence Olivier, which closed in 1968; to the right is the vicarage.

On the other side of the main door, the interior pulses with a riot of colour and pattern: tiles, brick, painting and gilding that extend from the walls and floor up to the very roof. The font is of various marbles with carved alabaster angels, and the pulpit is a weighty structure of geometrical mosaic.

On the north and west wall, mosaic patterns give way to impressive tile paintings that depict biblical scenes and characters. These compete with stained-glass windows that admit a muted light.

Almost a third of the length of the church is devoted to the chancel. To emphasise its importance, the abstract designs of the nave progress – as you pass through the gilt iron and brass gates set in the alabaster and marble chancel screen – to the richer gilded and painted decoration of the sanctuary.

In place of an east window (which is ruled out by the encroaching nearby buildings), there is an impressive three-tiered fresco. This outstanding piece of work inspired by 15th-century Italian creations acts as a reredos and extends on to the north and south walls.

Everywhere the eye rests in this unforgettable iconic church, it is met by a visual richness that is the equal to the most ornate medieval cathedral.

This page: *The glowing Italian-inspired tiered fresco above the altar of All Saints, Margaret Street.*

Brompton Oratory

Why visit: *Grand Baroque architecture, marble treasures and superb music*
Where: *Brompton Road next to the Victoria and Albert Museum, SW7 2RP (Tube: South Kensington)*

More correctly called the London Oratory, or the Church of the Immaculate Heart of Mary, this is the second largest Catholic church in London. Built in 1880–4 in a neo-Baroque style with a deliberate 'Italian Renaissance' feel, it has a large dome and cupola standing 61m (200ft) tall. The ornate interior is breathtaking, with a nave wider than St Paul's, pilasters and columns in Devon marble, and more exotic marbles in the apse and altars.

Huge marble figures of the Twelve Apostles, along with most of its 17th-century treasures, were brought to London from Italian churches. Bizarrely, during the Cold War the KGB supposedly used the porch to drop secret communiqués!

Covent Garden St Paul

Why visit: *Its impressive Tuscan portico facing onto Covent Garden piazza*
Where: *Bedford Street, WC2E 9ED (Tube: Covent Garden)*

The great Inigo Jones designed this Italianate masterpiece, completed in 1663. People often ask why the huge east door on to the piazza doesn't open. It was originally intended to be the main entrance, but tradition demanded that the altar be placed at the east end. So the portico door is actually a fake and the church is entered from a little graveyard off Bedford Street.

Among those buried at the church are Grinling Gibbons (master carver of the late 17th/early 18th century) and the pulpit is said to be his work. Also buried here is Margaret Porteous, the first known victim of the Great Plague.

St Paul's is widely known as the Actors' Church and has been associated with local theatres since it was built. Memorials in the church are dedicated to many famous actors, including Charlie Chaplin and Noel Coward.

Langham Place All Souls

Why visit: *The last surviving church by John Nash, George IV's favourite architect*
Where: *All Souls Place, just south of BBC Broadcasting House, W1B 3DA (Tube: Oxford Circus)*

This so-called Waterloo church was built in 1823, one of many commemorating Wellington's 1815 victory over Napoleon. Purists complained that Nash blithely confused different architectural styles, but it was designed for maximum impact, to provide an eye-catching monument for the newly laid-out Regent Street.

Constructed in Bath stone, which glows in the evening sunlight, it has a grand columned circular portico reminiscent of a classical temple, surmounted by a fluted spire. Inside is a large open hall with a wide nave surrounded by a gallery on three sides. At the east end, a spectacular painting of Christ hangs under a huge golden sunburst, one of the finest of its kind in England.

Trafalgar Square St Martin-in-the-Fields

Why visit: *The iconic Classical design, blueprint for churches around the world*
Where: *Trafalgar Square, WC2N 4JJ (Tube: Charing Cross or Leicester Square)*

In 1542 Henry VIII rebuilt the church already on this site to keep plague victims from being carried through his palace grounds – at the time, this was an isolated spot 'in the fields'. It was replaced in 1726

by this lovely temple, designed by James Gibbs, which boasts an imposing Classical pediment supported by huge Corinthian columns, and a tall steeple topped with a gilt crown – a design that looks, according to one critic, 'as though Wren had been to Italy'. Gibbs was certainly inspired by Christopher Wren, as the interior, with its ceiling of painted and gilded plaster panels, shows.

Ingenious renovations in 2007–9 have introduced more light, renewed the pews and stone flooring, and exposed the crypt's brickwork.

Westminster St Margaret

Why visit: *The church of the House of Commons since 1614*
Where: *Parliament Square, SW1P 3JX (Tube: Westminster)*

As nearby Westminster Abbey was a monastery church, local people needed a place to worship and so St Margaret's was founded in the 12th century. The building was begun in Tudor times, but in the 18th century the whole structure was enlarged and encased in Portland stone, causing the church to be described as 'a Tudor body in Georgian clothing'.

The stunning arcades and clerestory windows form a procession through the nave to a richly coloured Flemish glass window. Later windows commemorate William Caxton and Sir Walter Raleigh, and there are beautiful 20th-century windows by the artist John Piper.

This page: All Souls' spire in warm Bath stone (centre); the painted and gilded ceiling panels of St Martin-in-the-Fields (above).

WALES

The churches and chapels of Wales are brilliantly diverse, ranging from large and splendid parish churches in the English mould, to tiny, remote buildings that are quintessentially Welsh.

Generally speaking, the churches and chapels of Wales are not as celebrated as those of England, which is a disservice to the buildings and to potential visitors. Wales has hundreds of superb and interesting churches and chapels, often in outstanding locations.

They range from imposing parish churches, such as St Mary's in Tenby and St Mary's in Abergavenny, to minute buildings in very remote locations. Among the latter are chapel-churches that are as hidden away as any in Britain, and which are best discovered with the help of a large-scale OS map that shows all public footpaths.

Many of the churches described on the following pages have something in common: saints. Church after church has its roots far back in the earliest days of Christianity in Britain. They were most often originally founded as wooden buildings by wandering clerics whose courage alone surely justifies their becoming saints. They brought Christianity to places that must have been wildly remote and potentially dangerous. The dangers were just as much from humans as from the forces of nature, and many of the early clerics died at the hands of brigands and raiders.

Visiting such places today is a reminder of just how important Christianity was to bringing civilisation and stability to Britain. Churches were at the centre of every aspect of life from the time of those early saints through more than 1,500 years of British history.

The churches described here remain very important to their communities. There are remote churches that are lovingly tended and which still have loyal congregations who may have to make their way on foot to regular services, as well as keeping the churches open and cared for. Churches in towns and villages are also adapting to changing times by taking on roles that keep them relevant.

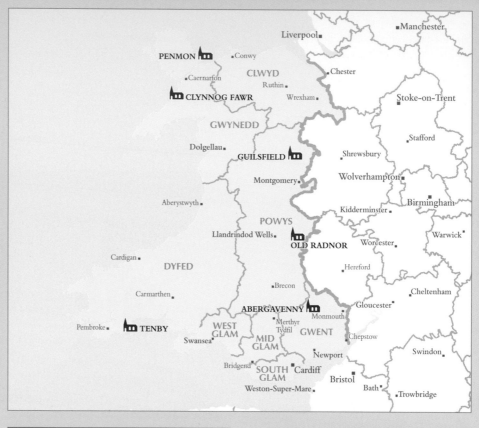

Opposite page: St Govan's Chapel at Bosherston clings to its cliff above the sea. This tiny chapel is the simplest possible building, and draws visitors for its long history as well as for its splendid setting.

THE FAR SOUTH-WEST

Much of this area is 'Little England beyond Wales', also known as the Landsker. It is an English-speaking part of the country, the actual area of which has moved over time. In the Middle Ages the Landsker included all of the churches in this tour, including those in the Presceli Hills, but now it takes in the land west of Laugharne and south of a wiggly line that emerges at St Bride's Bay. Long before the Normans came this was a Celtic realm, with strong links to Ireland, and no less than four of the churches here have Ogham stones among their treasures. Ogham is an alphabet of Irish origin created by marking lines on the edges of stones, the number and angles of the lines creating the letters. It reads from right to left.

Tenby St Mary

Why visit: *Large and impressive 15th-century church*
Where: *High Street, SA70 7JD*

Rows of pretty town houses in pinks, blues, greens and creams line the harbourside at Tenby, and above them all rises the spire of the parish church. The town was important in medieval times, with a castle and town walls, parts of which can still be seen, but by the 18th century it had slipped into forgotten decay. It was reinvented as a seaside resort in the early 19th century, which is when many of the handsome houses were built.

St Mary's dates from the 15th century although there was an earlier church on this site and the base of the tower is 13th-century. The interior is bright, neat and harmonious, partly because all the woodwork was cleaned and waxed in the

1960s. The eye is led to the altar by the 15th-century wagon roofs in both nave and chancel. These still have their bosses, with the ones in the chancel having such subjects as a mermaid, Christ's Passion and the four Evangelists. The altar is 10 steps up from the chancel floor.

There are chapels on either side of the chancel. The north chapel, dedicated to St Nicholas, was built in 1475 and was refurbished in 1966. In the north aisle is

a grim monument to John Denby, Archdeacon of St David's in the 15th century. His effigy is depicted as a rotting corpse – a memento mori or reminder that this is the fate awaiting us all. The south chapel, also 15th-century, is dedicated to St Thomas. Here is a memorial to mathematician Robert Recorde who died in 1510 and who is famous for having invented the equals (=) sign. Also in this chapel is an old curfew bell and the church's original font, now disused. The font used today is from 1886.

Bayvil St Andrew the Apostle FoFC

Why visit: *Picturesque setting; perfect early 19th-century fittings*
Where: *2 miles north-east of Nevern, off a track to a farm, SA41 3XN; keyholder lives nearby*

Set in a tree-lined, grassy and bracken-filled churchyard with a few leaning headstones, Bayvil's tiny church would be described by most as a chapel. It was built in the early 19th century, when most new religious buildings in Wales were Nonconformist chapels. However, this is an Anglican building. It was not restored by the Victorians, partly because being virtually new it did not need restoring, so it has kept its original furnishings virtually intact: pews, a three-decker pulpit and even the old funeral bier (carrier for coffin). When the Friends of Friendless Churches took it over in 1983 it was in a poor condition, but it is now returned to its former quiet dignity. Fortunately the resident bats stayed on.

This page: St Mary's, Tenby (top); monument to John Denby (centre).
Opposite page: Pebble floor at St Illtyd, Caldey Island.

Bosherston
St Govan's Chapel

Why visit: *Legend of St Govan*
Where: *1 mile south of Bosherston, on the cliffs at St Govan's Head, nearest postcode SA71 5DP; not accessible when the red flag of the firing range is flying*

Settings do not come much more dramatic than this. Approached down a flight of worn stone steps, (see page 87) the chapel is perched on a cliff face above the waters of the Atlantic. On a still day in summer it is lovely; when the autumn and winter gales blow it is very wild.

St Govan is said to have been a 6th-century Irish monk, who may not have come to Pembrokeshire until he was an old man, by which time he was an abbot. Legend says that he was being chased by brigands when a fissure opened in the cliff face, allowing St Govan to slip inside, and closed up after him.

After the brigands had gone St Govan emerged but stayed on, building the chapel and living in the tiny cell that can still be seen behind it. He died in 586 and is said to be buried under the floor of the chapel.

The building is tiny and very simple, its interior containing only the most basic stone altar. There is debate as to its age, some saying it is post-Norman, some saying 10th-century or even before.

In medieval times this was a place of pilgrimage, with a holy well (now long dry) the water of which was said to be good for such things as eye complaints.

Caldey Island St David

Why visit: *Atmospheric church in an island setting*
Where: *On Caldey Island, reached by boat from Tenby, SA70 7UH; boats visit the island from Easter to October; the island is closed in winter*

This is the parish church of little Caldey Island, where both islanders and monks are buried, their graves marked by wooden crosses. There may have been a church here as early as the 6th century, but the building as it stands today is a simple Norman structure, repaired in the 1800s, and restored twice in the

20th century. The font was designed by Eric Gill, and the stained glass was made in the 1920s by Theodore Bailey, one of the island's monks. The liveliest glass is in the Fish Window – a 20th-century take on the ancient Christian symbol – and the Tree of Life Window.

Caldey Island St Illtyd

Why visit: *Ancient church with roots in Celtic Christianity*
Where: *On Caldey Island, see St David (below left) for details, SA70 7UH*

With a Christian community since the 6th century, Caldey Island is one of the earliest Christian sites in Britain. Today it is a Cistercian abbey, farmed by the monks for produce and for flowers to make perfume. The abbey buildings and grounds are not open to the public, but parts of the island are open, as is St Illtyd's (and St David's, see left).

St Illtyd's is part of the buildings called the Old Priory, which have not been occupied since the Dissolution in the 16th century when the buildings were left to decay. The island was given over to farming until the monks returned in 1906 after a break of over 300 years and set up the community again.

As it stands today St Illtyd's dates from the 13th century, but the famous Caldey Stone, found in the grounds and now in the church, has a 6th-century Ogham inscription on it and also a later, 9th-century, Latin script. The church is simple and serene on the inside, with

pebble floors and stone walls, and very picturesque on the outside, with lichen-covered walls and a tall, spindly spire.

Eglwys Gymyn St Margaret

Why visit: *Historic church saved by a local antiquarian*
Where: *On the B4314, north of Pendine, SA33 4PD; church may be locked but keyholder lives nearby*

A low, simple building in a large round churchyard, St Margaret's dates from the 14th century. However, there was almost certainly a much earlier church here. The church had a thorough, though sensitive, restoration in the early 20th century, masterminded by G.G.T. Treherne, who had spent his childhood in this part of Wales. He subsequently studied at Oxford University, where he rowed in the 1859 Boat Race.

He was a passionate antiquarian and wrote widely about the history of Eglwys Gymyn and its area. He was responsible for saving the Avitoria Stone, which is inscribed in both Latin and Ogham, and is the greatest treasure of the church.

Gumfreston St Lawrence

Why visit: *Holy wells and ancient customs*
Where: *On a track south of the B4318, west of Tenby, SA70 8RA*

Like many Welsh churches, St Lawrence's is built within a 'llan', an early Christian enclosure that may date back to the first days of Christianity in Wales. However, the present building and its tall stone tower are from the late 12th or early 13th century. The interior of the little church is charming, with a low chancel arch adding to the ancient look and feel.

There are three holy wells in the churchyard, and they still attract pilgrims. The waters are said to have medicinal and healing properties. An old Easter custom called 'Throwing Away Christ's Nails' has been revived here in recent years. From Palm Sunday, members of the congregation carry a nail in their pockets, and after the Easter Day service they take the nails to the holy wells and throw them in. An older name for the custom was 'Throwing Lent Away'.

Haverfordwest St Mary

Why visit: *Carvings in wood and stone*
Where: *Top of High Street, SA61 2DA*

Set at the top of the tidal part of the Western Cleddau river, Haverfordwest was an important port in medieval times. It was a key town in 'England beyond Wales', a region that was so thoroughly taken over by the Normans and later incomers that the Welsh inhabitants and their language were subsumed.

The east end of St Mary's dominates the top of the High Street, making a stone full stop to the rows of pastel-coloured houses. It is a castle-like building, with a square tower and battlements. It dates mostly from the 13th century, and the piers and arches in the nave are particularly fine, lit by a later Perpendicular clerestory.

The lovely oak roofs are 16th-century, some of the superb bosses being in the shape of the Tudor rose. The roof is supported on stone corbels in the shape of human faces, and the capitals of the piers have detailed stone carving of foliage, people and creatures. There is more wonderful carving, this time in wood, on the bench-end of the Mayor and Sheriff's Pew. It shows a splendid, feathered St Michael, with raised sword and winged dragon at his feet.

Hodgeston FoFC

Why visit: *14th-century stonework*
Where: *Centre of Hodgeston; SA71 5JU*

The tower at Hodgeston is typical of this area – tall, thin and wider at the bottom. It is a late example of its kind, built in

about 1600. The limewashed interior of the chapel is simple and is especially noted for its 14th-century stone carving. This is seen at its best in the triple sedilia, which has ornate ogee-arched canopies. The church had fallen into disrepair by the 19th century and was restored in 1856 when the decorated tiles in the chancel were installed. Some of the pews are a recent introduction, having been made by W.D. Caroe in the late 19th century for St David's Church, Exeter.

Llandawke St Oudoceus FoFC

Why visit: *Lovely church in pretty setting*
Where: *Approached on foot through the private gardens of the Old Rectory, SA33 4RD*

Sitting on the side of a little dell, Llandawke's church can be glimpsed from the road as it approaches the hamlet. It is a lovely building with a short, stout stone tower topped by a pyramidal roof, and a simple nave and chancel. It dates from the 13th century, but was remodelled a century later.

In the church is a 6th-century memorial stone inscribed in both Ogham and Latin. From much later is the battered 14th-century effigy of a woman, found in the churchyard in 1902. This is said to be the effigy of St Margaret Marlos, niece of Sir Guy de Bryan, who had the church remodelled.

The church was in a bad state by Victorian times, and was rescued by the ladies of Laugharne, who raised some of the necessary funds by holding a grand bazaar and fete. The most remarkable item of that time is the carved wooden

altar. It has legs with statues, and also includes carvings of a variety of flowers, with birds at the corners.

The church was taken into the care of Friends of Friendless Churches in 2006, and much work has been done and continues to be done, to maintain and enhance the building.

Llandeloy St Eloi FoFC

Why visit: *Ancient church rebuilt using Arts and Crafts principles*
Where: *Off the A487, north-west of Haverfordwest, SA62 6LJ*

Standing in ruins since the 1840s, by the beginning of the 20th century this little 12th-century church was roofless and its walls were crumbling. There was talk of rebuilding and restoring it, and before World War I a significant amount of money had been raised for the purpose, but the war intervened and it was not until 1925 that work began. The architect was John Coates-Carter, by then officially retired. He was a follower of the Arts and Crafts Movement, that group of intellectuals, artists and craftsmen who believed that traditional crafts and skills could be combined with creative inspiration to create objects and buildings that were both useful and beautiful.

The building that Coates-Carter recreated adheres exactly to those principles. The church is simple and simply furnished, with a rood screen and rood made to Coates-Carter's designs and built in Cheltenham (Coates-Carter's place of retirement). The raised chancel and altar can be reached through the screen or via a tiny transept. Behind the stone altar is a highly idiosyncratic reredos that shows Christ reigning from the Cross, and with a background of the sun, moon and a rainbow.

Laugharne St Martin

Why visit: *Grave of Dylan Thomas*
Where: *Off Church Street, just to the north of village centre, SA33 4QE*

Thousands of people come here every year to see the grave of poet Dylan Thomas, marked by a simple white cross. The church dates largely from the 15th century, but was heavily restored in the 19th century. It contains 17th-century memorials and much Victorian glass.

From the church you can make a circular walk on footpaths to the estuary of the Taf (Thomas's 'heron priested shore'), down to the Boathouse (where Thomas lived), on to the castle and back up the village street. You will pass shops and pubs that Thomas always denied were the direct inspiration for *Under Milk Wood*, although the people of Laugharne (pronounced Larn) never seem to have a problem with this idea.

Nevern St Brynach

Why visit: *Ancient stones*
Where: *East of Newport, SA42 0NF*

Nevern is on the little River Nyfer, which winds to the north of the Preseli Hills. These hills have been inhabited for thousands of years, as the prehistoric Pentre Ifan burial chamber, or dolmen, proves. Pentre Ifan is only a mile or two south of Nevern and has spectacular views across the hills to Cardigan Bay.

Nevern's church and churchyard contain more chapters on the history of man in this area, although from a much later time. The earliest are stones with Ogham and Latin inscriptions on them; they date from the 5th or 6th century, around the time that Irish St Brynach came here and founded the church. One of the stones is now used as a sill in the church. Close to it is another stone, also used as a sill, this time from the 10th century, with an intricate Celtic cross carved on it.

There is another Ogham and Latin-inscribed stone in the churchyard, near to the church's chief treasure, the Nevern Cross. This dates from the late 10th or early 11th century and is one of the finest Celtic crosses in Wales. It is covered in intricate interlacing patterns, all beautifully preserved and nearly as clear as when the cross was carved. The stone from which it is made came from the Preseli Hills.

The church as it stands today has a Norman tower and Tudor nave, but it was rigorously restored in 1864.

Legends abound here: one of the yew trees is called the Bleeding Yew, and has dark blood-like sap that oozes year round. And the first cuckoo of spring is supposed to sing from Nevern Cross on 7 April – St Brynach's Day.

Stackpole Elidor
St James and St Elidyr

Why visit: *Excellent tower; monuments*
Where: *South of Pembroke, SA71 5BZ*

Tucked away on a sloping hillside in peaceful countryside, the most immediately obvious feature of this church is its tower – tall and thin even in comparison to the other churches in this area. The tower is the oldest part of the church, dating back to the 13th century. The body of the church was in poor repair by the mid-19th century and no less a person than the famous church architect and restorer Sir George Gilbert Scott was called in to bring the church back to life. His work was thorough, and today's church is very much a result of that restoration.

Several memorials are preserved inside, including one to Sir Elidor Stackpole and another to his wife, Lady Elspeth. They are 14th-century, so the Sir Elidor who is commemorated is presumably not the Elidyr in the church's dedication, though the names are clearly the same. In the Lort Chapel there is a fine 17th-century memorial to Roger Lort, shown with his wife Abertha, their seven sons and five daughters. There are also memorials to the Cawdors, who restored the church.

Opposite page: Interior at Hodgeston (left); the lovely church of St Oudoceus (centre); unusual reredos at Llandeloy (right).
This page: The Nevern Cross (left); exterior of St James and St Elidyr (above).

ALSO IN THE AREA

Angle St Mary the Virgin
Why visit: *Medieval seaside church with nearby 15th-century seamen's chapel*

Bosherston St Michael and All Angels
Why visit: *Lovely small 13th-century church close to the famous Lily Ponds*

Kidwelly St Mary
Why visit: *Impressive medieval church with wide nave and chancel*

Manordeifi St David FoFC
Why visit: *Setting; Georgian fittings*

Mwnt Holy Cross
Why visit: *Cliff-top setting*

New Hedges St Anne
Why visit: *Bright blue 'tin tabernacle' built in 1928*

BLACK MOUNTAINS BORDER COUNTRY

The Black Mountains are the ever-present backdrop to the churches here. In kind weather this is a wonderful area, almost completely unspoiled and full of birdsong and wildflowers. Many of the churches have a timeless, untroubled quality that brings visitors back to them again and again.

Abergavenny St Mary

Why visit: *Superb array of monuments*
Where: *Monk Street, NP7 5ND; open Mon–Sat 11am–3pm, Sun 2–4pm*

The parish church in Abergavenny was founded in the late 11th century as the church of a Benedictine priory. It is the only part to survive, apart from the later tithe barn. The church went through several re-orderings, restorations and rebuildings in the 19th century, partly to reflect changing religious practice, and in 1882 another restoration began, resulting in the nave and north aisle being virtually rebuilt in an endeavour to return to the original layout. In 1896 more was done to bring back into use the whole of the east end, including the chancel, parts of which had been used as a school.

Despite all these changes, the church contains a remarkable number of monuments, many of them medieval. The oldest is to Eva da Braose, of the Norman Marcher Lord family. She died in the mid-1200s. Her effigy holds a shield marked with her husband's crest of a fleurs de lis. The largest collection of monuments is in the Herbert Chapel. Here, ranks of effigies on their decorated table tombs fill the space and the walls. They range in date from the 15th to the 17th century and show the changes in faces, fashions and taste through that time.

There are two outstanding wooden carvings in the church. The earliest is the effigy of Sir John de Hastings, of about 1325. He is shown praying and in repose, his feet on a lion. The figure is beautifully made and very well preserved. Even more remarkable is the wooden figure of Jesse, made in the 15th century. He is literally larger than life-sized, and wonderfully carved, with flowing robes and a luxuriant beard. From his stomach protrudes the stump of what would once have been the Tree of Jesse, an enormous sculpture showing how Jesus was descended from Jesse, with all of the principal biblical persons depicted in between. The figure is a unique work of art, unlike anything else in Britain.

The church is at the centre of a thriving church community, with the 16th-century tithe barn housing an education centre and the newly built Priory Centre.

Capel-y-ffin St Mary

Why visit: *Setting and simple beauty*
Where: *In the Vale of Ewyas, between Llanthony and Hay-on-Wye, NP7 7NP*

Tiny, whitewashed and with a lop-sided bellcote, St Mary's is charm itself. Diarist and clergyman Francis Kilvert, who lived a few miles away, described it as 'squatting like a stout grey owl among its seven great black yews'. The setting is wonderful and wild: on the banks of the infant Honddu river, with the Black Mountains to the west and the great ridge carrying Offa's Dyke (and the Wales/England border) immediately to the east. To the north is Gospel Pass – the road over the mountains to Hay-on-Wye. In winter this is often impassable because of snow, and even in summer after heavy rain the road can be slippery and difficult.

The church was built in 1762, as a chapel of ease for the church at nearby Lanigon. Inside it is a simple, very small chamber, with a stone floor, wooden seating, minute gallery, pulpit and altar.

Cwmyoy St Martin

Why visit: *Remarkable leaning church*
Where: *Off the B4423, north-west of Llanfihangel Crucorney, NP7 7PS*

You can catch glimpses of Cwmyoy's 13th-century church from the B4423 as it winds up the Vale of Ewyas, and even from afar the leaning tower is very apparent. Closer to, the lean is even more dramatic, and it is not just the tower: the different elements of the building – tower, nave, chancel – are at different angles to one another.

But the church is stable, the tower buttressed, and the nave walls long braced with additional beams. All these leanings are because the church was built on what turned out to be an unstable hillside that was made up of debris from an Ice Age landslide. Inside, arches, floors and windows are at different angles, making

This page: Jesse figure, Abergavenny.
Opposite page: Leaning tower of Cwmyoy (left); ruins at Llanthony (centre).

the view up the nave into the chancel truly memorable. But it is also beautiful, neat and simple, with many memorials on the walls. The majority of these were made by the Butes, a family of stonemasons who carved memorials for churches across the Black Mountains.

In the nave is a stone cross with a figure of Jesus crucified upon it, possibly 13th-century. The cross was stolen in 1967 but, by good fortune, was spotted in a London antique dealer's shop by an expert from the British Museum and subsequently returned to Cwmyoy.

The tiny population takes great care of its wonderful, eccentric church, and feels very affectionate towards it, even though the responsibility of looking after such a special building is enormous.

Grosmont St Nicholas

Why visit: *Huge, late-Norman church*
Where: *On the B4347, north of Monmouth, NP7 8HP*

Grosmont sits within yards of the border with England, here formed by the River Monnow. The church is cruciform, with an unusual octagonal tower.

Inside, with its open timber roof, flagstone floor and round Norman piers, the nave could be taken for a castle hall. And there is a strong connection with the castle across the road, as the church was built partly for its garrison.

When it was restored in the 19th century by architect J.P. Seddon, the church was on the verge of collapse.

Seeing that the small congregation did not need regular use of the entire building, Seddon screened the crossing and chancel from the nave. Seddon's chancel is respectful of the origins of the church, but very much of its time.

Llanelieu St Ellyw FoFC

Why visit: *Setting; ancient, simple building with wonderful, battered screen*
Where: *East of Talgarth, off the A479, LD3 9DA; key at nearby house*

Lost in lanes east of Talgarth, Llanelieu's little church is the most simple of buildings, dating from the 13th century. Being so remote, the church escaped improvements until 1905, when work did some damage to ancient features. The bell turret dates from that time, but much remains just as it has done for centuries.

The highlight is the screen. Painted dark red and dotted with white roses, it rises up to the roof and is supported on wooden pillars. The partial outline of a cross stands out – the imprint of the crucifix that was ripped out at the Reformation. It dates from the 14th or 15th century; the earlier date would make it one of the oldest in Wales.

Llanthony St David's Church and Priory ruins

Why visit: *Ancient ruins; sublime setting*
Where: *Off the B4423, in the Vale of Ewyas, NP7 7NN*

Legend has it that St David himself stayed in this remote spot for a time while making his way through Wales. St David's

church dates from the early 12th century, but is almost certainly built on the site of an earlier church.

It is said that the ruins of St David's church attracted William de Lacy here. One of the Norman Marcher Lords, he renounced the world, and with a handful of like-minded men, established an abbey here in about 1100. After the Dissolution it fell to ruins, but parts have been restored and house a hotel and tea rooms.

Patrisio St Issui

Why visit: *Setting; rood screen*
Where: *Reached on lanes north of Abergavenny, west of the B4423, NP7 7LP*

Reached along tiny, winding flower-filled lanes (or by footpath), Patrisio's church sits on a south-facing slope looking over a tiny valley to the slopes of the Sugar Loaf mountain. A stone seat by the porch makes a perfect resting place.

Dating from the 11th century, the church's earliest part may be the tiny chapel at the west end, with its own doorway, altar and statue of St Issui. A wonderful 15th-century rood screen dominates the main part of the church. It is made of Irish oak, faded to a pale biscuit brown, and has superb foliage decoration with dragons at either end.

A wall painting of Time, shown as a skeleton, holds symbols of mortality: hourglass, scythe and shovel – when your time's up you'll be cut down and buried.

Skenfrith St Bridget

Why visit: *Tower; 15th-century cope*
Where: *On the B4521, off the B4347, north of Monmouth, NP7 8UH*

The most notable buildings in Skenfrith are its castle and its church, both dating from the 13th century. The exterior of the church is a delight, with a massively buttressed, squat square tower and built, like the nave and porch, of red sandstone.

The church has an unusual mixture of seating, dating from the 16th to the 20th centuries. Its greatest treasure is a late 15th-century cope (priest's cloak), found being used as a cover for the Communion table in the 19th century. It is now mounted behind glass.

AROUND RADNOR FOREST

The rounded hills of Radnor Forest dominate the landscape just west of the Wales/England border between Presteigne and Llandrindod Wells. This is a country of small towns, tiny hamlets and isolated farms. The grandest churches in this group are at Old Radnor and Presteigne, while most of the others are typical of Radnorshire: small, simple and often in wonderful settings.

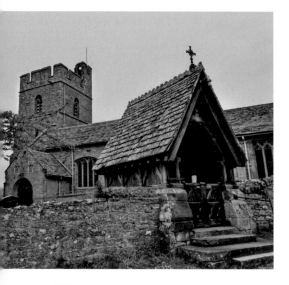

Old Radnor St Stephen

Why visit: *Britain's oldest organ case; boulder-like font*
Where: *South-west of Presteigne, LD8 2LD*

An important centre of the Welsh princedom of Powys before the Normans arrived, Old Radnor would have had a castle or administrative buildings. Across the lane from the church is a D-shaped raised earth platform with a ditch around it that some have suggested was where the castle stood.

There is a stone slab incised with a cross in the nave floor of the church, that is said to be the tombstone of Hugh Mortimer, rector of Old Radnor in the 13th century. The church was largely rebuilt in the late 15th or early 16th century. It is entered through the south porch, which has niches now occupied by handsome Victorian statues.

Just inside the door is a primitive-looking font – a circular block of stone with its top hollowed out to form a shallow bowl. It stands on four squat feet and may date back to the 8th century. The lovely wooden screen, stretching across the width of the church, is 15th-century, and is one of the best in Wales. Also of wood, and also lovely, is the organ case, a remarkable survivor from about 1500 and the earliest of its kind in Britain. The organ inside is Victorian, but was engineered so as not to damage or interfere with the remarkable case.

There are medieval floor tiles in several parts of the church, which also has its original roofs. In the north chapel there is a medieval vestments chest and 15th-century stained glass, including a figure of St Catherine.

Prominent in the churchyard is a huge block of rough-hewn stone that is the tombstone for the grave of Sir Herbert Lewis, 4th Baronet of Harpton Court. It may be a re-used prehistoric megalith. There are other memorials to members of the Lewis family in the church; the most interesting is to Thomas Lewis, who 'enjoyed a life full of years which on the 5th April 1777 he exchanged for the immortality of Heaven, aged 86 years and 5 months'.

To the north, the church looks over the open hills of Radnor Forest, so-called because it was a medieval hunting ground, an enclosed area that would have been the preserve of the monarch and important barons. Immediately to the south are large modern quarries, hidden by the lie of the land and by trees.

Bleddfa St Mary Magdalene

Why visit: *Pretty church; ruined tower*
Where: *Just off the A488, west of Knighton, LD7 1PA*

Bleddfa means 'the abode of wolves', and wolves were still to be found in Radnor Forest until Tudor times. The church dates from two main periods: the early 13th century and the latter part of the same century. However, the wooden bellcote dates from 1711, and the south porch is 15th-century. The interior is one large space, whitewashed and with its original wooden roof.

For many years a mysterious mound at the west end of the church was thought to be a prehistoric burial chamber, but when it was excavated in the 1960s it was discovered to be the base of a substantial stone tower to the church. Excavations showed that the tower had been burned down, and it is assumed this happened during the revolt of Welsh patriot Owain Glyndwr in the 15th century.

The church is the setting for the annual Bleddfa lectures, organised by the Bleddfa Trust, which seeks to unite creativity with spirituality through talks and activities.

Colva St David

Why visit: *Beautiful setting; ancient-feeling church*
Where: *On lanes south of Old Radnor; west of the B4594 at Gladestry; east of Builth Wells, HR5 3RA*

Colva's church stands more-or-less alone, peeping south through its bower of yew trees high up in the Radnorshire hills. The church is basically 13th-century, but with 15th-century additions, including the deep timbered porch with stone seats.

Inside, 18th-century memorials on the walls overlay traces of earlier wall paintings, and a skull-and-crossbones is a reminder of mortality. The font is 12th-century, probably from an earlier building that stood in this remote and beautiful place.

Cregrina St David

Why visit: *Norman font; quirky interior*
Where: *In the valley of the River Edw, east of Builth Wells, LD1 6YP*

Whitewashed, and with a minute bellcote, this is another delightful and remote Radnorshire church dedicated to St David. It is a building of the most simple kind on the outside. Inside everything is wonderfully askew: the chancel does not line up with the nave, the little medieval screen is tilted and the chancel timbers have warped with time. The font is Norman.

Disserth St Cewydd

Why visit: *Unrestored church with a wonderful roof and rows of box pews*
Where: *Off a lane west of the A483, south of Llandrindod Wells, LD1 6NL*

This is one of those extraordinarily atmospheric churches that escaped the Victorian improvers. Its interior is pretty much the same as it would have been at the beginning of the 19th century. The box pews, pulpit, altar rail and other fittings all date from the 17th and 18th centuries, while the wonderful wooden roof is 15th-century. There are even box pews either side of the altar. There are stone-flagged floors, wooden Georgian windows and traces of wall paintings.

The tower is from about 1400, while the whitewashed nave and chancel were built a century later. The church is tucked down a lane near to the River Ithon, sharing its setting with a caravan park.

Opposite page: Old Radnor (left); the entrance to St David's, Colva (right).
This page: The plain but delightful church at Cregrina.

Llananno St Anno

Why visit: *Outstanding rood screen*
Where: *Just off the A483, north of Llanbister, LD1 6TN*

This church was entirely rebuilt in 1877, and from the outside looks like hundreds of other chapel-churches built at that time. Although virtually everything else is Victorian, the little church contains one great treasure that must not be missed: the rood screen from the previous church on this site.

The screen dates from the 1490s and is a masterpiece by any standards. Ten lower panels have traceried wooden carving so delicate it is almost like lace. Each panel has a different pattern. Above them are decorated friezes that include foliage patterns and two wyverns, or dragons, with snakes for tails. Running the length of the top of the screen are 25 canopied niches, each one now filled with a Victorian figure, but the work has been done entirely in keeping with the spirit of the original.

The woodwork is full of intricate detail and the wood itself has faded to a silvery-brown – much more pleasing, to our eyes anyway – than the bright colours in which it would have originally been painted.

Llandegley
Pales Meeting House

Why visit: *Thatched meeting house with superb views*
Where: *On lanes north and west of Llandegley, which is on the A44, north-east of Llandrindod Wells, LD1 5UH*

This is the oldest Quaker Meeting House in Wales, and has been in continuous use since 1717. The present building dates from a little later than that, and is of brick and thatch. There are two rooms, one used primarily for meetings (every third Sunday) and the other used for other social events and so forth. It was a schoolroom in the 19th century. The views from the parking space just above the meeting house are truly memorable, with a panorama taking in valleys and hills stretching west, south and east.

Presteigne St Andrew

Why visit: *Fine town church*
Where: *Church Street, LD8 2AF*

Only just in Wales, Presteigne sits on the border, here formed by the River Lugg that flows a few yards to the north of the church. There may have been a church here as early as Saxon times, and there are traces of ancient stonework in the north aisle. That building was replaced by a Norman one, and again, clear signs of that structure can be seen, but most of the church as it stands today is 14th-century, with additions in the 15th century.

There were restorations and repairs in 1855, 1891 and 1927. The delicate screen dates from the 1891 renovation, and was designed by architect J.L. Pearson.

There are no pews in the church, and the nave is often cleared of its chairs to make space for concerts, performances and an annual art show that raises funds for the church.

Its greatest treasure is a large Flemish tapestry that hangs on the north wall. This dates from about 1510 and shows Christ's entry into Jerusalem. It has been in the church since 1737 and was restored in 1999.

ALSO IN THE AREA

Bryngwyn St Michael
Why visit: *Carved Celtic stone*

Cascob St Michael and All Angels
Why visit: *Setting; atmospheric both inside and out*

Glascwm St David
Why visit: *Larger-than-usual Radnorshire hill church*

Llanbister St Cynllo
Why visit: *Castle-like square tower*

Pilleth St Mary
Why visit: *Setting; holy well*

Rhulen St David
Why visit: *Tiny, remote church*

CHURCHYARDS

They have always been an important part of church life and today churchyards help to create the special atmosphere of peace and tranquillity that we associate with many churches. In cities they are among the most important green spaces. Country churchyards are often richer in wildlife than the fields around them, and a good number are managed to keep it that way. And, of course, many are rich in history, memorials and memories.

Early churchyards

Many churches are built on circular (or roughly circular) mounds, and usually these are said to have originally been places of spiritual significance before Christianity. The earliest Christian missionaries to Britain are thought to have chosen these places to show that the new religion was superseding the old, and also to provide a continuity between the old and the new. In places such as Rudston, Yorkshire, this seems self-evident, since the circular churchyard contains not just one but two prehistoric monoliths, one of them the tallest in England. At Avebury, Wiltshire, the church is built just outside the prehistoric

This page: The prehistoric monolith at Rudston, Yorkshire (above); a 'tea-caddy' tomb at Painswick (right).

arrangement of stones. More subtly, St Mary's, Old Basing, Hampshire, clearly seems to be built on a large mound, from which issues a spring called the Clear Well. Was this a pagan sacred spring?

In Wales the 'llan' prefix in so many place names indicates a roughly circular enclosure of land that may originally have been a pre-Christian tribal sacred space. These then came to be Christian enclosures and then churchyards.

Churchyard crosses

Early churchyards contained only one monument and that was the churchyard cross, which was the memorial to everyone buried there. The earliest are Saxon and fragments of these can still be found.

Ampney Crucis, Gloucestershire, has one of the few remaining intact crosses, with carvings of the Crucifixion and the Virgin and Child. Parts of ancient crosses can still be found in hundreds of churchyards. Some are complete apart from the top, such as at Alford, Somerset, where the cross of Ham stone is 13th-century.

Graves, tombs and burials

Until the 12th and 13th centuries the majority of people were buried in shrouds, not coffins, and the graves were not marked in any way. Those responsible for burying people began on one side of the churchyard and worked their way across until they reached the other side, at which point they returned to where the burials had started and began all over again, so that people were often buried on top of one another.

Stone coffins gradually came to be used for the more notable members of the community, and these developed slowly from simple hollowed-out stone containers to more elaborate carved ones. Eventually, some of these were marked by headstones, but this idea faltered in the 14th century.

Headstones did not become common in churches until after the Reformation, when more and more people were able to buy

Yew trees

Numerous legends, myths and theories surround the presence of yew trees in British churchyards. A convincing reason for them is that they represented both life, being evergreen, and death, being deadly poisonous. Many churchyard yews are said to be more than 1,000 years old, therefore older than the churches they shade. Some are said to be up to 4,000 years old, which may be unlikely. Venerable, ancient yews can be seen at Much Marcle, Herefordshire, hollow with seating inside, and Crowhurst, Surrey, complete with a 19th-century door to its hollow interior. Painswick, Gloucestershire, has 99 clipped yews, while Mere (*below*) in Wiltshire has 12 to represent the 12 Apostles.

a specific plot in the churchyard in which to be buried. The first headstones were of local stone where this was available, and in areas such as the Cotswolds, where the stone is beautiful, the churchyards were enhanced by their presence. The most graceful headstones are usually 18th- or early 19th-century, and some of these show beautiful use of calligraphy.

As stone, marble, slate and other materials became increasingly available and affordable, so the variety and style of memorials of all kinds grew throughout the 19th century. In some churchyards, such as that of St Mary's Church, Wolborough, Devon, the result is a visual history lesson of the whole period, with memorials to sailors, tradesmen, clerics and children often telling dramatic or tragic stories.

The simplest memorials are often the most moving, as the many thousands of plain grave stones that mark the resting places of those who died in the two World Wars attest. In the churchyard at Portchester, Hampshire, there is one to a volunteer in the Home Guard in World War II, which, along with his name and dates, says simply 'Well Done'.

Table tombs

The earliest table tombs, or chest tombs, date from the 14th century. They take their inspiration from the tombs with effigies that were placed within churches, but no churchyard tomb had an effigy. The early ones were simple boxes, but by the 18th century they had become elegant and very dominant in churchyards, especially in the Cotswolds. Here, a refinement were roll-top or bale tombs; Burford, Oxfordshire, is a good place to see excellent examples, as is Painswick, Gloucestershire, which also has 'tea-caddy' tombs, tall and looking very like large versions of their namesake.

This page: The ancient cross at Ampney Crucis, Gloucestershire.

OLD MONTGOMERYSHIRE

This group of churches is hugely varied: from the handsome town church in Welshpool to the little timber-framed church at Trelystan, and from the ancient pilgrim church at Pennant Melangell, to the 18th-century red-brick church at Llanfyllin. Several of the churches here are genuinely remote, so are a pleasure to track down.

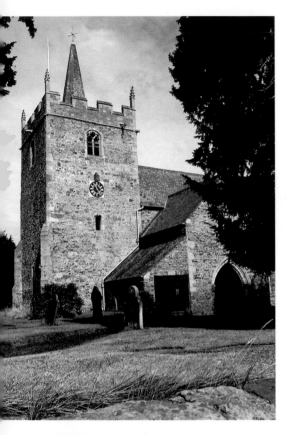

Guilsfield St Aelhaiarn

Why visit: *Medieval church with Victorian furnishings*
Where: *Church Lane, SY21 9NF*

St Aelhaiarn (also spelled Aelhaearn) was a 6th-century saint. As with many of the early Welsh saints, he was a member of the aristocracy – the son of one of the Welsh princes.

The earliest parts of the church here today date from the 14th century, including the core of the tower. The handsome south porch is 15th-century.

When the 16th-century clerestory was inserted the ceilings were renewed and raised. These are among the finest features of the church, with snowflake-like painted wooden bosses between the ribs.

The church was thoroughly restored by architect G.E. Street in 1879. Many of the furnishings that give the church its character today were designed by Street: the screens, pulpit, reredos and more besides. A model in the church shows what the church looked like before Street's work began.

Dolobran Friends' Meeting House

Why visit: *Isolated and remote 18th-century Quaker meeting house*
Where: *East of Pontrobert, north of the River Vyrnwy; walk north along track and footpath from Forge Farm at Dolobran-isaf, nearest postcode is TA4 4EB. A large-scale map is required to find this meeting house: the OS grid reference is SJ124124. Leave cars at Dolobran-isaf and walk*

Hidden among trees, and reached by track and footpath, this tiny Friends' meeting house is the most inaccessible place of worship in this book. It was built in about 1700, and consists of a brick-built cottage and meeting house under one roof.

Its story is entwined with that of the Lloyd family of nearby Dolobran Hall, who became Quakers in the 17th century. The meeting house eventually fell into disuse in the 19th century, at which time its furniture and fittings were dispersed. It was rediscovered in the 1950s and since then has been restored, with help from the Lloyd family. The interior is simple and friendly, with benches and a central table. There are meetings every Sunday.

Llanfyllin St Myllin

Why visit: *Unusual 18th-century red-brick church*
Where: *High Street, SY22 5BW*

Two rectors with very different views completely transformed this building. The first, John Edwards, disliked the old medieval church so much that he had it demolished in 1706 and replaced with a red-brick building, with an interior that was the height of fashion: an open space emphasising the pulpit instead of the altar.

More than a century later another rector, Robert Williams, disliked the 18th-century church as much as his predecessor had disliked the medieval one. He had three arches inserted to create a chancel, removed a lot of the pews to emphasise the altar, replaced the clear glass windows with stained glass, and introduced furnishings and fittings to make the interior look and feel richer.

Subsequently, under further rectors, changes were made to return the church to its former simplicity. The result is a very unusual building that has elements of both 'high' and 'low' ways of worship.

St Myllin, or Molling, after whom the church is named, was a 7th-century Irish monk who may have become Bishop of Ferns in County Wexford.

Llansantffraid-ym Mechain St Ffraid

Why visit: *Fascinating church with a many-layered history*
Where: *Church Lane, SY22 6AP*

On a hillock on the north side of the village, St Ffraid's is a lovely old building, its walls made up of stones of several different kinds, sizes and colours. The core of the church is probably 12th-century, extended and enlarged in the 14th and 15th centuries. There was considerable further work done in the 17th century, when the porch and spire were built. Yet more changes were made in the 18th and 19th centuries.

Throughout all these changes, very little was actually discarded, but was either re-used, modified or moved. The 14th-century east window was moved to the west end of the church to make way for a more 'appropriate' east window, and when the box pews were broken up in the 19th century their sides and doors were re-used as dados for the walls.

This page: St Aelhaiarn, Guilsfield.
Opposite page: Shrine of St Melangell.

A lot of the character of the church comes from the 17th-century work: the dormer window above the porch dates from then. Inside, the pulpit and choir stalls are also 17th-century.

In the early 18th century a transept was added that is entirely Georgian in style and look, providing yet another layer of interest. Even here materials were re-used from elsewhere in the church, including timber from the old rood loft. The late Victorian restoration added an arcade between the nave and the transept, and a new screen was put between the nave and chancel. The church is a visual testimony to centuries of change and adaptation.

St Ffraid was a 6th-century Irish saint, also known as St Bride and/or St Bridget.

Meifod
St Tysilio and St Mary

Why visit: *Historic church with early Celtic roots*
Where: *Centre of Meifod, SY22 6DD*

With its joint dedication and huge churchyard, this church is clearly out of the ordinary. And so it is, with a history stretching back as far as 550, when a chapel was founded here by St Gwyddfarch. This was the site of an important Celtic monastery, and at one time had three churches: one dedicated to St Gwyddfarch, one to St Tysilio and one to St Mary. Parts of St Mary's were still visible in the 18th century. The princes of Powys were buried here, and a carved stone in the church is said by some to be a memorial to one of them. As well as two crosses, the stone has complex patterning and carved knotwork on it, said to show Viking influence, and dating the stone to perhaps as early as the 9th century.

The church here today was founded by Madog Mareddud – one of the Powys princes – in the late 12th century. Parts of that building can still be seen at the west end. Rebuilding and alterations took place in the 14th and 15th centuries, which is when the tower was built. A 19th-century restoration brought many changes, including raising the original roofs. Woodwork includes a 17th-century pulpit and 19th-century pews that incorporated 17th-century elements.

Pennant Melangell
St Melangell

Why visit: *Shrine of St Melangell*
Where: *Off the B4391, on lanes west of Llangynog, SY10 0HQ*

This church is in the Berwyn Mountains, north of Llyn Vyrnwy, in a circular churchyard. It is a remote spot even now, and must have seemed as far from civilisation as it was possible to get in the 7th century when Irish hermit Melangell came here. She was discovered by chance by a Welsh prince when the hare he was hunting took refuge in her cloak. He was impressed by her courage and piety, and gave her the valley as a place of refuge.

The church as it stands today is from the 12th century onwards. The distinctive tower with its little wooden bell turret was built in the 17th century, as was much of the west end of the church. There have been several re-arrangements of the interior over the centuries, many to do with the placing of the church's great treasure – the 12th-century shrine of St Melangell.

The shrine had been dismantled and the pieces placed in various parts of the church, but it was reconstructed (using original pieces and modern replacements for missing parts) by archaeologist R.B. Heaton in the 1950s. It is a remarkable object: the sarcophagus is raised high above floor level on columns; above the sarcophagus is a steeply pitched stone roof with strange and unusual projecting crockets. The result is a blend of Saxon, Romanesque and Viking styles.

By the 1980s the church was in a very poor state of repair, and was rescued and restored by the Reverend Paul Davies and his wife, Evelyn. Work has continued on the church since, including rebuilding the apse in 1990.

Next to the church is the St Melangell Centre, which offers counselling and support, echoing the values the saint brought here more than 1,200 years ago.

Trelystan All Saints

Why visit: *Remote setting; timber-built church*
Where: *South-east of Welshpool, off the B4388, on Long Mountain, SY21 8LD*

This church is on the edge of woodland off a lane on the eastern slopes of Long Mountain, looking across the border to the Long Mynd, south of Shrewsbury.

Uniquely for this area it is timber-framed, though the panels were encased in white-painted brick in 1856. The timbered parts date back to the early 15th century, best seen in the roof, although this has been altered by the addition of metal strengthening rods. When the outside was sheathed in brick, the inside was covered with pitch pine, lending it a 'scout hut' atmosphere. The east window has a wooden frame with vivid stained glass. Part of an old oak screen with filigree tracery is still in place.

Welshpool St Mary

Why visit: *Handsome town church*
Where: *Centre of Welshpool, SY21 7DP*

Set on a walled and buttressed rise above the town, this is the largest church in old Montgomeryshire. The lower part of the massive square tower dates from around 1250. The chancel and two-storey south porch were built in the 1350s, while the nave as it appears today is 16th-century.

More rebuilding was done in the late 1700s; then in the 19th century the church was restored twice, the last time by architect G.E. Street. There are many memorials to the Herbert family, of nearby Powis Castle. There is also a modern memorial to Bishop William Morgan, translator of the Bible into Welsh, who was vicar here from 1575-9.

THE LLEYN PENINSULA

At the tip of the Lleyn Peninsula is Bardsey Island, a hugely important and popular place of pilgrimage in medieval Britain. All along the peninsula are churches that served as stopping places for pilgrims, and several of the churches were specially enlarged to cope with the numbers. Often, these churches had themselves been founded by early monks, who became saints, and whose churches often became places of pilgrimage in their own right. Today, the coast here is a popular holiday destination. Away from the sea the Lleyn has a landscape of hills and mountains, dominated by Yr Eifl and its amazing prehistoric town of Tre'r Ceiri. The churches on the peninsula range from the easy-to-find, in little towns and villages, to the downright hard-to-find, whether on mountains or coast.

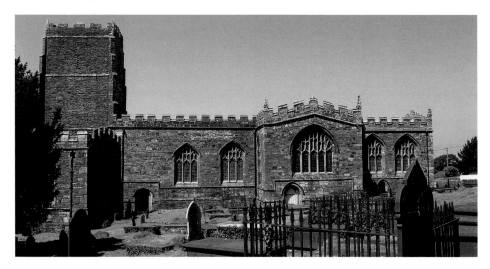

Clynnog Fawr St Beuno

Why visit: *A Christian site since the 6th century*
Where: *Just off the A499, LL54 5HN*

Descended from the royal princes of Powys, St Beuno was the most celebrated of the early Christian monks of North Wales. He founded the 'clas' at Clynnog Fawr in 616 and died here in about 640. A clas was an institution peculiar to the Celtic church, being a mixture of monastery and college – a place of prayer, teaching, ministry and mission.

Clynnog Fawr rapidly became an important ecclesiastical site, and was also a stopping place for those on pilgrimage to Bardsey Island. Sometimes known as the 'Island of 20,000 Saints', Bardsey was a hugely popular destination for pilgrims in medieval times, with three pilgrimages there being the equivalent of one to Rome.

Clynnog Fawr itself became a place of pilgrimage: the holy well near the church was said to have curative properties, and people spending the night on St Beuno's tomb were said to be healed.

The original church that stood here has long gone, though St Beuno's chapel, reached along a passageway from the church, is said to stand on the site of the old church and the saint's tomb. This little building has been used as a store and a lock-up in the past, and was rescued from ruin in 1913.

The church itself is a handsome building dating from the 15th and 16th centuries. Among the objects of interest inside is a set of dog-handling tongs. These are telescopic, with several sharp spikes at the business end. These were used in the days when dogs were permitted in churches and fights and other misdemeanours were common during services.

St Beuno's Chest is an ancient box, carved out of a single piece of ash wood. This was used to collect offerings from Bardsey pilgrims, and was also where sinners could 'pay' for their sins by putting in a financial contribution.

There is an intriguing 10th-century sundial in the churchyard, a relic from a time when clocks were unknown, but when the monastic pattern of the day needed to be adhered to.

Aberdaron St Hywyn

Why visit: *Historic pilgrim church*
Where: *In Aberdaron, LL53 8BE*

Aberdaron was the principal start point for pilgrims going to Bardsey Island, so was very busy in medieval times. The church had originally been founded by St Hywyn in the 5th or 6th century, but the present building dates from Norman times and later.

Only the doorway remains from the Norman church. It is very worn – not surprising since the sea is only yards away. The church was enlarged in the 14th century, and again in the 16th, when a second nave was added to make more room for the pilgrims.

Inside, the church is spacious and full of light that is reflected off the sea. The fine old timber roofs are from the 16th-century building work. Attached to the north wall are two large, smoothed stones, each inscribed in Latin. They are early 6th-century memorials to priests, found a few miles north of Aberdaron. Their age means they probably predate the monastery on Bardsey Island.

Llanengan St Engan

Why visit: *Excellent screens*
Where: *In the centre of Llanengan, LL53 7LL; the church may be locked, contact the churchwardens or vicar*

The church standing here today dates mostly from the 15th and 16th centuries – indeed the tower is dated to 1534 by an inscription on the wall. The first church on this site was built in the 6th century by Einion (or Engan), who is said to be

This page: Exterior of St Beuno's.

buried here. St Einion's Well nearby was traditionally sought out for its healing properties. This is another of the Lleyn Peninsula's churches that was enlarged in order to cater for the huge numbers of pilgrims who made their way to Bardsey Island.

St Engan's is most famous for its two 16th-century screens, said to be among the best of their kind in Wales. Also in the church is an ancient wooden chest, used to collect donations from the pilgrims.

Llangwnnadl St Gwynhoedl

Why visit: *Light and airy church*
Where: *On a lane to Morfa, off the B4417, LL53 8NN*

The sea is less than a mile away, but this handsome church is tucked away from storms in a sheltered, woody setting. There has been a church here since the 6th century, founded by St Gwynhoedl. Like St Beuno of Clynnog Fawr, he was a senior cleric in the early Welsh church. A stone set in the wall may be his gravestone.

As with so many churches on the pilgrim route to Bardsey, St Gwynhoedl's is far larger than any resident population could have needed. It was almost entirely rebuilt in the early 16th century as a large, virtually square space divided by two arcades. It was restored in the 1850s, at which time its rood screen was removed.

Penllech St Mary FoFC

Why visit: *Simple, atmospheric church*
Where: *On a lane off the B4417, north of Llangwnnadl, LL53 8DE*

Tiny and simple, the church at Penllech sits in open fields with a panoramic view over Caernarfon Bay. It was vested in the Friends of Friendless Churches in 2009, and they have brought it back into good repair with a light touch.

It was built in 1840, but its furnishings feel Georgian rather than Victorian. Everything is plain – pews, box pews, altar – except for the underside of the tester, or sounding board, above the pulpit. This has an embossed star on it with wavy rays; it is the only elaborate decoration in the building.

Pistyll St Beuno

Why visit: *Atmospheric and cared-for chapel-church; superb sea views*
Where: *Off the B4417 at Pistyll, LL53 6LR. Take a no-through-road lane heading towards the sea, opposite a large lay-by; the church is reached down a lane at the end of which is a caravan park*

St Beuno founded the church here, and he may have chosen this isolated spot as a place of quiet and retreat away from the comparative bustle of Clynnog Fawr. The building here now dates from the 12th century and was enlarged in the 15th. Externally it is extremely simple, with only a tiny bellcote breaking the outline of the slate roof. It is almost as simple inside - a single space with pews and an altar, lit by small windows. The walls are of stone and the roof is built of sturdy timbers - in fact the building has an almost barn-like feel, accentuated by the rushes and herbs that are strewn on the floor. These are renewed three times a year and make the little church feel different yet cared for.

The church has been a place of healing since St Beuno's time, a fact that the present congregation celebrates with the use of herbs inside, and by encouraging wild herbs and medicinal plants in the churchyard. In medieval times lepers came here, praying for healing, along with pilgrims making their way to Bardsey Island.

The actor Rupert Davies, who played Maigret in a long-running and loved TV series in the 1960s, is buried in the churchyard. His gravestone is engraved with the familiar theatrical symbol of two masks – one smiling and one sad.

Ynyscynhaearn
St Cynhaearn FoFC

Why visit: *Remote Georgian church*
Where: *Reached by track and footpath from Pentrefelin (on the A497 east of Criccieth), LL52 0DP; keyholder nearby, before visiting contact the FoFC; you will need a large-scale map to find this church*

There may have been a church on this site in the 7th century, founded by St Cynhaearn, but the building today is

from 1832. The rendered exterior is rather forbidding, as is the open landscape on a cold and windy day. But the interior is an immaculate and perfectly preserved Georgian church, complete with plastered ceiling and walls, a three-decker pulpit, pews, and a west gallery housing a tiny organ dating from 1834.

Reminders of an earlier church that stood here are a 17th-century carved chair and two 18th-century chests. The Commandment boards were painted by itinerant artist John Roberts when the present church was built.

There are two graves of special interest in the churchyard. One is to an ex-slave called Jack Black, brought to this area from the West Indies when he was eight. He became gardener to a nearby large house, and was given a cottage here along with a field and a cow. He died in 1791. A grave carved with a harp is that of 18th-century harpist David Owen, whose most well-known piece is Dafydd y Garreg Wen (David of the White Rock).

This page: Preserved Georgian church of St Cynhaearn.

ALSO IN THE AREA

Carnguwch St Cuwch
Why visit: *Tiny, remote mountainside chapel cared for by the Friends of Carnguwch Church; can only be reached on foot*

Nanhoron Capel Newydd
Why visit: *The earliest surviving Nonconformist chapel in North Wales, built in 1769, and still with its original furnishings and fittings*

ANGLESEY, YNYS MÔN

A large island, Anglesey has a distinctive character, which is due to the reflected sea light, the closeness of the mountains of Snowdonia, and the fact that there are often panoramic views to be had in the centre of the island. There are wonderful churches here, some of them in remote spots and needing a large-scale map to help track them down, such as that at Llantrisant. Four of the churches in this group are in the care of the Friends of Friendless Churches.

Penmon St Seiriol

Why visit: *Early Christian foundation; excellent stonework*
Where: *South-east Anglesey, LL58 8NE*

Located at the far south-east point of Anglesey, at the end of the public road, and with the sea only yards away Penmon has wonderful views southwards into Snowdonia. It would have been an utterly peaceful, very remote place when St Seiriol came here in the 6th century. Even this was not quite remote or quiet enough for him, and he is said to have had a cell on Puffin Island, just offshore. Danish raiders destroyed Seiriol's original building, and a new church was begun in the 12th century. That building remains at the core of the church, although the chancel was rebuilt by the Victorians.

There is excellent Norman stonework in the church, best seen in the tower arch with its chevron and chequerboard patterns. In the south transept more chevron patterns decorate the arches of a blind arcade. Here, a stone Celtic cross takes centre stage. It has interweaving, complex patterns on its shaft, and a cross within its round head. Other fragments of carving are set in the transept walls. The font, also with complex interweaving patterns, was hollowed out from the base of another cross.

The church does not stand alone. There are also the remains of some of the priory buildings, including the well-preserved refectory. Part of the priory is now a private house. Across the lane is a superb dovecote from about 1600 – later than the priory buildings.

Perhaps the most evocative part of the priory grounds is by the holy well. Here are the remains of a 6th-century cell. Could this be a building that St Seiriol knew and used?

Beaumaris St Mary and St Nicholas

Why visit: *Coffin of Princess Joan; carved misericords*
Where: *Church Street, LL58 8BN*

This is a large and handsome town church built in the early 14th century, with additions in the 15th century. The church was mainly for English people 'planted' here to establish English 'supremacy' over the Welsh, and protected by the town walls and Beaumaris Castle.

Many of the objects of interest in the church came from nearby Llanfaes Priory. The most notable of these is the stone sarcophagus of Princess Joan, wife of Llewellyn the Great and daughter of King John. It was used as a horse trough at the Dissolution of the Monasteries. Also from Llanfaes are the carved misericords, many depicting women. There is a very fine alabaster effigy to William Bulkeley and his wife dating from the late 15th century.

Llanbeulan St Peulan FoFC

Why visit: *Ancient church; stone font*
Where: *Reached on foot via a causeway off a lane between Dothan and the A55, LL63 5UR*

This is a modest building at the end of a raised causeway, reached on foot from the road. It is dedicated to St Peulan, a 6th-century monk whose foundation this was. His brother and sister were also clerics. The causeway itself is of interest, as it was made so that the congregation could reach the church without getting their feet wet – the surrounding land is prone to flooding. There is an evocative photograph from 1944 showing a bride being wheeled along the causeway in a bathchair after heavy rainfall.

The church is medieval, with nave, chancel, and a disproportionately large south transept. Some of the furnishings date from the 17th and 18th centuries, while the open timber roofs were renewed in the 19th century.

It is most well known for its stone font, which is rectangular and looks rather like a drinking trough. It has a Maltese cross in a circle carved on one end, and deeply incised patterns and decorations on two other surfaces. It used to be thought that it was Norman, but experts now think that it was originally a pre-Norman altar, hollowed out to become a font. This would make it unique in Britain.

Llaneilian St Eilian

Why visit: *Superb screen with painted figure of Death*
Where: *East of Amlwch Port, LL68 9LS*

The tower at Llaneilian seems to belong to another church, or even to another country: it is square, whitewashed and has a pyramidal cap, giving it a central European look. The rest of the church is stone, but with an unusual shape as it has a separate chapel set at an angle to the rest of the building and connected to it by an eccentric 17th-century passageway. This chapel, built in the 14th century, might very well be on the site of the original church that was built here in the 6th century by St Eilian.

The tower is 12th-century, with much of the rest of the church dating from the 15th and 16th centuries. Inside, the most outstanding feature is the lovely old wooden rood screen, still with its loft. Twisted and mellowed with age, it stretches across the width of the church, obscuring the chancel arch. It has fine and delicate carving, but standing out from the centre is a graphic painting of Death. Above, in Welsh, is an inscription that says, 'The sting of death is sin'.

There are other interesting features in the church, including 17th-century benches, an oak chest from 1667, and an 18th-century chandelier. In St Eilian's Chapel there is a rare medieval portable wooden altar. The pillar of a medieval preaching cross stands by the south porch.

Llanfigael St Figael FoFC

Why visit: *Unspoiled early 19th-century church*
Where: *East of the A5025 at Llanfachraeth, LL65 4DW*

Set on a leafy lane in unspoiled countryside in north-west Anglesey, this minute chapel-church is completely plain and simple on the outside. Inside it is almost completely unchanged since the first half of the 19th century. The ways of worship and social strata of those times is

laid out here: the centre of attention is the pulpit (rather than the modest altar table); the farm labourers had very simple, backless, benches with paddle ends; the farmers had box pews; and the squire had a separate box pew, next to the pulpit. The poorest people, described at the time as 'paupers', had to stand at the back.

The church has three fonts, two made of stone, and an unusual portable font made of wood. It is probably from the early 19th century. Like the rest of the church it is illuminated with candles.

St Figael's was rescued from closure and neglect by the Reverend Edgar Jones, who kept it weatherproof until the Friends of Friendless Churches were able to undertake its care in 2007.

Llangadwaladr
St Cadwaladr

Why visit: *King Cadfan's memorial stone; 15th-century stained glass*
Where: *Off the A4080, south of Llyn Coron, LL62 5HS*

The exterior of this church is made more decorative than many in North Wales by the lovely 17th-century window of the south chapel, called the Bodowen Chapel. The rest of the exterior is much more modest, with a low roof line broken only at the west end by a simple bell frame. It dates from the 13th and 14th centuries.

The church is renowned as the burial place of kings of Gwynedd, including King Cadfan, whose 7th-century memorial stone is set in the wall of the nave. It says that Cadfan 'was the wisest and most renowned of kings'. The stone was placed in the church by Cadfan's grandson, Cadwaladr (himself a king) and who may also be buried here. The origins of the church are even earlier than that, going back to the 5th century, when it was called Eglwys Ael, meaning the 'wattle church'.

In the chancel's east window is splendid, and rare, 15th-century stained glass showing the Crucifixion, and King Cadwaladr, wearing his crown.

On the exterior of the church are a number of strange stone creatures. One is a pop-eyed demon with long talons for feet and hands.

Llantrisant St Afran,
St Ieuan and St Sannen FoFC

Why visit: *Setting in remote countryside; 18th-century fittings*
Where: *West of Llantrisant hamlet, south of the lane going to Llanddeusant on a footpath beyond Ty-mawr, LL65 4HT; you will need a large-scale map to find this church*

Reached by footpath, this little church nestles on a hump of rock behind a high stone wall. It dates from the 14th century, with a south chapel that was added in the 17th century. Many of the simple wooden fittings are 18th-century, including benches, box pews and altar rails. They contrast with the rather grand 17th-century memorials to John Wynn and Hugo Williams.

Tal-y-Llyn St Mary FoFC

Why visit: *Panoramic countryside views*
Where: *Beside a lane south of Tal-y-Llyn hamlet, opposite Llyn Padrig, LL63 5TQ*

There are views through 360 degrees from this tiny church, which stands on a mound inside a circular churchyard. The building is medieval, with 16th- and 17th-century additions.

The inside is simple, with a low arch separating nave and chancel, and with huge beams in the nave roof. The altar rails are dated 1764. All but one of the original paddle-ended benches were stolen before the church was taken into the care of the Friends of Friendless Churches in 1999. They have been replaced with replicas made by a local craftsman who used the sole remaining bench as his model.

This page: The simple interior of Llanfigael (left); Tal-y-Llyn stands alone (above).
Opposite page: *St Seiriol, Penmon.*

CENTRAL ENGLAND

Stretching from the Welsh border across to the edges of East Anglia, and from counties close to London to beyond the River Trent, this is a very large area, with an enormous range of churches of many types and styles.

Opposite page: Stratford-upon-Avon's beautiful and ancient Holy Trinity church, which is also the resting place of Shakespeare.

The centre of England is a hugely diverse region, and as elsewhere in the country, there is a great range of church building styles and materials. The underlying geological structure of the area plays a very important role in what the churches were built of and look like.

Areas with good building stone, such as Gloucestershire, with its golden, easily worked limestone obviously benefit, as its glorious churches show. But Gloucestershire was also a fabulously rich county in medieval times, so its churches had the double riches of a superb building stone and the wealth to build in the grandest styles of the time.

Farther north and west, in counties such as Herefordshire and Cheshire, good building stone was not always so readily available,
but timber was, so some of the churches in those counties make use of wood, sometimes in spectacular ways.

Setting and landscape, also underpinned by geology, have a huge impact on the character of churches. Buckinghamshire and Hertfordshire, so often thought of as more-or-less on the doorstep of London, can feel very rural and remote, and their churches are often all the more enjoyable for being tucked away or overlooked.

Regional styles also make a big difference. Northamptonshire has its own design of spire, often copied in other areas but really special in its home county, while Worcestershire has a clutch of once very grand abbeys and priories that lend grace to areas that were once very wild and thickly forested.

THE SOUTHERN COTSWOLDS

A fortunate combination of Cotswold stone and wealthy wool merchants gave Gloucestershire a large number of truly splendid medieval churches, full of light and with exquisite structural and decorative carving that has not been equalled since. As a contrast to the grand town churches, this group also includes examples of the many small unspoilt churches found in the delightful Cotswold villages.

Cirencester
St John the Baptist

Why visit: *One of Britain's finest parish churches: huge, and lavishly built and decorated, both inside and out, mainly in the Perpendicular style*
Where: *Gosditch Street, GL7 2PE*

Dubbed the Cathedral of the Cotswolds, Cirencester's brilliant 'wool' church is the largest and, many would say, the finest of them all. The richly ornamented three-storey south porch and imposing tower certainly preside over the Market Place with all the grandeur of a cathedral, and the interior is just as astonishing.

Roman Cirencester (Corinium) had become the second most important town in Britain, and by late Saxon times there was already a very large church here. By the early 12th century Cirencester had an Augustinian abbey, and it was at about that time that the first church on the site of St John's was built.

Parts of it survive in the present church, most of which dates from successive renovations and additions throughout medieval times. So, for example, the Lady Chapel dates originally from 1235–50, the tower from around 1400, various chantry chapels from the mid-15th century, and the porch from about 1490. The nave was rebuilt between 1515 and 1530, acquiring the soaring, slender pillars and huge Perpendicular clerestory windows that are such key elements of the church's light-filled, elegant interior. It seems hard to believe that, little more than 100 years later, this glorious building was a temporary prison for more than 1,000 citizens of Cirencester, who were locked up here overnight by the Royalists after a Civil War battle in 1642.

Of the many interior features worth seeking out, don't miss the exquisite fan vaulting, or the wineglass pulpit – a stone masterpiece of about 1440, with delicate openwork tracery and decorative paintwork in burgundy and gold.

Bibury St Mary

Why visit: *Church of Saxon origin*
Where: *Church Road, GL7 5NR*

For a combination of ancient church and classic Cotswold village, Bibury is hard to beat. St Mary's has a Saxon core, evident still in the lower parts of the chancel arch and in the Saxon cross shaft set into the chancel wall. The original church was extended and embellished throughout the Middle Ages: there is a Norman north

doorway, a 13th-century south aisle with lancet windows, and a large Perpendicular window to the right of the porch.

The churchyard has a fine assortment of tombs and gravestones, a number of them commemorating the local clothiers and weavers who piously and generously financed the development of their village church over several centuries.

Duntisbourne Rouse
St Michael

Why visit: *Small Saxon and Norman church in a peaceful rural setting*
Where: *Off to the east of the small lane through the hamlet of Duntisbourne Rouse, which lies west of the A417 about 4 miles north-west of Cirencester, GL7 7AP*

This enchanting little church, stepped down the slope of a Cotswold hillside, is just as ancient as it looks and feels. The saddleback tower that helps lend the building its timeless air was a later addition to the rest of the church and dates from 1587. The nave is the place to look for the origins of the church. Here there are two Saxon doorways and other distinctive Saxon workmanship: herringbone masonry and quoins with long-and-short stonework. All but one of the windows are small and narrow, adding to the age-old feel of the building, and there are traces of early wall paintings. The tiny crypt chapel below the Norman chancel has a small, unglazed round-headed east window to let in the morning sun. A medieval cross in the churchyard completes the idyllic scene.

This page: St John's wine-glass pulpit *(left); exterior of St Mary, Bibury (above).*

Elkstone
St John the Evangelist

Why visit: *A mainly 12th-century church with much unspoilt Norman detailing*
Where: *On the east side of the lane through Elkstone village, east of the A417 about halfway between Cirencester and Gloucester, GL53 9PD*

The sturdy 14th-century Perpendicular west tower of St John's marks the highest church in the Cotswolds. This marvellous Norman church originally had a central tower, which perhaps did not survive the wild weather of these windswept Cotswold heights. Unfortunately it collapsed, or may have been dismantled, during the 13th century.

The rest of the Norman church remains, complete with an array of splendid carving ranging from the zigzag work of the broad chancel arch and the east window to a whole gallery of figures, from dragons and centaurs to angels and musicians, both inside and outside the building. Above the chancel is a rare columbarium or dovecote, reached by a spiral staircase.

Fairford
St John the Evangelist

Why visit: *Internationally famous for the most complete set of medieval stained glass in any parish church in Britain*
Where: *At the north end of the High Street, GL7 5AG*

Fairford's magnificent 'wool' church, rebuilt in the 1490s and hardly altered since then, deserves a place in any rollcall of fine Cotswold churches. However, the fame of the building is often eclipsed by that of its virtually complete set of late medieval glass, made between 1500 and 1517. The 28 windows tell many stories from the Old and New Testaments, culminating in the great west window that depicts Christ in Glory. Episodes from the early history of the Christian Church and its saints are also here.

The glass miraculously survived the scourge of the Reformation, only for the west windows to be badly damaged in a storm in 1703. It was removed from the church and put into safe storage during World War II. The glass has since been restored, repaired, partially renewed and cleaned through the centuries, but its survival as a set makes it unique.

There is much more to see inside the church, including a famous set of misericords, with such subjects as a woman beating her husband and a drunkard. Outside the church, don't miss the fascinating series of carved figures just below the roof parapet. The churchyard contains fine Cotswold tombs and monuments, some dating back to the 17th century. A favourite with visitors is more recent: a 1980 memorial with a stone sculpture of Tiddles, Fairford's much-loved church cat.

North Cerney All Saints

Why visit: *Unusual church with fine craftsmanship of several periods; lovely interior*
Where: *Dark Lane, a lane running west from the A435, GL7 7BX*

This unusual and lovely church gets its character from an eclectic mix of work from the 12th, 15th and 20th centuries. Transepts and a new roof were added to the original Norman church in the 1470s, creating a cruciform shape that makes an oddly charming composition with the saddleback tower at the west end.

The interior, full of colour and beautiful craftsmanship, owes much to a 20th-century benefactor. William Iveson Croome, a knowledgeable local churchman and historian who lived in North Cerney, worked with the architect F.C. Eden to restore and refurnish the church. Their thoughtfully executed work includes the rood loft, the gilded reredos, the contemporary glass and the purchase of period furnishings. The figures of saints in the side panels of the reredos are a reference to the church's dedication.

Northleach
St Peter and St Paul

Why visit: *Richly endowed 'wool' church with many fine 15th-century features*
Where: *Mill End, just west of the town centre, GL54 3HG*

The church at Northleach is a monument to the 15th-century glory days of this sleepy little town, when Northleach wool was the finest and the town's merchants the wealthiest. One of them, called John Fortey (commemorated in one of the fine collection of brasses here), took the church into another league by raising the nave roof and adding a lofty clerestory that fills the church with light. It includes an immense Perpendicular window above the chancel arch – a fine example of a feature that is special to Cotswold 'wool' churches. Other merchants of the time provided funds to enrich their church in other ways. The Lady Chapel and the elegant stone pulpit all date from this period, as does the pinnacled two-storey south porch: be sure to look up at the vaulting inside.

This page: *Stained glass at Fairford (left); St Peter and St Paul's imposing frontage at Northleach (above).*

ALSO IN THE AREA

Painswick St Mary
Why visit: *Churchyard with 99 18th-century yews, and table tombs*

Sapperton St Kenelm
Why visit: *Mainly early 18th-century church, with medieval origins; unusual bench-ends and collection of monuments*

NORTH GLOUCESTERSHIRE SPLENDOUR

Tewkesbury Abbey and Chipping Campden are the two grandest churches in this group, and each of these deserves a long visit, but the other churches here have something special to offer. Several of them, notably Deerhurst and nearby Odda's Chapel, have their roots firmly planted in Saxon times, while Bishop's Cleeve is Norman, and Winchcombe entirely 15th-century.

Tewkesbury
Tewkesbury Abbey

Why visit: *Monumental Norman architecture; burial place of Marcher lords*
Where: *Church Street, the A38 Gloucester road, GL20 5RZ*

With its enormous and imposing central tower, Tewkesbury Abbey is a Norman church built on a cathedral scale. The sheer size of the building is further emphasised by the west end, which is entirely made up of a huge arch that rises to the full height of the nave. The look and feel of grandeur is continued inside, where giant pillars soar up to the roof.

The abbey was founded by Robert Fitzhamon, one of William the Conqueror's most powerful barons, and was built between 1102 and 1121. Other Norman lords and their dynasties are connected with the abbey, and many of them are buried here. Two major changes to the Norman structure were made in the 14th century; first when the vaulted roofs were inserted. The second was when Lady Eleanor le Despenser, widow of one of England's most influential lords, transformed sections of the building to become, in part, a shrine to her husband and her family. So, in the chapels around the choir, are buried her husband (Hugh le Despenser), her ancestor Robert Fitzhamon, and her son and his wife.

Many other hugely important participants in the wars, feuds and politics of the Middle Ages are buried here, including Edward, Prince of Wales, the only son of Henry VI. Glittering down on all this is some of the finest medieval stained glass in England, much of it dating from Eleanor's time.

This page: Tewkesbury Abbey's imposing Norman interior.

Bishop's Cleeve
St Michael and All Angels

Why visit: *Excellent Norman architecture and decorative work*
Where: *In Bishop's Cleeve, off Church Road, GL52 8LJ*

Built on a Saxon foundation that may date back to the 700s, the present church here takes its shape and character from the 1170s, when it was rebuilt by the Normans and transformed into a large and splendid building. The Norman work is especially predominant in the west front, with its exuberant decoration. This is continued on the south doorway, where two dragons are portrayed.

Much further building and rebuilding work was done in the early 14th century, adding to the richness inside the church. A large gallery was erected at the west end in Jacobean times, and from then dates the elaborate tomb of Sir Richard de la Bere and his wife Margaret.

There is a small museum of the church's history over the south porch, which includes charming murals painted as visual lessons by a thoughtful Georgian schoolmaster.

Chipping Campden
St James

Why visit: *Quintessential Cotswold church with superb tower*
Where: *Church Street, at the northern end of Chipping Campden, GL55 6JG*

Chipping Campden is one of the loveliest Cotswolds towns, packed with buildings made from the famous honey-coloured stone. Its church is perfectly placed on a small hill away from the hurly-burly of the High Street, but still feels very much part of the town.

The tower is the first feature you see: solid and square, it was built in about 1500 and has a symmetry that makes it graceful for all its great size. It houses eight bells that date from 1618 to 1737, and a clock mechanism that was made in 1695, though this was retired in 1962 when a new mechanism was installed. The nave was rebuilt at about the same time, resulting in a feeling of great harmony throughout the building. Inside, the first impression is of grace and light, highlighted by the window over the nave arch, a Cotswolds speciality.

Treasures include a unique pair of altar hangings from about 1400. There are also excellent monuments, many to the rich wool merchants who poured their wealth into the creation of the building.

Deerhurst St Mary

Why visit: *Outstanding Saxon church, and nearby Saxon chapel*
Where: *On the west side of Deerhurst, close to the River Severn, GL19 4BX*

St Mary's is one of the most complete buildings to survive from before the Norman Conquest. It has a complex building history, as can be seen once inside the church, where there are many Saxon features, including tiny triangular windows, and high up on the west wall, a beautiful pair of windows with pointed tops and a carved baluster.

There are several excellent pieces of Saxon sculpture here, thought to date from the 9th century, including an angel in the ruined apse. Especially interesting is the font, rescued from use as a wash tub on a farm, and covered in intricate interleaving carved patterns.

Recently, an early painted figure was discovered on a panel high up in the east wall of the nave. It may date from the 10th century, which would make it the oldest wall painting in any church in Britain. Close to St Mary's is another Saxon church, called Odda's Chapel, which had been converted into a farmhouse and is accessible.

This page: Exterior of Deerhurst (above); gurning figure at Winchcombe (right).

Hailes

Why visit: *13th-century wall paintings*
Where: *Off Salter's Lane, opposite the ruins of Hailes Abbey, GL54 5PB*

This tiny church sits quietly down the road from its well-known neighbour, Hailes Abbey.

The church dates from, at the latest, the 12th century, but was given a thorough overhaul in the 13th century because of its close relationship with the then new abbey. Further changes were modest until the 17th century when the church was reorganised to reflect changes in religious thinking; those changes in their turn have been swept away. The stained glass in the east window is 15th-century and originally came from the nearby abbey.

During the 13th century the interior of the church was covered with wall paintings, many of which survive, albeit in a somewhat faded and fragmentary state. They include St Christopher carrying the Christ child, as well as mythical creatures.

Stoke Orchard
St James the Great

Why visit: *Rare wall paintings*
Where: *Stoke Road, west of Bishop's Cleeve, GL52 7SH*

Modest and unassuming from the outside, Stoke Orchard's little church has many features showing its origins in about 1170. It is the inside that makes the church so special, as its walls are covered in a wonderful jumble of paintings, with fragments and layers from many centuries on top of, behind, and around one another. The earliest paintings are the ones that are most celebrated. They depict the life of St James of Compostela and date from the early 13th century. They are the only ones of their kind in Britain. Parts of paintings from the 15th, 16th, 17th and 18th centuries also survive, some scraped back in the 1880s and 1950s to reveal more of the St James pictures.

The church also has a Norman font and many other features, ranging from the 12th to the 19th centuries.

Winchcombe St Peter

Why visit: *Perfect Perpendicular church, with gargoyles*
Where: *Gloucester Street, GL54 5LU*

This is a beautiful town church, built all of a piece in the first half of the 15th century. It is the only church of its age in Gloucestershire to have a nave arcade of eight bays, and the only one in the county without a chancel arch. This gives the church a wonderful light and airy feeling. It also draws the eye straight down to the east window and the bright masterpiece in stained glass, made in the late 1800s by John Hardman Powell. The window depicts Jesus walking on the water, with a faltering St Peter beginning to sink. The outside of the church is arrayed with a gallery of gurning stone figures, each one different.

ALSO IN THE AREA

Great Washbourne St Mary
Why visit: *Small church with details from many ages*

Little Washbourne
St Mary CCT
Why visit: *Little church in lovely setting, with 18th-century fittings*

OXFORDSHIRE AND WARWICKSHIRE

The places of worship in this largely rural area are extremely diverse, ranging from the very grand at Bloxham to the smallest imaginable at Ettington. What they have in common is that they are built of stone that was usually quarried locally. Each has a unique story to tell, whether it be a tower crashing down for no apparent reason or a stray bomb causing huge damage; an incredibly long-lived vicar, or connections with the Civil War Battle of Edgehill.

Bloxham St Mary

Why visit: *Soaring tower and spire*
Where: *Church Street, OX15 4PY*

Bloxham is in a small valley in the ironstone countryside of North Oxfordshire. On its southern side is the church of St Mary, outstanding even in an area of splendid churches such as Adderbury, Deddington and Broughton.

Little is left of a Norman church built here in the 12th century, apart from a few details in the chancel arch and windows, a rebuilt doorway in the porch and a fine doorway to the left of the altar. The south porch, with its stone vault, and the nave arcades, show good Early English work of the 13th century.

The following century brought the chief glory of St Mary's: its magnificent tower and soaring spire, a prominent landmark for miles around, giving rise to the rhyme 'Bloxham for length, Adderbury for strength, Kings Sutton for beauty'. The outside of the tower, the west door and the attractive parapet round the base of the spire all have a profusion of decorated ornamentation, typical of the early 14th century.

Above the parapet is a corbel table of heads, animals and birds, and the cornice on the outside of the north aisle shows grotesque figures: pigs, foxes, rabbits and two men fighting with a sword.

There is also fine window tracery in the north aisle, especially in the west window, which has carved heads outside, a curious and rare feature. During the same period both aisles were widened and the north transept added. More impressive carving can be seen inside the church, especially in the corbels of the nave and south aisle and a capital in the north transept. The latter has heads and linked arms in a pattern that seems to be unique to Oxfordshire.

In the early 15th century the nave roof was raised to allow more light through the new clerestory, and the superb Milcombe Chapel was built. The chapel has tall, elegant pillars and four massive windows that flood the church with light.

Between 1860 and 1870 much restoration work was done and fine stained glass was inserted, especially in the east window, designed by William Morris and Edward Burne-Jones.

The church's best monument is in the Milcombe Chapel, and is to Sir John Thorneycroft. Dating from 1725, he is wearing a periwig and flowing draperies and reclines languidly on one elbow, with his other arm gesturing upwards as if to warn Heaven of his impending arrival.

Adderbury St Mary

Why visit: *Glorious 15th-century chancel; superb stonework and carving elsewhere*
Where: *Mill Lane, OX17 3LP*

This splendid church is one of the greatest to be found in Oxfordshire. It has a tremendous tower and spire combination, and the walls seem as much glass as stone. The wide nave is 14th-century, and the transepts are 13th-century, with fine stone carving, including a capital showing the special Oxfordshire motif of linked arms.

The glory of St Mary's is the superb chancel, built in the early years of the 15th century by William of Wykeham, Bishop of Winchester and founder of Winchester College and New College, Oxford, whose family lived at the nearby village of Broughton.

Broughton
St Mary the Virgin

Why visit: *Setting of church next to Broughton Castle and its park*
Where: *West side of Broughton, on the approach to Broughton Castle, OX15 5EF*

St Mary's was built almost entirely in the early 14th century, at the same time as Sir John de Broughton was building the adjacent castle. Inside, the chancel and nave are separated by a rare stone screen. The chancel and the wide south aisle contain a remarkable collection of effigies and monuments commemorating the owners of the castle, from the 14th century to the present day. Another interesting feature is the large collection of hatchments of the Fiennes and Twisleton families from 1666 to 1847.

Burton Dassett
All Saints

Why visit: *Church on a steep hillside*
Where: *Burton Dassett Country Park, CV47 2AB*

The power of place that this building exudes is remarkable. The sparse interior is cloister-like and its setting in the Burton Dassett Country Park is second to none. The church is built into a hillside, so the climb inside from tower end to altar is considerable. On the walls are paintings from several centuries that have been restored. The stone altar in the Lady Chapel was wisely smuggled away in anticipation of the Reformation and buried for safekeeping. The pillars have intriguing carvings, among them a Green Man and several strange beasts chasing each other around the stonework.

Deddington
St Peter and St Paul

Why visit: *Light-filled church*
Where: *Church Street, OX15 0SA*

One evening in March 1634 the tower and spire of Deddington's church collapsed spectacularly, taking part of the church with it. The present tower, with eight handsome beflagged pinnacles, was built 50 years later with massive buttresses on each corner.

Inside, the nave and chancel are 13th-century. The clerestory window over the chancel arch and (unusually) clerestory in the chancel are a good demonstration of the late medieval passion for letting in light. Most of the windows are plain glass, but there is a pleasing Arts and Crafts east window in the north aisle.

Ettington The Old Quaker Meeting House

Why visit: *Tiny meeting house in pleasant surroundings*
Where: *Halford Road (the approach path is hard to find from the road so look out for a modest notice board), several hundred yards south of the parish church, CV37 7TQ; usually only open on Sundays, but can be opened on request*

Built between 1681 and 1684, this tiny meeting house – like most Quaker meeting houses – does not look at all like other buildings on this tour. It is a very simple single-storey building made of local stone with a slate roof, and it is just as modest inside. It stands in a peaceful garden that is also a Quaker burial ground.

Oxhill St Lawrence

Why visit: *Excellent Norman carvings; poignant grave of a slave*
Where: *Church Lane, north-east of Shipston on Stour, CV37 0RH*

Both the nave and chancel of St Lawrence's are 12th-century, and the north porch protects the original, beautifully carved, Norman north doorway. The porch and the sturdy little tower were built in the 15th century. On the south side of the church is another beautiful Norman doorway. Above it is a row of strange carved heads.

Inside is a 12th-century font with carvings of Adam and Eve in two of its 16 panels; the other 14 have trees, flowers and decorative patterns.

A gravestone in the churchyard commemorates Myrtilla 'Negro slave to Mr Thos Beuchamp of Nevis. Buried Jan ye 6th 1705'.

Somerton St James

Why visit: *Fermor family memorials; rare stone reredos*
Where: *Church Street, OX25 6LN*

This is an important Cherwell Valley church, built in the 13th and 14th centuries but embellished with battlements and pinnacles a century or so later. The south aisle became a chantry chapel for the Fermor family in the reign of Henry VIII, shortly before chantries were abolished. An exceptionally wide arch leads into the aisle from the chancel through a screen. Apart from the three rich marble Fermor family tombs, the church contains two rarities: an early 14th-century stone reredos depicting The Last Supper and a Holy Rood sculpted on the outside of the tower.

Opposite page: The spire at St Mary's, Bloxham (left); effigy of Sir John de Broughton at Broughton (right).
This page: *The many windows shed light on St Peter and St Paul, Deddington (left); the delightful Quaker Meeting House at Ettington (centre); Oxhill's squat tower (above).*

South Newington
St Peter ad Vincula

Why visit: *Exuberant porch; wall paintings*
Where: *High Street, OX15 4JF*

This handsome many-windowed Norman and Early English church is entered through a splendidly pinnacled porch, which gives it a particularly theatrical effect.

It is for its array of medieval wall paintings that St Peter's is celebrated. Those in the north aisle are oil on plaster and include a Martyrdom of Thomas a Becket and a delightful Virgin and Child – strongly coloured and sophisticated for such an early date (about 1300). Also depicted are St Margaret with the dragon that ate her, the execution of Thomas of Lancaster, and other scenes, some now very faded. Over the nave arcades are scenes from the Passion, which may be 15th-century. They are done in a much simpler, almost primitive manner.

This page: The Virgin and Child wall painting at South Newington (above); the chancel at Warmington (centre); St Peter, Whatcote (right).

Tredington St Gregory

Why visit: *Village setting; handsome building from many periods*
Where: *Mill Lane, off the A429, CV36 4NL*

Tredington's impressive church is made all the more so by a very tall spire. It has a long history, and elements of the original Saxon building can still be seen. Parts of the church were added or rebuilt between the 12th and 15th centuries, accounting for the attractive mixture of building styles evident from the outside. Stone benches set against the wall in the chancel have survived; these were the precursor of seating in the church.

Warmington St Michael

Why visit: *Battle of Edgehill burial place*
Where: *Church Hill, off the B4100, OX17 1JN*

The earliest part of St Michael's is the 12th-century nave. The church was subsequently enlarged with the additions of the north and south aisles towards the end of the 12th century, and enlarged again with much rebuilding during the 13th century. In the middle of the 13th century a chapel was built with a priest's chamber above it; it still has its fireplace and remains of its garderobe, or latrine.

The church is very close to the site of the Civil War battle of Edgehill and it is thought that many of those who died that day are buried here. There is a rare tombstone of the time in the churchyard, to a Royalist called Captain Gourdin.

Whatcote St Peter

Why visit: *Pretty stone church that was hit by a bomb*
Where: *Rectory Lane; east of the A429, south of the A422, CV36 5EB*

Whatcote is a tiny place at the junction of two Roman roads deep in rural Warwickshire. Its small size and remote location make it all the more surprising that the church was hit by a bomb during World War II. A great deal of damage was done, but in 1947 the church was restored. Many features of the old church can still be seen, including the 12th-century doorway on the north side of the nave. In the churchyard there is a tall medieval cross with an 18th-century sundial at its top.

In the 17th century the church had the same rector, John Davenport, for more than 70 years; he died aged 101 in 1668.

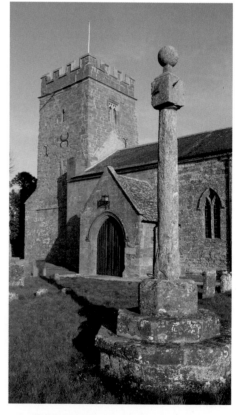

ALSO IN THE AREA

Sutton under Brailes
St Thomas a Becket
Why visit: *Simple 12th-century church*

WEST OXFORDSHIRE

Often described as the gateway to the Cotswolds, the much-visited town of Burford shared the great wealth of the Cotswold wool industry in the 14th and 15th centuries and held one of the most important medieval wool markets. This prosperity is reflected nowhere more than in its great church. The other churches on this tour are more modest and less well known but are typical of rural Oxfordshire, each full of charm, with some unexpected feature or story and always in a picturesque setting.

Burford
St John the Baptist

Why visit: *A richly endowed and embellished 'wool' church in a popular and pretty town*
Where: *Lawrence Lane, at the lower end of Burford High Street, beside the River Windrush, OX18 4RY*

St John's began life as a Norman church, of which the central tower and west wall, with its typical Norman door, remain. After this, its story is one of continual additions and 'improvements' over the years, making the history of the building fascinating although difficult to read.

The church was rebuilt in the 13th century, but its most admired features are the result of changes made in the 15th century, when the nave was remodelled with enormous Perpendicular windows and a fine clerestory. At the same time, a splendid three-storey porch was added. It has a wonderful vaulted ceiling inside. Other additions were the slender spire on top of the Norman tower, and the Sylvester chapel to the west of the porch, named after the merchant family who built and embellished it.

The interior of the church is full of interest. The tiny wooden chantry chapel that is opposite the door survived the Reformation thanks to the local squire,

who used it as a private pew. The many monuments include one to a local stonemason, Christopher Kempster, who worked on St Paul's Cathedral with Sir Christopher Wren. Another, of 1569, commemorates Edmund Harman, sometime barber-surgeon to Henry VIII.

St John's also contains sculptures of Native Americans – a remarkably early depiction of the New World. The brightly coloured pulpit was assembled in 1878 from fragments of 15th-century wooden tracery. In a small chapel north of the chancel is the magnificent early 17th-century canopied tomb of Sir Lawrence Tanfield, Lord Chief Baron of the Exchequer, and his wife. The sculpture of a skeleton below their effigies is an unusually late example of

the rather grisly medieval fashion for a memento mori. At their feet kneels their grandson, Lucius Carey, Viscount Falkland, the Cavalier courtier and poet who was killed at the Battle of Newbury in 1643. There is much good Victorian stained glass, notably the huge west window illustrating the stem of Jesse.

G.E. Street restored the church in 1877 and removed most of the original plaster, much to the displeasure of William Morris, who subsequently went on to found the Society for the Protection of Ancient Buildings (SPAB).

A modern plaque on the outside of the church commemorates three Roundhead soldiers who were executed in the churchyard in 1649. They were the ringleaders of a large band of mutinous troops (known as Levellers) whom Cromwell had imprisoned in the church. One of the prisoners inscribed his name on the lead font, and this can still be seen.

Charlbury
St Mary the Virgin

Why visit: *A welcoming church in a pleasing little country town; good Norman and Decorated work*
Where: *Church Lane, OX7 3PS*

The interior of the church at Charlbury is something of a surprise. It was much altered in the 19th century but the real transformation was in the early 1990s, when the main altar was moved to the west end. Purists may disapprove, but it seems to work: the church has become a more flexible space, and its architectural features are enhanced, particularly the fine Norman arcade to the north aisle. The five-light windows at the east end of both chancel and aisle are good examples of 14th-century Decorated tracery, in contrast to the plainness of the aisle windows, which are Tudor or later.

The tall, slender west tower is Early English, with a Perpendicular upper stage. A sundial of 1776 is preserved on a south-facing buttress.

This page: Effigy of Sir Lawrence Tanfield, who died in 1625, at Burford (left); exterior of Burford, with its elegant spire (centre).

Minster Lovell
St Kenelm

Why visit: *Unaltered 15th-century church in a lovely setting and with an intriguing historical mystery*
Where: *In Old Minster, on the lane that leads north-east out of Minster Lovell village, OX29 0RR*

Beautifully sited on the River Windrush, St Kenelm's stands next to the dramatic ruined manor house of the Lovells, who rebuilt the original priory church or minster in the mid-15th century. Soon afterwards, this once-great family made its exit from history with the 9th Baron, Francis Lovell, henchman and lifelong friend of Richard III. He disappeared in 1487, after the Wars of the Roses. His lands were seized by the crown and he was never heard of again.

The cruciform church has scarcely been altered since it was built. The central tower rests on four great pillars, with a fan vault over the crossing. In the south transept is a well-preserved Lovell tomb with a fine alabaster effigy and colourful heraldic symbols.

North Leigh
St Mary

Why visit: *Originally Saxon church with altered layout and interesting interior features, including the Wilcote Chapel*
Where: *Church Road, OX29 8TX*

The tall Saxon tower of St Mary's was not always at the west end of the church. The original nave, to the west of a central tower, was dismantled in the late Norman period. The Norman chancel became the nave, with a new chancel added in the late 13th century. The original roof line of the nave and the blocked-up arch can be clearly seen.

The interior of the church has many fascinating features. The dramatic, highly coloured Doom painting over the chancel arch has survived from the 15th century. Below it is an unusual and rather heavy Victorian stone screen. The Perrott aisle, on the north wall, is an Italianate memorial chapel of about 1700.

Don't overlook the tiny Wilcote chantry chapel, a superb example of mid-15th-century Perpendicular Gothic, with fan vaulting, a beautiful east window with original glass, and fine alabaster effigies. It is among the treasures of Oxfordshire.

Shipton under Wychwood
St Mary

Why visit: *Large, pleasingly situated medieval village church; 15th-century stone pulpit*
Where: *Church Street, just east of the main road through Shipton under Wychwood, on the far side of the village green, OX7 6BP*

The size and grandeur of St Mary's reflects the fact that Shipton parish used to include Ramsden and Leafield, villages that now have Victorian churches of their own. Shipton's largely 13th-century church stands between the Old Prebendal House and the village green. The tower and broach spire are typically Early English, with some fine detailing.

Inside, the church is quite plain, with aisles on both sides of the nave and late Norman capitals in the chancel arch. Most of the windows are from the 13th and 14th century. Several monuments commemorate the Reade family, squires here for 200 years. The 15th-century pulpit is carved from a single block of stone; the font is of the same period.

This page: Wall painting at North Leigh (left); the marble Fettiplace effigies at Swinbrook (right).

Swinbrook
St Mary

Why visit: *Lovely setting; Fettiplace monuments and Mitford graves*
Where: *Pebble Court, on the west side of Swinbrook village, in the Windrush valley east of Burford, OX18 4DY*

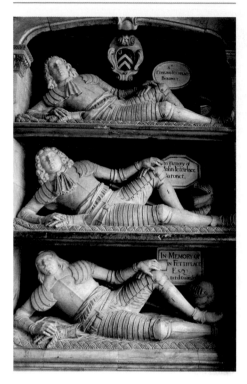

St Mary's is in a most attractive setting in the Windrush valley near Burford. The small church has a curious 19th-century tower and an enormous east window, which was blown out by an exploding land mine in 1940.

Yet nothing about the unassuming exterior hints at the extraordinary richness of the 17th-century monuments inside. They depict six members of the Fettiplace family, one of the great families of Oxfordshire until they died out in the late 18th century. The highly stylised marble effigies, laid out on shelves, each recline rather raffishly on one elbow. There are also brasses commemorating other Fettiplaces. Nearby Asthall Manor, the Fettiplace family seat, later became the home of the Mitford family. Four of the six Mitford sisters, Nancy, Unity, Pamela and Diana, are buried in the churchyard along with their parents, Lord and Lady Redesdale. The only Mitford son, Tom, killed in Burma in 1945, has a memorial inside the church.

IN AND AROUND OXFORD

Oxford has a great variety of churches, which are sometimes as important for their historical associations as for their architecture or fittings. Close to the city are churches that are astonishing buildings in their own right. Virtually in the city suburbs, at Iffley, is one of the most complete Norman churches in Britain.

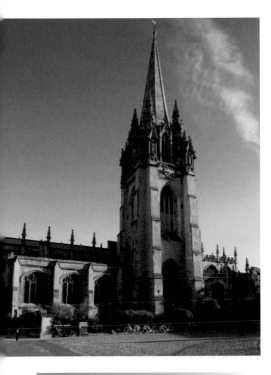

Oxford St Mary the Virgin, the University Church

Why visit: *Splendid architecture; the scene of many historic events*
Where: *High Street, OX1 4BJ*

St Mary the Virgin is both a parish church and the University Church, and in the Middle Ages was the centre of university life.

The steeple, one of the finest in England, dates back to the early 13th century. Much of the exterior fabric of the church has been enriched with decoration from later centuries, not least the Baroque south porch, dating from 1637 and reflecting the exuberance of its time.

The chancel is notable for its original oak stalls and misericords. Like the rest of the church, memorials to past worthies abound – clerical, academic and civic. None encapsulates the past more evocatively than a recently erected slab on the north wall, close to the screen.

It lists the martyrs of different religious persuasions who over the centuries have been associated with the church.

The trials of Bishops Latimer, Ridley and Cranmer took place in the nave in 1554–5; in 1774 John Wesley preached his famous sermon attacking the sloth of the unreformed university; and later, in 1833, John Keble and John Henry Newman began their Anglo-Catholic crusade from the same pulpit.

Oxford St Aloysius

Why visit: *Flamboyant building with a special character*
Where: *Woodstock Road, OX2 6HA*

The church of St Aloysius was built in 1873 by the Jesuits as the principal Roman Catholic church in Oxford. Cardinal John Newman had plans to establish an Oratory in Oxford in 1866 but they came to nothing. The present Oratory was only established in 1990. The building has a wide and spacious interior, with an equally wide apse with many Gothic features, fine lancet windows and a prominent rose window.

Oxford St Mary Magdalen

Why visit: *Associations with the three protestant martyrs*
Where: *Magdalen Street, OX1 3AE*

Dating from the 13th century, this church is significant for three reasons: for being just outside the old city walls, for its shape (as wide as it is long), and as the major Anglo-Catholic congregation in the city. There is also its physical association with the adjacent memorial to the Protestant martyrs. The Martyrs' Memorial, 1841, was devised by a Low Church group to commemorate the three martyrs, Bishops Latimer, Ridley and Cranmer.

Oxford St Michael at the North Gate

Why visit: *Saxon tower with many historic connections*
Where: *Cornmarket Street, OX1 3EY*

As its name implies, this church originally formed part of the town gate on the northern route out of the city and was connected to the ancient walls that protected the city and its inhabitants. Only a few traces of the northern wall remain, but the Saxon tower attached to St Michael's provides a vivid reminder of its role in medieval times as a prison. At street level a crudely blocked doorway indicates the exit made by the martyrs Latimer, Ridley and Cranmer before being burnt at the stake in the adjacent Broad Street. The site of the martyrdom is marked in the street there.

The tower is also significant as the oldest church tower in Oxfordshire, built in the first half of the 11th century.

The church as it stands today is mainly in the Perpendicular style, except for the fine Early English chancel with lancet windows at the east end. This is a church of town not gown, and it contains many memorials to Oxford worthies.

Oxford Wesley Memorial Church

Why visit: *Reminders of John Wesley*
Where: *New Inn Hall Street, opposite St Michael's Street, OX1 2DH*

One of Oxford's most elegant spires is surprisingly that of the Methodist Wesley Memorial Church. Built in 1878 in a conventional Gothic style, it has a spacious interior, with aisles typical of Methodism of the period but grounded in the Church of England. John Wesley remained an ordained priest of the latter until his death in 1791. The first Oxford meeting house where he preached was in a building opposite the present church, now 32–34 New Inn Hall Street, as signified by a plaque on the wall.

This page: *The 13th-century steeple at Oxford's University Church.*

Brightwell Baldwin
St Bartholomew

Why visit: *Monuments; brasses; fine medieval glass*
Where: *Cadwell Lane, north of Ewelme, west of Watlington, OX49 5NS*

Set in a little hamlet in unspoilt countryside, St Bartholomew's is a handsome 14th-century church, little altered except for some minor additions in the following century.

The interior is very interesting, especially the north chapel, which is completely dominated by 17th- and 18th-century monuments to the Stone family of nearby Brightwell Park. The chapel also contains fine medieval glass. In the nave the brass to John the Smith of 1371 is thought to bear the earliest known inscription in English.

Chalgrove St Mary

Why visit: *Wall paintings from the 1320s*
Where: *Church Lane, off the B480 north-west of Watlington, OX44 7SD; the church has limited opening times, but the key can be obtained from named keyholders listed by the north door*

It is the 14th-century chancel that makes this church so celebrated as it contains a remarkable and almost complete set of wall paintings dating from about 1320. The paintings are in four main sections and include scenes from the life of Christ, scenes from the apocryphal later life and subsequent death of St Mary, pictures of saints, and a Doom painting.

This page: Wall painting at Chalgrove (above); the Jesse window at Dorchester (centre); Alice of Suffolk at Ewelme (right).

Dorchester Abbey Church of St Peter and St Paul

Why visit: *Jesse window; Knight of Dorchester; very early medieval glass*
Where: *Junction of High Street and Queen Street, OX10 7HH*

Dorchester was the seat of the bishops of Wessex from 634 until the following century, when the bishopric was moved to Winchester. Subsequently the bishops of Mercia had their cathedral here until the see was moved to Lincoln shortly after the Norman Conquest.

In 1140 the church was refounded as a community of Augustinian Canons, and the building of a grand new abbey church was begun.

Only the wide Norman nave remains of that church which, with substantial additions in the 13th and 14th centuries, served its monastic community until the Dissolution. A rich resident of Dorchester called Richard Beauforest purchased the church for the use of the village and so saved it.

On first entering the church it feels rather bare, with an austere nave and a large open space on the right, which was used as a people's chapel in monastic times. There is nothing here to hint at the richness of the east end of the church, which was built between 1250 and 1340 in the Decorated style.

Beautifully moulded, slender arcades on either side lead the eye to the great east window with its finely sculpted tracery divided by a central buttress. Much of the glass is medieval, though the rose window at the top is Victorian. On the north side of the chancel is the remarkable and famous Jesse window, illustrating in both tracery and glass the descent of Christ from Jesse. To the south a smaller window carries the shields of various benefactors and patrons.

The sedilia and piscina below the south window are surmounted by richly carved and pinnacled canopies with many details of animals and foliage. Behind each seat is a tiny medieval glass window illustrating the life of St Birinus, thought to be among the earliest glass in England.

On the north side of the chancel is a small 13th-century chapel dedicated to St Birinus. It contains a charming medieval roundel in the east window showing the saint being blessed.

The 12th-century lead font is one of the very few in England. There are many monuments in the abbey, including the celebrated Knight of Dorchester, dating from about 1280. He is a remarkably vigorous, even truculent figure, and is shown twisting his body round while drawing his sword from its scabbard.

Ewelme St Mary the Virgin

Why visit: *Complete 15th-century group of buildings; tomb of Duchess of Suffolk*
Where: *Parson's Lane, east of Wallingford, off the A4130, OX10 6HS*

The church, almshouses and school here, all built by the Duke and Duchess of Suffolk in the mid-15th century, are a unique medieval complex and are justly celebrated. There was an earlier church, of which the tower survives, but otherwise the building was completely rebuilt in the Perpendicular style, with enormous windows lighting the nave and aisles.

Inside the door is a font with an extraordinary ornate cover stretching towards the roof. It dates from 1475.

St John the Baptist's Chapel, on the south side, is the chapel for the almshouses and contains the tomb of Thomas Chaucer (son of the poet Geoffrey Chaucer) and his wife. Their daughter, Duchess of Suffolk (Alice de la Pole), is buried in a magnificent tomb next to the altar. Her beautifully carved alabaster effigy shows her in simple habit and coronet and wearing the Order of the Garter on her left arm. Below is an effigy of the Duchess as a decaying corpse – a reminder of the fate of all, no matter how great or famous.

Iffley St Mary the Virgin

Why visit: *Perfectly preserved Norman church; superb carvings*
Where: *Church Way, 2 miles south of the centre of Oxford, off the A4158, OX4 4EJ*

St Mary's is a magnificent building, rightly famed as an almost perfect specimen of a Norman church, with unusually rich decoration both inside and out. Built between 1170 and 1180 it was the gift of a rich patron, the Remy family, who held the manor of Iffley in the second half of the 12th century.

It consists of a large, aisleless nave and chancel with a massive battlemented tower in the centre. The west front contains a superb doorway, richly carved with chevron and beakhead mouldings. The south door is equally splendid, with elaborately carved capitals. Inside, the principal features are the great Norman arches supporting the central tower, ornamented with zigzag carving and shafts of black marble.

Long Wittenham St Mary

Why visit: *Rare and unusual Norman lead font*
Where: *High Street, west of Dorchester, OX14 4QJ*

Two venerable yews flank the path leading to this church, entered through a charming 15th-century wooden porch. Inside, the chancel arch has survived from the original Norman church but the south arcade is 13th-century, with typical Early English stiff-leaf capitals. The roof was raised to make a clerestory in the early 16th century.

The lead font is Norman; only 20 or so such fonts remain in England, five of them in Oxfordshire. The south transept, now the vestry, contains a great curiosity – a piscina with a tiny effigy of a knight forming the lip of the bowl.

This page: Norman splendour at Iffley (left); St Mary's at Long Wittenham (above); the remarkable 14th-century stained glass at North Moreton (right).

North Moreton All Saints

Why visit: *Complete late 13th-century window with its original stained glass*
Where: *Junction of High Street and Wallingford Road, east of Didcot, off the A4130, OX11 9AT*

Parallel to the road, and with a handsome tower of stone and flint, this little church has a well-deserved reputation for being one of the finest in its area. It also contains the most outstanding medieval glass in Oxfordshire. This is found in the east window of the south, or Stapleton, chapel, built as a chantry by Sir Miles Stapleton late in the 13th century. He served with Edward I on the king's campaign in Scotland, and died at the Battle of Bannockburn in 1314.

The glass in the window has survived virtually intact, which is remarkable. The brightness of the colours, still vibrant after 700 years, makes it really memorable. There are 15 panels, with scenes from the lives of Jesus, the Virgin Mary, St Peter, St Paul and St Nicholas. The central scenes are of the Scourging, Crucifixion and Resurrection of Jesus.

There are fragments of medieval glass elsewhere in the church, including the figure of St John the Baptist. Other windows, by Victorian architect J.F. Bentley, are worth studying.

There is a Norman tub font, medieval tiles in the chancel and three 13th-century tomb slabs in the south chapel.

SHAKESPEARE COUNTRY

This part of Warwickshire is full of Shakespeare connections, both actual and more tenuous. His family were of prosperous yeoman stock – and there were lots of them. Stratford is the epicentre of the Shakespeare tourist industry, but the church where he is buried is a wonderful building in its own right. Most of the other churches in this group take you far away from the Shakespeare throngs, to gentle countryside and winding rivers.

Stratford-upon-Avon
Holy Trinity

Why visit: *Shakespeare's tomb and memorial; outstanding church*
Where: *Avonside, beside the River Avon, CV37 9BG*

Even if you wanted to, there is no escaping the Shakespeare industry in Stratford. But the church, somehow, escapes the worst of the crowds of tourists, saved by the fact that it is a short walk away from the town centre.

But, of course, the church is where Shakespeare is buried, and so it is inevitably on the tourist itinerary. He is buried in the chancel, where his grave and memorial can be found.

Commissioned by his widow in 1616, the memorial is said to be his best likeness.

The church itself is outstanding, and would be celebrated even without the Shakespeare connection. Its origins are pre-Norman, but the present building dates from the 13th century and later. It is a large building, full of light, with a central tower crowned by a tall and beautiful spire erected in 1763. The architect G.F. Bodley restored the church in a sensitive way in the 19th century, and the organ case that he designed sits splendidly above the crossing arch in the centre of the church.

There are many memorials and other items of interest, with the Clopton Chapel being particularly packed. Here, one of the finest monuments is the early 17th-century tomb of George Carew and his wife Joyce Clopton. In the chancel are 26 misericords from about 1450. These include some of the most famous of all such carvings.

Hampton Lucy
St Peter ad Vincula

Why visit: *Grand Victorian church in village setting*
Where: *Church Street, CV35 8BE*

Architects Thomas Rickman and Henry Hutchinson built this village church on a cathedral scale in the 1820s. Thirty years later, one of the greatest Victorian church architects, Sir George Gilbert Scott, added a chancel that completed the Gothic effect.

The east window depicts the life of St Peter, but it had to be pieced back together after an American Flying Fortress aircraft crashed nearby in World War II, blowing out the glass.

Such a large church in such a modest village is accounted for by the fact that it was funded by the Lucy family of nearby Charlecote Park. A member of the family was rector at Hampton Lucy for 59 years; at that time most of the villagers were employees of the estate.

Loxley St Nicholas

Why visit: *Lovely church; beautiful setting*
Where: *Wellesbourne Road, CV35 9JP*

On a sloping site in a wildflower-speckled churchyard, Loxley's church has a battlemented tower that dates back to the 13th century. The origins of the church are much older than that, and in 1983 parts of the Saxon building of about 950 were discovered, and can now be seen. Much of the church was rebuilt in the 18th century, and from then date the large windows in the nave with their clear glass and many of the internal fixtures and fittings. There are excellent monuments, many to the rich wool merchants who poured their wealth into the creation of the building.

Oldberrow St Mary

Why visit: *Simple and charming small church*
Where: *In Oldberrow hamlet, just off the A4189, B95 5NU*

St Mary's is a small church, crowned by a jaunty timber-framed bell turret with a tiny broach spire. The church's plan is very simple since the nave and chancel are one. Much of it was in fact rebuilt in 1875, although many original features were kept and so the church feels old and friendly.

The 12th-century font is particularly notable, as is the east window, which is dedicated to the Reverend Samuel D'Oyley, who was rector here for 67 years between 1792 and 1859.

The churchyard is an especially important site for nature conservation, with untouched grassland that is full of wildflowers and grasses in spring and summer. Unspoiled and unsprayed grassland such as this is very rare in the wider countryside now, and churchyards can be wonderful places for wildlife.

Snitterfield
St James the Great

Why visit: *Font with faces; literary connections*
Where: *Church Lane, Snitterfield, off the A46, CV37 0LG*

Much of this church was built during the 13th and 14th centuries; the tower was built in at least two distinct phases, with construction interrupted by the Black Death (1348–9). One of the most interesting features of the church is its 14th-century font, which, like others in Warwickshire, has carved heads round the base of the bowl. Time has weathered and chipped at these faces giving their expressions an enigmatic appearance. They are still commanding centuries after they were first carved.

The church has several literary connections. Poet Richard Jago was a curate here in the 18th century, and was buried in a vault in the church in 1781. His poems have not weathered as well as the faces on the font; they include a long account of the Battle of Edgehill, which took place nearby.

William Shakespeare's family came from Snitterfield, and his grandfather Richard was a churchwarden. His Uncle Henry had a farm in the village, but had a poor reputation with regard to the church, being fined for dressing inappropriately, and eventually excommunicated for non-payment of his church tithes.

Studley Nativity of the Blessed Virgin Mary

Why visit: *Setting; churchyard; varied building materials*
Where: *East of Studley, on Church Lane, end of Castle Road, B80 7AB; open term-time weekdays*

Set in quiet countryside close to the River Arrow, Studley's church has a history dating back to the 12th century, and parts of that original building can be seen in the north wall. Most of the rest of the church was built in the 14th and 15th centuries, including the handsome tower with its pleasing mix of pink and white stone.

Among the objects of interest in the church is a 13th-century coffin lid decorated with a beautifully carved cross entwined with flowers. It was found in 1931 on the site of the priory that once existed in Studley. The 17th-century altar rail is a reminder that dogs were once allowed in churches; rails (effectively a fence) such as these were erected in churches to prevent the dogs getting too close to the altar. A recent addition to the church is the Millennium Room, created in 2002 to provide a special space for children. The churchyard is managed to promote wildlife.

This page: Studley's tower (above); knight at Wootton Wawen (right).
Opposite page: Holy Trinity, Stratford-upon-Avon (left); Loxley (right).

Wootton Wawen St Peter

Why visit: *Architecture, furnishings and fittings from Saxon times to present day*
Where: *Next to the entrance to Wootton Hall, off the A3400, B95 6EE*

From the main road, the very large, red-roofed south chapel of St Peter's looks almost as big as the rest of the church. The tower nestling modestly behind it looks Gothic but is in fact Saxon in its lower stages, as becomes clear when you enter the church. The base of the tower is used as a kind of sanctuary, with an altar and modern stained glass in its north window. On either side of the tower are the nave and chancel, with an aisle and the large chapel to the south.

The church is packed with a fascinating mixture of furnishings, fittings, memorials and memorabilia, all interpreted and explained. The font with its unsettling carved heads is 14th-century; there are 15th-century bench-ends, and many monuments. Perhaps the most notable of these is that to Francis Smith; it dates from the early 17th century and has an effigy of him in armour and with a long, neatly combed beard.

ALSO IN THE AREA

Billesley All Saints CCT
Why visit: *Charming small church with long history and Shakespeare connections*

Binton St Peter
Why visit: *Windows commemorating Scott of the Antarctic*

Charlecote St Leonard
Why visit: *Victorian church with excellent collection of 17th-century monuments*

THE HEART OF WARWICKSHIRE

The area around Coventry, Rugby, Warwick and Leamington Spa has plenty of urban sprawl and might not seem an obvious place to visit country churches. Yet with the exception of the outstanding St Mary's in Warwick, all the churches in this group are either in villages or in secluded spots that could easily be far away from the built-up Midlands. Most of these churches have long stories: this area, close to the Roman Fosse Way, is steeped in history.

Berkswell
St John the Baptist

Why visit: *Norman church with Saxon crypt and half-timbered porch*
Where: *Beyond the school in Church Lane, Berkswell, CV7 7BJ*

This stout country church proclaims its Norman origins as you approach, with its collection of five round-headed east windows. Perhaps even more striking is the quaint half-timbered porch, like a miniature cottage on stilts above the south door. It dates from the 16th century and was formerly used as a schoolroom. The south doorway itself is another survival from the 12th-century church. Inside the church, steps lead up to the chancel, with the five Norman windows framed by a round 12th-century chancel arch. Don't miss the well-preserved rib-vaulted Norman crypt, which has a separate octagonal chamber and some stonework believed to date back to the 8th century.

Warwick St Mary

Why visit: *A stately landmark of a church, with a fine Norman crypt and medieval chancel; spectacular 15th-century Beauchamp Chapel with magnificent monuments*
Where: *Old Square, CV34 4AB*

There's no mistaking the importance of this great church, which dominates most views of Warwick from its hilltop site, with the best view from the castle. The landmark pinnacled tower dates from the early 18th century. The reason for this comparatively late date was the huge fire that devastated Warwick in 1694, destroying much of the old church so that the tower and nave had to be rebuilt. The oldest part of the church to escape the blaze was the Norman crypt, a wonderful vaulted space where the base of a ducking stool is kept on display.

Other surviving parts of the medieval church miraculously include the 15th-century chancel and the Beauchamp Chapel, one of the finest chantry chapels in the whole country. With no expense spared, it was created in the mid-15th century for Richard Beauchamp, 5th Earl of Warwick, a close associate of Henry V who died in France in 1439. Beauchamp's gilded effigy, resting on a marble tomb, is the centrepiece of the chapel, which is magnificent in every detail. Another tomb here is that of Robert Dudley, Earl of Leicester and dashing suitor to Queen Elizabeth I, who granted him the nearby castle of Kenilworth. Famously, he entertained the Queen there at vast expense for three weeks in 1575. Eventually he married Lettice Knollys, whose effigy lies here beside his.

This page: The Beauchamp Chapel at Warwick (above); the Norman crypt at Berkswell (right).
Opposite page: Chesterton (top centre); Ladbroke (below centre); nave and chancel, Offchurch (right).

Much of the woodcarving in Berkswell church is by Robert Thompson, a well-known craftsman from Yorkshire. He was born in 1876 and became known as 'the Mouseman of Kilburn' because of his 'signature', a mouse carved in oak. Nine examples of this signature can be found in the woodwork at Berkswell.

Birdingbury St Leonard

Why visit: *Small, little-known country church that is a curious but successful mixture of Georgian and Victorian*
Where: *Adjacent to Birdingbury Hall, on the road leading north out of Birdingbury village, between Leamington Spa and Rugby, CV23 9RP*

With its pale walls and red-tiled roof, its Tuscan west front and its charming little cupola, this tiny parish church could almost have been transplanted from some Greek or Italian village.

The impression is reinforced inside by the beautiful painted and gilded ceiling in the Gothic apse, which was added to the original Georgian church in 1873, along with the screen, altar rails and chancel stalls. The font, box pews and pulpit belong to the 18th-century church. The chancel window depicting St Leonard was given by Sir Theophilus Biddulph of neighbouring Birdingbury Hall.

Chesterton St Giles

Why visit: *Remote rural church with historic connections and fine monuments*
Where: *Just under 2 miles east of Chesterton Green on an unclassified road (cul de sac), CV33 9LG*

As the crow flies, Chesterton church is barely a mile from the noise and bustle of Warwick Services on the M40, but it feels amazingly remote. The church owes its isolated status to repeated bouts of the plague, which drove the medieval villagers away to nearby Chesterton Green. The site of St Giles is a historic one: a Roman villa close by has been partially excavated, and there was a Roman encampment on the Fosse Way (B4455), just to the west.

The church stands in open country on a hilltop – a long, low, castellated building of limestone. Notice the 18th-century painted sundial above the south door, with its motto: 'See and be gone about your business'. The core of the building is early 13th-century, with some older fragments. The fine 16th- and 17th-century monuments are to members of the Peyto family, whose manor house stood near the church. They include

Sir Edward Peyto, who commissioned the unmistakable landmark that can be seen on a hill to the north-west: Chesterton Windmill, built in 1632.

Ladbroke All Saints

Why visit: *Unusual tower; fine 14th-century sedilia*
Where: *On the north side of Church Road, leading west out of Ladbroke towards Harbury, CV47 2DF*

The unusual 'striped' tower of Ladbroke church gets its effect from alternating layers of sandstone and limestone. Like much of the rest of the church, it dates from the 14th century. Notable features of the same period include the pinnacled sedilia or clergy seats, on the south side of the chancel. The clergy records go back to 1290, and earlier parts of the church include the 13th-century east window, with Victorian stained glass, by John Hardman & Co, depicting more than 80 figures. Much of the stained glass dates from the 1876 refurbishment of the church by architect and church restorer Sir Gilbert Scott.

Offchurch St Gregory

Why visit: *Norman and later village church with ancient origins*
Where: *Near the junction of the village street and School Hill, in Offchurch (just east of Leamington Spa), CV33 9AW*

This ancient village close to the Fosse Way takes its name from the Saxon king, Offa, who is recorded as having founded a church here to commemorate his dead son. A stone coffin discovered beneath the porch may have been that of King Offa himself. The present sandstone church is mainly Norman, with a 15th-century tower. The noticeably crooked sides of the chancel arch recall its rebuilding in the 14th century after it collapsed. The north doorway has fine Norman carvings that had been plastered over and were uncovered in 1833. Later work includes the 18th-century oak pulpit and some good 17th- and 18th-century monuments.

ALSO IN THE AREA

Churchover The Holy Trinity
Why visit: *Norman and Early English church with fine 17th-century Dixwell family monuments*

Dunchurch St Peter
Why visit: *14th-century rebuild of a Norman church, in a pleasing setting*

Monks Kirby St Edith
Why visit: *Largely unaltered medieval priory church*

Stoneleigh St Mary
Why visit: *Norman origins; mainly 12th-century tower, chancel and font with carvings depicting the apostles*

CENTRAL NORTHAMPTONSHIRE

Something like 1,200 years of varied histories link these churches. Two of England's most interesting Saxon churches – Brixworth and Earls Barton – are to be found in this group. Two of the others are almost complete churches of their period: Finedon from the 14th century and Whiston from the first half of the 16th century. In the centre of Northampton is St Peter's, an outstanding Norman church that was rescued from an uncertain fate in the 20th century, while All Saints in very rural Cottesbrooke was restored in the 18th century.

Higham Ferrers
St Mary

Why visit: *Tower, spire and entrance doorway; associated medieval buildings*
Where: *Off High Street, Market Square, NN10 8DL*

Set around St Mary's is a clutch of fascinating medieval buildings that make this part of Higham Ferrers feel rather like a modest cathedral close. The Bede House, Chantry Chapel and, farther away, Chichele College were all founded by Henry Chichele, who was born in the town in 1362 and went on to become Archbishop of Canterbury.

The church has a splendid tower of the 13th and 14th centuries, with a superb double entrance doorway surmounted by a series of 13th-century carvings in roundels. Each roundel contains a biblical scene; the Mary and Child at the centre is a modern replacement. The tower is crowned by a tall, beautifully decorated spire. The top of the tower and the spire collapsed in the early 17th century and were rebuilt to the original designs.

The interior of the church is large and spacious, with ironstone arcades leading to a screen over which is a rood designed in the 20th century by Sir Ninian Comper. Of the monuments in the church, the brass on the tomb between

the chancel and the Lady Chapel deserves special mention and is reckoned by many to be one of the best in England. It is to Laurence St Maur, who died in 1338. Above the figure of Laurence is a group of saints with Abraham at the centre.

Archbishop Chichele contributed much to the church, including the choir with its 20 stalls, still complete with their original misericords.

Brixworth All Saints

Why visit: *Famous Saxon church*
Where: *Off Church Street, NN6 9BZ*

This is a remarkable survivor from the 9th or 10th century, with virtually the entire nave and chancel remaining from that time. From the outside the church retains much of its Saxon feel, with the exception of the top half of the tower and the tall spire, which are both from the 14th century.

The best Saxon architecture can be seen inside, where the arches are made of re-used Roman tiles. At one time the church was even bigger than it is now, and must have been a very important centre in Saxon times. The origins of the church go back to a monastery that was founded here in 675.

Cottesbrooke All Saints

Why visit: *18th-century fittings; monuments to Langhams and Redes*
Where: *Close to the entrance to Cottesbrooke Hall, NN6 8RL*

All Saints is a handsome battlemented medieval church in an immaculate churchyard. The inside is full of surprises. The church was restored in the 18th century 'in the Wrenian manner', and so has a rounded ceiling with painted edges and hanging candelabra. It also has a three-decker pulpit, box pews and a family pew for the Langham family of nearby Cottesbrooke Hall. 'Family pew' is an understatement for what is

This page: The magnificent rood and screen of St Mary's, Higham Ferrers (top); the church's beautifully decorated spire (below).

essentially a raised private room approached by an elegant staircase. Behind this are monuments to members of the Langham family, and to their predecessors, the Redes. There are other Langham monuments in the nave, one festooned with what appears to be decaying foliage.

Earls Barton All Saints

Why visit: *Saxon tower; painted saints and butterflies*
Where: *High Street, NN6 0JG*

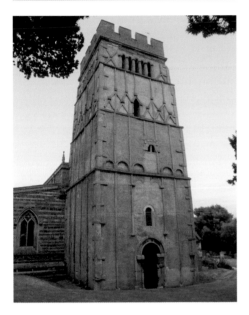

All Saints has one of the most celebrated of all Saxon towers. It dates from about 970, but is famous not so much for its age as for the decorative stonework, patterns of vertical lines and rounded and diamond shapes that rise up the tower, culminating in a stage with Saxon windows. The battlemented top stage is 15th-century.

Much of the rest of the church is Norman, including the south door, complete with a frieze of strange heads. The interior is dominated by a restored rood screen, painted by Henry Bird in 1935. In the lower panels he painted saints in modern-day dress, and in the upper parts hundreds of butterflies. The entire screen is bright with golds, blues and reds and is an idiosyncratic delight.

This page: The Saxon tower of All Saints, Earls Barton (above); Raunds' much-lauded spire (right).

Finedon St Mary

Why visit: *Unified 14th-century architecture; unusual strainer arch; strange Green Men*
Where: *Church Hill, NN9 5NR*

Built of local ironstone, St Mary's dates almost entirely from the 14th century, with the nave and chancel from the beginning of the century and the tower and spire from about 50 years later. The result is a very pleasing and harmonious whole. Externally, one of the most impressive features is the large east window, its elegant five lights crowned by an ogee head. Internally, there is a most unusual architectural feature, a strainer arch inserted in the late 14th or early 15th century to prevent the church collapsing. Its function may be purely structural, but it was made in such a delicate way that it looks decorative.

There are other surprises: there are at least five Green Man carvings in the church. As always, their meaning is enigmatic and their feeling unsettling. They are often thought of as pagan figures, but many experts think they depict the fate of those who only lead material lives, and are entirely Christian symbols.

Northampton St Peter CCT

Why visit: *Northamptonshire's finest Norman church*
Where: *Marefair, Centre of Northampton, NN1 1SR; open Wed–Sat, 10am–4pm*

Sitting on an island of grass and trees, St Peter's is a wonderful church, safe in the care of the Churches Conservation Trust. The outside is brilliant, with a mixture of Norman and later detail re-used in the 17th-century tower. A striped pattern is created by alternating courses of limestone and ironstone. The stripy effect is continued on the Norman arches inside, and these are supported on superb carved capitals with foliage, birds, beasts and monsters. These carvings had been plastered over in the 17th century and were painstakingly uncovered in the 19th century by local antiquarian Anne Elizabeth Baker. It took her 11 years to complete the job.

Raunds St Peter

Why visit: *Steeple; wall paintings*
Where: *Church Street, NN9 6JB*

In church enthusiasts' lists of 'best steeples' Raunds always comes near the top, and its combination of magnificent tower and soaring spire is stupendous. Much of the church is 13th-century, and the east window is especially beautiful. The inside is full of interest, with a series of wall paintings that include scenes of St Christopher and the deadly sins, as well as three living men meeting their skeletal (dead) counterparts.

Whiston St Mary the Virgin

Why visit: *Perfect 16th-century church*
Where: *Just east of Whiston, NN7 1NP*

Whiston is a very small village tucked away in the countryside east of Northampton. Its church is on a hill a little way to the east and is reached along a track. Although there are traces of earlier work, the church is almost entirely of a piece, and can be dated with accuracy to 1534, when it was built by the Catesbys, lords of the Manor. It is a handsome building very typical of the Perpendicular style, but built late, just before the Reformation that effectively brought church building in England to a halt for 100 years. Many Catesbys have memorials in the church.

NENE VALLEY CHURCHES

Northamptonshire's Nene Valley is remarkably untouched by the blight of modern building developments, and its villages and countryside are, by and large, a pleasure to visit. The county is famous for its steeples, spires and towers, and all the churches in this cluster have a tower or spire, or both, to be proud of – worth visiting for those alone. Fotheringhay is by far the most widely known, but Warmington, Lowick and Titchmarsh are equally memorable in different ways. Likewise, Aldwincle has not one, but two beautiful and historic churches.

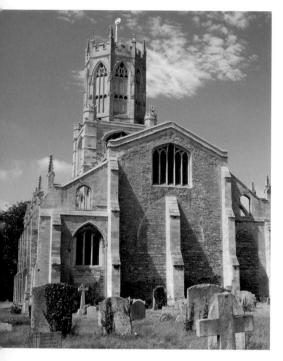

Fotheringhay
St Mary and All Saints

Why visit: *Memorable lantern tower; royal monuments*
Where: *In Fotheringhay, by the River Nene, PE8 5HZ*

The elegant octagonal lantern tower of St Mary's can be seen for miles around, and the flying buttresses that sprout in abundance from the church make it doubly distinctive. The combination of the lantern and the window-filled base of the tower is striking, all the more so because the body of the church appears truncated in comparison. It looks like this because the chancel was demolished after the Reformation, along with cloisters and college buildings that used to stand here.

Elizabeth I ordered that monuments to various nobles that had been left in the ruins of the demolished buildings be moved into what had been the nave. These include those of Edward, Duke

of York, who was killed at the Battle of Agincourt in 1415, and his nephew Richard, Duke of York, killed in 1460 at the Battle of Wakefield.

On the wall of the north porch is a carved stone lion, one of a pair that once guarded Fotheringhay Castle. All that is left of the castle today is a grassy mound, but it explains the historic importance of Fotheringhay and its church. Richard III was born in the castle, and Mary Queen of Scots was held prisoner here from 1586 until her execution on 8 February the following year.

Aldwincle St Peter

Why visit: *Excellent steeple; carved stonework*
Where: *Thorpe Road, west end of Aldwincle, NN14 3EP*

St Peter's is legitimately another claimant for the title 'best Northamptonshire steeple'. All the elements are in place:

handsome lower stages leading up to an elegant broach spire with three stages of spire-lights (or lucarnes), each one smaller than the one below. The earliest parts of the church are 12th-century, with the north aisle being built in 1190, and other elements, including the spire, added in about 1375. The south aisle was built in 1520. There are also mysterious and enigmatic carvings both inside and outside the church. One at least is clearly a Green Man, while another might be a musician; others could be tortoises, but on closer inspection are they dogs?

The church has some fine stained glass, most Victorian but some medieval, and a modern window to commemorate the Millennium. Some of the furnishings were inherited from All Saints, at the other end of the village, when that church became redundant.

Aldwincle All Saints CCT

Why visit: *Beautiful building that is open and airy inside*
Where: *Thorpe Road, east end of Aldwincle, NN14 3EA*

Aldwincle's two churches are linked by a long, very pretty and unspoiled village of houses; both modest and grand. All Saints is on the eastern edge of the village, next to open country, with the old parsonage opposite.

The poet John Dryden was born in Aldwincle in 1631, and baptised in All Saints. His father, Henry Pickering, was rector here for 40 years, and his gravestone is now inside All Saints.

The church is 13th- and 14th-century in the main, with its splendid pinnacled tower, the porch and south chapel dating from the 15th century.

Aldwincle did not need both its churches, so for many years All Saints stood empty and disused, and these

days is cared for by the Churches Conservation Trust. In a bold move it was decided to leave the church with few furnishings and fittings, resulting in a remarkably light and airy interior, and the excellent architecture speaks for itself.

Apethorpe St Leonard

Why visit: *Extraordinary Mildmay memorial*
Where: *Bridge Street, PE8 5DP*

On the edge of the grounds of Apethorpe Hall, St Leonard's is a handsome church built of limestone. The body of the church is late 14th- or early 15th-century, while the tower and its spire were built in 1633. Also 17th-century is the Mildmay Chapel, built by the then owners of the Hall to house their monument. Under a huge and overwhelming marble structure lie Sir Anthony Mildmay and his wife, their hands clasped in prayer. Around them stand four figures representing Piety, Charity, Wisdom and Justice.

There are other monuments in the church, as well as rare stained glass from both the 17th and 18th centuries.

Lowick St Peter

Why visit: *Splendid tower and monuments*
Where: *Main Road, on the northern edge of Lowick village, NN14 3BH; locked – keyholder in village*

Seen from the road, Lowick's church is like something from a fairytale, its tower crowned by an octagonal lantern surrounded by a thicket of pinnacles each with its own tiny flaglike weathervane.

The outside is almost surpassed by the riches inside. First, there are four windows in the north aisle with medieval stained glass of the highest quality. The glass (from about 1320) originally came from one very large window that depicted the story of the Tree of Jesse, which may have been broken up in 1644 to remove its 'superstitious' images.

Then there are the monuments, like an art gallery of church monuments from the 1400s through to the 18th century. Sir Ralph Green (died 1419) and his wife are shown in alabaster on an elaborate table tomb; they are holding hands, and he is in armour while she wears a headdress that resembles a gigantic pair of earmuffs. Also of alabaster is the memorial to Edward Stafford, 2nd Earl of Wiltshire, who died in 1499.

There is a brass to another Green, Sir Henry, from the 1460s. There are much later memorials of various sorts, including that to Lady Mary Mordaunt, shown leaning with her elbow on a skull. She died in 1705.

Titchmarsh
St Mary the Virgin

Why visit: *Lovely tower and harmonious 15th-century architecture*
Where: *Church Street, NN14 3DB*

Titchmarsh (or Tichmarsh as it is also spelled) has yet another of Northamptonshire's memorable towers, but this one looks as if it might have been designed for Somerset, as it has a West Country look.

It is of four stages, with statue niches in the lower three stages, and pinnacles crowning the top stage. The statues in the niches are 20th-century replacements for the original ones. Like most of the rest of the church the tower is late 15th-century, and is a splendid example of the Perpendicular style. Over the south porch is a room that was built as a private pew for the Pickerings, lords of the Manor. The church is in a street of pretty stone cottages, some of them thatched.

Warmington
St Mary the Virgin

Why visit: *Superb Early English architecture; wooden roof with Green Man bosses*
Where: *Church Street, PE8 6TE*

Warmington's church has one of the most famous of all Northamptonshire's steeples. Built in the 13th century (as is the rest of the church) its square lower part has three stages, the top one with decorated belfry windows. Above that is a broach spire, with large spire-lights (or lucarnes). Inside the church is a rare survivor from the 13th century, a wooden roof rather than a stone one. There are nine Green Man bosses on this roof, each one different; one appears to be snarling while another has foliage growing out of his eyes.

Some of the detailing of this magnificent small church was used as inspiration by architect William Butterfield when he came to build his famous church of All Saints, Margaret Street, London (see page 84).

This page: All Saints, Aldwincle (left); Titchmarsh (centre).
Opposite page: Fotheringhay exterior (left), and colourful 15th-century pulpit (centre).

ALSO IN THE AREA

Cranford St Andrew CCT
Why visit: *Memorials to the Robinson family of next-door Cranford Hall. Open summer weekends; keyholder nearby*

Dene St Peter CCT
Why visit: *13th-century church with memorials to the Brudenells, including James Brudenell, Earl of Cardigan, who led the Charge of the Light Brigade; keyholder nearby*

RURAL BUCKINGHAMSHIRE

Large parts of Buckinghamshire are remote, rural and very pretty. The only actual town church in this cluster is St Mary's in Aylesbury, standing in a quiet enclave of greenery and old buildings. Some churches here are built on a 'town' scale but are tucked away in delightfully out-of-the-way locations, while others stand in villages where time certainly feels slower and its effects more gentle.

Wing All Saints

Why visit: *Famous Saxon church*
Where: *Church Street, LU7 0NX*

A famous Anglo-Saxon church with later additions, All Saints stands in a large churchyard on the edge of the village, from which it is approached through a fine 20th-century lychgate. The Saxon apse is seen at once and is worth looking at closely. Probably built in the 10th century on top of the 9th-century crypt, it is seven-sided and has typical Saxon blank arcading with remains of triangular arcading above with two original round-headed windows, now blocked. The large windows were inserted in the 15th century, but at ground level there are more ancient round-arched windows lighting the earlier, stone-vaulted, crypt.

From the external view the rest of the church appears to be medieval, with 14th- and 15th-century windows, tower and south porch. But on entering you find yourself in a large and complete

Saxon church. The three semi-circular arches on each side of the nave are late Saxon or early Norman, and led to aisles, which were replaced by the present ones in the 14th century. The chancel arch is probably 9th-century like the apse, but was altered at some stage. Above it is the only complete Anglo-Saxon window, a two-light opening with arches of Roman bricks and a central column. The building of the massive bell tower in the 15th century destroyed the Saxon west end.

In the 15th-century south porch, which is the main entrance, is the base of an 'Aylesbury' font, while inside is the 15th-century font now in use. Above the nave is a remarkable 15th-century timber roof, carved with angels with outstretched wings and saints and kings along the sides. In the south aisle are fragments of medieval stained glass.

In the north aisle stands a monument commemorating Sir Robert Dormer, who died in 1552. Whether of this date or slightly later, the monument is one of the finest of its period in England.

Aylesbury St Mary

Why visit: *Distinctive Norman font*
Where: *St Mary's Square, HP20 2JJ; open daily 9am–2.30pm*

The parish church of Buckinghamshire's county town, St Mary's is used for all ceremonial county services, dominating the old part of Aylesbury. It has its own little cathedral-like close in St Mary's Square, surrounded by old houses. It is an example of a large town church of the 13th century and is cruciform in plan with a massive central tower. The tower is surmounted by a square lead-clad clock-stage with arcaded parapet and pinnacles, above which rises a short lead-clad spire, known as a Hertfordshire spike.

Sir George Gilbert Scott carried out extensive restoration work here in the 1850s and 60s, including replacing the late Perpendicular east window. In fact, he has been criticised for destroying the medieval fabric by doing so.

In the north transept is an alabaster monument to Lady Lee, who died in 1584. She is kneeling with her daughter and in front of her is a vase of red flowers that are always kept fresh.

The highlight of the church is its Norman font, one of several in Buckinghamshire called 'Aylesbury' fonts. It is shaped like a chalice and has delicate carving based on foliage.

This page: *Saxon apse at Wing (left); Norman font at Aylesbury (above).*
Opposite page: *Interior at Hillesden (centre); Jordans Friends Meeting House (right).*

Chetwode
St Mary and St Nicholas

Why visit: *Setting; 13th- and 14th-century stained glass*
Where: *South-west of Buckingham, on lanes off the A4421, MK18 4JX*

In a remote part of Buckinghamshire near the border with Oxfordshire, this predominantly 13th-century church stands almost alone, with only an old gabled stone house and farm buildings for company. After the Dissolution of the Monasteries the church and house (part of an Augustinian priory) were purchased by the Risley family, who incorporated the south transept into their house and demolished the nave. Their attempts to drive out the parishioners failed and the chancel became the parish church. The present plain bell tower was built on the site of the nave and serves as a porch.

The church is wide, spacious and very much in the Early English style, as exemplified by the wonderful group of five lancets at the east end, and the two groups of three lancets a little to the north and south. Two of the southern lancets contain wonderful stained glass from the 13th and 14th centuries, notably lozenge-shaped panels. The east window has 19th-century glass in a matching style.

Hillesden All Saints

Why visit: *Superb early 16th-century church*
Where: *Church End, at the south end of Hillesden, south of Buckingham and Gawcott, MK18 4DB*

Called 'The Cathedral of the Fields', this magnificent church stands in an isolated hamlet on a slight hill, so that while it can appear suddenly in distant views, reaching it involves negotiating miles of winding narrow lanes. Apart from the late 15th-century tower, the entire church was rebuilt in about 1500.

On the north side, the main approach is to a two-storey vestry attached to the north chapel, with an octagonal stair turret terminating in a beautiful stone 'crown' formed of flying buttresses. The porch has stone panelled sides, a fan-vaulted ceiling and an original oak door.

Inside all is light from the unusual clerestory and the large windows, some with their original stained glass, including the story of St Nicholas in the upper lights of the east window of the south transept. The chancel and north chapel have stone panelling and in the chancel there is a frieze of angels with musical instruments. The flat plaster ceilings are decorated with oak ribs, copied from the original ceilings probably in Sir George Gilbert Scott's restoration of 1873-5.

The tall, carved rood screen is original, as is the linenfold panelled screen to the north chapel. There is a family pew from the late 17th century and earlier, although restored, benches with linenfold panelling. In the north chapel are two fine monuments to the Denton family, who became lords of the manor after the church was built.

In the churchyard is an almost complete 14th-century preaching cross.

Ivinghoe St Mary

Why visit: *A grand town church in a village*
Where: *Church Road, in the centre of Ivinghoe, LU7 9EW*

Essentially, St Mary's is a building of the 13th century, though the tower and the great arches supporting it are 14th-century, inserted into the earlier building. Externally the walls are rubble limestone with dressings of clunch, chalk stone quarried at Totternhoe (in next-door Bedfordshire). In places this soft stone has been replaced by harder wearing limestone, but inside the advantages of an easily carved stone are apparent in the moulded piers and arches of the nave arcades, and particularly in the stiff-leaf ornament of the capitals.

Above the arcade is a 15th-century clerestory, but the outline can also be seen of the earlier circular windows that it replaced. Some of these beautiful, circular windows survive in the west-facing walls of the transepts. High above the nave is an excellent 15th-century timber roof with carved angels and with the Apostles on the wall posts.

The fine Jacobean pulpit has an hourglass stand, and the lectern is 15th-century with a double-sided revolving bookrest.

Jordans
Friends Meeting House

Why visit: *England's most famous Quaker meeting house*
Where: *Southern edge of Jordans, at the junction of Jordans Lane and Welders Lane. Jordans is east of Beaconsfield, west of Chalfont St Peter, HP9 2SN*

Standing in a beautiful valley deep in the Chilterns, this Quaker meeting house dates from 1688 and was one of the first to be purpose-built. It is a simple brick building with a hipped tiled roof, restored after a fire in 2005.

The interior is plain and unassuming with simple panelling to the lower walls, raised a little higher on the left-hand end wall to mark the elders' seats. There is a fixed wall bench all around the room, and open-backed benches. Both the ground and first floor rooms are separated from the main room by screens with shutters. The men, women and children usually met in three separate rooms, but by opening the shutters the three spaces could be united.

William Penn, the founder of Pennsylvania, returned to England and is buried in a marked grave in front of the meeting house.

Little Missenden
St John the Baptist

Why visit: *Ancient-feeling, idyllic setting*
Where: *Abbott Road, west of Amersham, HP7 0QY*

St John's tower, with its prominent battlemented semi-octagonal stair turret, is 15th-century, and escaped refacing in knapped flint in the 19th century. The mixture of local building materials is part of the charm of this church – the south aisle has a mixture of brick and flint, but the wide south porch is timber framed.

Inside, the church feels very ancient; experts argue whether it is Saxon or Norman. The simple semi-circular arches have a primitive appearance and the extensive medieval wall paintings, which have been uncovered, give the interior an 'early Christian' feeling. The step down into the chancel and the old tiled floors contribute further to the atmosphere.

North Marston St Mary

Why visit: *Exceptional chancel*
Where: *In Church Street, MK18 3PH*

This is a parish church of architectural magnificence. The nave is 13th-century in origin, with fine piers and arches to the arcades. A parish priest at this time was John Schorne, who achieved fame by reputedly capturing the Devil in a boot. His shrine became a place of pilgrimage, but the Canons of Windsor removed it in 1478 to Windsor where they were trying to raise funds to complete St George's Chapel. It is said that they built the new chancel and nave clerestory at North Marston as a sop to the parishioners.

The church was transformed about this time. The nave was raised by the addition of the clerestory with three four-light windows each side, and a battlemented parapet above. The crowning glory was the new chancel, bigger than the nave, with battlements, stepped buttresses carrying tall pinnacles, traceried windows, and the unusual feature of an original two-storey vestry on the north side.

This page: Stoke Poges' churchyard, immortalised in Gray's Elegy *(centre); old fittings and uneven floor at Twyford (right).*

Stewkley St Michael

Why visit: *Outstanding Norman church*
Where: *West of Leighton Buzzard, off the A4146, LU7 0HL*

St Michael's is one of the best-preserved Norman parish churches in England, built around 1150-80. At some stage, probably in the 15th century, the roof pitch was reduced and was then raised back up to follow the line visible on the tower wall in the tactful restoration by G.E. Street in 1844.

The west front of the church faces the road and has a central door with a Norman arch and tympanum carved with dragons. The south doorway, protected by Street's porch, has chevron ornament on the arch. The bulky central tower has blind arcading at belfry level in the form of intersecting round arches that produce pointed arches.

Stoke Poges St Giles

Why visit: *The famed inspiration for* Elegy in a Country Churchyard
Where: *Church Lane, SL2 4NZ*

The churchyard here is famously said to have inspired Thomas Gray to write his *Elegy in a Country Churchyard* in 1750, and he is buried close to the east wall of the church. There is a large monument to him in the adjoining field, now owned by the National Trust.

The large brick chapel is the Hastings Chapel, built by Lord Hastings in 1558. Its windows are closer to the domestic Tudor style than Gothic. The main church, built of a mixture of flint and stone, is basically Norman but with a 13th-century north nave arcade, chancel and tower.

Twyford The Assumption of the Blessed Virgin

Why visit: *Atmospheric interior*
Where: *Brook Street, north-east of Bicester, south of Buckingham, RG10 9PP*

Twyford's impressive church is set in a big, tree-dotted churchyard in which there is a cross of very early date, probably 13th-century, with remains of arcading and carved figures. The church itself has a splendid Norman south doorway; the nave is 13th-century, while the clerestory windows are 15th-century, as are the fine timber roof and elaborately carved bench-ends.

ALSO IN THE AREA

Dinton St Peter and St Paul
Why visit: *Famous Norman doorway*

Drayton Beauchamp St Mary
Why visit: *Lovely 15th-century church*

Haddenham St Mary
Why visit: *Delightful village setting*

Little Kimble All Saints
Why visit: *14th-century wall paintings*

Nether Winchendon
St Nicholas
Why visit: *Ancient fixtures and fittings*

Quainton
St Mary and Holy Cross
Why visit: *18th-century monuments*

Winslow
Baptist Meeting House
Why visit: *17th-century chapel with Georgian fittings*

HIDDEN HERTFORDSHIRE

A number of lovely Hertfordshire churches give the lie to the widely held belief that the county has been taken over by new towns, motorways and London overspill. Being so close to London, this is certainly a densely populated county with a lot of urban sprawl, but there are still surprisingly quiet, green corners, interesting old villages, and market towns where the streets tell of a long and often prosperous history. Timber, cob, brick and thatch are a reminder that Hertfordshire lacks natural building stone, and many of the old churches are built of flint.

Hitchin St Mary

Why visit: *Large and lovely historic church, with rich embellishments from many centuries*
Where: *Church Road, east of the High Street, SG5 1HP*

Hitchin's unpretentious and delightful church has the air of having been very well loved for a long time. The church mentioned in the Domesday Book was not the first here: its predecessor was an 8th-century Benedictine monastery.

The sturdy tower is 12th-century but its massive buttresses were added after an earthquake in 1298. Otherwise most of the present building dates from the 14th and 15th centuries, with many additions funded by medieval and later merchants in wool, leather and corn, who helped make Hitchin a busy and prosperous place. These features include the elegant Perpendicular porch and windows, the exquisite carved screen, the font and its cover, and the many chantry chapels and monuments. Allow plenty of time to explore this varied and absorbing church – and don't forget to look up at the angels and many other beautiful and sometimes intriguing roof carvings.

Anstey St George

Why visit: *Fine Norman and Gothic cruciform church with an ancient font*
Where: *Near St George's End, SG9 0TJ*

St George's is reached through a 15th-century lychgate that incorporates a small lock-up, said to have been made in 1831 to punish drunkards. The building shows clear evidence of its Norman origins both at the crossing and in the extraordinary pillared font, with its frieze of four mermen clutching their tails. The upper part of the tower is 14th-century and has a slender spire known as a 'Hertfordshire spike'.

St George's is a lucky survivor. A US bomber from nearby Nuthampstead fatally crashed on the castle mound behind the church during World War II, but miraculously its bombs did not explode. The incident is vividly depicted by Patrick Reyntiens in a memorial window in the church, which was dedicated in 2000.

This page: The tower at Hitchin, complete with its 'Hertfordshire spike'.

Ashwell St Mary

Why visit: *Large church and tall tower built of clunch; unusual 14th- and 15th-century graffiti*
Where: *Mill Street, SG7 5QQ*

This historic and well-manicured village in the far north of Hertfordshire has a delightful array of vernacular buildings as a backdrop to its dazzling 14th-century church tower. The church is built of a type of hard chalk known as clunch, and can look almost pure white in a certain light. Clunch is softer than limestone and was often used to construct domestic buildings, or for interior work, but seldom used for a whole church. Though showing signs of wear that have been exacerbated by acid rain, Ashwell's thick-walled tower is Hertfordshire's tallest. Its original height is marked by a row of crenellations halfway up. The top half was added in the 15th century, followed by the leadwork 'Hertfordshire spike' on top.

The soft stone may have been a catalyst for the church's most renowned detail: extraordinary medieval graffiti that can be seen on the nave pillars and inside the base of the tower, which includes a detailed sketch of old St Paul's in the City of London. One piece of graffiti on the south side of the nave includes a complaint in Latin, presumably from a disappointed architect or clerk of works. It translates: 'The corners are not jointed properly. I spit on them'.

Ayot St Lawrence
St Lawrence

Why visit: *Late 18th-century Greek revival church*
Where: *Off to the north of Bibbs Hall Lane, AL6 9BZ*

Ayot St Lawrence is known mainly for the National Trust property of Shaw's Corner, the Arts and Crafts house where George Bernard Shaw lived from 1906 until his death in 1950. Ayot's parish church could hardly be more different. Replicating a temple from Ancient Greece, it was built in 1778 for Sir Lionel

Lyde, a wealthy landowner who wanted something impressive to enhance his view from Ayot House. His architect was Nicholas Revett. A few hundred yards east of the white stuccoed church with its colonnades and portico – very avant-garde for its day – stands what remains of its medieval predecessor. Lyde had dismantled this into a forlorn, roofless ruin before the Church authorities could object, in the belief that it would make a picturesque addition to his landscape.

Bishop's Stortford
St Michael

Why visit: *Hilltop site, elegant exterior; 15th-century fixtures and fittings carved in wood and stone*
Where: *Windhill, CM23 2ND*

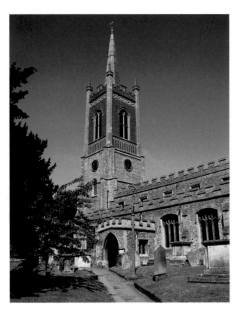

St Michael's is a large and imposing church, dominating town and country from its hilltop site. The distinctive and rather elegant brick belfry, which contains a ring of 10 bells, was added in 1812, but most of the rest of the church is 15th-century and has preserved its original fittings inside, such as the beautifully carved screen and choir stalls, complete with their misericords.

Look up to see the excellent range of stone corbels, with their representations of a whole cast of characters from the customary angels to a cook and a gardener. The hexagonal pulpit – fitted with a foldaway false floor that can be raised up to give shorter preachers a

'higher profile' – dates from 1658. The square Purbeck marble font is the sole survivor from a Norman church on this site, and was discovered buried in 1868.

St Paul's Walden
All Saints

Why visit: *The family church of Queen Elizabeth, the Queen Mother*
Where: *Bullocks Hill, in the centre of the village of St Paul's Walden, south of Hitchin, SG4 8DL*

The late Queen Elizabeth, the Queen Mother, was born and brought up just to the south of the village at St Paul's Walden Bury, home of the Bowes-Lyon family since the 18th century. A wall tablet in All Saints' commemorates her baptism here in 1900, and a memorial in the churchyard commemorates her life.

The church is Perpendicular, with an extraordinary, incongruous baroque chancel, installed in 1727 as the gift of Edward Gilbert, the first Bowes-Lyon ancestor to live in the parish. One of the treasures of the church is a 14th-century window depicting the Virgin and Child, recently restored.

South Mimms
St Giles

Why visit: *Historic village and church with interesting family monuments*
Where: *Blanche Lane, in South Mimms village; reached on the B556 or, from the M25 or A1(M), via the roundabout near the motorway services, EN6 3PD*

Sandwiched between the M25 and the A1(M) is the comparatively calm oasis of South Mimms (or Mymms) and its medieval flint church. First recorded in 1136, it has a 13th-century chancel and a Perpendicular tower and nave.

In 1877 the church was restored by G.E. Street. The gilded font cover of 1939 is by Sir Ninian Comper. He also designed the glass above the altar in the 15th-century Lady Chapel, which was built in 1448 as a private chantry for the Frowyke family who were lords of the Manor of South Mimms. The tomb of Henry Frowyke the Younger and the carved screen both date from the 1520s.

In the chancel, a 13th-century grave slab (the oldest), and a canopied tomb of the mid-16th century (the latest) each commemorate Henry Frowyke the Elder.

Stanstead Abbotts
St James CCT

Why visit: *Unspoilt country church*
Where: *Roydon Road, Stanstead Bury (off the minor road leading north-west from Stanstead Abbotts), SG12 8JZ; open Jun–Sep on Sunday afternoons 2.30–5pm*

Despite limited opening hours, this delightful but disused hilltop church, dating from the 12th century, is well worth seeking out. A marvellous 15th-century rustic porch, built of massive timbers, is the unlikely precursor to an unspoilt Georgian interior with tall box pews and a three-decker pulpit. The original king-post roof also survives, and there are a number of interesting Elizabethan and later monuments.

This page: Bishop's Stortford's early 19th-century brick belfry.

ALSO IN THE AREA

Hatfield St Etheldreda
Why visit: *Historic church associated with neighbouring Hatfield House; lavish monuments to the Cecil family*

Hemel Hempstead St Mary
Why visit: *12th-century church with fine Norman stonework; early clerestory*

Knebworth St Martin
Why visit: *Idiosyncratic early 20th-century church, by Sir Edwin Lutyens for his wife's family of Knebworth*

Little Hormead St Mary the Virgin CCT
Why visit: *Small rural church with marvellous Norman chancel arch and doorways, and exquisite 14th-century font*

Ware St Mary
Why visit: *Spacious Perpendicular cruciform church; outstanding 14th-century font carved with angels and saints*

ALONG THE GREAT OUSE

Felmersham is one of a number of old villages set amid the loops and bends of the River Great Ouse as it meanders its way across the gentle landscapes of north Buckinghamshire and Bedfordshire. Church, river and village or town make a series of pleasing pictures here, with inspiring churches that vary from Saxon to Victorian in settings ranging from secluded, timeless Clifton Reynes to decidedly urban and modern Bedford.

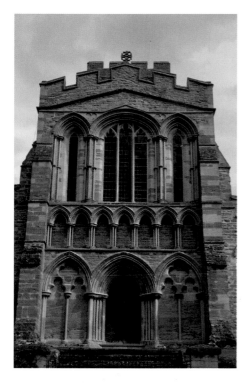

Felmersham St Mary

Why visit: *Unusually impressive 13th-century church generally unspoilt by later alterations*
Where: *Church Road, MK43 7JP; open daily in summer months*

This is a building to delight all visitors who enjoy church architecture purely for its own sake. The majestic appearance of this 13th-century cruciform church is enhanced by its elevated site above the river, and the first view of the amazing west front, with its blind arcades and grand portal, will not easily be forgotten.

Much of the building is unadulterated Early English: it was completed within about 20 years, from 1220. The main later additions were the 15th-century tower and clerestory. The interior is equally awe-inspiring, with plenty of natural light to enhance the graceful piers and soaring

arches of both nave and crossing. The chancel is very long, with lancet windows, though these are the result of a 19th-century restoration. The intricate tracery of the 15th-century oak screen is still painted in its original sumptuous colours – all the more effective because the simple furnishings and plain decor of the church are not a distraction. However, this may not always have been the case: traces of paint on one of the nave pillars and in the ringing chamber suggest they were once embellished with wall paintings. The south door still has its sanctuary ring: anyone holding it could claim the protection of the church.

Bedford St Paul

Why visit: *Large and welcoming town church, mainly Victorian but with surviving medieval features*
Where: *St Paul's Square, near Town Bridge, MK40 1SQ*

Bedford's principal parish church has an imposing site at the heart of this busy town, close to the main bridge over the river. Much of the building, including the tall spire, is Victorian or later but it has a much older core. The general style is Perpendicular, with a spacious and lofty feel to the interior: the piers are slender and the aisles are the same height as the nave. Earlier features that remain include the two-storey Early English south porch and the 15th-century roofs of the nave and south aisle, with fine carving that can be viewed at closer range from the gallery.

Many striking pieces of original craftsmanship were skilfully re-used in the restoration of the choir stalls, with

This page: The west front of St Mary, Felmersham (left); battlemented walls at Clifton Reynes (right).

misericords that include one of Bedford Castle, and in the stone pulpit, which was made in 1680 from recycled medieval stonework. It was used by John Wesley to preach a famous sermon in 1758. The Trinity Chapel is another medieval survivor, from 1416, and this was 'adopted' by the BBC during World War II, when it was used for broadcasting the *Daily Service*.

Clifton Reynes St Mary

Why visit: *Secluded village location; early monuments*
Where: *Church Lane, at the north-west end of the village of Clifton Reynes, east of Olney, MK46 5DT*

Topped with rows of neat battlements like a church from a medieval fairytale, Clifton Reynes' church sits at the end of its secluded village surrounded by open country, in a bend of the River Great Ouse. The tower is Norman with a 14th-century top, and much of the church is medieval though some parts were later rebuilt.

Special features of the church are the 14th-century octagonal font, carved with figures in arched niches, and the unusual monuments, including two pairs of early oak effigies. These depict 14th-century knights and their ladies, each with a dog at their feet. They are thought to be

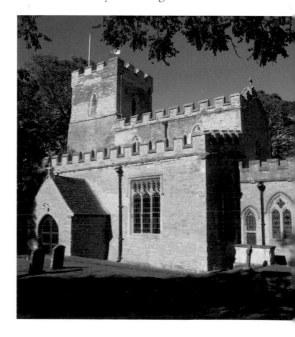

members of the Reynes family, who were lords of the manor here. Others are commemorated in later monuments, including a fine stone table tomb and a 15th-century brass to Sir John Reynes.

Elstow Abbey Church of St Mary and St Helena

Why visit: *Impressive former abbey church with a detached tower*
Where: *Church End, off the A5134 at the northern end of Elstow village, on the southern outskirts of Bedford, MK42 9XT*

Elstow's mighty 13th-century bell-tower, one of only a handful of freestanding church towers in the country, looks out across the spacious village green and stands side by side with the remaining part of a Norman abbey that is now the parish church. The three bays towards the east end are a surviving fragment of the original cruciform abbey church, which was founded by William the Conqueror's widowed niece, Judith, in 1078. The east wall, with its Perpendicular windows, was added after the Dissolution.

A handsomely vaulted 13th-century room from the original abbey is now used as a vestry. Two 19th-century windows in the church commemorate John Bunyan, author of *The Pilgrim's Progress*, who was baptised here in 1628 and later joined the church's bellringing team. The church is on the route of the John Bunyan trail, a long-distance path linking places connected with him.

Gayhurst St Peter

Why visit: *Attractive classical church in a parkland setting; grand 18th-century monument*
Where: *Off the B526 north-west of Newport Pagnell, in the grounds of Gayhurst House, MK16 8LG*

The parkland of Gayhurst House, an impressive Elizabethan mansion, provides the backdrop to this classical church, with its pleasing square tower topped by finials and a leadwork cupola. It was built in 1728 for the Wright family, who settled here in 1704, bringing to a close a turbulent period in Gayhurst's history. One previous owner was Sir Francis

Drake, who sold the former house here almost immediately after Queen Elizabeth I had given it to him; another was Sir Everard Digby, hanged as a conspirator in the Gunpowder Plot.

The finely dressed, periwigged figures of Sir Nathan Wright and his son George (who commissioned the church) still preside over the airy interior from their large, rather theatrical marble monument in the squire's pew. The classical columns and pilasters, the gilded reredos and altar rails, and the ornate plasterwork of the ceilings, all make a suitably grand and elegant setting for them.

Olney St Peter and St Paul

Why visit: *14th-century church with handsome steeple and interesting associations, in lovely riverside setting*
Where: *Church Street, off the High Street, MK46 4AD*

The dignified 14th-century stone steeple of Olney church makes a distinctive landmark in its setting beside a bridge over the winding River Great Ouse. The rest of the church is of the same period, with very tall windows and 14th-century tracery, though this has been much restored and the glass is Victorian or modern. One window depicts the church, and also the 18th-century poet and hymn-writer William Cowper, who lived in Olney and co-wrote the Olney Hymns of 1779 with curate John Newton (the composer of *Amazing Grace*). Quotations from some of Cowper's now familiar hymns also appear in the window.

Another notable Olney resident was architect George Gilbert Scott, who was brought up here. The 1870s restoration of the nave and chancel was by him. Olney's village sign depicts the famous pancake

race that still takes place here every Shrove Tuesday. It finishes at the church with a Shriving service. The tradition dates back to 1445.

Turvey All Saints

Why visit: *Church with Saxon origins and features dating from almost every era since; outstanding 13th-century wall painting*
Where: *High Street (off to the north of the A428), MK43 8EP*

The 13th-century bridge that crosses the Ouse in this harmonious old stone village is a relative newcomer in comparison with the church, which dates back to around 980, and possibly even to Roman times. The outlines of two small round arches above the southern nave arcade are the most visible feature of the original Saxon church. The nave roof above, with its 12 graceful angels and carved bosses, is thought to date from a 15th-century expansion of the church, when the nave was heightened and the north aisle was also built.

The older south aisle incorporates a Lady Chapel at its eastern end; here, the alcove next to the sedilia has a well-preserved 13th-century wall painting of the Crucifixion. The Elizabethan tomb opposite is one of four monuments to members of the Mordaunt family, who later became earls of Peterborough.

ALSO IN THE AREA

Broughton St Lawrence CCT
Why visit: *Medieval wall paintings*

Hanslope St James
Why visit: *Soaring steeple (a clear landmark west of the M1); Norman nave and chancel*

Marston Moretaine St Mary
Why visit: *Detached tower*

Willen St Mary Magdalene
Why visit: *Classical 1680s church at the edge of Willen Park*

This page: *Sir Nathan and George Wright in St Peter's, Gayhurst.*

ACROSS HEREFORDSHIRE

Herefordshire is a large, mostly rural county, often remote-feeling, especially on its western border with Wales. Here, the difference between Wales and England is often difficult to detect, whether in landscape or buildings, and many of the churches have a Welsh feel. Rivers give a special character to much of the county, and several of the churches chosen here are in deeply rural loops of the River Wye. The Norman Herefordshire School of mason-sculptors flourished here, creating an unsurpassed body of work.

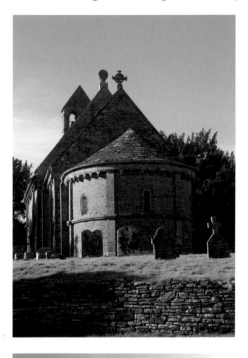

Kilpeck
St Mary and St David

Why visit: *Finest collection of Romanesque carving in Britain*
Where: *Northern edge of Kilpeck village, HR2 9DN*

Kilpeck is a modest village hidden away in west Herefordshire, but its church is world-famous for its 12th-century sculpture and carving, made by a group of mason-sculptors known as the Herefordshire School. The church is small, built of red sandstone, and set on the edge of the village, with beautiful countryside surrounding it. At first glance it looks unexceptional, except perhaps for the apse at the east end. In fact the whole church – nave, chancel and apse – is pretty much as it was built in the early 1100s, and is astonishingly well preserved.

This page: St Mary and St David, Kilpeck.

The south door draws attention first. It is alive with figures and foliage patterns. There are warriors, birds, snakes or dragons, monsters and, near the top, an angel. The work is fluid, sophisticated and beautifully carved. The doorway is fantastically well preserved; until Victorian times it was protected by a porch. Now it is exposed to the weather, but monitored very carefully for signs of wear.

Next to look at on the outside are the carvings on the corbel table, which runs round the entire church below the roof line. Here are men, animals and monsters. Some are identifiable, others are more enigmatic. A few are missing; it is said that some of the carvings were too earthy for a local Victorian lady and she had them removed. One of the carvings, a sheila-na-gig (a lewd female figure), is very earthy indeed. There is more superb carving inside the church, particularly the chancel arch and in the rib-vaulting of the apse. From a much earlier date are the font and the stoup – unmissable, with two enormous stone hands clasping the bowl.

Abbey Dore St Mary

Why visit: *Atmospheric former abbey church (Dore Abbey)*
Where: *On the B4347, at the southern end of the Golden Valley, HR2 0AA*

This will be the first church that many people visit when exploring the beautiful and aptly named Golden Valley. It is all that is left of a Cistercian abbey founded here in 1147, and consists of what had been the presbytery, crossing and transepts of the abbey church. Much of it dates from the 12th and 13th centuries, though the tower is 17th-century.

At the Dissolution the abbey buildings were sold and much of the fabric was demolished. By 1632 cattle were using parts of it as a shelter. It was at this time that Viscount Scudamore, whose great-great-grandfather had bought the abbey, began to restore the church, including building the tower. Much of the building work re-used stone from the rest of the old abbey buildings, including items such as the bosses which had been carefully saved from the nave roof.

Many of the fittings are from this time, including the ornate wooden screen. The musician's gallery, also of wood, dates from the early 18th century. The church needed restoring again by the end of the 19th century, and this essential rescue included revealing, protecting and re-using many original features and items.

Bredwardine St Andrew

Why visit: *Norman church; Kilvert's grave*
Where: *Church Lane, HR3 6BU*

You could come here for the setting alone: beautiful green Herefordshire countryside, with the River Wye only a few yards away, and a churchyard full of trees, and snowdrops in the spring. The church is Norman, although there is evidence of a Saxon church on this site. Parts of the chancel may be of Saxon date. The chancel is at such a pronounced angle to the nave that some members of the congregation cannot see the altar.

There is early stone carving on the lintels of both the south and (blocked) north doorways; the north doorway has two figures, one with a bird's head and the other, perhaps, with a monkey's head. In the church are a huge bowl-shaped Norman font and the effigies of two knights; one from the 13th century and the other from the 14th century. The latter is of Sir Roger Vaughan, who died defending Henry V at the Battle of Agincourt in 1415.

In the churchyard, on the north side, is the grave of Francis Kilvert, rector here for two years until his death in 1879. His diaries record the lives of the people of this area, and his descriptions of the seasons, the weather and the Border countryside and its way of life are among the best of their kind.

133

Brinsop St George

Why visit: *St George in stone and in glass*
Where: *Signposted off a lane just north of the A480, HR4 7AT*

Brinsop's 14th-century church, at the end of a cul-de-sac lane, is famous for its ancient depictions of St George – one in stone, the other in glass. The stone one is a re-set tympanum showing the saint killing the dragon. It is one of the great works of the 12th-century Herefordshire School of mason-sculptors. The glass sculpture of St George is from the 14th century and is in the east window, along with other figures from the same period.

Poet William Wordsworth was a regular visitor to Brinsop, as was Francis Kilvert (see page 133), whose diary records that he visited the church on 13 March 1879. It is the last entry in the diaries.

There is much 20th-century work in the church by Sir Ninian Comper, including several windows, one of which is in memory of Wordsworth.

Brockhampton All Saints

Why visit: *Unique early 20th-century church*
Where: *In Brockhampton-by-Ross, north of Ross-on-Wye, off the B4224, HR1 4SE*

This is a church like no other, a genuinely unique building that was the last major work of its architect, William Lethaby. He was commissioned to build the church by the owners of nearby Brockhampton Court, the old church having fallen into disuse. The new church, completed in 1902, was built on a new site, north-west of the house.

Lethaby had been an apprentice to leading architect Norman Shaw, was a disciple of William Morris and active in the Arts and Craft movement. All of these influences are clear in the building.

The exterior is idiosyncratic and enchanting: a short central tower of sandstone; a square wooden bell-tower; thatched roofs; and windows that range from long and thin to small and square.

The inside is just as unusual, from the almost tent-shaped lime-washed concrete roof to the stonework of the windows, and full of brilliant detail, from hanging lamps to door fittings. It is a masterpiece; a tribute to Lethaby's vision.

Clodock St Clydog

Why visit: *Setting; oak furnishings*
Where: *Hunthouse Lane, just east of the Welsh border under the slope of the Black Mountains, HR2 0PD*

This is a quintessential Borders church, built of red sandstone with a sturdy, castle-like tower, and in a very rural setting. Its nave is Norman, the chancel a little later and the tower later still.

It is lucky for us that the church is so remote, for it was never 'restored' and so has preserved its 17th-century box pews, pulpit, stalls, communion table and very rare bench. This is where the parishioners sat while waiting to receive Communion.

There is much more to see and enjoy in this special church.

Eaton Bishop
St Michael and All Angels

Why visit: *Superb medieval stained glass*
Where: *Rectory Meadow, west of Hereford, HR2 9QJ*

St Michael's has a Norman tower crowned with a later broach spire that is a prominent landmark. Much of the rest of the church is from the 13th century.

It is for its medieval glass that the church is famous. This was probably made in the 1330s and is in the east window of the chancel and the adjoining north and south windows. The figures depicted in the east window are the Madonna and Child, St Michael, a bishop, the Archangel Gabriel and the head of Christ. This is agreed by experts to be among the finest stained glass anywhere in Britain.

Hoarworthy St Catherine

Why visit: *Southern Italy in Herefordshire*
Where: *North-west of Ross-on-Wye, east of the A49, HR2 6QH*

This is not what you expect to find on the lanes of Herefordshire: a church seemingly plucked from southern Italy and plopped down beside the Wye. But there it is – a campanile, colonnades and apse, and interior to match, with four enormous marble columns leading the eye to the east end with its golden mosaic of Christ in Glory.

The architect was J.P. Seddon, who created this remarkable building between 1874 and 1903 at the request of the then vicar, who did not like the chapel that stood there at the time.

King's Caple
St John the Baptist

Why visit: *17th- and 18th-century fittings; 19th-century monuments*
Where: *Signposted at the crossroads, across the Wye from Hoarworthy, HR1 4TX*

Caple means chapel, and the 'King's' part of the name suggests that the people of this area owed direct allegiance to the Crown. St John's dates from the

This page: Brockhampton's unique nave (left); the Norman tower at Eaton Bishop (above).
Opposite page: *Carved doorway at Ledbury.*

13th–15th centuries, and has kept its 17th-century pulpit and some of its box pews, plus an 18th-century west gallery.

There are two particularly interesting early 19th-century monuments in the church: one is by John Flaxman, the other by Sir Richard Westmacott – the best-known ecclesiastical sculptors of their time.

Ledbury
St Michael and All Angels

Why visit: *Detached bell-tower; Norman 'portal' windows; monuments*
Where: *Worcester Road, Ledbury centre, HR8 1PL*

From Norman times onwards St Michael's was Herefordshire's biggest and most important church. As it is seen today, the church has elements from the three great periods of English church architecture: Early English, Decorated and Perpendicular – from the 13th and 14th centuries, and some from the 15th century. There is also original Norman work, as can be seen in the west door and in some of the piers and arcades of the nave and chancel. The unusual detached bell-tower (there are only seven in Herefordshire) dates from the 13th century, with its upper stage and spire being added in 1733.

Features of special interest include the circular 'porthole' windows high up in the walls of the chancel. They serve no function now, but they once allowed light into the whole length of the church before higher aisles and chapels were built, making them redundant. St Michael's has many notable monuments, ranging in date from the

13th century (a priest in vestments), to 1851 (a child named John Hamilton, made by Mary and Thomas Thornycroft).

Leominster Priory Church of St Peter and St Paul

Why visit: *Norman and later church with three naves*
Where: *Church Street, leading on to The Priory, HR6 8EQ*

This is a big, spacious church, with a building history that has left it with an unusual layout, consisting of what can be thought of as three parallel naves. What can be seen today is only a part of the original priory church, which stretched farther to the east. At the Dissolution the town kept the nave(s), but the cloisters, transepts, presbytery and chapels were all demolished.

A church has stood here since at least as early as 660, and there are stories that St David – of Wales fame – may have founded a church here a century earlier.

The story of the building that stands here today goes back to 1121 when Henry I re-founded the monastery (it had been closed down in 1046), and buildings on a grand scale were erected. The first nave was built at this time, while the second dates from the 13th century, and the south aisle (as big as the second nave and bigger than the first) from the 14th century.

Many of the best architectural features are on the outside of the church, especially the Decorated windows of the south aisle. The outstanding 12th-century decoration on the west doorway was made by the same mason-sculptors who worked at Kilpeck and Shobdon.

Madley Nativity of the Blessed Virgin

Why visit: *Imposing church full of interest*
Where: *Brampton Road, off the B4352, west of Hereford, HR2 9LX*

Madley village is small and modest; its church is large and sumptuous. The original building here was Norman, but much of that was replaced in the early 13th century, making the church bigger. Another rebuilding took place in the

14th century, and it was at this time that the church became so splendid, and gained its unusual features.

The ground at the east end of the church falls away quite steeply, a feature the 14th-century buildings took advantage of by building a crypt under the new and splendid polygonal apse (itself very unusual in English churches). The crypt was restored in 2007, and this space, with one central pier, is now a tranquil place for private prayer.

Much Marcle
St Bartholomew

Why visit: *Monuments; churchyard yew*
Where: *Opposite the junction for Monks Walk, off the B4024, HR8 2PL*

St Bartholomew's is a fine, interesting and much-loved church. The nave and side aisle roofs were renewed in 2009, the latest work in a building that dates from about 1220. The church is particularly famous for its monuments. One of the best of these is from the 14th century and is thought to be of Sir Hugh Audley and his wife Isolde. They lie in the Kyrle Chapel, where there are many monuments to the Kyrle family, who have lived at nearby Homme House since 1580. In the north aisle is another famous monument: that of Sir Walter de Helyon. Made of oak, his effigy dates from about 1360 and is very well preserved. Such wooden effigies are very rare. However, the colours were controversially renewed for an exhibition in 1972.

St Bartholomew's has one of the most celebrated churchyard yews in Britain: it is hollow and has a seat inside it. Despite its empty trunk and being very gnarled it is still growing; this yew is believed to be over 1,500 years old.

Pipe Aston St Giles

Why visit: *Setting; Norman tympanum*
Where: *By Whalley House, west of Ludlow, SY8 2HG*

Tiny, remote and very rural, the church here has a great treasure: a Norman tympanum showing the Lamb of God flanked by a griffin and a winged bull. It is thought to have been sculpted by one of the mason-sculptors who later worked at Kilpeck. The little church is full of interest, including several Norman architectural features, a 12th-century font, 14th-century nave roof and fragments of wall painting.

St Margarets St Margaret

Why visit: *Setting; outstanding rood loft*
Where: *St Margaret's Close, above the Golden Valley, off the B4347, HR2 0QW*

So often with Herefordshire churches setting plays a huge part in the impact of the building. Here, the little church is in a hamlet with an old farmhouse next door, and with wonderful views away to the south and west. The church is very simple: chancel and nave, with a wooden bell-turret over the west end. Its chief treasure is its beautiful rood loft, a rare survivor in a church, and particularly well preserved here. It dates from about 1520.

Shobdon
St John the Evangelist

Why visit: *Gothick confection; Norman ruins*
Where: *At Shobdon Court, north of Shobdon village, off the B4362; signposted to 'Shobdon Arches', HR6 9LZ; closed for essential works in 2011, check via the internet for the latest update*

From the outside St John's looks a normal parish church, but the inside is quite different – an iced and piped creation of the late 18th century. Whites and blues dominate the colour scheme and there are ogee arches everywhere. There is a three-decker pulpit, pews with Gothick

bench-ends, and a large private pew for the family of the estate, complete with large fireplace.

Of the Norman church that stood here before all that remains are the 'Shobdon Arches', re-erected fragments of carving put up when the church was being refurbished in the 18th century. They are very weatherworn now but were once among the best work of their kind by the Herefordshire School of mason-sculptors.

Weobley
St Peter and St Paul

Why visit: *Spire; rose window*
Where: *Church Road, north side of Weobley, HR4 8SD*

Weobley is famous for its half-timbered 'black-and-white' buildings, many of which line the main street, Broad Street. The tower and spire of the church are at the far end of the street, and are the most prominent element in the landscape. The spire is altogether impressive; very tall and connected to elaborate pinnacles by flying buttresses. The tower is 14th-century; the spire was rebuilt in 1675 and again in 1898.

Although the earliest church here was Norman, most of what can be seen today dates from the 13th and 14th centuries. Of special interest is the rose window in the south aisle. Near it is a coffin lid with foliage carving. Monuments include an effigy of Sir William Devereux from 1402, and a statue of Colonel Birch, MP, who died in 1691.

This page: *The pretty interior at Shobdon (left); Weobley's impressive spire (centre).*

Yarpole St Leonard

Why visit: *Detached bell-tower*
Where: *Green Lane, off the B4361, HR6 0BD*

This is a story of two halves. The first is about St Leonard's detached tower, which, after examination of is timbers by dendrochronology (tree-ring dating) can be dated very accurately to the winter of 1195–6. This makes it one of the oldest timber structures in Britain.

It is a fascinating building, made of four massive oak posts (each a single tree about 200 years old when felled), encased in a stone skirt wall that may be of the same date. The tower was altered in the 14th and 16th centuries. The church itself was virtually rebuilt in Victorian times.

Yarpole is a very small village, so the threatened loss of its shop and post office resulted in re-thinking the way the church was used. In 2010 part of it became a shop and post office. The rest of the church keeps its original function, and this may be a way forward for other churches that need to re-think their role and function in the 21st century.

ALSO IN THE AREA

Foy St Mary
Why visit: *Setting in a loop of the Wye; 16th- and 17th-century screen*

Hereford All Saints
Why visit: *Excellent town church dating from the 13th century onwards*

Holme Lacy St Cuthbert
Why visit: *16th- and 17th-century Scudamore monuments*

Peterchurch St Peter
Why visit: *Unusual internal arrangement of four parts; dramatic apse*

Richard's Castle
St Bartholomew CCT
Why visit: *Views; detached bell-tower*

Vowchurch St Bartholomew
Why visit: *Lovely setting; atmospheric interior; Norman font*

SOUTH WORCESTERSHIRE

Worcestershire once had more abbeys and priories than any other county, and three of them – Great Malvern, Little Malvern and Pershore – are included in this cluster of churches. These are impressive buildings, framed by the county's famously hilly southern and western landscapes. At the other end of the visual scale are delightful churches in village settings such as Elmley Castle and Besford.

Great Malvern Priory of St Mary and St Michael

Why visit: *England's best collection of medieval glass*
Where: *Church Street, WR14 2AY; open weekdays*

When the priory was founded in the 11th century, this part of Worcestershire was a densely wooded forest, probably as remote as anywhere in England at that time. The natural landscape of the Malvern Hills is still an important component in the look and feel of the priory and the town, with the slopes of the hills a prominent visual backdrop.

The remoteness probably helped to preserve the priory's treasures in the years after the Dissolution in the 16th century; elsewhere, wonderful stained glass of the kind still seen here was smashed as it was considered to be 'popish', or superstitious.

The core of today's priory church – all that is left of what had been a monastic foundation – is the Norman architecture

that can be seen in the nave and in the blocked south doorway. But much of the building we see now dates from a major rebuilding that happened in the last half of the 15th century.

The chancel, together with its enormous east window, probably dates to around 1440. The tower was complete by 1460. Work went on until 1500 and later to transform the priory church into a building on a par in some ways with Gloucester Cathedral.

Barely 40 years later Henry VIII's Dissolution brought a complete change. The townspeople bought the church for £20, while the rest of the priory buildings were either leased or sold off, often to be demolished.

Between 1540 and the 19th century very little work was done to maintain or repair the church, which meant that much that might otherwise have been 'modernised' or removed was left in place. Between 1860 and 1915 an huge amount of repair and restoration work took place, including repairs to the stained glass.

And it is the stained glass that is the finest treasure at Great Malvern: it is among the finest collections of medieval glass in England. It can be seen in many of the windows, particularly the east window, the chancel clerestory, St Anne's Chapel, north transept and west window. It was installed between 1450 and 1501. Scenes include several with Mary at their centre, the Passion and Crucifixion of Jesus, and Old Testament stories. Renowned figures of the time are shown, some dead, some living. These include Prince Arthur and Henry VII.

Many other wonderful things can be seen in the church, including medieval stalls and misericords, a remarkable collection of medieval wall and floor tiles (made in kilns near the priory), and many monuments.

Beckford St John the Baptist

Why visit: *Norman doorways with enigmatic carvings*
Where: *Main Street, GL20 7AD*

This limestone church stands in an attractive village on the eastern slopes of Bredon Hill. It comprises a central tower, nave, chancel and porch. The nave is

This page: The Priory at Great Malvern (left), and its superb stained glass (above).

Norman, and has two excellent Norman doorways. The southern one is better preserved, protected by a 15th-century porch. Its tympanum is particularly interesting, with a carving of a cross, above which are a circle and a bird, and flanked by two strange creatures. As so often, the meaning of these symbols and creatures is open to interpretation. The Norman north doorway is weathered, but shows the Harrowing of Hell.

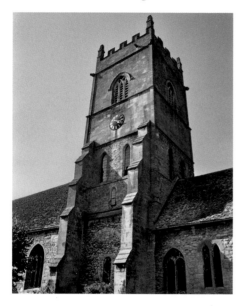

There is further Norman stonework on the chancel tower arch, with zig-zag decoration, and also with human heads and a centaur. Among the furnishings are a number of 15th-century bench-ends and a font of about the same date.

Besford St Peter

Why visit: *Woodwork of many kinds from many centuries*
Where: *St Peter's Lane, WR8 9AP*

At first glance, Besford's little church looks Victorian, as indeed are the neat wooden-framed and shingled bellcote and the chancel. But a closer look at the sides of the nave shows it to be timber-framed, and this 14th-century structure is unique in Worcestershire.

Inside the theme is wood: from the roof, to the pews, pulpit and altar rails; from the walls – panelled using old pews – to the beautiful, original medieval rood loft. Wood features too in one of the monuments – that to Richard Harwell of Besford Court, who died in 1576

aged 15. His alabaster effigy is surrounded by a wooden lattice. And there is a painted wooden triptych in the nave. It dates from the end of the 16th century, and its panels shows scenes that are reminders of the passage of time and the inevitability of death.

Croome d'Abitot
St Mary Magdalene CCT

Why visit: *An attractive 'period piece' and a telling illustration of 18th-century architectural and landscaping trends*
Where: *In Croome Park, off the A38 or A4104 (M5 junction 7), WR8 9DW*

The 6th Earl of Coventry, of Croome Park, clearly kept up with the times and subscribed to (or perhaps helped set) the trend for sweeping away the old. In the 1750s, he replaced his Jacobean house, commissioned Capability Brown (his first landscape assignment), demolished the old church and built this one instead.

Completed in 1763, the new hilltop church in Bath stone was one of Brown's planned 'eye-catchers', and an early and successful attempt at Gothic Revival. It would have been designed to resemble an elaborate, almost fantastical medieval church, when seen from a distance.

The airy Georgian Gothic interior, like that of the earl's new house, was by Robert Adam. Slender quatrefoil piers lead up to an elliptical vault with moulded plasterwork and coving. Decorative ogee-shaped plasterwork frames give the windows and chancel arch a gothic touch. Note the elegant pulpit, on a slender stem and with an elaborately carved tester. The chancel serves as a mausoleum to the Coventry family, and includes a number of ornate monuments from the old church.

Elmley Castle St Mary

Why visit: *Norman carvings and other early details; 17th- and 18th-century memorials*
Where: *Parkwood, Elmley Castle, south-west of Evesham, WR10 3HT*

The 'castle' – long since ruined – in the name of this lovely village was that of the Beauchamp family and once stood

just above the church, on the north slopes of Bredon Hill. The Beauchamp coat of arms appears on the 15th-century font. From the outside, St Mary's appears to be of the same period, with its battlements and its Perpendicular tower, north transept and porch. But a look inside the porch reveals fragments of Norman carvings – a pig and a rabbit – that betray the building's much earlier origins, and the chancel's outside walls have herringbone masonry that is probably from the 11th century.

Two fine monuments are in the north transept. One is a dignified memorial to William Savage, who died in 1616. It features his son, daughter-in-law and grandchildren, all carved in loving detail. Opposite, in contrasting style, stands the huge early 18th-century pedimented tomb of the first Earl of Coventry, with his wigged effigy framed by marble columns and allegorical figures.

Little Malvern St Giles

Why visit: *Impressive building in a spectacular setting, with many medieval features remaining unaltered*
Where: *Beside the A4104 on the eastern side of the Malvern Hills, WR14 4JN*

Although a sandstone tower and chancel are the only remaining parts of the priory church here, they make an imposing building, set against a wooded slope of the Malvern Hills, with the Severn valley away to the east. The priory was founded in the 12th century, but the Perpendicular features of the present church date from a

This page: Beckford tower (left); Little Malvern's St Giles (above).

1480s rebuilding by Bishop Alcock of Worcester after he visited the priory to investigate its poor state.

The exceptional east window still has most of the glass that was installed at that time to commemorate the church's restoration. It depicts members of the family of King Edward IV and Elizabeth Woodville, reflecting Bishop Alcock's royal appointments: he was president of the royal council and Chancellor of England. Other medieval work that survives in the priory includes locally made tiles, the choir stalls and screen, and some re-set roof bosses.

Pershore Abbey (Holy Cross and St Eadburgha)

Why visit: *Magnificent abbey church*
Where: *Church Row, WR10 1BL*

It seems incredible that this soaring church, which is still glorious both inside and out, should be a mere fragment of the one that once stood here. The abbey of today comprises only the chancel, south transept and crossing tower, now supported by great buttresses where once the Norman nave stood.

The building carries distinct echoes of two English cathedrals: the tower is similar to Salisbury's and the 13th-century arcades to those of Wells. This was one of only three Norman churches in England to have been fully vaulted in stone – though two fires in the 13th century destroyed the original barrel-vault and the tower, which was rebuilt in 1330. The chancel arches and vault were replaced in Gothic style, contrasting superbly with the Norman crossing.

Look up inside the tower to see an extraordinary piece of design by Sir George Gilbert Scott, who restored the abbey in the 1860s. Instead of a belfry floor, there is a suspended platform high inside the lantern, so that the inside of the tower, with its beautiful traceried panelling, is visible from below.

Ripple St Mary

Why visit: *Lovely setting; fine set of 15th-century misericords*
Where: *Station Road: on the eastern edge of Ripple village, off the A38 leading north from junction 1 of the M50, GL20 6HA*

The distinctive appearance of the church in this village near the River Severn is due mainly to the contrasting balustraded top section of the tower. An 18th-century afterthought in sandstone, it looks surprisingly attractive on the large 12th- and 13th-century cruciform building of much paler lias stone.

Inside, the highlight is the choir stalls, installed for the canons of Ripple's mother church, Worcester Priory, who would have taken services here. The set of 16 misericords is a medieval country calendar, depicting the labours of the months and the four elements, including a charming one of the man in the moon.

Wickhamford St John the Baptist

Why visit: *Picture-book setting, with interesting associations*
Where: *Sally Close, at the north end of Wickhamford, off the A44 south-east of Evesham, WR11 7SD*

Wickhamford's handsome limestone church makes a wonderful composition with the large half-timbered manor house next door, bought in 1549 by the Sandys family. It had formerly been a grange of Evesham Abbey. It later became the home of George Lees-Milne, who restored the church in 1949, and his son James, the architectural historian and conservationist, who was a leading light of the National Trust in its early days.

A previous restoration in the 17th century gave the church much of its character and its furnishings, but the core is 13th- and 14th-century. A medieval wall painting survives in the chancel, where there is also a 17th-century memorial to Sir Samuel and Sir Edwin Sandys and their wives. Father and son both died in the same year, 1623.

This page: The amazing soaring interior of Pershore Abbey (left); St John the Baptist at Wickhamford (above).

ALSO IN THE AREA

Churchill St Michael CCT
Why visit: *Tiny, atmospheric medieval village church*

Evesham St Lawrence CCT
Why visit: *16th-century church with Victorian and later stained glass*

MONUMENTS AND TOMBS

Some experts have estimated that there are 18,000 significant monuments in Britain's parish churches, an astonishing number and a remarkable record of changing religious attitudes, ideals, fashions and art. They range in date from the 12th century to now, and can be found in churches almost everywhere, including in those that otherwise are not of great importance. Some are overwhelming in their size and presence, but perhaps the most moving are often the most modest.

Norman beginnings

The earliest monuments to individuals are carvings of figures on top of coffin lids, dating from Norman times. These developed into carved reliefs, but fully sculpted effigies did not appear until the 13th century.

Then, important people's effigies were placed on tomb chests. Such figures may not have been true likenesses of the person, as the heraldry and symbols associated with the effigy would have made the person's identity clear. However, the clothing and other details such as armour and head-dresses are accurate, meaning that monuments can be used to learn a great deal about the lives of the people commemorated.

Early monuments are most often in alabaster (from Derbyshire) or Purbeck marble. A few wooden ones survive,

including that to Sir Alexander Culpeper and his wife at Goudhurst, Kent, which is still brightly coloured. He died in 1537.

At about that time Renaissance ideas began to influence art, and so, for example, monuments without effigies began to be made. However, the popularity of effigies only dipped, as exuberant Jacobean monuments show.

By the 18th century marble was the preferred material, and the colour used was considered less important than the quality of the workmanship. Religion also often seemed to take a back seat, with memorials

This page: One of the 16th-century Culpeper monuments at Goudhurst, Kent (above); the monument to Thomas Spenser at Yarnton, Oxfordshire (right).

Brasses

Monuments in the form of flat sheets of engraved brass set into stone, brasses have been made in England since the 13th century, and are still made for churches today. There are more brasses in England than in the whole of the rest of Europe.

The most commonly depicted figures are knights and clerics. A fine, very early, example of a knight is Sir John D'Abernon at Stoke D'Abernon, Surrey, dating from 1277, while a superb priest's brass is that of Laurence de St Maur, at Higham Ferrers, Northamptonshire. It dates from 1337.

Some churches have particularly fine collections of brasses. Places worth a special mention include Cobham, Kent *(right)*, and Northleach, Gloucestershire.

There was a revival of interest in brasses in the 19th century, when architects and artists such as Augustus Pugin, inspired by Gothic ideals, created brasses rich in colour and ornament.

with few if any obvious Christian elements. An example is the monument to Sir Thomas Spenser at Yarnton, Oxfordshire. He is depicted life-size, in draped, Classical clothing, flanked by his wife and son, who are also life-size. The monument dominates all around it.

One of the most celebrated sculptors of the 18th and early 19th centuries was John Flaxman (1755–1826), who initially made his living working for the Wedgwood ceramics company. His ambitions to become a 'proper' sculptor were realised after he visited Italy.

Another of the famous monumental sculptors was Sir Richard Westmacott (1775–1856), one of whose monuments can be found at Stanford on Avon, Northamptonshire. The figure is of Robert Otway Cave and shows him asleep among his books. The work of such artists was often imitated by lesser sculptors, and this resulted in a rash of over-sentimentalised, maudlin monuments that sometimes overshadow the brilliant spectrum of church monumental sculpture.

Collections of monuments

Some churches have outstanding collections of monuments. Especially renowned are the 'Aldworth Giants', a collection of nine effigies dating from the mid-1350s at Aldworth, Berkshire. These effigies to members of the De La Beche family were already famous by the reign of Elizabeth I, who made a detour especially to see them.

Bottesford, Leicestershire, has monuments to the earls of Rutland from the 1st to the 8th, dating from 1543 to 1679. That to the 8th earl is by Grinling Gibbons. At Elmley Castle in Worcestershire, is the monument of 1631 to Sir William Savage, his son and grandchildren. In the same church is the early 18th-century monument to the 1st Earl of Coventry.

At Strelley, Nottinghamshire, the monument of about 1410 dedicated to Sir Sampson Strelley and his wife shows him wearing armour and her clothed in a fine gown. They are shown at peace and holding hands in the most tender way.

There are other Strelley monuments in the church, including a particularly fine one from the early 1500s to John de Strelley and his wife Sanchia. They are shown praying together rather than holding hands.

This page: *A view taking in just some of the monuments at Bottesford, Leicester.*

SOUTHERN SHROPSHIRE

The sandstone country of southern Shropshire, with the valleys of the Rivers Teme and Severn, forms the backdrop to several of the churches here. Some are in villages, amid historic half-timbered buildings; others surrounded by rolling fields and parkland. Ludlow's sumptuous parish church may seem far from rural, but like many medieval town churches it might have been a more modest affair without the wealth generated by a sought-after commodity from the countryside around: the wool that sustained the cloth trade of the Middle Ages.

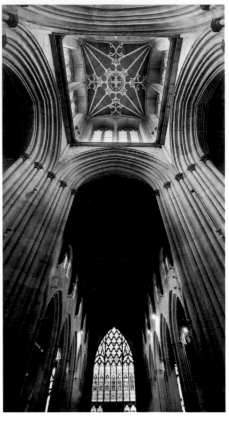

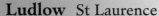

Ludlow St Laurence

Why visit: *Dazzling medieval craftsmanship in stone, wood and glass in almost every part of the building.*
Where: *College Street, behind the Buttercross, SY8 1AN*

Ludlow possesses one of the great parish churches of England, and one of the largest. St Laurence's is known, with good reason, as the Cathedral of the Marches. With the castle, the lofty 15th-century tower stands proud in any distant view of the town, though it can only be glimpsed from the warren of old streets and passages that lead to it: the best view is from the north.

Set in a loop of the River Teme, Ludlow's hill was always a natural site for a stronghold in these turbulent border lands and the first church was built soon after the Norman castle of 1085. There are few obvious remains of that church or of its 12th-century successor, which was nearly as big as the present building. Improvements and additions were made through the 13th and 14th centuries, including the unusual hexagonal south porch (one of only three of its shape in the country). By the late Middle Ages, Ludlow's burgeoning prosperity from cloth and other trades enabled the various guilds to be generous in funding a transformation of the church into the masterpiece of Perpendicular style, which had emerged by the late 15th century.

The work touched almost every aspect of the building: the chancel, which is just as long as the nave; the west front; and the tower, with its soaring fluted arches flooded with light from the large windows above. The height of the nave and transepts was increased. Interior detailing included exquisitely carved roof bosses and corbels, as well as furnishings such as the misericords in the choir stalls, which portray a whole cast of colourful characters: human, animal and mythical.

A good deal of medieval glass has survived, restored in the 19th century but not spoiled. The east window in the chancel depicts the life of St Laurence, while the Lady Chapel, with its excellent screen, has a restored 14th-century Tree of Jesse window. There is more fine medieval glass in the windows of the north (Palmer) chapel.

St Laurence's has a fitting collection of elaborate 16th- and 17th-century monuments, some with finely costumed effigies. Outside, near the north door, is a wall memorial to the poet A.E. Housman (1859–1936). He is also commemorated by a cherry tree in the churchyard, recollecting famous lines from *A Shropshire Lad*.

This page: *St Laurence's commanding exterior (left), and dramatically high stone fluted arches (above).*

Bridgnorth
St Mary Magdalene

Why visit: *Classical church of the 1790s, designed by Thomas Telford*
Where: *East Castle Street, WV16 4AQ*

There are two church towers that punctuate Bridgnorth's pleasing hillside townscape, which slopes steeply up from the River Severn. St Leonard's – now cared for by the Churches Conservation Trust – is Victorian Gothic and of red sandstone. St Mary's, less than a century earlier, is a complete contrast. This grand but restrained Classical building of pale grey stone was designed by the engineer Thomas Telford when he was county surveyor for Shropshire.

Built in 1792–4, the church is aligned north–south, with the altar at the south end. The unusual orientation was chosen to give the façade more impact from East Castle Street. Telford's original interior was light, stark and simple, and any embellishments are later additions, including the Victorian chancel screen and pulpit, and the apse of 1875. The stations of the cross in the side aisles were installed in 1987.

Bromfield
St Mary the Virgin

Why visit: *Lovely setting; painted chancel ceiling*
Where: *Off to the south of the A49, north-west of Ludlow, SY8 2JP*

A pleasant hour's walk above the River Teme leads from Ludlow to St Mary's, which began life as a Norman priory church and still shares its riverside setting with the old Priory Gatehouse. With its sturdy stone base supporting a half-timbered upper floor, this looks as though it could have been uprooted from rural Normandy. The church was part of a private house for more than 100 years after the Dissolution, but a mid-17th-century renovation returned it to its rightful purpose. In 1672, Thomas Francis painted the ceiling of the restored chancel with a stylised assemblage of clouds, angels and scrolls bearing biblical texts. Also of interest is the ornate gilded Victorian triptych above the altar.

Claverley All Saints

Why visit: *Medieval church in attractive village setting; early wall paintings*
Where: *Church Street, off the A454 between Wolverhampton and Bridgnorth, WV5 7DS*

This church has pride of place in the historic hilltop village – making a photogenic composition with the black-and-white houses around it. The chancel is believed to stand on Roman foundations, and the oldest visible parts of the building are early Norman.

Inside, the north arcade is Norman and the south Gothic. The long 14th-century chancel suggests that this was a church of importance – a fact borne out by the varied collection of 15th- and 16th-century monuments to distinguished local families.

Today, visitors travel here to see the outstanding medieval wall paintings, especially the long, early 13th-century frieze high on the north wall of the nave. With its representations of battling knights on horseback, it has been compared in style to the Bayeux tapestry.

Kinlet St John the Baptist

Why visit: *Church of Norman origin with several good 15th- and 16th-century monuments*
Where: *About a mile north-west of Kinlet village, in the grounds of Kinlet Hall (now Moffats School), DY12 3BL*

Kinlet church no longer has a village around it, but stands in a rather remote location in the grounds of Kinlet Hall. The medieval church is distinctive for its little black-and-white half-timbered clerestory: an unusual 15th-century take on a vernacular building style that is typical of Shropshire. Inside is a fine collection of Tudor and earlier monuments to the Blounts of Kinlet Hall and other local families. Have a look at the canopied alabaster tomb of local squire Sir George Blount, kneeling with his family. He died in 1584, and one local legend claims that his ghost is contained in a sealed bottle in the base of the tomb.

Morville St Gregory

Why visit: *Historic church with much surviving Norman work; associated with* The Morville Hours
Where: *Off to the south of the A458, before Morville Hall, WV16 5NB*

A backdrop of wooded hills and parkland, with the grand stone buildings of neighbouring Morville Hall, create an idyllic setting for this ancient country church. Originally a Saxon minster, it later became a cell of Shrewsbury Abbey, with a prior in residence until 1540. Records show that a new parish church had been dedicated in 1118, and some features of that church remain, including the chancel arch, the south door and perhaps the richly carved Norman font. The bells of the church, and its monastic past, were the inspiration for Katherine Swift's popular book *The Morville Hours*. Published in 2008, it is about the garden the author created at the Dower House at Morville Hall.

This page: Bridgnorth's Classical interior, in soft colours.

ALSO IN THE AREA

Aston Eyre
Why visit: *12th-century church with a well-preserved Norman tympanum*

Quatt St Andrew
Why visit: *Interesting church with a medieval core and Georgian brick exterior; 17th-century monuments*

Stottesdon St Mary
Why visit: *Norman church with an outstanding font from about 1160*

AROUND SHREWSBURY

For a town of its size, Shrewsbury is amazingly well endowed with churches of almost every period. At least a dozen are within easy walking distance of the town centre, including three that are rather grand and special in their different ways. Within half an hour's drive of Shrewsbury, a great variety of more modest Shropshire churches will repay a visit. Each has outstanding elements, memorable either for its architectural or historical interest, and sometimes both.

Shrewsbury St Mary CCT

Why visit: *Large church with clear and interesting evidence of its development from Norman times; outstanding collection of stained glass*
Where: *St Mary's Place, off St Mary's Street, SY1 1DX; not open Sundays*

St Mary's is as good an introduction to the development of Gothic architecture through the ages as you are likely to find anywhere. It stands on the site of a Saxon church, and has been Shrewsbury's largest for a long time. The spire is one of the tallest in England, topping a tower that has very clear Norman origins in its lower part. A walk round the outside from the splendid Norman west doorway takes in the lancet windows of the transepts (Early English), the 14th-century windows of the Trinity Chapel (Decorated) and the 15th-century ones of the south aisle (Perpendicular).

The interior has a similarly wide range of work. In the nave, slender shafted piers of early Gothic style support great rounded Norman arches. The arcades lead up to a pointed Gothic chancel arch that frames the enormous Decorated east window. Here can be found one of the treasures of Shrewsbury, a superb Tree of Jesse in 14th-century stained glass. The window is only a part of St Mary's superb collection of stained glass of different periods, including much fine German and Flemish glass.

Shrewsbury Holy Cross (Shrewsbury Abbey)

Why visit: *Norman west tower with Perpendicular window*
Where: *Abbey Foregate, SY2 6BS*

Roger de Montgomery, 1st Earl of Shrewsbury, was a close associate of William the Conqueror and one of the great landowners of post-Conquest Britain, with holdings in many counties. Roger owned most of Shropshire, and it was he who founded this Benedictine abbey, on the site of a small Saxon church, in 1083. He is said to have been buried here when he died in 1094.

The abbey church became a place of pilgrimage after relics of the Welsh Saint Winefride were brought here. It remained important until the Dissolution, when the east end was demolished, leaving the nave to serve as a parish church. Fortunately the mighty Norman tower survived. The west doorway, at its base, would seem remarkable in any other church, but here it is eclipsed by the astonishing Perpendicular window above it, which almost spans the entire width of the tower with its seven lights and ornate tracery. The statue at the top depicts

Edward III. Plans for a substantial 19th-century restoration of the abbey church resulted in the successful rebuilding of the chancel in 1887, but the rest of the work was not completed. Most of the interior furnishings and fittings, such as the monuments, have come from other churches in Shrewsbury or farther afield.

The font is reputedly made from a Roman capital from nearby Wroxeter. Among the names on the war memorial in the church is that of Wilfred Owen, the World War I poet.

Shrewsbury St Chad

Why visit: *Stately Classical parish church built to a unique design*
Where: *St Chad's Terrace, SY1 1TH*

This rather extraordinary parish church, set on a spacious green hill above the River Severn, stands in stark contrast to Shrewsbury's medieval streets and mainly Tudor townscape. Dating from 1790–2, it is a Classical church, and is built from a

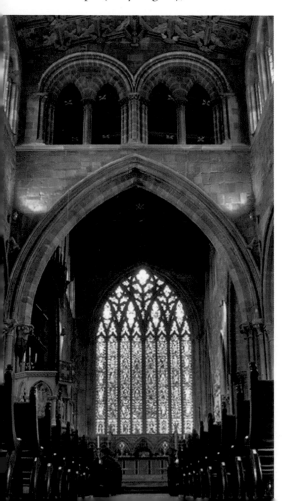

This page: The view towards St Mary's east window (left); the font of Holy Cross, possibly made from a Roman column (above).

pale stone that sets it quite apart from the red sandstone and half-timbering that are the usual materials of Shropshire. What is more, it is a Classical church with a difference: the nave is completely round.

Opinions differ as to how successful a building this is. The tower, from some angles, looks almost unrelated to the rest of the church, being separated from it by a rounded antechamber. But the interior is light, bright and uncluttered. Slender white columns (made of local cast iron) support a gallery that sweeps right round the church.

Acton Burnell St Mary

Why visit: *Unspoilt 13th-century church with much fine-quality craftsmanship*
Where: *East of the village centre, near Acton Burnell Castle, SY5 7PE*

Acton Burnell Castle was the home of Robert Burnell, a close associate of Edward I who became Lord Chancellor and Bishop of Bath and Wells. Sharing its setting here with the atmospheric ruin of his fortified house stands the pleasing early Gothic church that he built in the 1270s.

It has survived basically unchanged, though the attractive little tower is a Victorian addition. The church is by no means ostentatious, but the craftsmanship and materials have all the hallmarks of a wealthy and fashionable patron of the time. These include fine detailing, Purbeck marble shafts and some windows that have progressed from Early English plain lancets towards the Decorated style, with trefoil and cinquefoil patterns. Some

This page: St Chad's unusual circular nave – the rounded antechamber to the tower can also be seen from this side.

of the original medieval floor tiles remain, and there is a tomb with a fine brass of 1382 to Nicholas Burnell, the 1st Lord Burnell. The much more elaborate 16th-century tomb in the north transept is that of Sir Richard Lee and his wife.

Melverley St Peter

Why visit: *Unusual 15th-century timber-framed church beside the River Vyrnwy*
Where: *Church Lane, west of Shrewsbury near the Welsh border, SY10 8DE*

The Welsh border country has timber-framed buildings of many kinds, but only a few are churches. Here, in a tiny hamlet right on the Welsh border, is a rather special example, black-and-white both inside and out, and wonderfully picturesque and rustic-looking in its setting. Built from local oak in 1406 and restored in 1878, the church stands right beside the river: too close for comfort, perhaps, especially in the floods of 2007.

The interior is divided into three by oak frames: one supports a gallery while the other serves as a chancel screen. The windows are mainly Victorian, and there is a slender Jacobean pulpit, panelled and beautifully carved.

Moreton Corbet St Bartholomew

Why visit: *Dramatic setting; fine interior features commemorating the Corbets of Moreton Corbet Castle*
Where: *Opposite Castle Farm, off to the east of the B5063, SY4 4DW*

The ruins that stand beside St Bartholomew's look far more dramatic than the church itself: one part is the gaunt shell of an elegant Elizabethan mansion, the other a crumbling fragment of a medieval castle, with a later gatehouse. But the story of the Norman church is bound up with theirs, so be sure to go inside. The building was continually improved and embellished, often extravagantly, by many generations of the Corbet family, who lived in the castle. Different generations of the family added features from the grand 14th-century south aisle to the squire's pew of 1778,

and a Victorian restoration of the whole church in 1883 was funded by Sir Vincent Corbet. The fine collection of Corbet monuments is worth a close look. Their family emblem, an elephant and castle, appears on some, and Corbet elephants feature in the reredos, which is by Sir Ninian Comper. He also designed the east window.

Wroxeter St Andrew CCT

Why visit: *Ancient church built on an important Roman site, with good Jacobean woodwork and Elizabethan monuments*
Where: *In the middle of Wroxeter village, off the B4380 south-east of Shrewsbury, SY5 6PH*

Wroxeter village stands on the site of Viroconium, a town of some 5,000 people that was one of the most important settlements of Roman Britain. St Andrew's has 11th-century origins and incorporates fragments of ancient masonry, such as the huge Roman stones in the north wall of the nave.

Near the top of the south wall is an embedded fragment of an Anglo-Saxon cross shaft. The font was carved out of the capital of a Roman column, and the churchyard gateway has Roman pillars on either side. Later work inside the church includes fine Jacobean fittings such as box pews and pulpit, and an outstanding collection of Tudor monuments.

ALSO IN THE AREA

Battlefield
St Mary Magdalene CCT
Why visit: *A beautiful 15th-century church that was endowed by Henry IV after the Battle of Shrewsbury in 1403, as a poignant memorial to the slain*

Condover
St Andrew and St Mary
Why visit: *Hammerbeam roof; monuments*

Meole Brace Holy Trinity
Why visit: *Outstanding stained glass by William Morris and Sir Edward Burne-Jones*

STAFFORDSHIRE TOWN AND COUNTRY

It would be hard to think of a greater variety of churches than this group in Staffordshire. There are urban churches ranging from impressive former collegiate foundations in Penkridge in the south, to one of England's largest Methodist chapels in Hanley, Stoke-on-Trent in the north of the county. In between are rural churches varying in style from High Victorian at Hoar Cross to the historic village church of nearby Abbots Bromley, with a most unusual church at Ingestre, thought to be the work of Sir Christopher Wren.

Hoar Cross Holy Angels

Why visit: *A Victorian masterpiece by G.F. Bodley*
Where: *Maker Lane, the road leading south out of Hoar Cross, DE13 8QR*

This amazing Gothic Revival church is quite a surprising find in a remote hamlet in rural Staffordshire. With good reason it is sometimes known locally as 'the cathedral in the woods', the 'woods' being the formerly vast ancient woodland of Needwood Forest.

It was built as a memorial to Hugo Meynell Ingram of nearby Hoar Cross Hall, a rambling Victorian mansion that is now a health spa. The church was commissioned by Meynell Ingram's wife Emily, widowed after only seven years of marriage when he died in a hunting accident. Her choice of architect was G.F. Bodley, the leading 19th-century

exponent of Gothic Revival style. This church is considered to be his finest work. Begun in 1872, in collaboration with Bodley's partner Thomas Garner, the church has an imposing tower (disciplined yet not severe), and a huge, tall chancel that unusually for a church, faces south rather than east.

The interior, suffused with a dim, pinkish light from the colour of the sandstone, gradually reveals a very fine and harmonious collection of High Victorian design and craftsmanship. This includes the roof vaulting to the delicate chancel screen and the exquisitely carved stone reredos with its figures of saints and angels.

The ornately decorated organ was built from parts of a former organ from Bangor Cathedral. A collection of Meynell family tombs and memorials in the Chantry chapel include those of Hugo and Emily Meynell Ingram.

Abbots Bromley
St Nicholas

Why visit: *Historic church associated with the Abbots Bromley Horn Dance*
Where: *Set back from the High Street, behind the Goat's Head pub, WS15 3BP*

One of the most unusual features of St Nicholas's is six huge pairs of painted reindeer antlers hanging in the north chapel: for hundreds of years they have been among the essential, rather remarkable, props for Abbots Bromley's famous Horn Dance. It takes place each September, and the church is the traditional starting point for the dancers, who travel some 10 miles around the neighbouring villages and farms during the course of the day. The origins of the church may even predate those of the ancient dance: a building was recorded as being here in 1002 and the list of priests goes back to 1086. The medieval church, dating from the 12th and 13th centuries, was extensively restored during the 19th century but much older work is still evident. The Classical tower was built in 1688 to replace its collapsed predecessor.

Hanley Bethesda Methodist
Chapel HCT

Why visit: *A fine and large 19th-century town chapel, currently being expertly restored*
Where: *On the corner of Albion Street and Bethesda Street, ST1 1QF*

This huge 19th-century chapel was once the most popular place of worship in what was to become the city of Stoke-on-Trent, a federation of the six towns of the Potteries. The building largely dates

from an 1819 renovation of an original chapel of 1798, which accommodated 600 worshippers. Enlarged twice to meet the growing demand for seats, it eventually held 2,000 people, many of them in a vast tiered oval gallery – making it one of the largest chapels outside London. The stuccoed frontage on Albion Street, Italianate in style and with a grand Classical portico, was added in 1859.

The chapel was closed to the public after many years of deterioration in the 20th century but is now undergoing a major restoration programme, thanks to the Historic Chapels Trust. The restored building will find a variety of uses from concerts to film shows and from weddings to conferences.

Ingestre St Mary

Why visit: *The only known church outside London designed by Sir Christopher Wren*
Where: *At the end of the cul-de-sac lane leading to Ingestre Hall, off the A51 between Rugeley and Stone, ST18 0RF*

Sir Walter Chetwynd of Ingestre Hall, the 17th-century politician and antiquary, was a friend of Sir Christopher Wren and a fellow member of the Royal Society. So when a drawing labelled 'Mr Chetwynd's tower' turned up among Wren's papers, it began to seem fairly certain that this fine church of the 1670s was indeed the work of the architect of St Paul's Cathedral.

The quality of the interior at Ingestre, such as the carved screen and the exquisite plaster ceilings, is certainly worthy of a building designed by a master. The richly carved pulpit and tester are by the renowned Dutch-born wood-carver Grinling Gibbons, and carry his peapods motif. The Chetwynd coat of arms sits above the door; several family tombs and monuments are in the church.

Penkridge St Michael and All Angels

Why visit: *A handsome and important church with a long and interesting history; good collection of monuments*
Where: *Church Road, off the A449, between the station and river, ST19 5DN*

The church at Penkridge had already been granted collegiate status by Royal Charter in the 10th century, indicating its importance from early times. It was a wealthy foundation with extensive lands and quite a collection of buildings, including a chapter house and a refectory, close to the site of the present church. Most of these buildings were lost at the time of the Reformation, though the Old Deanery and Church Farm date from the church's collegiate days.

The structure of the present handsome and rather grand sandstone church dates from the 13th century, though the tower and porch are a century later. Alterations during the 16th century gave the exterior much of its Perpendicular character but the church retains the original 13th-century arcades inside, and the east window is in the Decorated style. There are some distinguished 16th- and 17th-century monuments, notably the double-decker tomb of a father and son both called Sir Edward Littleton, of nearby Pillaton Hall, who died in 1610 and 1629 respectively.

Wolverhampton St Peter

Why visit: *A grand and historic 15th-century church; fine original stone pulpit; many monuments*
Where: *Off Wulfruna Street, WV1 1TS*

Standing, cathedral-like, on high ground in central Wolverhampton, St Peter's is one of the great city parish churches of the Midlands. A plaque in the porch records the endowment of a monastery by a 'noble matron' called Wulfrun at 'Hamtun' in 994. Her statue stands outside the west end of the church. The oldest part of the present church dates from the 12th century, but most of the present church is 15th-century except for the chancel, which was rebuilt in 1867.

The various chapels contain an interesting collection of monuments spanning many generations, from the bronze statue of Sir Richard Leveson, who helped to defeat the Spanish Armada, to John Marston (1836–1918), a Victorian manufacturer and a pioneer of the early days of the motor industry here.

Don't miss the carved faces on the choir stalls, nor the wonderful stone pulpit. Carved in about 1450, it still has its original staircase, curving round one of the sandstone piers. It is guarded by a large and mournful-looking stone lion.

This page: Fine plaster moulding at Ingestre (left); battlemented splendour at Penkridge (centre); Wolverhampton's grand parish church (above).
Opposite page: High Victorian at Hoar Cross (left); the interior of Hanley's Methodist Chapel (right).

ALSO IN THE AREA

Mavesyn Ridware St Nicholas
Why visit: *Almost two churches in one – a combination of medieval and Georgian, with remarkable monuments to the Mavesyn family*

Tutbury St Mary
Why visit: *Norman priory church with outstanding 12th-century west doorway*

SANDSTONE AND TIMBER IN CHESHIRE

Cheshire's churches are remarkably diverse in character and feel, but sandstone and wood unite them. Several of the churches selected here are as grand as any in England. They include St Mary's in Nantwich and St John's in Chester. Much humbler in appearance, but as important and as interesting, are the churches at Lower Peover and Marton, perhaps the two oldest timber-framed churches in Europe.

Nantwich St Mary

Why visit: *One of the finest parish churches in England*
Where: *Town Square, CW5 5RQ*

St Mary's is Cheshire's finest parish church. Like so many Cheshire churches it is built of sandstone, and it dates largely from the mid- to late-14th century. Weathering has scoured some of the exterior stonework, adding to the character of the building, which is crowned by an octagonal bell-tower. Inside the church, the stonework is almost as pristine as it was when first built, and since most is 14th-century it feels harmonious.

From the nave with its elegant piers and arches, a tall arch leads through to the choir and chancel. The choir stalls are of the same age as the church and are among the most splendid of their kind, with tall canopies and, underneath the seats, one of the most famous sets of misericords in England. These include figures of two men wrestling, a fox in robes and with a hunting bow, and a

bird-like creature with a human face for its rear end. The stone pulpit here also dates from the 14th century.

Among contemporary additions to the church are a set of kneelers that include images of tractors, cars and a diesel train.

Bunbury St Boniface

Why visit: *Church packed with interest from the 14th century to the present day*
Where: *On the corner of Bowers Gate Road and Wyche Road, CW6 9PN*

Although there has been a church here since Saxon times, much of the story of Bunbury's church revolves around a colourful 14th-century knight called Sir Hugh de Calveley. He founded a college and chantry here in 1386 after a life spent as a fighting soldier, during which he had gained both fame and notoriety. Sir Hugh was said to be 2m (7ft) tall, with the appetite of two men and the fighting ability of 10. His tomb and effigy are in the church, still surrounded by the original spiked railings, eight of which were made to hold candles.

Much of the church was rebuilt and subsequent work carried out in the 15th century. Disaster struck in 1940 when an enemy plane returning from a raid on Liverpool dropped a bomb that seriously damaged the church, including blowing out the windows. Impassioned fundraising meant that the church was eventually fully restored, and this included new stained glass designed by Christopher Webb in the 1950s. The east window shows bold and colourful local scenes with people in 1950s clothes, as well as biblical scenes and characters.

There is much else to see in the church, including the brightly painted tomb of Sir George Beeston, a descendant of Sir Hugh de Calveley. Like Sir Hugh, he was a warrior, best known for his role in fighting the Spanish Armada. He died in 1601 and was possibly as old as 101. In the south aisle is a carved figure of Jane Johnson, who died in 1741. The sculpture was buried in the churchyard when a rector took exception to its generous figure. It was dug up and rescued in 1882.

Chester St John

Why visit: *Impressive Norman church, once a cathedral*
Where: *Vicar's Lane, CH1 1SN*

As well as its cathedral Chester has at least six ancient churches, several of them now no longer serving as such. Two, St Peter's (of many ages and possibly with Roman masonry in its fabric) and St John's are of particular interest, and are the joint parish churches of Chester.

St John's was a cathedral for a short time in the 11th century, and its surviving Norman architecture is on a cathedral scale. The building fell into ruin twice: in the 16th century, when it only survived at all because it had become a parish church, and in the 19th century. What remains is very impressive, particularly the great Norman piers in the nave. The church still plays an active role in the life of Chester after 1,000 years.

This page: *St Mary, Nantwich, with its octagonal tower.*

Daresbury All Saints

Why visit: *Lewis Carroll connections*
Where: *Daresbury Lane, the turning opposite the pub, WA4 4AE*

Daresbury and its church are most well known because of the connection with Charles Lutwidge Dodgson, world famous as Lewis Carroll, author of the *Alice* books. His father was vicar at Daresbury; Charles was born here in 1832 and baptised in the church.

Built of sandstone, most of the church was rebuilt in the 1870s, but the handsome tower is from the 1500s. Inside, panels from the 16th-century rood screen, destroyed during the Victorian rebuilding, are preserved. The pulpit is 17th-century and elaborately carved. But it is the window in the Daniell chapel that draws attention as it contains scenes from the *Alice* books. The brilliantly realised figures are based on John Tenniel's *Alice* book illustrations. The five scenes include the Mad Hatter's Tea Party, with the dormouse asleep in the teapot, and an eccentric March Hare with straw in his hair. The stained glass artist was Geoffrey Webb, whose brother, Christopher, designed some of the glass at Bunbury.

Great Budworth
St Mary and All Saints

Why visit: *Fine 15th- and 16th-century church*
Where: *Church Street, CW9 6HH*

Great Budworth is a very pretty village with houses of many ages and kinds, and at its heart sits St Mary's, a lovely red sandstone church dating mainly from the 15th and 16th centuries, though the Lady Chapel dates back to the 14th century.

All the exterior walls are battlemented. Inside, there is much to see, including a fine 15th-century font, and five 13th-century oak stalls, thought to be the oldest of their kind in Cheshire. There are several memorials to the Warburton family, including one made of alabaster to Sir John Warburton from 1575, and one to Sir Peter Warburton from 1813. Next to the lychgate, which was erected in 1920 as a memorial to the dead of World War I, are 18th-century stocks.

Lower Peover St Oswald

Why visit: *Timber-framed church*
Where: *The Cobbles Lane, off the B5081, WA16 9PZ*

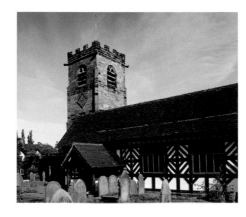

Tucked among a small group of buildings that includes a pub, an old school and cottages is one of England's most ancient timbered churches. The first sight of St Oswald is a real pleasure, with the patterned black-and-white timbered walls contrasting with the 16th-century sandstone tower.

The oldest parts of the church date back to the 14th century, which would make it one of the oldest timber-framed churches in Europe (but also see Marton, right). Inside is a brilliant assemblage of timber columns and huge beams. Much of the nave and chancel are 14th and 15th century, while the side chapels date from the 17th century. Originally, the church was all under one roof, but architect Anthony Salvin gave different parts their own roofs when he restored the church in the 1850s.

Simple 17th-century box pews, some with original doors, fill the body of the church. Much older is a wooden chest carved from a single lump of oak, as old as the most ancient parts of the church.

Malpas St Oswald

Why visit: *Monuments from the 16th and 17th centuries; 15th-century roof*
Where: *Church Street, SY14 8PD*

One of Cheshire's most handsome churches, St Oswald's dates primarily from the late 15th century, though the tower is from the 14th century. It is built of sandstone and is battlemented, and

on the outside are something like 70 gargoyles and other stone carvings. Many are very worn, but among them are a muzzled bear, a musician, and several dragons whose faces have weathered to make them appear endearing rather than frightening.

The interior is spacious and light, with a superb wooden nave roof, constructed in the late 15th century, and with gold-painted bosses and angels. On either side of the nave are chapels: one to the Breretons and one to the Cholmondeleys. Each contains a fine monument; that to Sir Randal Brereton and his wife is of about 1522, while that of Sir Hugh Cholmondeley and his wife is from 1605.

Marton
St James and St Paul

Why visit: *Perhaps the oldest timber-framed church of its kind in Europe*
Where: *On the A34, SK11 9HE*

With a founding date of 1343, Marton's church just pips Lower Peover to the post to make it possibly the oldest timber-framed church of its kind in Europe. The outside is lovely – weathered upright and horizontal timbers and cottagey windows stand out against the white walls, while over all is a shingled tower and spire.

The inside, apart from some Victorian restoration and modern pews, is essentially still as it was in the 14th century, with large wooden piers supporting the timbered roof, and all lit by the rows of little windows.

This page: St Oswald, Lower Peover.

ALSO IN THE AREA

Astbury St Mary
Why visit: *One of Cheshire's finest medieval churches*

Thornton Le Moors
St Mary CCT
Why visit: *13th-century village church*

Warburton St Werburgh CCT
Why visit: *Especially atmospheric timber-framed church*

IN AND AROUND DERBY

This group is a wonderful mixture of churches, from the grandest Derbyshire has to offer, at Wirksworth and Ashbourne, to two of its most idiosyncratic, at Dale and Trusley. They span a huge range of time, from the Saxon carvings at Wirksworth, to the very modern at Mickleover. Derby itself is represented by two contrasting churches: Gothic Revival at its most light and airy at St Mary's, and a rare surviving medieval bridge chapel.

Ashbourne St Oswald

Why visit: *One of the finest parish churches in Britain*
Where: *Church Street, on the west side of Ashbourne, DE6 1AJ*

Widely said to be Derbyshire's finest parish church, and a contender for one of the best churches in England, St Oswald's is splendid both inside and out.

The exterior is dominated by a large central tower and tall, thin, elegant spire. Much of the church dates from the 1200s, including the chancel with a huge east window from a later date, which contains some medieval glass. There are examples of all the great ages of English church architecture – Early English, Decorated and Perpendicular – throughout the church, especially in the windows.

In the north transept are serried ranks of excellent monuments to the Cockayne, Bradbourne and Boothby families. Among the finest are those to Joan and Edmund Cokayne from 1404, Sir John Cockayne and his wife from 1447, and Sir Humphrey and Lady Brabourne from 1581. Also here is the much later memorial to Penelope Boothby, who died in 1791 in her sixth year. The monument shows Penelope as if asleep and is generally considered to be a masterpiece of its kind. Penelope was already celebrated when alive, having been painted by Sir Joshua Reynolds.

Wirksworth St Mary

Why visit: *Saxon and medieval carvings*
Where: *Church Walk, DE4 4DP*

The earliest parts of St Mary's as it stands today are from the 13th century and include the lower part of the tower and the massive crossing piers. There was much further work done in the 14th and 15th centuries, and the church was thoroughly restored in the 19th century by Sir George Gilbert Scott.

St Mary's is most famous for carvings from a church or churches that stood on this site going back to Saxon times. These can be found throughout the church, mounted into the fabric of the walls. Far and away the most renowned of these is the Wirksworth Stone. It was found buried below the chancel in 1820, covering a grave with a complete skeleton in it. The stone, parts of which are missing, shows scenes from the life of Jesus, and other biblical or apocryphal stories. Each scene is distinct but constructed by the sculptor so that they work together as a composition. The

stone may have been made before 700. Nearly as famous is 'T'owd Man of Bonsall' a carving of a medieval lead worker, holding the tools of his trade. Elsewhere in the church are dozens of other fragments of carving, sometimes in groups (a king and queen, heads of assorted creatures, odd bits of jumbled stonework), and sometimes singly (Adam with a sinuous serpent seemingly eating the apple), all adding up to a gallery of early sculpture.

This page: St Mary, Wirksworth, looking dramatic in the snow (left); enigmatic carved fragments at Wirksworth (centre); the elegant tower and spire of St Oswald's (above).

Dale Abbey All Saints

Why visit: *Tiny, old, semi-detached church*
Where: *The Village, off the A6096 north-east of Derby, DE7 4PN; usually open weekend afternoons or ask for key at the Dale Christian centre*

At the end of a rural village street, and feeling far from industrial estates nearby, Dale Abbey is one of England's most idiosyncratic churches. It is picturesque, tiny and takes up one side of a building, and so is effectively semi-detached, the other part being a private house.

There was an abbey here in the 12th century, but it has long been in ruins, and the little church is all that remains intact from these buildings. It even has a fragment of 13th-century wall painting inside to prove its credentials. The interior is packed with a remarkable jumble of old furniture and fittings, some from the 17th century.

Derby St Mary

Why visit: *Elegant church designed by A.W.N. Pugin*
Where: *Darley Lane; can be approached on foot from Queen Street in Derby centre, DE1 3AU*

Augustus Welby Northmore Pugin was one of 19th-century England's foremost architects and designers, a proponent of the Gothic Revival style, and the mastermind behind much of the look of the Houses of Parliament in London. St Mary's was one of his first ventures into the Gothic Revival, and its foundation stone was laid on 28 June 1838, Queen Victoria's Coronation Day.

The church is elegant inside and out, and benefits from a footbridge that was built over the A601 in 2007, which gives the best view of Pugin's design.

Derby St Mary on the Bridge

Why visit: *One of only six surviving bridge chapels in Britain*
Where: *Duke Street, north of the cathedral, by the River Derwent, DE21 4RZ; open Tue and Sat, May–Sep, 2–4pm*

Dating largely from the 14th century, this little chapel originally stood on the first arch of a medieval bridge over the Derwent; the springing of the arch can still be seen below the east wall. It is one of only six bridge chapels surviving in Britain. It offered spiritual reassurance to travellers setting out into the wild lands beyond the bridge.

After a long and varied career, including being used as a prison and a carpenter's workshop, it fell into ruin, and was eventually restored by the Haslam family in the early 20th century. Work on embellishing the interior has carried on since, and today the chapel is a fully functioning place of worship.

Mickleover Our Lady of Lourdes

Why visit: *Modern church with new, light-filled vestibule*
Where: *Uttoxeter Road, DE3 9GE*

Dating from 1982, and with a vestibule added in 2004, this modern, octagonal church is a striking new addition to Derbyshire's churches. It is built of brick, has low walls and is crowned by a little cupola. The new gathering area is a bold addition, with big wooden pillars, and is flooded with light. The inside is very simple, but effective.

This page: 'Semi-detached' All Saints at Dale Abbey (left); the unusual octagonal church at Mickleover (above).

Morley St Matthew

Why visit: *Medieval glass; 16th- and 17th-century monuments*
Where: *Unnamed road off Church Lane, DE7 6DE; open Sat 2–4pm; summer only*

St Matthew's is a handsome church with a tall spire, the history of which can be traced back to 1378. Most of its interest lies in the North Chapel, where much of the fabric, including the floor tiles, was brought from nearby Dale Abbey. There are four beautiful windows here from Dale, containing some of the best medieval glass in the country. Virtually filling the chapel is a collection of monuments to the Sacheverell family, many from the 16th century.

Norbury St Mary and St Barlok

Why visit: *Medieval glass*
Where: *Norbury Hollow, DE6 2ED*

Norbury's church is tucked down a lane near Norbury Manor (a National Trust property), dating from the early 14th century. From the outside it is unusually arranged, with its tower in the middle of the south aisle over the porch. The chancel is taller than the nave, has four huge windows on each side, and is the highlight of the building. These windows are full of 14th- and 15th-century glass. In the chancel are tombs and memorials of the Fitzherbert family, lords of the manor and builders of the church.

Trusley All Saints

Why visit: *18th-century building complete with original fixtures and fittings*
Where: *Taylor's Lane, west of Derby, DE6 5JG; open summer weekends*

In a small, very rural hamlet, Trusley's formal little church is a surprise, being built of red brick in the Classical style and dating from 1713.

Its porch is a grand baroque affair, so grand that it is suggested it was brought from elsewhere. The Georgian atmosphere is retained perfectly inside, with the original box pews, three-decker pulpit and other furnishings.

BETWEEN LEICESTER AND THE TRENT

This cluster of churches straddles the Leicestershire/Derbyshire border, and includes two of England's most splendid churches, at Repton and Melbourne. Both are in Derbyshire. Leicester itself has a number of interesting churches, two of which are included here. In between are churches of many kinds, ranging from small and unobtrusive at Foremark to Breedon on the Hill with its nationally important collection of Saxon sculpture.

Repton St Wystan

Why visit: *The Saxon crypt and its fascinating story*
Where: *Willington Road, DE65 6FH*

St Wystan's has a fascinating and complex history, much of it forgotten or misunderstood until Dr Harold Taylor began to study it in the 1930s. He worked on the story of the building for over 50 years, including working with archaeologists who did much to uncover its early history in the 1970s and 80s.

From the outside it is a very handsome medieval church, not unlike so many others in this area. Its spire is remarkable, immensely tall and thin and dates from the 15th century, as does the tower. It has a clerestory that was built at about the same time. Other features are from the 14th century, including the south porch.

It is at the chancel end of the church, however, that the story becomes so interesting; for here, under the chancel, is a Saxon crypt, complete with beautifully carved stone piers. And

much of the chancel is also Saxon, changed and altered many times through the intervening centuries.

For a long time the crypt was entirely forgotten, lost beneath later work and by a ground level that had risen considerably over the years. It was only when a workman fell into it during building work in 1779 that it was rediscovered.

The 18th century was a bad time for the church; much of the fabric was altered, and many monuments and fittings mistreated or destroyed. More work was done in the 19th century, some of it to conserve the building's structure. In 1998, the crypt underwent a major restoration.

The crypt is a vital part of the story of the Saxon kingdom of Mercia, of which Repton was once the capital. The crypt was a royal mausoleum, where King Aethelbald was buried in 757 and King Wiglaf in 840. Wiglaf's grandson, Wystan, was murdered in 849 and buried at Repton. Wystan became venerated as a saint, and the crypt became a place of pilgrimage. In the 10th century Wystan's remains were removed to Evesham, and gradually the importance of the crypt was forgotten. Now it is celebrated as one of the oldest places of worship in Britain.

Appleby Magna
St Michael and All Angels

Why visit: *14th-century church with an early 19th-century interior*
Where: *Church Street, DE12 7BB*

With its stone tower and spire, and windows of the Decorated period, Appleby Magna looks every inch a medieval church. It is indeed an excellent example of its kind. But the interior was given a complete overhaul in the first four decades of the 19th century, transforming it into a space with very high ceilings culminating in plastered rib-vaulting. At the same time the furnishings were completely renewed,

box pews were installed throughout and the west gallery was rebuilt. The north and south doors were closed off, and the main entrance became the west door under the tower. The chancel was remodelled during the 1870s.

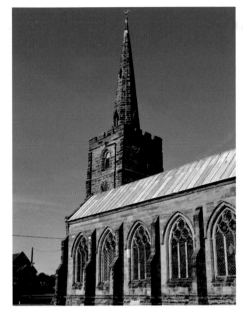

The oldest part of the church is the chapel in the north-east corner. There is the battered effigy of Sir Edmund de Appleby, who fought with Edward III at the Battle of Crecy in 1346. His moated manor house was just to the east of the church.

Ashby-de-la-Zouch
St Helen

Why visit: *Historic connections; 15th-century architecture; monuments in the Hastings Chapel*
Where: *Lower Church Street, off Market Street, in the town centre, LE65 1AB*

The story of St Helen's is very much tied to the story of the ruined castle just to the south. The keep of the castle and the church were built in the 1470s by Lord Hastings, one of the most influential and important noblemen of his time. He was deeply involved in 15th-century politics and was eventually beheaded in the Tower of London on the orders of Richard, Duke of Gloucester (who was very shortly to become Richard III).

Much of the 15th-century church remains, but considerable changes and additions were made by architect

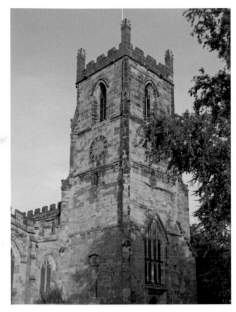

J.P. St Aubyn between 1878 and 1880. There is a great deal to be seen inside the church, particularly in the Hastings Chapel.

Among the many monuments here is a splendid alabaster tomb to the Second Earl of Huntingdon and his wife from about 1561. Around the base of the tomb little figures called mourners, each one different, are separated by elaborate shields. There is also a monument to Selina, Countess of Huntingdon. In 1783 she founded an evangelical movement called the Countess of Huntingdon Connexion.

Breedon on the Hill
The Priory Church of St Mary and St Hardulph

Why visit: *Saxon sculpture*
Where: *Off Melbourne/Squirrel Lane; just west of a large quarry, DE73 8AJ*

Breedon Hill is an oddity: a prominent outcrop of limestone in a landscape that is otherwise sandstone. It has attracted the interests of man from very early times, and was a hill fort in the Iron Age. The views from the hill are outstanding.

A monastery was founded within the ramparts of the old fort as early as the 7th century, and it became an important Christian centre in the Kingdom of Mercia. The monastery may well have been sacked by Vikings in the 9th century. However, the buildings survived with a change of ownership and use, and

remained a priory until the Dissolution in the 16th century. By then the Saxon church and its associated buildings had been altered several times, with a major rebuilding in the 13th century.

At the Dissolution, Francis Shirley had purchased the priory church for use as a burial place for himself and his successors. The parishioners successfully petitioned to be able to use that part of the church for the parish; what was then the nave was 'ruinated'. The nave, including most of what remained of the Saxon building, was subsequently demolished.

Much later, in the 18th century, the church nearly fell down of its own accord, but was repaired. What survives today is essentially the eastern end of the priory church plus the tower.

The Shirley family is very much in evidence: the extraordinary family pew – an enormous and sumptuously carved wooden box – dates from 1627. It was intended to give privacy to the family, and looks rather like a small prison. Shirley monuments from the 16th century dominate the northern part of the church.

This page: Decorated windows at Appleby Magna (left); St Helen's, Ashby-de-la-Zouch (centre); Saxon carving at Breedon on the Hill (above).
Opposite page: St Wystan's medieval exterior (top); its Saxon crypt (below).

But the Shirley family items, for all their ostentation, are firmly upstaged by the Saxon carved stonework and sculpture that is embedded at various places in the walls of the church. Some of this was discovered during the 18th-century repairs, others were placed in the church in the 1930s. Some may still be in situ from Saxon times, but this has not been confirmed. Taken together, this constitutes the largest known collection of such stonework in Britain.

Large amounts originally formed a decorative frieze that went around both the inside and the outside of the church. There are also fragments of another frieze: figures, mostly saints, in panels under arches; free-standing crosses; and, most famous of all, the 'Breedon Angel'. There are several stylistic variations in this work, and much of it is superb by any standards. Details in the clothing, attitudes and overall appearance of the figures has enabled experts to date them to the 8th or 9th century – back to the beginning of the story of this remarkable church.

Coalville
Mount St Bernard Abbey

Why visit: *Cistercian abbey with church designed by A.W.N. Pugin*
Where: *Off Oaks Road, between Coalville and the Blackbrook Reservoir, LE67 5UL*

This was the first Cistercian foundation in England since the Dissolution of the Monasteries in the 16th century.

The church, designed by A.W.N. Pugin in the late 1830s and extended a century later in the 1930s, is at the centre of a working abbey, but visitors are welcome to the church, and to see a little of the monastic way of life.

Pugin became a devout Catholic, and believed that the best architectural expression of Catholic faith was the Gothic style. The abbey church here still bears the imprint of his passionately held beliefs, but the changes made in the 1930s altered the layout that he designed.

Foremark St Saviour

Why visit: *Complete 17th-century church and fittings*
Where: *Between Repton and Melbourne, just south of the River Trent; immediately west of Repton Prep School on a lane signposted 'HGV Entrance Only', DE65 6EJ*

St Saviour's was built in 1662 re-using stone from a ruined chapel at nearby Ingleby. It is built in such a convincing Perpendicular style that from the outside only an expert could tell the true date of this building.

It is a different story inside, because the simple interior is entirely and clearly 17th-century. Everything is of a piece, from the box pews to the three-decker pulpit. The little church is essentially one space, but the east end is divided from the west by a charming wooden screen.

Leicester St John the Baptist

Why visit: *High Victorian masterpiece*
Where: *Clarendon Park Road, LE2 3AD; usually open Mon–Thu, contact details on notice board*

Built in 1884 to the designs of Joseph Goddard, senior partner in Leicester's most prolific firm of church architects, St John's is a relatively plain and austere brick-built town church on the outside, its only playful detail being a needle-like spirelet. The surprises come on the inside, with one very impressive tall open space, along the edge of which are stout round piers supporting a gallery that extends the entire length of the church on both sides. It is an ingenious and very

unusual conception. The sumptuous reredos, high altar and other fittings at the chancel end of the church were all added later in the 20th century.

Leicester St Mary de Castro

Why visit: *Extraordinary arrangement of the tower built within the south aisle*
Where: *Castle Yard, off Castle Street, LE1 5WN; open Mon–Fri 12–2pm, Sat 2–4pm*

St Mary's is set in a part of Leicester where the city's medieval past can still be imagined: here are the castle mound and the castle walls, approached from the south via a castle gateway. The church itself is big and imposing, with a tall spire originally built in 1400, but altered and shortened in the intervening centuries.

The origins of the church go back to the 12th century, when it was the castle chapel. It was much enlarged later in the 12th century, when the splendid Norman chancel as it is today was created. By the late 13th century much more space was required, so a south aisle was built that is bigger than the nave and choir put together. Its timber roof, dating from the 15th century, has the widest span of its kind in England.

At the west end of the south aisle is St Mary's biggest visual surprise: the base of the tower grows out of the floor and rises up through the roof. It is thought that this remarkable arrangement came about because there was simply nowhere else to put it, there being no room outside on the crowded castle green.

Melbourne
St Michael and St Mary

Why visit: *Norman magnificence*
Where: *Church Square, DE73 8EN*

This is one of the most splendid Norman churches in England, built in the early 1100s. The reason for there being such a

cathedral-like church here is that Melbourne is a mile or two south of the River Trent, once a strategically important demarcation line between southern and northern England.

As originally planned, the church had three towers, a huge and very expensive undertaking for an ordinary church. It also has an unusual feature in that there is an upper gallery at the western end of the church, with walkways linking it to the east end, which once had an upper chancel. The lines of this upper chancel can still be traced in the external stonework of the tower. Perhaps these elaborate arrangements were so that King Henry I could have, in effect, a private church above the rest of the church.

The church was not finished when Henry died; the tower was given an upper stage only in the 17th century, while the present nave was substantially altered in late medieval times. By this time the building was simply a parish church.

The Norman work can be seen at its best in the nave, where great round columns support round-headed arches. Details to look out for include the rich and enigmatic carvings on the capitals of the chancel arch. They include the Melbourne Cat, which is smiling across the chancel entrance to a snarling dog on the other side. There is a man pulling the dog's tail, presumably so it cannot reach the cat.

Orton on the Hill St Edith

Why visit: *Lovely old church with many interesting features*
Where: *The Green, CV9 3NG; open Sat and Sun, when locked, keyholder details in porch*

St Edith's dates almost entirely from the 14th century, but the tower and clerestory are from about a century later. The church was much larger until 1763 when the north aisle was demolished. The spire is oddly truncated, as in 1950 it was thought to be in a dangerous condition and was therefore reduced in height.

Inside, the church is charming and unspoiled, with furnishings, fittings and memorials dating back to the 13th century. The box pews and pulpit are from the 18th century, as is the eccentric stone font, inscribed 'S.S. Perkins Esq'; Samuel Steel-Perkins lived at Orton Hall, where he died in 1808. On the brick floor next to the font is an intriguing gravestone with a cross carved on one end and a man on horseback on the other. It has been restored, but may date back to the 13th century.

There is a small mausoleum in the north wall of the church, containing the effigy of a 14th-century Cistercian monk.

Staunton Harold
The Ferrers Chapel of the Holy Trinity

Why visit: *Private chapel built in defiance of Oliver Cromwell*
Where: *North-east of Ashby-de-la-Zouch, on the Staunton Harold Estate, next to Staunton Harold Hall, LE65 1RT; open Jun–Aug, Wed–Sun, 1–4.30pm; also Apr–Oct, bank holidays 1–4.30pm*

Staunton Harold Hall and its estate are privately owned, but the chapel was given to the National Trust in the 1950s when the estate was up for sale. The chapel is in an idyllic position, with the big house on one side and a lake on the other. It is a building entirely in the Gothic style, but was actually built during the 17th-century Commonwealth.

Its builder was Robert Shirley, and inscriptions in the church tell much of the story. Over the chancel arch is written: 'Sir Robert Shirley Baronet Founder of this church anno domini 1653 on whose soul God hath mercy'; and over the entrance: 'When all things sacred were throughout ye nation Either demolisht or profand Sir Richard Shirley Barronet founded this church whose singular praise it is to have done ye best things in ye worst times…'.

In other words, Sir Richard built his chapel in direct and public defiance of the Commonwealth and Oliver Cromwell, who was outraged and demanded that Shirley make compensation. Sir Richard refused, was imprisoned in the Tower of London and died there aged only 27. Completed after Sir Richard's death, and following his detailed plans, the chapel is as handsome inside as out, with its 17th-century fittings surviving, astonishingly in light of the story above, virtually intact.

Opposite page: Pugin's design at Coalville (left); part of the tower at St Mary de Castro, Leicester (right).
This page: Norman church at Melbourne (left); the charming interior at St Edith's, Orton on the Hill (centre).

ENGLAND'S SMALLEST COUNTY

Rutland's entire population is barely 35,000 – about the same as the nearby market town of Grantham. This is a county of villages and farms, with a long tradition of rural prosperity. Over the centuries, wealth has combined with fine building stone, from the limestone ridge in the east and north, to give Rutland a splendid array of churches, a good proportion of them of a remarkably early date.

Oakham All Saints

Why visit: *Impressive, light-filled nave with slender columns, and capitals with rare medieval figurative carvings*
Where: *Market Place, in the centre of Oakham to the west of the castle, LE15 6XT*

The very splendid church of Rutland's county town presides over a delightful jumble of old inns, houses and school clustered around the market place with its buttercross. Close by is the great hall of the Norman castle. The south doorway of All Saints, the earliest part of the present building, dates from the early 13th century. The outside, with its clerestory, pinnacles, battlements and large Perpendicular windows, has the distinguished look of a later church:

15th-century for everything except the magnificent tower and slender spire (which are a century older).

Most of the interior structure is 13th- or 14th-century. Be sure to look up at the series of intricately carved capitals on the tall, narrow piers of the nave – lively medieval depictions of a whole host of creatures and Bible stories. There is also a fine example of a Green Man, with leaves flowing out of his mouth. The corbels have intricate carvings, too, including one of baby birds in a nest.

The earliest feature in the church is the font, made in the late 12th or early 13th century and carved with intersecting arcades. Most of the other furnishings and fittings are Victorian, as is the chancel with its ornately stencilled and gilded ceiling. It dates from the 1850s, when the church was restored by Sir George Gilbert Scott. A new organ, its oak case bearing the Rutland coat of arms, was installed in 1995. It plays a key role in a programme of concerts and recitals, for which this spacious, light-filled church makes a wonderful setting.

Brooke St Peter

Why visit: *A delightful, unspoilt church, well off the beaten track; a curious mixture of Norman and Elizabethan*
Where: *In Brooke, south of Oakham, LE15 8DG*

This long, low church, with its rather dumpy 13th-century tower, is an unlikely but harmonious mix of styles. The doorway has two rows of unmistakably Norman zigzag carving, and inside a Norman north arcade with a Norman font beneath one of its rounded arches.

Otherwise this is an Elizabethan building, with clear mullioned windows and a remarkable set of 16th- and 17th-century fittings including pulpit, screens

and box pews. The effect is delightful, mainly because the church has remained largely unaltered since the late 16th century, despite a restoration of 1879. The simple interior has one particularly good monument, with a painted alabaster effigy of Charles Noel, who died in 1619.

Edith Weston St Mary the Virgin

Why visit: *Interesting history and associations; monuments*
Where: *Church Lane, on the southern shore of Rutland Water, LE15 8EY*

The long history of St Mary's opened a new chapter during the construction of Rutland Water. It became linked with the neighbouring church of St Matthew, Normanton. Now jutting into the lake close to Edith Weston, Normanton church was deconsecrated and would have been submerged when the reservoir was filled in 1979. Luckily, however, the upper part was saved as a museum. A plaque in St Mary's commemorates 22 people whose remains were exhumed from Normanton and then cremated.

Also remembered here is Sir Gilbert Heathcote of Normanton Park, who was Lord Mayor of London in 1711 and governor of the Bank of England. His 18th-century wall memorial, with an inscription full of praise for his noble character, is among those brought here from Normanton, along with the medieval altar stone in the north aisle. A modern stained glass window shows Jesus and the disciples in a fishing boat, with Normanton church in the background.

Exton St Peter and St Paul

Why visit: *Collection of 14th- to 18th-century monuments of outstanding quality*
Where: *In Exton Park, west of Exton village, LE15 8AN*

The Noel family of Exton Park, earls of Gainsborough, have held the manor here since the 17th century. Noel family monuments are among the highlights of an exceptional collection of memorials in the fine, secluded medieval church.

There is work here by sculptors who were the foremost of their age, including a rare sculpture in marble by the 17th-century master woodcarver Grinling Gibbons. This monument, to Viscount Campden, cost £1,000 when it was completed in 1686 – a fortune at the time. But as the Viscount had four wives and 19 children – all represented and named on this huge and lavishly ornamented marble monument – perhaps the sum was not excessive.

Two of the later Noel monuments are by Joseph Nollekens, a very successful 18th-century sculptor who was a co-founder of the Royal Academy in 1768. An earlier memorial, with its figures dressed in exquisitely detailed costumes, is the alabaster tomb of 1580 commemorating lawyer Robert Kelway and his family.

Hambleton St Andrew

Why visit: *Pleasant setting and interesting history*
Where: *Upper Hambleton, at the junction, east of Oakham, LE15 8TH*

The hilltop setting of St Andrew's ensured its preservation when much of its parish disappeared beneath Rutland Water in the 1970s. It now presides over a pretty and much-visited village surrounded by water. Hambleton would be on an island in the reservoir, but for a strip of land connecting it with Oakham.

Its large and imposing church was once the most important in the county. It is recorded in the Domesday Book as one of three in Hambleton, which had at one time been the capital of Anglo-Saxon kings in Rutland. The oldest features of St Andrew's visible today are the Norman capitals, the arch of the south doorway and the unusually shaped font (believed to date from the 12th century). Much of the rest of the church is 13th-century except for the chancel and its arch, which were rebuilt as part of an 1890s restoration. The Victorian stained glass, as well as the unusual lectern and ornately carved organ-case, all date from this time.

This page: The breathtaking chancel arch at St Peter's, Tickencote.
Opposite page: All Saints, Oakham.

Teigh Holy Trinity

Why visit: *Unusual and charming Georgian interior with unique pulpit*
Where: *Village centre, north of Oakham; the church is usually locked but details of keyholders are posted outside, LE15 7RX*

With a population of barely 40, the village of Teigh (pronounced 'tea') has an appropriately small but most unusual church. With its 13th-century tower, this could pass for a medieval church, though in fact the rest of the church is a 1782 rebuilding.

The interior is Georgian, but features a delightfully quirky take on the typical box pews and three-decker pulpit. Go into the nave through the west door below the tower. Look back, and you will find you have just walked underneath the pulpit! It is flanked by a pair of reading desks with ogee-shaped canopies, and behind it in the tower arch is a large trompe l'oeil window with 'leaded lights' and a 'view' of trees and sky beyond.

The aisle is flanked by rising tiers of box pews, set parallel to the aisle, facing each other as though for a choir. A Georgian mahogany font and a plaster ceiling complete this curious but pleasing church. Part of the 1995 BBC adaptation of *Pride and Prejudice* was filmed at the nearby Georgian rectory.

Tickencote St Peter

Why visit: *Outstanding original Norman chancel arch*
Where: *Off the B1081 north-west of Stamford, PE9 4AE*

Perhaps Rutland's most photographed church, St Peter's is the result of combining a Norman church of about 1170, the surviving part of which includes an early architectural masterpiece, with a late 18th-century reconstruction in Romanesque style. The stupendous chancel arch is part of the former, while most of the rest of the church belongs to the 1792 rebuilding.

The east front was rebuilt to extraordinary effect, with round-headed windows and blind arcading filling almost the whole height. This design was loosely based on its predecessor. The restoration

was commissioned by Miss Eliza Wingfield (commemorated in the south porch), with Samuel Pepys Cockerell as architect. The original Norman chancel arch was left intact, and is often considered the finest in England.

Each of its six orders of arch has a different decoration – beakheads, zigzags, crenellations, and a row of heads comprising a delightful array of humans, animals and grotesques. The detail demands close inspection, and the effect of the whole is electrifying.

ALSO IN THE AREA

Ashwell St Mary
Why visit: *14th-century church restored in 1851 by the eminent Victorian architect William Butterfield*

Greetham St Mary
Why visit: *Elegant 14th-century steeple; fragments of Norman carving embedded in the south wall; unusual Norman font*

Manton St Mary
Why visit: *Unusual church with a wonderful assortment of headstones, carved in local limestone, in the churchyard*

North Luffenham
St John the Baptist
Why visit: *15th-century angel roof*

Stoke Dry St Andrew
Why visit: *Ironstone tower; rare oriel window; amazing Norman carvings*

Whissendine St Andrew
Why visit: *Spectacular limestone tower; 16th-century screen from St John's College, Cambridge*

NEWARK AND THE TRENT VALLEY

The broad flat plain of the Trent in eastern Nottinghamshire has much more in common with neighbouring Lincolnshire than with the Nottinghamshire of Sherwood Forest to the west. This landscape of wide skies and distant views is a perfect setting for the conspicuous church spires and towers that beckon from every direction, drawing attention to some of the most interesting churches of the East Midlands.

Newark-on-Trent St Mary

Why visit: *Large, magnificent medieval church with many interesting fittings*
Where: *Between Church Street and Appleton Gate, near the market place, NG24 1JS*

Usually ranked among the very best parish churches of England, St Mary's dominates town and country with its immensely tall 14th-century spire of Lincolnshire limestone. The church was already destined for grandeur before the spire was built. The crossing, and the lower part of the tower, including the wonderful west doorway, date from a 13th-century building phase. Records show that six oaks from Sherwood Forest were donated to the building project by Henry III.

The church later acquired fine features of the Perpendicular period, such as the spacious, high nave with its slender piers,

beautiful clerestory, and the pinnacled two-storey south porch. The huge windows of the transepts and the east end are now the largest in the church, with Victorian glass of 1864 in memory of Prince Albert. The rood screen and the choir stalls, with their 26 misericords, are of a similar date, as is the unusually long row of sedilia in the Lady Chapel.

A much more recent highlight of the interior is the gilded reredos above the High Altar, a 1937 work by Sir Ninian Comper. The stained glass is nearly all Victorian or later, but the Holy Spirit Chapel has a window remade in 1957 using many assorted fragments of St Mary's surviving medieval glass. The glass on the north side of the church was almost all blown out by a freak storm in 1903, after which nearly 4,000 individual panes had to be replaced.

An intriguing feature on the outside of the Markham Chantry Chapel, south of the high altar, is a macabre yet creepily endearing painting of a dancing cadaver – one of two surviving panels depicting the Dance of Death, (intended as a memento mori). Among Newark's collection of interesting monuments, note several smartly coloured and gilded 17th-century wall tablets; the Markham monument of 1601 with figures framed by Classical columns and pediment; and the large Flemish brass of 1361 to wool merchant and church benefactor Alan Fleming.

This page: St Mary's fine sandstone exterior (left); the beautiful gilded reredos (above).

Coddington All Saints

Why visit: *Glass, decorations and furnishings by William Morris's partnership*
Where: *Chapel Lane, NG24 2PW*

From a distance, All Saints could be a little red-roofed medieval country church, but in fact the appearance of the present building is largely the result of a restoration of the original 13th-century church in 1864–5.

The main advantage of this is the interior decor and fittings by William Morris and his Pre-Raphaelite partners. There is a painted ceiling and a canopied seat in the chancel, as well as fine-quality stained glass. The east window has a beautiful small Annunciation panel by Sir Edward Burne-Jones and a nearby window depicts St Catherine and St Cecilia, the patron saint of music, who is playing a small pipe organ. The St John the Baptist, in a lancet window in the tower, is believed to be the work of Morris himself. Stencilled paintwork on the window tracery originally extended to the walls, too, but whitewashing has covered up much of this.

East Markham
St John the Baptist

Why visit: *Grand 15th-century church; 15th-century brass; good window by Comper*
Where: *Church Street, on the southern edge of East Markham village, NG22 0SA*

East Markham's grand Perpendicular church has a fittingly imposing site on a ridge overlooking the Trent valley to the east. The building rises in three stages, with battlements on each: the aisles at the lower level, then a splendid large-windowed Perpendicular clerestory and rising again to the fine tower, complete with decorative detailing such as pinnacles and gargoyles.

The interior is spacious, airy and full of light. Have a close look at the glass in the east window, fine early work by Sir Ninian Comper with beautiful detailing in the clothing and ecclesiastical regalia. The figures are the Virgin and Child flanked by four saints. The church is known for its outstanding 15th-century brass to Dame Millicent Meryng. Her second husband was Sir John Markham, a former lord of the manor and church benefactor. His tomb is in the chancel.

Egmanton Our Lady of Egmanton Parish and Shrine

Why visit: *Ebullient late 19th-century interior by Sir Ninian Comper*
Where: *Tuxford Road, Egmanton (south of Tuxford), NG22 0EZ*

From the outside, this looks like an unexceptional medieval church, but its interior underwent an extraordinary transformation in 1896–8, thanks to the staunchly Anglo-Catholic 7th Duke of Newcastle-under-Lyne, of nearby Clumber. The church and shrine of our Lady of Egmanton here had long been (and still is) a place of pilgrimage, and the duke commissioned Sir Ninian Comper to give the church the most lavish of face-lifts. The result is unbelievably ornate and colourful, with organ-case, font cover, pulpit, rood loft and screen all in a riot of red, blue, green and gold.

Hawton All Saints

Why visit: *Easter sepulchre and other 14th-century carvings, considered among the finest in England*
Where: *In Hawton village, just south of Newark, NG24 3RN; the church is usually locked, but a keyholder is nearby*

The tiny rural village of Hawton might seem a surprising place to find an astonishing gallery of medieval carvings in stone, but its handsome and unspoilt church is just that. The late 15th-century pinnacled tower serves as a fine landmark to guide visitors to All Saints.

Inside, the lovely chancel of about 1330, with light pouring in through its seven-light east window, makes a fitting home for a superlative series of works by

outstanding master masons of the late 1300s. The beautiful screen at Southwell Minster, a few miles to the west, was made in about the same period, and it seems that the same skilful hands may have carved these treasures at Hawton. On the north side, next to a beautiful carved doorway and the tomb recess of Sir Robert de Compton, who endowed the chancel, is the exquisite Easter sepulchre. This masterpiece illustrates the story of Christ's death and resurrection, with a series of figures framed by the most finely detailed decorative stonework. At the base are dozing Roman soldiers guarding Christ's tomb. Christ and the three Marys are in the central recess, with the Ascension depicted at the top.

A three-seated sedilia opposite the sepulchre is just as intricate, with figures of saints and a pelican. A double piscina, in the same style, completes the group.

Holme St Giles

Why visit: *Unspoilt and delightful rural church, with much late 14th-century work*
Where: *Langford Lane, off the A1133 north of Newark, NG23 7RY*

Now separated from North Muskham and the Great North Road, just to the west across the River Trent, Holme was

a much more frequented place until the 16th century, when the river changed course to leave it isolated on the eastern bank. A century or so before that, Holme's 13th-century church had been extensively renovated and embellished, in fine 15th-century style, by a wealthy wool merchant named John Barton. He died in 1491 and his will survives, documenting his family and his last wish to be buried here. His effigy lies beside that of his wife Isabella (and above a cadaver), on their tomb, between the chancel and the chapel he built next to it.

Since Barton's day little has changed in the church, though it was sensitively restored in 1932 by local historian Nevile Truman. Evidence of Barton's generosity remains in many features and details, including the large Perpendicular windows and the ornate gabled two-storey porch with its heraldic shields, some referring to sheep and the wool trade, and gargoyles. A motif on Barton's tomb that is repeated in the roof and elsewhere is a pun on his name: it depicts a bar and a barrel, or tun. Among other carved treasures are the screen and the wonderful bench-ends in Barton's chapel. Each of the poppyheads on top is flanked by a pair of expressively carved creatures, from angels to dogs and birds.

This page: The superb 14th-century Easter sepulchre at Hawton.

ALSO IN THE AREA

Balderton St Giles
Why visit: *Very fine Norman doorway; 15th-century screen, and many unusual poppyhead carvings on bench-ends*

Laxton St Michael the Archangel
Why visit: *Perpendicular clerestory and tower; Easter sepulchre and good monuments; historic village*

Newark-on-Trent Barnbygate Methodist Church
Why visit: *Typical Wesleyan chapel of 1845 with Classical interior features; still in use; not always open, but caretaker next door*

EASTERN ENGLAND

For church enthusiasts eastern England is one of the best places in Britain. Norfolk, especially, is famous for its wonderful churches, but Suffolk, Essex, Lincolnshire and Cambridgeshire also have superb collections, including individual churches that are the best of their kind.

Eastern England is rich in churches, and full of surprises. Perhaps the biggest surprise is Essex. The county is dismissed by some as being virtually an extension of London, and therefore suburban in look and feel. But, even surprisingly close to the capital, there is countryside as green and unspoiled as anywhere in England, and with some of the country's prettiest villages and lovely churches. Perhaps Essex's best churches are the ones hidden away at the end of long, leafy lanes, or those that seem to draw the visitor to an Essex of wide landscapes and the tang of saltmarshes.

Suffolk's landscapes and churches are much better known – after all, artists such as John Constable painted them hundreds of times. And some of Suffolk's churches are world-famous. Long Melford and Lavenham are two; 'wool' churches, built from the immense wealth that the wool trade brought to the whole of East Anglia in the Middle Ages. Those two buildings are grand statements in flint and stone, but it is often the detail in the smaller churches that lingers in the memory.

Norfolk has more medieval churches than any other county in England but, like Essex, is surprisingly little-known. The richest concentration of churches in Norfolk – and with some of the very best churches in the whole of Britain – is contained within a tiny area west of King's Lynn. And Norwich has so many medieval churches that there seems to be one in most streets, although many are now no longer in use.

The Fens is an area shared by west Norfolk, parts of Cambridgeshire and southern Lincolnshire. The complex history of this region – rich at differing times from fen produce, water-borne trade and agriculture – means that it has superb churches. Lincolnshire as a whole is huge, and is another of the eastern counties with churches, which include some of the best in the country, in some tucked away and unexpected places.

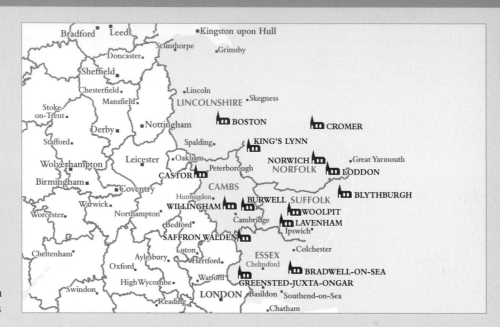

This page: St Andrew,
Greensted-juxta-Ongar, with
its distinctive weather-boarded
tower and 'tree-trunk' nave.

SOUTH-WEST ESSEX

This group of churches begins with one of the most famous in Britain. St Andrew's at Greensted is rightly celebrated for being the oldest wooden church in the world. But it keeps its feeling of quiet rural charm, even with all the visitors and its proximity to East London. Other churches in this tour are more rural, especially Lambourne, tucked away in lanes as pretty as you'll find anywhere.

Greensted-juxta-Ongar
St Andrew

Why visit: *Fascinating ancient church; nave built from tree trunks*
Where: *Signposted to 'Greensted Church' off Greensted Road, west of Chipping Ongar, CM5 9LD*

Greensted's church is the oldest timber building of its kind in Britain and Europe, and is proud to call itself the oldest wooden church in the world. Tree-ring analysis in the 1990s provided a date range of between 1063 and 1100. It is the upright timbers of the nave that are so ancient; these make the church akin to the stave churches of Scandinavia. The timbers are huge logs split vertically and placed side-by-side; each log has a groove down it into which fillets of wood are fitted for a weatherproof seal.

The church looks very different today to when it was first built. Modifications include a 16th-century brick chancel, 18th-century tower and spire, and much Victorian restoration that saved the building from a ruinous state. The timber and brick sill on which the ancient timbers now rest dates from that time.

Excavations have shown that a much earlier wooden church once stood here, perhaps dating back to the time of St Cedd, who built so many churches in this area in the 7th century.

Blackmore St Laurence

Why visit: *Outstanding timber tower*
Where: *Church Street, CM4 0RN; open Wed, Fri, Sun 2.30–4.30pm May–Oct, but check the website: www.stlaurenceblackmore.org.uk*

The tower of St Laurence's is one of the best of its kind in England, and is remarkable both inside and out. From the outside it looks tremendous: a lower half-timbered stage with three lean-to roofs, then a smaller middle stage with vertical weather-boarding, then another yet smaller stage, but this time with horizontal weather-boarding, and finally a shingled broach spire. Inside, there is a formidable array of timbers to support the tower, with a complex arrangement of posts, braces and struts. These have recently been ring-dated to about 1400.

The tower masks the west end of the original Norman priory church that stood here. This has a doorway, an upper round window and two round-headed windows. Parts of the rest of the church are Norman, while the north arcade is early 14th-century, and the south arcade is Tudor, with piers of red brick. Nothing of the other priory buildings remains, the only visible clue to their existence being two blocked doorways in the church that may have led to the cloisters. The priory closed in 1527, with the church continuing as the parish church, minus its choir.

Hatfield Broad Oak
St Mary

Why visit: *Former priory church with fascinating furnishings and monuments*
Where: *High Street (B183), CM22 7HG*

St Mary's is a large and impressive church in a big churchyard. It was founded as a priory in about 1135 by Aubrey de Vere II, Earl of Oxford, incorporating an earlier parish church. Parishioners and monks disagreed violently in 1378, resulting in the church being permanently divided by a wall. At the Dissolution everything east of the wall was demolished – the rest stayed as the parish church. It was largely rebuilt in the 14th and 15th centuries.

Fixtures and furnishings from the 18th century make a real impact inside, from the huge brass candelabra, to the impressive wooden symbols of the Evangelists: lion, ox, eagle and angel. Also 18th-century is the seating and panelling in the chancel. The handsome wooden roof dates from 1843.

The church has many wall-mounted monuments. One to Sir John Barrington includes at the top a skull and bones. Below that is an urn flanked by

This page: Interior of St Andrew's, Greensted-juxta-Ongar.

chubby putti, one of which is sobbing into its handkerchief.

Other monuments include motifs such as wilting foliage and draped urns. Much more commanding is the battered effigy to Robert de Vere of about 1300. He is shown in armour and with a shield, in the act of drawing his sword.

Lambourne
St Mary and All Saints

Why visit: *Setting; 18th-century furnishings and fittings*
Where: *North-east of Lambourne village; at the end of Church Lane, signposted 'Lambourne Church' from the A113, RM4 1AH*

This is a rural church to savour. It lies at the end of a lane approached not from Lambourne village, but from the main road. It is a small, white-painted building with a neat weather-boarded belfry crowned by a lead-covered broach spire.

On the outside are obvious clues to its origins: two Norman doorways, the north one with good zig-zag decoration. Inside, the 12th-century and later 15th-century work is almost entirely

disguised by 18th-century decor and fittings. There is a fine west gallery, donated by a London ironmonger, an 18th-century font, and many 18th- and 19th-century memorials.

In 1951 repairs uncovered parts of a medieval wall painting of St Christopher; his bearded face is beautifully painted. And from the 17th century are panels of exquisite Swiss stained glass.

Waltham Abbey   Holy Cross and St Lawrence

Why visit: *Remnant of once great abbey church; Victorian restoration; monuments*
Where: *In the centre of Waltham Abbey, Highbridge Street, EN9 1DJ*

The church that stands here today is a truncated remnant of what was once a great abbey church. Of the original, two-thirds bigger than what is left, nothing remains, and there is little of the other abbey buildings.

Waltham Abbey was founded in 1030 in what was then a thickly forested part of what we now call Epping Forest. It was rebuilt in 1060 by King Harold, and it was here that his body was brought after the Battle of Hastings. Henry II greatly enlarged the abbey in the 12th century as part of his penance for the murder of Thomas a Becket. At the Dissolution everything, except the part of the church that had been used as a parish church, was demolished.

The outside of the church today is a pleasant jumble of work in differing materials from many ages. The tower is 16th-century, with a top stage built in 1905. Inside, the feeling is very different, with great Norman piers marching towards an east end that was created by architect William Burges in the 19th century. His solution for finishing what was left of the abbey church is generally considered to be masterful, with work by some of the finest artists and craftsmen of the 19th century, including stained glass by Edward Burne-Jones.

Contrasting with this grandeur is the Lady Chapel, dating from the 14th century and with beautifully detailed window tracery. A Doom painting was discovered on the walls here during restoration work.

Monuments in the church include a brightly painted one to Sir Edward Denny and his wife. It dates from about 1600, and as well as effigies of the husband and wife, leaning on their elbows, there are smaller figures of their 10 children.

The marble tomb of sea captain Robert Smith (died 1697) shows his ship, the *Industria*, in full sail on an ocean full of dolphins. Round this scene are carved some of the tools of his trade: a sextant, hour glass, cannon, cutlass and pistol.

Willingale Doe and Spain
St Christopher and St Andrew and All Saints CCT

Why visit: *Two churches sharing the same churchyard*
Where: *The Street, CM5 0SJ*

Here are two churches side by side, separated only by a row of trees and an expanse of the churchyard that they share. They make a fine composition in the gentle Essex landscape.

The older is St Andrew's, now in the care of the Churches Conservation Trust. It was given to nearby Blackmore Priory by William de Hispania (hence the 'Spain' part of the village's name) in 1120, and it has several 12th-century features, including doors and windows. Roman bricks were re-used for much of that work. The chancel and belfry were added in the 15th century. The dainty white-painted belfry is supported inside the church by an interesting arrangement of a tie-beam with four arched braces.

St Christopher's has a 14th-century nave, chancel and tower, and a south porch from the 15th century. A great deal of reconstruction was undertaken in the 19th century. The 'Doe' of the village's name comes from the D'eau family.

This page: Lambourne's rural church (left); the monument to Sir Edward Denny, at Waltham Abbey (centre).

ALSO IN THE AREA

Great Warley   St Mary
Why visit: *Arts and Crafts masterpiece*

ESSEX FARMLAND AND COAST

Some parts of Essex are remarkably remote, reached by lanes that become narrow and deserted as they reach the coastal inlets and marshes. Some of the churches are at the ends of such lanes, making them most rewarding when discovered. And some have histories stretching back to the 7th century when St Cedd built churches here.

Bradwell-on-Sea
St Peter-on-the-Wall

Why visit: *One of Britain's oldest churches*
Where: *On the coast, reached on foot by track from the end of East End Road, east of Bradwell-on-Sea, CM0 7PX; there is parking at the start of the track*

Reaching St Peter's is a small adventure, leaving the modern world behind as you get closer to the sea. When the lane stops being metalled, a footpath continues to the little chapel, right beside the mudflats.

This is one of the oldest churches in Britain. It was built on the site of the gateway of a Roman fort using the fort's stone, some time after 653. The builder was St Cedd, from Lindisfarne, who founded many churches. Only the nave remains, but the outlines of the eastern apse and north and south porticus can be seen on the ground.

A monastery that was also here was destroyed during Danish raids in the 9th century. The church was still in use in the 16th century, and partly owes its survival to its use as a seamark for fishermen and sailors. In the 17th century it became a barn, and holes were punched in the walls to make barn doors. Restoration and reconsecration took place in 1920, and today the inside of the chapel is simple and serene, with benches and an altar and wall-mounted crosses at the east end.

There is a popular, annual pilgrimage to the chapel from the village, and many people visit the chapel throughout the year on their own private journeys.

Boreham St Andrew

Why visit: *Extended porch; Saxon details; Sussex monument*
Where: *Church Road, CM3 3EQ*

St Andrew's is a fascinating building with a long history, yet with a comparatively recent and eccentric addition. This is an extension to the porch that stretches across the churchyard to the roadside. Built of timber and with a tiled roof, it was originally constructed for the wedding of a colonel's daughter in 1843. It was later demolished, but rebuilt in memory of Canon Hulton in the 1920s.

The story of the church can partly be told from the outside: the central tower has a Saxon core, later enlarged by the Normans, and heightened again in the mid-16th century. Later changes, all in flint, make the exterior a visual pleasure. There are memorable stone carvings on the 15th-century north aisle windows in the form of human heads, some smiling, some frowning, some grimacing.

Inside, original Saxon details (arches of re-used Roman material) can be seen embedded in the tower arches. The church was enlarged and altered in the 13th, 14th and 15th centuries, with elements from each of these periods still visible. The most impressive monument in the church comprises three side-by-side alabaster effigies to the first three earls of Sussex, made in the later part of the 16th century. At the foot of each earl is a monkey wearing a hat.

Copford
St Michael and All Angels

Why visit: *Remarkable wall paintings*
Where: *Off Aldercar Road, between Copford Green and Copford, CO6 1DG*

Tucked away from its village, and next to Copford Hall, St Michael's is one of Essex's most important Norman churches. It has a remarkable collection of original wall paintings from the 1140s.

The outside gives clues to the special nature of the church. A great deal of Roman brick was used to build it; this is noticeable in the apse at the east end.

Inside, the paintings immediately claim attention, but it is worth looking at the structure of the building. The original Norman building had a barrel-vaulted nave, an exceptionally rare example in England that was replaced by the present timber structure in about 1400. Remains of the springers that held up this roof can still be clearly seen. However, the apse has its original Norman vault. As well as making use of Roman brick, 12th-century builders extending the church used bricks of their own time – one of the earliest examples in England of locally made medieval bricks.

Some of the paintings have been restored, repainted and renovated more than once, but the original scheme is intact, as is the feeling of sophistication; this is church art of the highest standard. In the apse, Christ is shown in Glory, surrounded by saints and Apostles. The apse arch bears the signs of the zodiac, while elsewhere there is complex decorative patterning. The 15th-century screen, Norman font and gilded Hanoverian Royal arms are outshone by the paintings, but merit generous praise.

Layer Marney
St Mary the Virgin

Why visit: *16th-century brick church; Marney monuments*
Where: *Roundbush Road, CO5 9UR*

Here the church goes with the house, or rather tower, for the outstanding feature of Layer Marney Tower is the huge brick gatehouse built by Sir Henry Marney, who became the first Lord Marney. He also built, or rather rebuilt, the church. Both are in red brick and date from the early 16th century. The Marneys had lived here since the 12th century, but it was only in the time of Henry VII and Henry VIII that the family, in the person of Sir Henry, came to be nationally important. The tower and church reflect that status and wealth.

The church is built with patterning (called diapering) in blue brick. This is especially noticeable in the tower, which also has stone-dressed buttresses, and the overall effect is very harmonious. The plan of the church is unusual in that it has two south porches; one giving entrance to the chancel.

Inside, the church is beautifully kept, light and airy. There are two screens, wall monuments and even an old plough to draw the eye, but it is the memorials to three Marneys that stand out. First is Sir William, whose early 15th-century alabaster effigy was in the earlier church on this site. Then comes Sir Henry himself, in black marble, under an ornate terracotta canopy. Last is his son, John, 2nd and last Lord Marney, who died in 1525. Each figure has a lion at its feet.

Maldon All Saints

Why visit: *Unique tower; 14th-century stone roses*
Where: *Top of High Street, CM9 4PY*

All Saints is unique: it has the only triangular tower in England. The tower dates from the 13th century, and owes its shape to the fact that it had to fit between the then nave (replaced in 1728 with the present one) and a fish market. Flint-built, and with a shingled spire and three shingled spirelets, it is a striking sight. Inside, the south aisle is quite

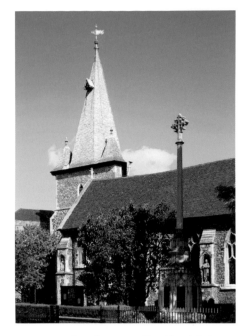

unexpected and extraordinarily rich in decorative stonework from about 1340. Rows of little ogee-headed arches form an arcade lining the south and west walls. Above the arcade, the framing of the windows is decorated with trailing tendrils of stone roses.

Maldon St Mary

Why visit: *Attractive church; ancient roots*
Where: *Church Street, CM9 5HN*

Looking out over the River Blackwater, St Mary's is an attractive church in an attractive setting, and is Maldon's most distinctive landmark. It has a squat brick and flint tower with massive buttresses; an early 17th-century top stage is crowned by a pretty but idiosyncratic 18th-century spire.

The nave is Norman, while the south aisle dates from 1886. A handsome polygonal extension called the Octagon was opened in the early 1990s. In the south aisle is a stained glass window dedicated in 1991 and commemorating the Battle of Maldon 1,000 years earlier, in 991. It may be that the church built on this site by St Cedd was destroyed by the Vikings who won the battle.

Opposite page: One of the oldest churches in Britain at Bradwell-on-Sea (left); wall paintings at Copford (right).
This page: The triangular tower at All Saints, Maldon.

Mundon St Mary FoFC

Why visit: *Remote atmospheric church with fascinating details*
Where: *South of Maldon, east of B1018, at the end of Vicarage Lane, CM9 6PA*

At the end of lanes after miles of flat, rural farmland, St Mary's is as remote as anywhere in Essex. When The Friends of Friendless Churches took it over in 1975 it was in a dangerously ruinous condition. It had always suffered from subsidence, and had the misfortune (given its remote setting) of being damaged by a World War II flying bomb in 1944. Work to stabilise, restore and repair the buildings has resulted in a wonderfully atmospheric place, immediately recognisable by its tower with lower pantiled 'skirt' and upper timbered bellcote.

The inside is equally atmospheric, with 18th-century box pews and pulpit beyond the massive timbers of the tower. Between the nave and the chancel is a rudimentary screen, above which is painted 'Behold the Lamb of God' in fading golds and reds. The east end of the chancel has a visual surprise – painted trompe-l'oeil curtains above the window, and painted boards on the north and south walls, hung on (painted) strings.

Tillingham St Nicholas

Why visit: *Setting; Norman doorway*
Where: *The Square, CM0 7SU*

Tillingham's grassy square is lined with weather-boarded cottages and a pub. The church sits back a little but is an integral part of the village scene. Its tower is a jaunty affair, largely from the 14th century but with later battlements. Much of the rest of the church is 13th and 14th century, with a Norman north doorway and font. Inside, a Victorian rood screen and rood with Christ on the Cross separate the nave from the chancel.

ALSO IN THE AREA

Little Braxted St Nicholas
Why visit: *Tiny Norman church; its entire interior is covered in decoration*

NORTH ESSEX

No less than five of the churches in this group are enhanced by being set in pretty villages or towns that have lovely houses and cottages close by. The combination is irresistible, and has resulted in one at least – Finchingfield – becoming for many the quintessential English village scene. The churches themselves vary from the noble and splendid, as at Saffron Walden, to the unusual, as at Debden and Little Dunmow.

Castle Hedingham
St Nicholas

Why visit: *Outstanding Norman and later church*
Where: *Church Lane, in the centre of the town, CO9 3ER*

Pretty cottages in pastel shades snuggle up to the churchyard walls here. It is an idyllic scene.

The church, and the castle from which the village takes its name, were built within 50 years of each other by the powerful de Vere family in the late 11th and early 12th centuries.

From the outside the chancel is clearly Norman, while the nave appears later and the tower and south porch, of red brick, are 16th-century. Inside, the church reveals itself to be predominantly Norman, with piers leading to a chancel arch that has a pointed apex, showing that it was built on the cusp of the Gothic period. Beyond the chancel arch is the rare Norman wheel window at the east end. Even the great south door is Norman, as are two other doors in the church.

Saffron Walden
St Mary the Virgin

Why visit: *Glorious early 16th-century nave with clerestory windows*
Where: *Church Street, CB10 1BP*

Coming into Saffron Walden from the west, St Mary's appears over ancient roofs in much the same way that it has for hundreds of years. The immediate approach to the church, up Church Street, takes you through the unspoiled heart of the town.

The church is very large, one of the biggest in Essex, and was almost entirely rebuilt between 1450 and 1525. It is especially noted for the size and grandeur of its nave and aisles. However, the exterior is dominated by the very tall tower and spire, which were designed in the 1830s by architect Thomas Rickman. He also did much work at Cambridge – only a little distance away across the county boundary.

The Cambridge connection goes back to the nave, which was built by Simon Clark and John Wastell, master masons at King's College Chapel. Their work at Saffron Walden is outstanding: the nave is very tall and elegant with clerestory windows in pairs and blank panelling below them. At the top of the piers upon which these rest, the spandrels (triangular panels between the arch and its frame) are richly carved, and include saffron crocus, the flower that gave the town its name, and its fame and fortune.

The wooden roofs of the nave and aisles are original and have bosses that include Tudor roses. The fine chancel screen dates from 1924. The church's brasses have been moved from their original places on to the walls. The best monument is to Thomas, Lord Audley, who died in 1544. It is of black marble and a fine piece of work; 17th-century historian Thomas Fuller wrote that the colour was no blacker than the soul of Audley himself.

The chancel screen is from the early 15th century, and the superb double hammerbeam roof dates from about 1535. In the churchyard is a Norman cross that

was removed from the churchyard at the Reformation and used as a pillar in the cellar of a local pub until it was put back in 1921 to become a war memorial.

Debden St Mary the Virgin and All Saints

Why visit: *Church of many ages and with an eventful history*
Where: *At the end of Church Lane, west of Debden village, CB11 3LD*

At the end of a lane leading away from the village, Debden's church is a mixture of building dates and styles from the 13th to the 21st century.

The original early 13th-century church was rebuilt in the 14th and 15th centuries, and for the next 250 years nothing very eventful happened. But then, in 1698, the steeple collapsed. It was rebuilt, but just 19 years later it collapsed again and this time there was no money for repairs.

After several years, during which parts of the church were in ruins, a building campaign began in the then fashionable Gothick style. The most dramatic element of that work is the octagonal 'chapel' that was built beyond the nave in 1792. This has all the classic elements of Gothick design – complex pendant shapes and use of plasterwork. Here is the tomb chest of Richard Chiswell, who commissioned all this work, but then committed suicide in 1797 after a financial disaster. Misfortune struck again in 1878 with a serious fire. The west end of the church, including

the troublesome steeple, was rebuilt in 1930, and in 2000 the 'New Room' was added, with pinnacles to match the rest of the building.

Finchingfield St John the Baptist

Why visit: *Setting; chancel screen*
Where: *Church Hill, best reached on foot through the archway under the former guildhall, CM7 4NW*

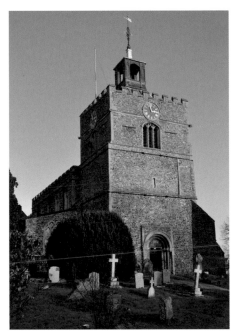

The tower of Finchingfield's church looks out over one of the best-loved villagescapes in England.

Much of the body of the church is from the 13th and 14th centuries. The 15th-century chancel screen is both delicate and elaborate and draws the eye along the nave.

The south chapel also has a lovely screen from the 14th century. In this chapel are brass effigies to Sir John Berners and his wife from the mid-1500s. There are many other monuments in the church, particularly in the chancel and the Kempe Chapel.

Opposite page: The grand nave of St Mary the Virgin, Saffron Walden (left); Norman doorway at Castle Hedingham's St Nicholas (right).
This page: Debden's much-renovated church (left); Finchingfield's tower with cupola (above).

Little Dunmow St Mary the Virgin

Why visit: *Remarkable remnant of much larger church; Fitzwalter monument*
Where: *St Mary's Place, on the south side of Little Dunmow, CM6 3HX*

This is a fragment of a very much larger priory church that was demolished at the Dissolution. It had been the Lady Chapel, and dates from about 1360. The finest thing about the exterior is the windows and their wonderful tracery. And the oddest thing about the exterior is the strange, spindly brick belfry, described by some as looking like a chimney. It dates from 1871.

Inside, the church is dignified, and full of light because of the enormous windows along the south side. The north side has 13th-century piers that were once the link between this part of the building and the priory chancel. Between and below the south windows and the east window is blind arcading that includes carvings of animals and foliage.

The finest monument is that to Lord Fitzwalter and his wife Elizabeth, of about 1431. Their effigies are made of alabaster and the detailing of clothes and faces is superb. They look like portraits rather than idealised images.

Radwinter St Mary the Virgin

Why visit: *Excellent Victorian rebuilding of a medieval church*
Where: *Off Walden Road, CB10 2SW; open first Sat each month, 10–1pm*

The story of Radwinter's church as it appears today revolves around the Reverend J.F.W. Bullock, who was vicar here from 1865 to 1916 and whose family had been lords of the Manor. He commissioned architect Eden Nesfield to virtually rebuild the church between 1869 and 1870.

Some elements of the old church were kept, including the 14th-century porch, to which Nesfield added a charming upper storey. Further work was undertaken later by Temple Moore, an eminent architect, who rebuilt the tower and spire.

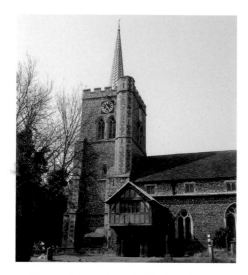

More of the original old church can be seen inside, including the 14th-century nave roof. There is fine Victorian work as well, particularly the chancel screen. The reredos is what many consider to be St Mary's greatest treasure. It is Flemish and from the early 16th century and shows scenes from the Life of Our Lady. Like much at St Mary's, it is here because of Reverend Bullock, who bought it in a London saleroom.

Thaxted St John the Baptist, St Mary and St Laurence

Why visit: *Impressive church in a lovely townscape*
Where: *Watling Lane, CM6 2QY*

Thaxted's pretty houses, painted in yellows, blues, pinks and greens, are a perfect foil for its battlemented and pinnacled church. In medieval times Thaxted was a wealthy place, its riches coming from the cutlery industry. The church was rebuilt in the 14th and 15th centuries with some of the proceeds of that trade. Its tall spire is a landmark for miles around, and its imposing grandeur reflects the riches that were put into it.

The interior is much plainer than the outside, with largely white walls and a feeling of great spaciousness enhanced by the floor space that is kept clear of seating. The white paint and clear glass in most of the windows, including those in the clerestory, means that features such as the original wooden roofs stand out.

There is much to see here, including many carved bosses, the 15th-century font and its ornate wooden cover. Also

note the 17th-century pulpit, the organ (played by Gustav Holst who lived in Thaxted for many years), and an eagle lectern. The latter is brightly coloured, and rather like a parrot.

Tilty St Mary the Virgin

Why visit: *Very rural setting; exceptional east window*
Where: *North-east of Stansted airport, off a lane between Broxted and Duton Hill, signposted 'Tilty Church', CM6 2JN*

St Mary's looks like two, or even three, churches magicked together. The chancel is rather grand, with an exceptional east window that is often cited as an example of Decorated window tracery at its finest. The ochre-coloured nave is much smaller in scale, and with its elaborate little cupola looks rather central European. And on the north side is a brick-built extension with crowstepped gables that could be from the Netherlands.

This little church has a fascinating story. The oldest part is the nave, which was originally 'the chapel outside the gates' of the Cistercian abbey of Tilty. All such abbeys had a chapel like this, for passers-by, workmen, and for women, who were not allowed in the precincts. Of the abbey itself nothing now remains except for lumps of masonry in a field nearby.

The nave is 13th-century. Its porch is 17th-century, and the little belfry and its cupola date from the 18th century. The brick extension is a Victorian vestry. The chancel was added in about 1330, and has outstanding features, especially the east window with sinuous reticulated tracery.

Inside are elements from every part of the church's history, including sedilias and piscinas in both parts of the building. Those in the chancel are as grand as its

windows. There are also brasses, medieval floor tiles, hatchments and a 15th-century roof on the nave.

Wendens Ambo St Mary the Virgin

Why visit: *Setting; wooden tiger*
Where: *Church Street, off the B1039, CB11 4JZ*

The combination of church and cottages here is rural England at its most appealing. The church itself is beautiful, with flint walls and a collection of roofs at different angles, best seen from the south-east. The tower, which has a little spire called a Hertfordshire spike, is Norman, and has re-used Roman bricks in the west doorway. The nave and chancel are later – the chancel was rebuilt around 1300. Inside, there are remains of medieval wall paintings showing scenes from the life of St Margaret, a 16th-century font cover and a medieval screen and benches. One has a renowned carving of a tiger on it.

This page: The 14th-century porch at Radwinter (left); St Mary's colourful exterior at Tilty (centre); Wendens Ambo (above).

ALSO IN THE AREA

Great Dunmow St Mary
Why visit: *15th-century wooden gallery*

Hadstock St Botolph
Why visit: *Setting; oldest working door in England (Saxon)*

Little Maplestead St John the Baptist
Why visit: *Unusual round church*

SOUTH SUFFOLK

Suffolk is justly famous for its churches, and this group includes what many would consider to be the two finest: Lavenham and Long Melford. But all the churches here are outstanding in their different ways, making this as rich a collection as you will find anywhere. Very often it is the setting, whether in town, village or countryside, that gives the buildings even more of an edge. There are so many wonderful churches here because from the 14th to the 16th century Suffolk was immensely wealthy, its riches gained from the woollen cloth trade.

Lavenham
St Peter and St Paul

Why visit: *One of England's greatest churches*
Where: *Church Street, west side of Lavenham, CO10 9RR*

Lavenham's church stands on the edge of the town, with open fields just beyond. Both town and church are world famous for their beauty, and the fact that there is a breathing space of countryside beyond the church actually adds to the pleasure of the setting.

For about 150 years, between the end of the 14th and the middle of the 16th century, Lavenham was one of the richest towns in Britain. Its wealth was built on the cloth trade – especially the making of kersey, a woollen cloth named after the nearby village of the same name. Many of Lavenham's splendid timber-framed buildings date from this prosperous period, as does the church.

The church itself was built, or rather rebuilt, in the years immediately following the Tudor victory at the Battle of Bosworth, in 1485. The instigator was John de Vere, 13th Earl of Oxford, one of the most powerful men in England. Lavenham was one of his many estates in East Anglia. He worked on the church in partnership with Lavenham's richest and most important clothiers, particularly the Spring family.

Work began with the stupendous tower, built of flint dressed with limestone imported from Northamptonshire. Set into the tower – and clearly visible from the ground – is the de Vere star, one of their symbols. The other de Vere symbol, a wild boar, can be seen in the south porch and in the nave. Next to be rebuilt was the nave; the only feature left from the 14th-century nave was the rather odd spirelet, kept to hold the Sanctus bell. The chancel was not rebuilt, and retains its fine 14th-century arch.

The glory of the interior is the nave, with its elegant piers and fine

This page: *The impressive and finely worked exterior of St Peter and St Paul.*

15th-century roof, the rare 14th-century chancel screen and the screens at the ends of the aisles. These two parclose screens are outstanding. The north one, made in the 1520s, is the finest and was built by the Spring family. It has wonderful, intricate wood carving. The south screen is less elaborate and was built by the Spourne family.

There are excellent misericords in the chancel. They include musicians, a jester, an ibis and a spoonbill, reminders that East Anglia in the Middle Ages was very much wilder and wetter than it is now, and these two birds, very rare in Britain today, were common then.

Boxted Holy Trinity

Why visit: *Setting; Poley monuments*
Where: *On lanes south-west of Boxted, beyond Boxted Hall, IP29 4LN*

Holy Trinity is closer, both physically and perhaps in spirit, to Boxted Hall than it is to the village. From the churchyard there is a beautiful view over the little Glem Valley to the hall, seat of the Poleys (pronounced Pooley).

The church has a modest exterior dating mostly from the Perpendicular period with a later red-brick chapel on the north side. The fascination of this church lies within as it contains a remarkable collection of memorials to generations of Poleys.

The nave has an early 16th-century tie-beam roof and an excellent carved pulpit complete with sounding board, dated 1618. The chancel was enlarged in the 17th century and has an unusual hammerbeam roof and three-sided communion rails typical of this period. There are hatchments on the walls and many ledger-stone memorials set into the floor.

On the south wall of the chancel is a splendid Elizabethan tomb with rare black oak effigies of William and Alice Poley. The stained glass in the east window commemorates Hugh Weller-Poley, killed while in the RAF during

This page: The picture-perfect setting of St Mary's, Cavendish (centre); Clare's 14th-century south nave doorway with ornate carvings in the surround (right).

World War II. Both hall and church are shown in the glass, along with rabbits and partridges.

On the north side is the Poley Chapel, with more Poley memorials including two magnificent alabaster monuments of soldier and adventurer Sir John (1558–1638) and his wife Dame Abigail (died 1652). They were erected long after their deaths and are in the baroque style. Sir John is particularly flamboyant and wears a curious frog earring. It is often suggested that the rhyme 'A Frog he would a wooing go, with a Rowley, Poley, Gammon and Spinach' may refer to the Suffolk families Roley, Poley, Bacon and Greene.

Cavendish St Mary

Why visit: *Village setting; eagle lectern, Flemish reredos*
Where: *Just off the village green in Cavendish, CO10 8AZ*

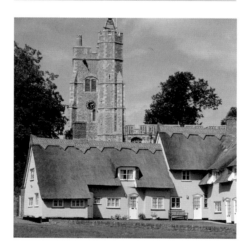

From the west and south, the combination of village green, cottages and church at Cavendish is perfect, and makes one of the loveliest and most famous English village scenes. The church's prominent tower and turret staircase date from about 1300, as does the porch. This still has its original door, complete with sanctuary ring. The 14th-century south aisle is plain flint, but rising above it is a fine 15th-century clerestory with excellent flushwork and battlements.

The interior is especially light, with exceptional late 15th-century arcades and elegant slender piers. On the wall of the north aisle is a great treasure –

a 16th-century Flemish alabaster reredos of the Crucifixion given to the church in 1953. It is set in an elaborate 20th-century frame made by Sir Ninian Comper. The chancel dates from the 1380s, with a magnificent window filling the east wall.

Unusually, the ground floor of the tower has a vaulted ceiling with a large central boss depicting a Green Man. Displayed on the rear wall of the tower are World War I battlefield crosses brought back from the Western Front.

St Mary's has an ancient brass lectern in the shape of an eagle, one of only 50 medieval lecterns of this type to have survived the Reformation. There is another just along the road at Clare.

Clare St Peter and St Paul

Why visit: *Features from many periods, including a medieval eagle lectern*
Where: *Town centre, CO10 8PB*

Clare's church is in the centre of the little town, with handsome houses on all sides. It is a large building in the Perpendicular style, reflecting the prosperous times in which it was built. The west tower has a 13th-century door with dog-tooth moulding, and there are also two distinctive turrets at the east end of the nave. The porch is 14th-century with a finely carved stone head at the centre

of the vault and stone carving, including Green Men, around the 15th-century oak door. Over the porch is an 18th-century sundial on which is inscribed 'Go about your business'.

The interior is light and spacious, with graceful nave arcades divided from the clerestory above by a well-preserved string course with carved figures and foliage. From between the arches a variety of medieval heads look down – kings, queens, merchants and perhaps even a jester. The 15th-century chancel had fallen into disrepair by the 17th century but was rebuilt in 1617. From this time are the clergy stalls and the fine altar rail, and the benefactors who paid for the work are commemorated in the east window.

William Dowsing, the famous Puritan zealot who went from church to church in East Anglia in the 1640s looking for and destroying what he thought of as 'superstitious' or 'popish' objects and images, claimed that he 'brake down a 1,000 pictures superstitious' at Clare on 6 January 1643. It is unlikely that there were '1,000 pictures' to destroy here, but he did break most of the stained glass. Not, however, such surviving pieces as those with heraldic images in them, as these did not count as either popish or superstitious.

The brass eagle lectern here is one of the few medieval lecterns of this type to have survived the Reformation and is a fine example. On display nearby is a curious beer jug called 'The Gotch', which holds 32 pints and was presented to the bell ringers in 1729. The unusual 17th-century gallery was once a private pew and is now incorporated into St John's Chapel, within the church.

Denston St Nicholas

Why visit: *Perfect Perpendicular church*
Where: *East of the A143, CB8 8PP*

It is difficult to believe that this beautiful and well-cared-for church was neglected for many years, and almost ruinous by the 1970s. Now, fully repaired and restored, it is considered to be one of the finest small churches in England.

It was established as a collegiate church between 1475 and 1485 with a bequest

from John Denston, of nearby Denston Hall. An existing 14th-century tower was retained, joined to a beautifully crafted new Perpendicular exterior.

Outside the porch is a conspicuous and well-preserved holy water stoup. The impressive interior is beautifully proportioned, with nave, aisles and chancel all of a piece. Elegant arcades rise to a lofty timber roof, which has marvellous carved animals running along its edges.

Seven-sacrament fonts are an East Anglian speciality, and Denston has one of the best-preserved of the few that survive. It dates from the 15th century. Fonts like this were obvious targets after the Reformation as they show scenes from the Catholic sacraments. The Denston font shows a confirmation, a mass, last rites, and so forth.

The oak benches are original, with delightful carved finials featuring a variety of animals. The best known is a carving of what is usually described as an elephant, but of an imagined, or perhaps mythical kind, with what looks like a duck's bill rather than a trunk and swept-back ears that resemble a fancy hair-do. The lower part of the rood screen is still here, as is the original, and rare, rood beam (on which the figures of Jesus,

Mary and St John would have stood). The chancel has priests' stalls with misericords including an excellent carving of a crane, and the east window contains a large number of glass fragments. There is a fine brass of Henry and Margaret Everard, and a table tomb with two macabre shrouded effigies is thought to be of John Denston and his wife.

Kersey St Mary

Why visit: *Hilltop setting; excellent flint patterning*
Where: *At the top of Church Hill, IP6 6EF*

St Mary's stands on high ground above its very pretty village, which prospered during the late medieval cloth-making boom in this part of Suffolk. Kersey was a particular kind of woollen cloth, named after the village.

It is an interesting church partly because a 14th-century reconstruction in the Decorated style of the chancel, north aisle and base of the tower was brought to a sudden halt by the Black Death. The rebuilding was only completed half a century later, this time in the Perpendicular style.

The handsome tower has lower courses of neat flushwork and the battlemented upper stage has particularly effective flint patterning. Both north and south porches are in use; the south porch is more elaborate, with marvellous flint flushwork panelling, carved niches and pinnacled buttresses. It has an intricately carved

This page: An exemplary Perpendicular church at Denston (top centre) with its rare and original rood beam (below centre); Kersey's light interior (above).

wooden ceiling, which is most unusual and was only revealed during repairs in 1927.

The interior is light, with the large north aisle separated from the nave by a fine seven-bay arcade with interesting carving. The nave has an excellent wooden roof. Of interest here are the early 15th-century font with decorated panels, the unusual wooden lectern with a delicate 15th-century stem, and a later eagle reading desk. At the east end of the north aisle is a beautiful piscina and sedilia. On display is part of a 15th-century rood screen with six panels in the original colour of kings and prophets, including an especially good St Edmund the Martyr depicted with his symbolic arrow (he was used as a target by archers before being beheaded).

Long Melford Holy Trinity

Why visit: *Superb 'glass and light' church*
Where: *North side of Long Melford, CO10 9DT*

With many of the finest East Anglian churches, setting and position play a crucial part in the impact of the building. Long Melford's Holy Trinity is perhaps the finest example of this. It is not in the central part of the long and beautiful main street, but in a group with other buildings on a hill to the north, across the Chad Brook, past the pepper-pot towers of Melford Hall, and beyond what must be one of the biggest village greens anywhere. It is a truly memorable scene; best savoured on foot.

During the Middle Ages Long Melford was one of the richest towns in the country, and the great wealth of the merchants who made fortunes in the cloth trade is evident throughout the

town (the 'Long' part of the name is wholly accurate) and its church. The three greatest benefactor families to the church were the Cloptons, the Cordells and the Martyns.

The church itself, one of the most celebrated in Britain, gained its present magnificent appearance when it was rebuilt in the late 15th century. The immediate impression is of flint and glass, and of the late Perpendicular style at its most majestic.

The main body of the church was completed in 1484, and stands in a large churchyard with Sir William Cordell's hospital of 1573 to the south. A large, sumptuous, and entirely separate Lady Chapel was added to the east end of the church in 1496, giving the building an even more distinctive profile.

Lightning destroyed the original tower in 1710 and what we see today was completed in 1903. Its flintwork is every bit as fine and complex as in the nave.

The interior is of cathedral proportions, with wide nave and aisles, and is flooded with light from the immense windows. To increase the dramatic effect there is no chancel arch, and a single superb wooden roof extends the entire length of nave and chancel.

One of the finest collections of late medieval glass in England is contained in the north aisle windows, including a 15th-century figure of Elizabeth Talbot,

Duchess of Norfolk, said to have inspired Tenniel's depiction of the Duchess in *Alice's Adventures in Wonderland*. The tiny 'rabbit' roundel nearby, of three rabbits with shared ears, is famous and is thought to be a symbol of the Trinity.

Also in the north aisle is a fine alabaster bas-relief of the Adoration of the Magi dating from about 1350. The tomb of the knight in armour is Sir William Clopton, who died in 1446. His son John was the founder of the church and is commemorated in the Clopton Chantry Chapel, which is beautifully decorated with a painted and carved roof, the east window containing a rare 'lily crucifix'.

John Clopton's tomb dates from 1497 and is between the chapel and the chancel. It was originally also the Easter Sepulchre and has a painting of Christ underneath its canopy. On the south side of the chancel is the Renaissance tomb of Sir William Cordell, Speaker of the House of Commons during the reign of Queen Mary and Master of the Rolls to Queen Elizabeth.

The east end of the south aisle is the Martyn Chapel, which has excellent brasses. Roger Martyn, who died in 1684, remained loyal to Rome and left a rare description of the church and its ritual before the Reformation.

The distinctive Lady Chapel is, most unusually for a parish church, situated at the east end and is a delightful building in its own right. It is light and bright with a central sanctuary surrounded by an ambulatory (walkway). Its cambered tie-beam roofs have well-preserved carvings. After the Reformation it became a school room, and a multiplication table is still visible on the north-east wall.

Polstead St Mary

Why visit: *Beautiful setting; many features, including Norman brick arches*
Where: *Off Water Lane, on a track west of Polstead, CO6 5BS*

Yet another Suffolk church in a superb setting, St Mary's is located on a hill, away from the road, overlooking the valley of the River Box. It has many unusual features for a Suffolk church, including a stone medieval spire (the only one in the

county). Also, it was not rebuilt in the Perpendicular style (much of it is Early English and Decorated) and it has many Norman features (including Norman bricks). The metal roof of the nave is a recent addition, dating from the 1980s.

The interior is very special, for the Norman brick arches may be built of the earliest-known locally made bricks in Britain, dating from about 1180. Historians have differed in their views about the bricks, some saying they are Roman, or even Tudor, but the current balance of expert opinion favours a 12th-century date.

Bricks were also used to make the font, a most unusual material for such a purpose, and perhaps dating back to the 13th century. The north porch has fragments of wonderful medieval glass. There is much else to see in this lovely old church, but it is the churchyard that draws many visitors, as somewhere here (there is no gravestone) is the grave of Maria Marten, victim of William Corder in the notorious 'Red Barn Murder' case of 1827. The grave of Percy Edwards, of radio and television birdsong impersonation fame, can also be seen.

Stoke-by-Nayland St Mary

Why visit: *One of the great Suffolk churches, especially renowned for its tower*
Where: *In the village, CO6 4QU*

Painted by Constable and many others, and in the top tier of Suffolk churches, St Mary's is beautiful inside and out. Its huge tower, built of flint, pebble, brick and limestone, is a landmark for miles around. Dating from the mid-1400s, it is a little later than most of the church.

The interior was heavily restored in Victorian times, especially the east end,

but the west end is very much as it was originally built. This includes the wonderful, soaring tower arch. Many will think this is the single most unmissable feature of the church.

Below this arch is the late 15th-century font, which has very clear, detailed carvings. These include the four Evangelists. Also very special is the south door – original, oak and covered in a delicate filigree of carving that includes a Tree of Jesse. It is one of only a very few surviving medieval doors in Suffolk.

Monuments include large memorials to Lady Anne Windsor with her two daughters, of about 1612, and one to Sir Francis Mannock, of about 1634. There are also a number of brasses, including one to Sir William Tendring. His coat of arms can be seen on the tower, as he was one of St Mary's main benefactors.

Stratford St Mary St Mary

Why visit: *Fantastic flintwork*
Where: *On the B1029, just east of the village, CO7 6LS*

Chopped off from its village by the main Ipswich trunk road, and right beside the B1029, Stratford St Mary's church is perhaps best first viewed from the quiet lane (the Dedham road) just to the east.

But it needs to be looked at close-to as well, because it has really excellent, and very unusual, flintwork. Below the windows appears, in flint flushwork, a lengthy inscription inviting prayers for the soul of a benefactor, Thomas Mors, a cloth manufacturer who died in 1500.

His wife, who died in 1510, left money for an elaborate porch to be built. However, when constructed in 1532 it tactlessly obscured the end of her husband's pious inscription. Higher up on the walls there are letters of the alphabet in flintwork. Apart from demonstrating Thomas Mors' wealth to the passers-by (work with such detail would have been very expensive), experts differ as to the significance or meaning of the letters. By the 19th century the church was in a poor condition, and so was heavily restored in the 1870s by architect Henry Woodyer.

This has given the interior a Victorian flavour, but it remains a handsome church with a lofty perpendicular nave with four bays of slender columns, two aisles and a clerestory. At the east end are two chapels, and the chancel has an east window with Victorian glass. High on the chancel wall above the arches is a striking Victorian mural of Old Testament scenes and The Last Supper.

Opposite page: *A view of Long Melford's grand church (left) and the Elizabeth Talbot stained glass window (centre).*
This page: *Polstead's unusual brick font (left); Stoke-by-Nayland's landmark church (centre); intricate flintwork at Stratford St Mary (above).*

ALSO IN THE AREA

Acton All Saints
Why visit: *14th-century brass of Sir Roger de Bures*

Hadleigh St Mary
Why visit: *Steeple; setting alongside Hadleigh Deanery*

173

NORTH-WEST SUFFOLK

Almost every part of Suffolk offers a wealth of fine churches to visit and it is easy to be spoilt for choice. The county's medieval craftsmen were second to none, and in this area around Bury St Edmunds their work is evident in many guises. Enjoy spectacular woodcarving in many elaborate 'angel' roof structures, and the characteristic flushwork: striking patterns in stone and knapped flint, shaped and built with masterly precision, that adorn porches, clerestories and towers.

Woolpit St Mary

Why visit: *Outstanding 15th-century porch; angel roof; 15th-century bench-ends*
Where: *In the centre of the village, north-west of Stowmarket, IP3 9QP*

This ancient village was on the pilgrimage route to Bury St Edmunds and is full of history and legend. The church here was attached to the abbey of St Edmundsbury from pre-Norman times, but the oldest parts of the present building – the chancel and south aisle – are early 14th-century.

The spire, with its delicate flying buttresses, is Victorian. Its style may not belong to Suffolk, but it is distinctive and looks especially striking when lit up at night. It was added after the original tower was partially destroyed by lightning in 1852.

The exceptional two-storey porch is large and beautifully proportioned, with a fine stone entrance (unusual for Suffolk) surrounded by Perpendicular niches that once contained figures. It is topped by a lovely openwork parapet, and there is excellent chequerboard flushwork on the east wall, echoing the

similar panels on the clerestory. Be sure to look up inside to see the fine bosses on the vault. The porch dates from the mid-15th century.

Of the same period, inside the church, is the astonishing angel roof. Every part of its double hammerbeam structure is alive with angels and other figures. Many of them are 19th-century replicas of originals that were destroyed by the Puritans. Although also restored, with bright paintwork in the lower panels, the screen has pleasing ogee arches and delicate open tracery above. High above it, over the chancel arch, is an unusual, rather gaudily painted canopy of honour. The brass eagle lectern – a design much favoured by the Victorians – is in fact a rarity. Dating from around 1520, it is one of only about 40 to have survived the ravages of the Reformation.

Woolpit's famous benches have poppyheads and traceried ends and a great variety of creatures to identify and admire, including monkeys, dogs and birds. As well as the medieval bench-ends in the nave and chancel, there are Victorian ones by Henry Ringham, the master woodcarver from Ipswich, who expertly repaired the angel roof.

Earl Stonham St Mary

Why visit: *Superb hammerbeam roof*
Where: *On the north side of the A1120 through Earl Stonham, IP14 5EE*

East Anglia possesses an unparalleled gallery of woodcarving in its church roofs, and here is one of the best, so take binoculars with you! Every part of the structure bristles with ornamentation: foliage, animals, Green Men and many angels (some headless since they were attacked by the iconoclasts of the 17th century). Other features to look for in the church include the well-preserved Doom painting above the chancel arch, and the finely carved 17th-century pulpit behind which are three hourglasses for timing sermons. The church is a rather stern-looking cruciform building, set on a windy hill with a handsome, solid-looking tower. The fine clerestory, with flushwork panels, was built around 1460.

Hessett St Ethelbert

Why visit: *Exterior stonework; rich interior; medieval wall paintings*
Where: *In the centre of Hessett, east of Bury St Edmunds, IP30 9AX*

The elaborate stonework of its exterior immediately confirms that this is a truly special church. The porch and tower are particularly fine, with intricately carved stone parapets, pinnacles and East Anglian flint flushwork, all bearing witness to the wealthy 15th-century patrons who are celebrated in shields and inscriptions.

The inside of the building lives up to this promise, with its grand Perpendicular nave arcades and, everywhere, powerful evidence of the medieval church. This includes the delicate tracery of the screen; the clergy stalls in the 14th-century chancel; lovely stained glass; and the richly carved octagonal font of about 1451. Several wall paintings survive, including a graphic Seven Deadly Sins dating from the 1370s. Beneath it is a rare 15th-century Christ of the Trades, depicting various medieval tools.

This page: Woolpit's marvellous angel roof.

Mildenhall St Mary

Why visit: *Exceptional angel roofs in nave and aisles; huge 14th-century east window*
Where: *On the west side of Mildenhall High Street (B1102), IP28 7EE*

The Breckland town of Mildenhall was well on the way to prosperity by the time of the Norman Conquest, as is reflected in the grandeur of its impressive church, which was rebuilt between the 13th and 15th centuries. Much distinguished medieval craftsmanship makes it one of the great churches of East Anglia. The tall 15th-century west tower and the huge Decorated east window are the features that strike most people first. The two-storey north porch of about 1420 makes a fittingly grand entrance, with its fine stone vault and roof bosses.

Even more remarkable are the extravagant roofs above the nave and both aisles, which are embellished with throngs of carved angels and biblical figures. The nave, especially, is a remarkable survival: unable to reach the immensely high carved angels to destroy them with their bare hands, the iconoclasts tried to shoot them to pieces instead. Many of the figures are still peppered with gunshot.

Stowlangtoft St George

Why visit: *Harmonious exterior; interior woodwork*
Where: *On the road through Stowlangtoft village, off the A1088, IP31 3JR*

Unlike many East Anglian village churches that have evolved over the centuries, this dignified and harmonious building set on the elevated site of a Roman camp was built in a single phase between about 1370 and 1400. Its benefactor, Robert de Ashfield, is buried in the chancel, having died in 1401.

The interior is a rare and very varied gallery of woodcarving: most of it medieval, but with some Victorian detailing that competently emulates the original. There is a wonderful collection of bench-ends with poppyheads and choir stalls with misericords, a 15th-century screen, and a series of Flemish panels of the same period, to either side of the altar. These were stolen in 1977 but eventually returned to the church. There are also wall paintings of a faded St Christopher in his customary spot on the north wall.

Thornham Parva St Mary

Why visit: *Thatched rural church with rare 14th-century altarpiece; early wall paintings*
Where: *In the scattered farming hamlet of Thornham Parva, west off the A140 near Eye, IP23 8EY*

Fields and trees surround this wonderful ancient church, which seems connected to the East Anglian landscape around it by its walls of flint cobbles and its roof of reed thatch. Dating back to pre-Conquest times, it has a small Saxon window in the west wall and two Norman doorways. The setting and the building are enchanting in themselves, but there is more inside: notably a rare, beautifully painted and gilded nine-panel retable vividly depicting saints, in glowing colours, flanking a Crucifixion panel. Thought to have been made in the 1330s for the Dominican priory at Thetford, this extraordinary masterpiece was discovered in a stable by Lord Henniker of Thornham Hall in 1927. The panel has a matching altar frontispiece, which somehow found its way into the Musée de Cluny in Paris. Yet another treasure at Thornham Parva is a series of very early wall paintings depicting the life and martyrdom of St Edmund.

Troston St Mary

Why visit: *A quiet, little-known rural church with medieval wall paintings*
Where: *Church Lane, on the east side of the village, IP31 1EX*

There are interesting features of many periods in this unassuming village church, which had a thatched roof until 1869. The chancel is the oldest part, with its Early English lancet windows from the 13th century. The nave and tower came a century later, and there is a typical 15th-century Suffolk porch, with panels of stone and flint. The three-decker pulpit is Jacobean, and a notable addition of recent times is the contemporary stained glass in the east window. This depicts the story of Christ's appearance on the road to Emmaus. The rather dim light inside the church makes it difficult to see the remarkable medieval wall paintings, but look closely to see St George and St Christopher on the north wall, and a Doom above the chancel arch.

This page: Stained glass at Mildenhall (left); the thatched church at Thornham Parva (centre).

ALSO IN THE AREA

Euston St Genevieve
Why visit: *17th-century church in the style of Sir Christopher Wren; in Euston Park; key at estate office*

Gipping Chapel of St Nicholas
Why visit: *Flintwork walls; medieval stained glass; Perpendicular windows*

Shelland King Charles the Martyr
Why visit: *Remote country church with charming 18th-century Gothick interior*

Stonham Parva St Mary CCT
Why visit: *Unusual tower; double hammerbeam roof; 15th-century font*

EAST SUFFOLK

The landscapes of east Suffolk range from windswept coasts to quiet farming country, dotted with outstanding churches. In addition to a wealth of quintessential Suffolk features, such as wonderful roof structures, incomparable flintwork and medieval carvings on bench-ends and stalls, the churches here contain rare examples of craftsmanship that are among only a handful of their kind in the country.

Blythburgh Holy Trinity

Why visit: *Exterior flintwork; superb light interior with famous angels*
Where: *Church Lane, IP19 9LP*

Blythburgh church is sometimes called the Lantern of the Marshes, looking out as it does over the tidal River Blyth and its marshes and meadows.

An Augustinian priory was founded here in 1130, which probably accounts for the size and splendour of the church. In 1412 Henry IV granted permission for it to be rebuilt, transforming it into one of Suffolk's finest Perpendicular churches. The tower remains from the earlier building. The exterior is an amazing mix of flint and glass, with intricate decorative stonework and carving along the parapets of the porch and south aisle. Set into the east end below the window are enigmatic carved letters.

Inside, the aged wooden roof, still with its original faded paintwork, stretches the entire length of the church. On it are the 12 famous wooden angels that are celebrated in Blythburgh's town sign. There used to be more, and some of those that remain have been repaired or renewed. One story tells that they were shot at by Puritans, trying to dislodge them. Shot has been found in some of the roof timbers, but this probably dates from the 18th century, when people were paid to shoot at the jackdaws that inhabited the church. By then it was in a poor state, and by the late 19th century the congregation sat in their pews under umbrellas as the roof leaked so badly.

Restoration began in the 1890s and continued for nearly a century, but was all done with a light touch, so that the church feels both ancient and loved.

The interior is light and airy, largely due to the clerestory windows which, like the roof, extend the whole length of the nave and chancel. The font has detached stone stools surrounding it, which are unusual. There are marvellous 15th-century poppyhead bench-ends depicting the Seven Deadly Sins, the four seasons and the Seven Acts of Mercy.

In the chancel are stalls carved with figures of saints and Apostles, which may have been part of the base of the rood screen. Each carries his own symbol so that he can be recognised. The figures are beautifully made and very sophisticated, with neatly combed beards and hair.

Bramfield St Andrew

Why visit: *Detached round tower; screen panels with original painted figures; 17th-century Elizabeth Coke monument*
Where: *Walpole Road, leading west out of the village on the A144, IP19 9HT*

It is clear from the first glimpse that this is a church out of the ordinary. The simple thatched building and its detached, round flintwork tower, with its ring of five bells, share a churchyard but appear to have always been otherwise unrelated. Such towers are often assumed to be Norman, but it is now thought that church and tower may both be of 14th-century date. The Domesday Book records a previous church on the site, but no evidence of Norman work is obvious in either building.

The church has some very special treasures inside. The wonderful carved and gilded rood screen somehow escaped destruction at the Reformation, and its painted panels of the Evangelists and St Mary Magdalene are 15th-century originals. Only the canopy has been restored. The monuments in the chancel deserve a close look, both for their workmanship and for the interesting stories they reveal. The beautiful alabaster effigy of Elizabeth Coke holding her baby is especially moving; she died in childbirth in 1627.

Dennington St Mary

Why visit: *Interior fittings and furnishings, especially parclose screens and bench-ends*
Where: *Near the junction of the A1120 and the B1116 in Dennington village, IP13 8AA*

Dennington's large 14th-century flint church is imposing enough, but the outside gives little clue to the rare treasures inside.

An immediately striking feature is the parclose screens, complete with their lofts, which separate the two side chapels from the body of the church. The effect

This page: *Holy Trinity at Blythburgh, seen rising from the marsh landscape.*

of their painted and gilded tracery is astonishing, both from a distance and close-up. In the south chapel, be sure to look at the monuments, notably the beautiful 15th-century effigies of William Bardolph and his wife. Every detail of the interior of St Mary's is noteworthy, from the three-decker pulpit to the 16th-century font cover with its charming finial.

Look too at the stunning chancel windows and the medieval pyx canopy, a carved wooden spire-shaped cover hanging above the altar. This rarity (one of only four in England, it is said) was used to store consecrated bread and wine for use in administering Communion to the sick. Above all, perhaps, spend some time with the menagerie of extraordinary creatures carved on the many medieval bench-ends.

Framlingham St Michael

Why visit: *Chancel with Howard tombs; concealed hammerbeam roof; rare organ*
Where: *In Church Street, the road leading towards the castle, IP13 9AZ*

St Michael's stands between the centre of the pleasing little market town of Framlingham and the great curtain wall of its 12th-century castle. This was the fortress of the Howards, Dukes of Norfolk – a wealthy and influential family at the time of Henry VIII.

The great chancel of the Perpendicular church, larger than the nave, was built by the 3rd duke in 1550 as a family mausoleum. Remains of members of the Howard family from before the Reformation had to be moved from Thetford Priory when it was dissolved, and here were joined by later family

This page: Howard tomb at Framlingham (above); Southwold's roof and screen (right).

burials in increasingly extravagant tombs, such as that of Henry Howard, Earl of Surrey. He was beheaded, aged 30, in 1547 but his gilded tomb dates from 1614.

The 12th-century chancel arch remains as evidence of an earlier church, as does a 14th-century wall painting of the Trinity on the northern arcade. The nave roof above it, probably dating from the 1520s, is a masterpiece of carpentry, with the hammerbeams concealed behind traceried timber vaulting. A masterpiece of a different kind is the ornate organ, built in 1674 by Thomas Thamar and still in use. Its case may be older, and is a rare survivor of the destruction of such organs ordered by Cromwell in the English Civil War.

Southwold
St Edmund King and Martyr

Why visit: *Excellent flintwork; superb painted screens*
Where: *In the centre of the town, IP18 6JA*

St Edmund's is one of Suffolk's greatest Perpendicular churches, the mightiest survivor of a chain along the coast here, built in the 15th century, when the county was one of the richest in England.

Its exterior has superb examples of the art of flintwork. This is particularly fine at the west end of the tower. Here, panels of flint framed in stone rise above the window to a Latin inscription that translates as 'St Edmund Pray for Us'. Above that is chequerwork panelling of flint and stone.

The two-storey south porch is just as good, with 'M' for St Mary picked out on the lower panels. Above the door, framed by two windows, is a modern statue of St Edmund, shown bound in the ropes that tied him to a tree while he was used by Danish archers as a target.

The interior is packed with interest, from the 15th to the 20th century. Outstanding are the medieval screens separating the nave and aisles from the chancel and chapels. These retain much of their original colour, and the paintings are of the disciples, prophets and angels. On the eastern side of the chancel screen are stalls with carvings that include armrests in the shape of men, animals and fantastical creatures.

The painted and gilded pulpit and font cover are successful 20th-century restorations and recreations of medieval decorative woodwork. The font itself is original, but scraped of the seven sacraments that were once carved on it. Near the tower is a figure called Southwold Jack. Still with some of his 15th-century colour and in fine clothes of the 1470s, he was made to ring a bell at the beginnings of services.

ALSO IN THE AREA

Badingham St John the Baptist
Why visit: *Hammerbeam roof; seven-sacrament font*

Fressingfield St Peter and St Paul
Why visit: *Fine 15th-century porch, roofs and bench-ends*

Ufford St Mary
Why visit: *Unforgettable 15th-century carved telescopic font cover that rises in six pinnacled tiers right up to the roof*

Walpole The Old Chapel HCT
Why visit: *One of the earliest Nonconformist chapels in England, converted from a late 16th-century house*

Wenhaston St Peter
Why visit: *Unique medieval Doom painting on wooden boards*

Westhall St Andrew
Why visit: *Remote, lovely church with Norman doorway, painted screen panels and seven-sacrament font*

PEWS, BENCHES AND SEATS

Early churches did not usually have seating for the congregation, as services were short and sermons rare, so sitting was not necessary. But from the 13th century onwards seating began to be introduced, and by the early 19th century most churches were crammed with seating of different kinds. Today, we rarely see churches without any seating at all, but a church with the seating temporarily removed feels completely different.

Early seats

The earliest church seats look rather like low stone sills built against the walls of the church. These were for use by the ill and the elderly, hence the expression 'the weakest go to the wall'. Such seats can still be seen at Buckland, Gloucestershire, where they are partly concealed behind

much later (early 17th-century) wooden seats with backs and canopies. Acton, Cheshire, has stone seating around the whole church.

In the body of the church, the earliest seats were very simple wooden benches, most often supported on a wooden platform. Bench backs came later, developed from a single rail and then becoming a panelled back. In some churches the bench backs have elaborate linenfold panelling. Many early benches were adapted and re-used through the centuries, often because they were narrow and uncomfortable.

St Mary's Church at Dunsfold, Surrey, has what many think are the earliest surviving wooden benches. Dating from the late 13th century, these still have holes in them made to contain candles.

Benches and bench-ends

During the 15th and 16th centuries carpenters made benches that were highly decorated and marvellously carved. Many of these survive, and are a particular speciality of the West Country and East Anglia. It is the bench-ends that draw the eye. Here, the carpenter could display his skills to the best advantage, with the flat surface being carved with an enormous variety of images, from biblical characters to domestic scenes and from mythical creatures such as mermaids to religious symbolism. They are superb galleries of late medieval art.

Bench-ends fall into two main types: square-headed, developed in the West, and poppyheaded, developed in the East. The two forms meet in the middle of England, where variations on the two principal themes might be encountered. Poppyheaded benches usually have a carved top-most finial with two lower carvings on either side of it.

Cornwall has superb collections of carved bench-ends, a perfect example being those at St Winnow. Here, there are 16th-century images of a sailing boat blown by a strong wind, a Cornishman in a kilt drinking cider, religious symbols, and much else. There are more than 30 different bench-ends in this one church.

In East Anglia the finest examples are found at Wiggenhall St Germans and nearby Wiggenhall St Mary, both in Norfolk. Taken together, these two churches probably have the finest collection of bench-ends in England, with figures of saints, sinners, animals and symbols.

Occasionally, the craftsmen who created these small masterpieces can be seen, as at Great Doddington, Northamptonshire, where one is shown carving a Tudor rose.

Box pews

Enclosed seating, called box pews, was introduced in the 17th century, and reached its most opulent in the Georgian period. Box pews were often for particular families in the congregation. Some were fitted with locks, others were upholstered for even further warmth and protection from the draughts in the unheated churches – one of the main reasons for their popularity.

Thousands of box pews were removed by the Victorians, but many remain, including at St Mary, Puddletown, Dorset, which has rows of box pews, installed in 1635. The little church of St James, Cameley, Somerset, is crammed with box pews, some labelled with the names of the people who sat in them. Mildenhall, Wiltshire, has a complete set of box pews and other wooden fittings all put in place at the same time, in 1816. 'Private pews' were exactly that, built for and looked after by individuals and families. Some included fireplaces and comfortable upholstered seats.

Galleries

Some galleries were for ordinary members of the public, others were built especially for the gentry and important people. A church might contain both sorts of gallery, a rural example being at Minstead, Hampshire, where private pews as well as galleries for musicians and school children almost fill the space. The most famous example of a church crammed with galleries is St Mary, Whitby, Yorkshire, with a labyrinth of beautifully cared-for galleries.

Opposite page: Bench-end at Alford, Somerset, showing the 'Pelican in her Piety' – she pecks her own breast so that her young can feed on her blood.
This page: 18th-century box pews, pulpit and screen at Winterborne Tomson, Dorset.

Misericords

Seating in the chancels of parish churches was provided for the priest, parish clerk and any other clerics or dignitaries that were present. Such stalls, usually a single row on each side of the chancel, and sometimes one facing east with its back against the screen, were equipped with carved seats that tipped up. On the underside of the seat was a ledge called a misericord (derived from the Latin for pity). This was provided so that during very long services the user could lean back against the ledge and show every appearance to the congregation of standing up while, in fact, half-sitting.

Many misericords were carved, and since they could not generally be seen, they had on them an even wider range of images than elsewhere in the church. These range from scenes of domestic life – cooking, drinking, arguing, and so on – to sports, games, mythology, and even ribald humour. The misericord shown below is at Ripple, Worcestershire.

SOUTH AND EAST CAMBRIDGESHIRE

The churches in this tour include St Mary's in Burwell – a legacy of the time when the nature of this countryside was quite different. Many of these churches have monuments to notables who have contributed to the building and maintenance of the buildings. Look for the touching memorial to the Jenyns couple at Bottisham and the ancient brass to Sir Roger at Trumpington.

This page: Burwell's spirelet tops its tower (top); inside is magnificent timberwork in the roof and a rose window over the chancel arch (below).

Burwell
St Mary the Virgin

Why visit: *Rose window; intricate carving*
Where: *High Street, CB25 0HB*

St Mary's is a grand church, reflecting a time when Burwell was an inland port. There are traces of Norman work in the church, but the nave was almost entirely rebuilt in the mid-15th century, and the chancel in the 16th century. It is in classic Perpendicular style: soaring piers, large windows and a window-filled clerestory. There are hints of the influence of Ely Cathedral in the octagonal top of the tower, topped by an unusual 18th-century spirelet.

One of the most eye-catching features of the interior is the rose window above the chancel arch. It is surrounded by very intricate stonework, and there is much carving in stone and wood throughout the church. Some of the finest is in the woodwork of the roofs, where many creatures are depicted and the stone corbels are in the shape of angels.

In the churchyard is a gravestone on which is carved a winged stone heart with flames coming out of it. This commemorates 76 people who were killed when a barn caught fire. They had all been inside watching a puppet show; it happened on 8 September 1727.

Balsham Holy Trinity

Why visit: *Rood screen; chancel stalls; 15th-century brasses*
Where: *Church Lane, north side of Balsham, CB21 4DS*

The most memorable feature of the outside of the church is the square tower with its massive buttresses. They are not just at the corners, but in the centre of the sides as well; the west one has obliterated the west door. The buttresses are of various dates, some perhaps original, but one at least is from 1598 (it is dated), and further reinforcing work was carried out in the 1970s. The tower itself dates from the late 13th century. The nave clerestory appears to be built of yellow brick, but this is only a refacing done in the 19th century.

The church houses a magnificent screen, all the more special because it still has its loft, complete with ribbed coving. In the chancel is a complete set of 14th-century stalls. Their main decorative motif is ogee-headed arcades, but they also have carvings of a much less formal nature on the armrests and on the misericords. These include birds, animals, mythical creatures and people.

On the chancel floor are two large brasses to former rectors of Holy Trinity: John Sleford, who died in 1401 and John Blodwell, who died in 1462. Both are magnificent, but that to Sleford marginally more so. He was no mere vicar, but also, among other things, Keeper of the Wardrobe to Edward III.

Bottisham Holy Trinity

Why visit: *Beautiful medieval architecture; Jenyns monument*
Where: *High Street, CB25 9BA; keyholder at nearby garage*

The first thing the visitor sees at Holy Trinity is unusual: a 13th-century west porch, properly called a galilee, that stands in front of the west tower. The whole building is handsome, with the nave from about a century later than the galilee.

The architecture of the nave is especially fine, with grey stone used for the delicate and complex piers. In between nave and chancel is an especially elegant and simple stone rood screen composed of three equal arched openings. The chancel has elements from both the 13th and 14th centuries, with Victorian windows. There are two other intricately carved screens, each side of the rood screen, from the 14th century.

Behind these screens, which are not quite in their original state or position, are collections of monuments.

Notable on the north side are those to Thomas and Margaret Pledger, from about 1600, and one to a brother and sister, who died in 1638. Part of their inscription runs: 'These ye worlds strangers come not heere to dwell, They tasted, liked it not, and bad farewell'.

On the south side is the monument to Sir Roger and Dame Elizabeth Jenyns. They are shown sitting on a mat, each with a book, and lightly holding hands. She was 62 when she died in 1728; he died in 1740 aged 77. Their affection for each other is set in stone.

Harlton Church of the Assumption

Why visit: *Vast windows; monument to Sir Henry Fryer*
Where: *Coach Drive, CB23 1ET*

Huge windows make Harlton's church immediately interesting, and they dominate its character inside as well as out. Parts of the church date from the 13th century, but the immense windows may be as late as the mid-15th century.

The church still has its original stone screen. It was stripped of all its sculpture and decoration at the Reformation, but its elegant uprights are a reminder of past glories.

By far the most memorable element in the church is the monument to Henry Fryer, who died in 1631. It is very large and impressive and consists of Sir Henry himself in bright green armour, flanked by his parents who are dressed in black. They in turn are flanked by white figures, one male and one female. Below this group is a reclining female figure, book in one hand, handkerchief in the other. It is a melancholy tableau.

Ickleton St Mary

Why visit: *Norman wall paintings*
Where: *Church Street, CB10 1SL*

The exterior of St Mary's is a pleasing, rather homely mixture of roofs and walls clustered around a central tower and spire. Parts of the church are Norman, as the west doorway shows, but nothing on the outside prepares the visitor for the interior. Ancient round piers support arches above which is a series of very rare late Norman wall paintings. They are frescoes, and show martyrdoms, including those of St Andrew and St Peter, scenes from the life of Christ and parts of a 14th-century Doom painting.

Many of these marvellous pictures were only discovered in 1979, after an arsonist had set fire to the church. The paintings began to be revealed during subsequent cleaning work.

Kirtling All Saints

Why visit: *North monuments*
Where: *North of Kirtling, off Kirtling Road; on the footpath signposted to Kirtling Church, CB8 9PA*

Kirtling's church sits close to Kirtling Towers, a large Tudor gatehouse. This is the most substantial remaining part of a castle and great house that was the seat of the North family. Their monuments are in the church's North Chapel.

The church itself has a fine Norman south doorway, complete with a very ancient door. Much of the rest of the building is 16th-century, including the North Chapel (actually the south chapel).

The most remarkable monument is to Roger, 2nd Lord North. It consists of six elaborately carved pillars that support a canopy, on top of which is a brightly painted, box-like structure with yet more elaborate carvings, including coats of arms and figures. The whole structure looks rather like an over-the-top wedding cake. Beneath it is a tomb chest on which lies an effigy of Lord North. At his feet is a snarling dragon with a curly tail.

This page: *The memorial to the Jenyns at Bottisham (left); exterior of St Mary and St Michael at Trumpington (right).*

Trumpington
St Mary and St Michael

Why visit: *Memorial brass of Sir Roger de Trumpington*
Where: *Grantchester Road, CB2 9LH*

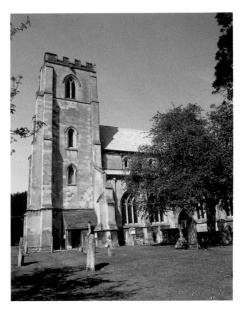

Virtually a suburb of Cambridge, Trumpington still retains its character. The church is on the west side of the village, close to open farmland.

It is a stern-looking building on the outside, re-faced in Bath stone in the 19th century, when the church was over-thoroughly restored by William Butterfield. Inside, rather more of the history of the church is evident. Much of it dates from the early 14th century, though the earliest parts are from a century before that. There are fragments of medieval glass in some of the windows (though most have dark Victorian glass), and an array of ancient coffin lids.

The church is renowned for having one of England's earliest brasses. This is to Sir Roger de Trumpington, who died in 1289. He is shown wearing chain mail, and his shield bears the Trumpington coat of arms. The brass lies on a table tomb with a canopy above that is of a later date than the brass.

ALSO IN THE AREA

Isleham St Andrew
Why visit: *Peyton tombs*

THE FENS AND THE GREAT OUSE

With wide skies and long views that seem to stretch to infinity, the Fens north of Cambridge make a memorable setting for fine churches. Towers and spires compete as distant landmarks, each one distinct from the rest. The higher ground of Fenland 'isles' was colonised in earliest times and the choicest sites were reserved for parish churches, not only in the Fens, but also in towns and villages of the different landscapes on the slow-flowing Great Ouse in old Huntingdonshire.

Willingham
St Mary and All Saints

Why visit: *Unusual 14th-century tower and many intriguing features, including wall paintings and a possible anchorite's cell*
Where: *Church Street, north of Cambridge, CB24 5HS*

The Fenland village of Willingham owes its exceptionally interesting church partly to its location on a medieval processional route. This ran from Cambridge to the cathedral at Ely, whose bishop was a landowner and had a manor here.

The intricately constructed 14th-century spire, with its pinnacles, windows and little flying buttresses, makes a distinctive landmark. Fragments of ornate Norman stonework set into the porch wall suggest an earlier church of some importance. The pieces came from the south wall of the chancel, rebuilt as part of a restoration in the 1890s.

The work of that time, carried out with great sensitivity, uncovered historic treasure: astonishing medieval wall paintings of varying dates. An early figure is thought to be Etheldreda, founder of the original monastery at Ely. Above the north arcade is a 14th-century painting of St Christopher crossing a river teeming with fish. The south side has a very clear 15th-century depiction of the Visitation of Mary to her cousin Elizabeth.

The arcades support a splendid but rather curious-looking double hammerbeam roof. After the previous roof collapsed, it was rather ingeniously replaced by a complete roof that was brought in pieces, on carts, from the priory church at Barnwell in Cambridge.

The original roof at Barnwell had been dismantled after the Dissolution. The 'new' roof differed slightly in size: look closely for the signs that it didn't quite fit!

Perhaps the most unusual feature at Willingham is a small 14th-century room to the north side of the chancel. Variously described as a sacristy or a treasury, it is now thought possible that it was an anchorhold – a cell built to house a long-term recluse known as an anchorite (or anchoress). The steeply pitched stone roof is supported by beautifully crafted arches of fine stonework.

Gamlingay
St Mary the Virgin

Why visit: *Grand exterior; 15th-century screen and choir stalls*
Where: *At the junction of Church Street and Church Lane, on the eastern side of Gamlingay, SG19 3JJ*

The exterior of St Mary's successfully blends elegant Perpendicular lines with rustic stone – partly fieldstone and partly a type of deep golden greensand known as carstone. This came from a nearby quarry known as The Butts. The 14th- and 15th-century exterior of the large church conceals an earlier core, evident in details such as a 13th-century lancet window in the north wall and three early roundels above the pillars of the south arcade. The interior of the church was much restored in the 1880s. The fine woodwork in the chancel was repaired at that time, and remains one of the best features of the church. The Perpendicular screen still has its entrance gates into the chancel, and behind it are 15th-century choir stalls with misericords.

Great Paxton Holy Trinity

Why visit: *Rare surviving Saxon features that make this a unique church*
Where: *Church Lane, on the north side of Great Paxton village, PE19 6RG*

Holy Trinity gives the impression of a fine Perpendicular church at first sight: from the outside there are few clues that the building is an exceptional rarity. For as well as being Saxon and a minster church, it is also cruciform, with aisles.

The original crossing piers survive, as does the tall arch of the north transept and both the nave arcades, complete with their Saxon capitals. A 1971 excavation discovered the lower parts of the transept walls in the churchyard. This all makes the church a unique survival in England. It is thought to have been built about 20 years before the Norman Conquest.

Long Stanton
St Michael CCT

Why visit: *Thatched 13th-century church*
Where: *At the southern end of Long Stanton village, north-west of Cambridge, CB24 3BZ; open Sunday afternoons, keyholder is available at other times*

There is something quintessentially English about this charming church. It feels ancient, with its heavily buttressed west end, its thatched roof – eaves only a few feet from the ground – and its simple interior. The chancel was rebuilt in 1884 but it is thought that the lancet windows and other features faithfully reproduced the medieval originals. In the south wall is a lovely 13th-century double piscina with intersecting arches, while a north wall window has glass of the same period. Until the 1880s, a holy well in the churchyard was used for baptisms.

Over St Mary

Why visit: *Wonderful stonecarving almost everywhere; south porch*
Where: *Church End, on the north-western edge of Over village, CB24 5NH*

The immensely tall and elegant 14th-century spire of St Mary's beckons across the Fens: no-one with an interest in

church architecture should ignore it. Dating back to 1254, the church was under the patronage of Ramsey Abbey; no expense was spared in its construction using the finest Barnack stone.

The exterior is a gallery of wonderful carving, from the Perpendicular west doorway, with its figure of the Virgin Mary, to the many extravagant gargoyles and other heads. The spacious south porch, with its twin pinnacles, and four windows at the sides, makes a spectacular prelude to the mainly 14th-century interior, where there is much to enjoy, from the grand, well-proportioned structure to the detail of yet more fine detailed carving, in both stone and wood. Don't miss the misericords in the choir stalls, nor the Jacobean pulpit with its lofty onion-domed tester.

St Neots St Mary

Why visit: *Splendid, tall, richly embellished tower; grand interior*
Where: *At the junction of Church Street and Brook Street, PE19 1QD*

The 9th-century monk who this town is named after lived and died at St Neot in Cornwall. His relics were later brought here, so a second town is named after him.

The large church presides over a spacious churchyard and reflects the size and importance of the town – the largest in Cambridgeshire and still growing. The imposing, pinnacled Perpendicular tower

dates from the 1530s and has a peal of 10 bells. Inside St Mary's, the lofty arcades and tall chancel arch lead the eye up to the nave roof. Have a good look at the cornices around the edge, with their carvings of angels and animals including hares, eagles and camels.

The font is Norman, but most interior woodwork is Victorian, including the pews and pulpit. The windows, with glass from the second half of the 19th century, depict events from the life of Christ.

Sutton St Andrew

Why visit: *A majestic 14th-century Fenland church with an outstanding tower*
Where: *High Street, CB6 2RH*

There are strong echoes of the famous octagon of nearby Ely Cathedral in the silhouette of St Andrew's, proudly set on its ridge and visible for miles across the Fens. Completed some 50 years after Ely, in 1388, Sutton has two octagons, one on top of the other, crowning its square tower. This was the last construction phase of a building that was completed within little more than 25 years under the direction of two bishops of Ely.

The magnificent vaulted two-storey south porch forms the centrepiece of the south front, which is rich in refined detailing: buttresses, battlements, gargoyles and lovely window tracery. The interior space has an appropriately grand feel, with soaring arcades and a tower arch, blind arcading along all the walls, and an immense and exuberant east window in late Decorated style.

Opposite page: Interior at Willingham (left); medieval wall painting (right).
This page: The spire of St Mary, Over.

ALSO IN THE AREA

Diddington St Lawrence
Why visit: *16th-century brickwork tower; fine brasses and stained glass*

Waresley St James
Why visit: *Attractive Victorian church of 1857 by William Butterfield, includes unusual polychromic tiles in the chancel*

SOUTH-EAST NORFOLK

A mainly rural area, south-eastern Norfolk has only two sizeable towns – Attleborough and Wymondham – both of which are on the busy A11 road to Norwich. Both have excellent and intriguing churches, shorn of their east ends. Loddon is a large village whereas other churches in this group are in smaller villages or hamlets, some of them almost lost along winding Norfolk lanes.

Loddon Holy Trinity

Why visit: *Screen and font*
Where: *High Street, NR14 6EX*

A large village on the River Chet, Loddon's church is a handsome building in a big churchyard just off the High Street. It dates almost entirely from the 15th century, and is built of flint, stone and brick, with excellent flintwork on the porch. Above the porch door is a rare survival, a statue of the Holy Trinity (albeit God has a new head); images such as this were usually either destroyed or defaced during the Reformation, or later, by Puritan iconoclasts.

The interior is high and light, with clerestory windows adding both daylight and elegance to the nave. The church is particularly noted for its font and screen. The former is a seven-sacrament font and is raised on beautifully carved stone steps. The font itself retains its canopied panels, but the seven scenes that were once depicted within the panels have been erased. The screen dates from the 15th century, and many of its painted panels are in very good condition. Among the scenes depicted are the Virgin and Child, the Adoration of the Magi and the Ascension.

Among the monuments is one to Lady Dionysius Williamson, who made a significant financial contribution to Sir Christopher Wren's rebuilding of St Paul's Cathedral after the Great Fire of London.

Attleborough St Mary

Why visit: *Excellent screen*
Where: *Church Street, NR17 2AW*

From the outside St Mary's looks rather odd because the tower is at the east end, where the chancel should be. In fact the tower was once the central part of a cruciform building, but the chancel was demolished at the time of the Reformation. The base of the tower is Norman, but much of the rest of the church dates from the 14th century.

The spacious interior is dominated by a wonderful late 15th-century screen that stretches the entire width of the church. It is one of Norfolk's best, but has had a chequered history, having been repainted in the 16th and 17th centuries, nearly sold to an antiques dealer in the 19th century and consigned to the back of the church until 1931.

Other items of interest in the church include an intriguing metalwork lectern and some wall paintings above the screen.

East Harling
St Peter and St Paul

Why visit: *Stained glass masterpiece*
Where: *Church Road (B1111), south of the A11, NR16 2NB; the church is not always open, keyholder telephone numbers are given in the porch*

The first feature the visitor will notice about East Harling's church is the very distinctive pinnacled wooden and lead-cased spirelet, or fleche, crowning the tower. The church was almost entirely rebuilt in the 15th century, in magnificent style, largely with funds provided by Anne Harling, after whose family the village is named.

The most outstanding feature is the enormous 15th-century stained glass east window. It was donated by Sir Robert Wingfield, second husband of Anne Harling. The glass was removed from the church during the 17th century and taken to East Harling Hall, perhaps to protect it from iconoclasts. At some point after 1736, when the hall was sold, the glass was put back in the church. It was removed once again during World War II and put back in 1947. The glass depicts many scenes from the life of Christ. The faces, clothes and backgrounds are beautifully observed. There are lovely stained glass angels in the north clerestory but these are not so easy to view.

The church contains many memorials, including the tomb of Anne Harling. In the south aisle there is an excellent 15th-century screen, and the hammer-beam roofs are very good.

This page: Painted screen at Loddon.

Hardwick St Margaret

Why visit: *12th-century church*
Where: *Church Road, village of Topcroft, NR35 2BH*

On the lanes just south of Shelton, Hardwick's little church is a contrast to its elegant neighbour. It looks old and battered with an assortment of windows and the remains of a round tower. But it has character, evident inside and out.

The 15th-century rood screen still has some of its original colour. It was repaired in 1661 by churchwardens John Ebbers and Joseph Cock. There is a faded wall painting of St Christopher on the north wall, and at the west end what was once a private pew is used as a vestry.

Pulham St Mary

Why visit: *South porch*
Where: *Opposite Church Close, on the B1134, next to the Post Office, IP21 4RD*

St Mary's dates mostly from the 15th century. Its two most striking features are the flint-built tower and the beautiful south porch of stone and flint. The stonework on the front of the porch is outstanding. There is an Annunciation on either side of the doorway, rows of angels playing musical instruments, a row of stone shields above the doorway, and above that two delightful windows. This is all crowned by a filigree parapet and pinnacles with mythical beasts. Inside there is much of interest, including the 15th-century screen with its tracery and faded paintings of the Apostles. Of the same date are the simple benches and a good deal of the glass.

Shelton St Mary

Why visit: *Beautiful exterior; excellent stained glass*
Where: *Low Road, NR15 2SD*

In a tiny hamlet tucked away among Norfolk's lanes and fields, St Mary's is a church of distinction and beauty. It was begun by Sir Ralph Shelton in the 1480s. The tower is earlier, from the beginning of the 15th century and is built of flint, unlike the rest of the church, which is made of brick with stone dressings. From the outside the two-storey porch, large aisle windows and glasshouse-like clerestory make a striking composition.

The interior is just as pleasing, with tall piers above which are canopied niches and stone panelling. In the chancel there are many monuments to Sheltons, including one to Sir Ralph, but perhaps the most interesting is that to Sir Robert Houghton. It shows four kneeling figures under a canopy on which is painted a chilling skull and crossbones.

There is excellent early 16th-century stained glass in the church, especially in the chancel, where the three east windows have panels that include figures of Sir John Shelton and his wife, Anne Boleyn (not *that* Anne Boleyn but actually a close relative). Sir Ralph and his wife are shown in the central window.

South Lopham St Andrew

Why visit: *Superb Norman tower*
Where: *Church Road (B1113), just north of the A1066, IP22 2HT*

St Andrew's magnificent castle-like central tower has five stages and a changing rhythm of blind arcades. It is clearly Norman, but also has traces of Saxon work. Inside, there is further Norman work to be seen, particularly in the arches of the crossing, but there are also later elements. The handsome font is 14th-century, as is the arcade.

One feature of special interest is the lowside window, complete with wooden shutter. This was placed so that those not attending a service could hear the Sanctus bell ringing and pause for prayer.

On the floor of the nave is a massive, ancient dugout chest, its body made from a single tree trunk. It was discovered during repairs to the tower in 1968, and may date back as far as the 900s.

Wymondham The Abbey

Why visit: *Two towers*
Where: *Church Street, west of village, NR18 0PJ*

Wymondham's church has an unusual profile due to the large towers at either end. It is evidence of a dispute between the monks of the abbey that once stood here and the townspeople, who had rights of access to parts of the building. The two sides fell out to the extent that each had a tower, and each built its tower higher to outdo the other. The octagonal tower was for the monks, while the great west tower was for the townspeople. The octagonal tower has a strange appearance. It was once at the church's centre, but the east end was demolished at the Dissolution, leaving an open space beneath it.

Inside, the nave has magnificent Norman stonework. At the east end is a huge glittering reredos designed by Sir Ninian Comper in the 20th century. The 15th-century nave roof is superb, with immense wooden angels and great wooden star shapes for bosses.

This page: South porch at Pulham (left); stained glass at St Mary's, Shelton (centre).

IN AND AROUND NORWICH

Norfolk is famed for its large number of churches, and this is nowhere seen more clearly than in Norwich, where there seems to be a church everywhere you look. The city has more than 30 medieval churches. Most of them are now adapted to other uses, but this remains a city to delight the church visitor. Most are open on certain days, and others by prior arrangement. The other churches in this group include some of the finest in the country.

Norwich St Peter Mancroft

Why visit: *Interior space; tower; medieval glass*
Where: *St Peter's Street, NR2 1NH*

Far more than the cathedral, tucked away in its quiet close, the church of St Peter Mancroft is in the very heart of Norwich. It stands cheek by jowl with the daily bustle of the city's lively market, and there is a wonderful contrast between the huge, still space within the church and the hectic outside world that reaches almost up to its walls.

The church encapsulates everything that is splendid about the Perpendicular style. It is a vast, airy space, punctuated by slender, soaring columns of the arcades and filled with light from the huge, clear windows of both aisles and clerestory. Construction was in a single phase of about 25 years, in the mid-15th century; only the top of the tower carries later significant additions in the form of the slender spirelet, parapet and 'pepperpot' pinnacles, added in 1895. The church owes its existence to the commerce of an earlier age, with no expense spared by the wealthy medieval merchants and craft guilds – from the two vaulted porches to the lavishly embellished tower that now houses 14 bells. The great east window has some of Norfolk's best 15th-century glass in its 42 panels, much of it collected from other windows in the church.

Norwich St Peter Hungate

Why visit: *Interesting 15th-century church in an attractive setting, now redundant but rejuvenated as a centre for medieval church art; open Thu–Sat; entrance fee*
Where: *Princes Street, NR3 1AE*

Set amid cobbled streets and old cottages near the top of Elm Hill, this church dates from the 15th century but looks older than other Perpendicular examples in Norwich – perhaps partly because of its dumpy, pyramid-topped tower. This was the result of emergency repairs in 1906 – part of a long struggle to keep the church standing. Saved from demolition, the building became a museum of church art in 1936, providing a home for fixtures and fittings from the city's other disused medieval churches. Now called Hungate Medieval Art, it is an interpretation centre focusing on the stained glass and other medieval artefacts of Norwich churches. Temporary exhibitions are held here, as well as activity workshops for adults and children.

St Peter Hungate itself has excellent stained glass, and a fine hammerbeam roof with carved angels, and there are good bench-ends from elsewhere.

Norwich St George Tombland

Why visit: *Pleasing exterior; varied and interesting fittings, monuments and glass*
Where: *In Tombland, west of the cathedral, NR3 1AF; open most mornings*

Conveniently close to the cathedral, St George's is an attractive blend of styles: Perpendicular at heart, with 17th- and 18th-century work evident in the brick clerestory and the topmost part of the tower. A Victorian restoration spared fine older furnishings inside, such as the 18th-century pulpit and dark wooden reredos, and also installed some earlier Flemish stained glass. Other glass in the church includes an Arts and Crafts window from the 1930s, and two small but lovely 15th-century roundels. The extravagant, heavily pillared 17th-century font cover is topped by a gilded Victorian figure of St George on horseback, with the dragon literally snapping at his heels.

A colourful 17th-century monument near the organ commemorates Alderman Anguish and his family, and another of 1609 remembers John and Olive Symonds, who left a generous bequest to the poor of the parish 'to continue for ever', of two shillings a week.

This page: *Slender arcades inside St Peter Mancroft, Norwich.*

Cawston St Agnes

Why visit: *Hammerbeam roof with angels; painted screen*
Where: *Church Lane, off the B1145 in Cawston village, some 15 miles north-west of Norwich, NR10 4AG*

Cawston's enormous cruciform church has treasures that are well worth travelling for. Its lofty, rather stern tower will guide you there. There have been remarkably few changes to this church that was built in the early 15th century, largely at the expense of the influential de la Pole family. And the expense must have been considerable to cover the cost of transporting fine stone to a region where there is none, and paying craftsmen and artists to create features that are among the finest of their kind in East Anglia. These include a wonderful roof with many angels (including one standing on the end of each hammerbeam), and a tall, exquisitely carved and painted screen with depictions of 20 saints in the panels.

East Dereham St Nicholas

Why visit: *Detached bell-tower, seven-sacrament font*
Where: *Church Street, NR19 1DN*

Doubly impressive, Dereham's church is not only a grand town church complete with integral tower, but it also has a massive, quite separate, bell-tower. This detached tower is early 16th-century,

while the central tower in the body of the church has Norman foundations but is mostly of the 14th century.

The church is entered through the south porch, which itself is a key element of the building. It dates from the 15th century and has a rich array of carvings on it, including an Annunciation and angels. The interior has features from the Norman period through to the early 16th century, including lovely 15th-century roofs in the transept chapel. Parts of the chancel are 13th-century, and it too has a lovely old roof. One of Dereham's great treasures is its seven-sacrament font, with remarkably intact carvings. It is accurately dated to 1468.

St Withburga is Dereham's own local saint and founded a convent here in the 7th century. There are several reminders of her in the church, including a window from 1957 and a picture of her on part of a rood screen rescued from a nearby church. A well is dedicated to her in the churchyard and may date back to medieval times.

Ranworth St Helen

Why visit: *15th-century screen*
Where: *Panxworth Church Road, edge of Ranworth Broad, NR13 6HT*

St Helen's is famous for its remarkable screen, a masterpiece made in about 1450. One of the features that makes it so special is that it still retains much of its original colour. It stretches the entire width of the church, and the figures on it include the Twelve Apostles, St George, St Mary, John the Baptist and other saints. The paintings are superb, perhaps especially St George and St Michael, and would be outstanding in any art gallery.

The church itself is an attractive and interesting building, with a tall tower that gives splendid views over the Broads, and flint walls interspersed with elegant windows from the Perpendicular period.

Although the screen overshadows the rest of the church contents, some are clearly special. They include 15th-century bench-ends, misericords, a linenfold pulpit and a 15th-century cantor's desk – a kind of lectern with two sides. One side has a painted eagle on it, the other a scrap of weathered musical notation.

Salle St Peter and St Paul

Why visit: *Fine 15th-century church*
Where: *The Street, NR10 4SE*

This is one of Norfolk's most splendid churches, and is in the 'top 10' for many enthusiasts. One aspect that makes it a connoisseurs' church is the fact that the building itself and many of its rich contents all date from the 15th century.

The sheer scale of such a church in what is a remote rural setting appears baffling. But it is a 'wool' church, built by people who had become immensely rich from the woollen cloth trade. At the time it was customary to reflect your earthly wealth in celebrating God by investing in his House. The most obvious sign of the money poured into the building is that it is entirely built of imported Barnack stone, rather than making use of abundant local flint.

The coats of arms of the benefactors are over the west door, along with two famous feathered angels. The interior is spacious with a long nave, generous transepts and a large chancel. Over each of these parts of the church are wonderful wooden roofs, culminating in the chancel with its throngs of angels and bosses that depict the life of Christ.

Salle has Norfolk's finest seven-sacrament font, with its scenes intact, and fine detail such as angels below each scene holding the relevant symbol. The font cover is an impressive piece of architecture in itself, suspended from an immense beam.

This page: *An angel standing on the end of a hammerbeam at St Agnes, Cawston.*

ALSO IN THE AREA

Elsing St Peter
Why visit: *14th-century church with superb font cover*

Heydon St Peter and St Paul
Why visit: *Setting; wall paintings*

Ringland St Peter
Why visit: *Setting; outstanding roofs; screen; stained glass*

THE NORTH NORFOLK COAST

Beginning at Cromer, these churches stretch westwards along the edge of the North Sea towards The Wash. As with so many coastal areas, the feeling of the sea and its influences on the light and atmosphere reaches a long way inland. North Norfolk is a popular holiday and weekend destination, but some churches here feel surprisingly secret and tucked away. Some would say this landscape and its churches are best enjoyed in the bracing autumn and winter months.

Cromer St Peter and St Paul

Why visit: *Impressive town church with Norfolk's tallest tower*
Where: *Off Church Street, NR27 9HA*

The story of the town's changing fortunes is told by Cromer's church. Like so many East Anglian towns and villages, it was very wealthy in the Middle Ages, but by the beginning of the 19th century it had declined to little more than a seaside village. The railway, and the boom in tourism towards the end of the 19th century, brought prosperity back again.

The church is very large and grand, and was built almost entirely in the 15th century. The decline was already well set in by the 17th century, during which time the chancel was demolished, before it fell down of its own accord. By the 19th century it was almost derelict. Architect Sir Arthur Blomfield came to the rescue in the 1880s, rebuilding the chancel, and repairing the nave and tower. Today the church is a popular, friendly place, its enormous nave full of light and space. There is excellent glass at the east end made by William Morris's company to the designs of Edward Burne-Jones, and elsewhere there is modern glass celebrating and commemorating the places and people of Cromer.

The outside of the church is magnificent, with superb architectural detailing. Crowning all is the great tower, at 50m (160ft) one of Norfolk's tallest. It is a popular attraction in its own right because of the views from the top.

Blakeney St Nicholas

Why visit: *13th-century chancel*
Where: *Off Cley Road, NR25 7NW*

The earliest part of this church is its chancel, from the late 13th century. It has a beautiful rib-vaulted roof and, most unusually, a seven-light window. There is only one other like this in England. Also of interest in the chancel are several misericords. The nave and tower are 15th-century, and there are also fragments of 15th-century stained glass.

Blakeney's church has a mystery: as well as the main tower, attached to the chancel is another tower. But this one is much too small and spindly ever to have been built for bells. Many reckon that it was built as a shipping beacon, but would the main tower not have been sufficient?

Burnham Deepdale St Mary

Why visit: *Norman font; medieval glass; round tower*
Where: *On the A149, just west of School Pastures, PE31 8DD*

The cluster of seven Burnham parishes can be confusing, but each church (one a ruin) is distinctive. St Mary's has one of East Anglia's many round towers. This one, although much restored, is an early example, and has Norman features and Saxon roots. Time and three restorations, one as early as 1796, have not robbed it of its charm. The interior of the church is simple and whitewashed, and contains one of north Norfolk's 11 distinctive square Norman fonts. It stands on four dumpy legs, and is best known for its carvings of the Labours of the Year, including scenes of men tilling and harvesting.

The church also has rare, and beautiful, medieval glass, some of it collected from elsewhere by a Victorian rector. One of the best pieces is of a full moon with a human face; it is in the south porch.

This page: *Norfolk's tallest tower at St Peter and St Paul, Cromer (left); rib-vaulting and the seven-light window at St Nicholas, Blakeney (centre); the square font at Burnham Deepdale (above).*

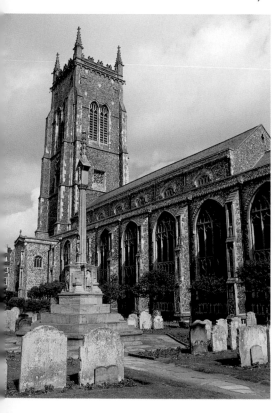

Burnham Norton
St Margaret

Why visit: *Wineglass pulpit; Norman font; round tower*
Where: *Just north of Burnham Market, Bellamy's Lane, PE31 8ES*

Norton's church is large and handsome, with a round tower that is Saxon in origin. It is best known for its wonderful wineglass pulpit, made in 1450 and paid for by John and Katherine Goldale. It is painted with the figures of the Four Latin Doctors: Saints Ambrose, Gregory, Augustine and Jerome. It escaped being destroyed or disfigured at the Reformation, unlike the figures on the screen. The church also has a fine Georgian pulpit with steps up for the preacher. Also here is another square Norman 'Norfolk' font. This has patterns of arches and diamonds on its sides.

Burnham Overy
St Clement

Why visit: *Unusual internal arrangement*
Where: *Just east of Burnham Market, at the junction of Mill Road and the B1155, PE31 8JB*

St Clement's is the most distinctive of all the Burnham churches. It has a large, square, Norman tower, and either side of it are the chancel and the nave. It was once a complete cruciform church, but the transepts have gone, and the tower itself had to be lowered as it was in danger of collapse. Now truncated, it is surmounted by a charming bell turret.

In order to shore up the tower, walls were built inside the church almost

This page: Burnham Norton's tower (above); the rood screen at Upper Sheringham (right).

blocking the tower crossing arches, meaning the building is virtually in two parts, with a passageway linking them under the tower. Both nave and chancel have altars. There is a faded medieval wall painting of St Christopher in the nave.

Cley Next the Sea
St Margaret

Why visit: *Superb church with features from the 14th and 15th centuries*
Where: *Church Lane, NR25 7UD*

An important port on this coastline in medieval times, Cley brought wealth that enabled St Margaret's to be rebuilt on a grand scale in the 14th century. But before it could be completed the Black Death struck here in 1348, killing many of the townsfolk. Cley never fully recovered: the port silted up, and what was once open water is now grass.

The church, however, did recover, but perhaps not in ways the original builders would have envisaged. The tower remains from the 13th century and there are large 15th-century windows in the aisles. Also from the 15th century is the splendid south porch. Reminders of what might have been include the south transept, a beautiful ruin from the 14th century.

There is much of interest inside the church, including 15th-century bench-ends, misericords and a seven-sacrament font. From the 17th century are the pulpit, altar table and a royal arms, originally that of Charles II but repainted for Queen Anne. Also here are interesting brasses from the 15th and 16th centuries.

Great Walsingham
St Peter

Why visit: *Superb set of medieval benches*
Where: *Church Road, in Great Walsingham, NR22 6DZ*

Great Walsingham is much smaller than its neighbour Little Walsingham, which gets all the attention because of the shrine and other buildings associated with Our Lady of Walsingham.

St Peter's is a fine 14th-century building with a 15th-century porch. It has no chancel, giving it a somewhat curtailed appearance, but this does not

detract from the beauty of the windows, among the best of their kind. The church's special treasure is its 40 benches dating from the 15th century. These still stand on their original wooden sills, a most unusual survival. The carving on many of the benches is exceptional, especially those with latticework backs. Some have linenfold panelled backs, a further refinement of medieval seating. There are carvings of saints on some of the benches, and others have animals and imagined creatures on them.

Upper Sheringham
All Saints

Why visit: *Rood screen and bench-ends*
Where: *Limekiln Lane, NR26 8TG*

Set in a large churchyard in quiet countryside inland from the sea, Upper Sheringham's church has features from both the 14th and 15th centuries. Inside, many of its fittings are from the 15th century, including the excellent and well-preserved rood screen that includes the front panel of its original loft. Also 15th-century are some of the bench-ends, with carvings including a baby in a shroud, a monkey and a mermaid. The font is 14th-century; the beam that held a font cover in place can still be seen.

ALSO IN THE AREA

Burnham Thorpe All Saints
Why visit: *Lord Nelson connections*

Little Walsingham St Mary
Why visit: *Seven-sacrament font, which survived a terrible fire in 1961*

South Creake St Mary
Why visit: *Setting; modern fittings*

THE NORFOLK MARSHLAND

Norfolk is full of wonderful medieval churches, and this far-flung, western edge has some of the very best the county has to offer. The area is called Marshland, and it has distinctive and very recognisable boundaries: the Nene on the West, the Ouse on the east and the Wash to the north. The landscape is divided by a complex pattern of waterways – some tiny, some huge – and by roads that often make abrupt sharp turns. In among them are straggly villages and their superb churches, some of which are among the finest anywhere.

King's Lynn St Margaret

Why visit: *West front; impressive brasses; wonderful medieval woodwork*
Where: *The Saturday Market Place, PE30 5EB*

Almost of cathedral size and impact, this great church is a pivotal part of the townscape of King's Lynn. It has twin towers at the west end, both of which have Norman origins. The north-west tower had to be rebuilt in 1452 as its foundations were giving way, and you can still see clear signs of subsidence inside the church. There was also once a huge central tower, but this is now very much reduced in height.

The west end of the church is a tremendous affair: between the two towers are a huge west window and a grand porch. Set into the south-west tower is an unusual 17th-century clock that tells the phases of the moon and the state of the tides on the Great Ouse. Written round its face are the words 'Lynn High Tide'.

The original Norman church was enlarged in the 13th century, and more work was done in the 15th century. Disaster struck on 8 September 1741 when a gale brought the spire of the south-west tower crashing down, destroying the lantern of the central tower and doing huge damage to the body of the church. The rebuilding work was completed in 1744, in the Gothic style, an unusual form to use at this time, and is generally regarded as a success.

Restoration work was done late in the 19th century, and it is from this time that the very large and unusual round east window dates. Inside, the church has differing architectural features from its eventful history and is packed with interest. Here are two of the largest and most impressive brasses in Britain – the earliest is to Adam de Walsoken, who died in 1349, and the other is to Robert Braunche, who died in 1364. Both men were mayors of the town.

The stalls and their misericords are from the late 14th century, as is the screenwork behind them. There are also screens with excellent woodwork from the 15th and 16th centuries.

The beautiful wooden pulpit is Georgian, and the eagle lectern is a rare brass one of the 16th century. The sumptuous reredos dates from 1899.

King's Lynn
St Nicholas CCT

Why visit: *South porch; angel roof*
Where: *St Ann's Street, PE30 1QS*

Although St Nicholas is a large and imposing building, it served as a mere chapel of ease for nearby St Margaret's. It was completely rebuilt in grand style

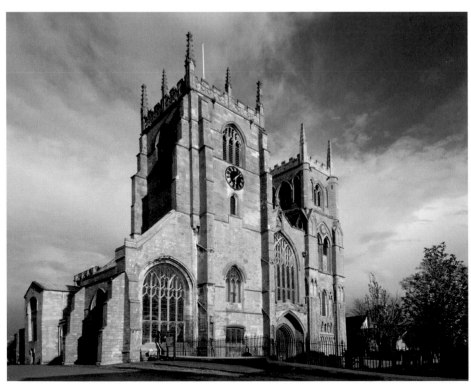

in the 15th century, and its south porch is an outstanding example of Perpendicular architecture. This is covered in a wealth of rich and complex carving, including a row of statue niches. Above them are two panels of carving of the most elaborate kind. The tower is crowned by an elegant spire built in the late 1800s to the designs of Sir George Gilbert Scott. Also very striking from the outside is the enormous west window. The spacious interior is dominated by its superb wooden roof, lined with angels. The font was presented to the church in 1627 by Bishop Harsnett. There are many tombs and memorials, one of the most noticeable being that to Benjamin Keene, made in 1757 by famous Scottish architect Robert Adam. It resembles a huge stone sugar bowl on top of an even larger stone cube.

Terrington St Clement
St Clement

Why visit: *Detached tower; font cover*
Where: *Churchgateway, north of the A17, PE34 4LZ*

A grand 15th-century church, St Clement's has a massive tower (also 15th-century) that is detached from it, but only by a short distance. This was a not-infrequent solution when church builders feared that the ground was too unstable for the body of the church to support a big tower. The west end of the church is elegant, with a large central window framed by two pairs of pinnacles, the outer ones very tall and thin. In comparison, the south porch appears low, rather like a beautifully carved railway tunnel entrance.

Inside, the greatest treasure of the church is its font cover, which was made in the 17th century. It is a very tall and ornate wooden structure that opens at the base to reveal painted biblical scenes in landscape settings. There are large Jacobean boards painted with the Lord's Prayer and the Ten Commandments, and a Georgian west screen.

Terrington St John
St John

Why visit: *Unusual priest's house*
Where: *Church Road, off the A47, PE14 7RY*

This church has an unusual-looking exterior: the tower is slim in comparison to the nave and is connected to the body of the church by an odd little extension called the Priest's House. This has a staircase that allows access to the external nave roof. Adding to the distinctive look are the clerestory windows, which are alternately circular and round-headed. The interior of the church is plain and simple, with 17th-century features that include the roof of about 1688 and a font dating from 1632.

Tilney All Saints All Saints

Why visit: *Excellent woodwork*
Where: *Church Road, between the A17 and the A47, PE34 4SJ*

With an imposing 13th- and 14th-century tower topped by a stone spire and corner pinnacles, Tilney's church stands out in its Marshland setting.

The core of the church is Norman, as the lovely arcades of the nave show. These run through both nave and chancel, and their capitals have a wide range of carved decoration. Among and in between the Norman columns are woodwork screens dating from the 15th to the 17th century. The Jacobean rood screen is particularly good, with two delicately carved lower stages and an upper stage with the favoured Jacobean motifs of obelisks and balusters.

The screen still has its original doors. Ancient benches and stalls add yet more to the character. Looking down on all this woodwork is a magnificent double

hammerbeam roof, with a complex array of carved timbers among which are wooden angels with outstretched wings.

Upwell St Peter

Why visit: *Ancient roofs; Georgian galleries*
Where: *Small Lode, PE14 9AA*

Beside the Wisbech Canal, a navigable arm of the River Nene, stands St Peter's. It has a 13th-century tower with an octagonal upper stage, and the body of the church is very handsome, made uniform by the battlements on porch, aisles, clerestory and chancel.

The inside is dominated by very fine medieval roofs – still with some of their original paint – and early 19th-century galleries. H. Munro Cautley, whose 1949 book *Norfolk Churches* is a classic of its genre, described these galleries as 'abominable', a view that would have been shared by the Victorians, no doubt. But the galleries give the church a particular character, and are an expression of changing church usage and fashion. They enable the visitor to get close to the wonderful carvings on the medieval roof, which include angels with outstretched wings and fantastical creatures. Also here is a rare medieval brass eagle lectern, rows of poppyhead benches, an ornate wooden pulpit and several interesting monuments and memorials, including one to 67 people who died of cholera in 1832.

Opposite page: The twin towers of the west front at St Margaret's, King's Lynn, (left); St Nicholas' beautifully carved porch (right).
This page: Terrington St Clement's nave exterior (left); St Peter's, Upwell (above).

Walpole St Peter St Peter

Why visit: *One of England's most famous churches*
Where: *Church Road, south of the A17, PE14 7NS*

This is one of England's most celebrated parish churches, and for many church enthusiasts it is one of the – if not the – best in the whole country. What makes it so special is that as well as being an exceptionally fine building in itself, it is full of fixtures and fittings from many periods, and these include outstanding examples of their kind.

The earliest part of the church is the tower, dating from the 14th century, while the whole of the rest was built between the late 1300s and 1450. It is a very large building, with huge windows in the nave and chancel. These have clear glass, so that you can see through the building from the outside, and it is flooded with light on the inside.

An unusual feature of the exterior is the passageway under the chancel. The reason for its being there is not entirely clear. Some experts wonder if it was part of a processional route, and others think it was to accommodate a right of way. It was certainly used at some point to secure horses during church services, as the tethering rings show.

The spectacular two-storey south porch is almost a building in itself, with superb carving on the outside and excellent vaulting to its ceiling.

One of the features that makes the interior so unique is the amount of lovely old woodwork. First, there is the splendid west screen, made in about 1630. Then, there are ranks of 17th-century benches in the nave. The painted base of the rood screen still separates the nave from the chancel, where the stalls have fine carvings from the 15th century. Best of all, perhaps, are the 15th-century benches in the south and north aisles. Those in the south aisle are in tiers; all have a variety of carved panels on their backs and superb poppyhead ends.

Also of wood is the screen to the south aisle chapel, the font cover of about 1600, the poor box (inscribed 'Remember the poore 1639') and the

'hudd', a shelter made so that the parson and his vestments would not get wet when officiating at funerals.

In the nave is an enormous brass chandelier dating from 1701, and also made of brass is the early 16th-century lectern. Look for the three endearing lions at its feet. Adding drama to the church is the fact that the chancel is significantly higher than the nave, and the high altar is higher still.

Walpole St Andrew
St Andrew CCT

Why visit: *Brick tower, Jacobean woodwork*
Where: *Kirk Road, south of the A17, PE14 7LL*

All of a piece from the 15th century, this church has a pretty brick tower with stone detailing. Built into it is a mysterious small room that may have been an anchorite's cell. At the east end of the nave, beyond the clerestory windows, are two little turrets that are an extension of stairs that led up to the rood loft.

Inside there is a Jacobean pulpit and other woodwork from the same period, and an earlier stone bracket for a pulpit that would have been reached via the rood loft stairs.

This page: The interior of St Peter, Walpole.

West Walton
St Mary the Virgin

Why visit: *Detached tower, 13th-century architecture*
Where: *Junction of Mill Road, Wisbech Road and School Road, PE14 7EU*

Before it became surrounded by a sea of modern developments, the impact of West Walton's detached tower in this flat landscape must have been awe-inspiring. Perhaps the nearby homes actually underline the architectural brilliance of this great crag of masonry. It has an open ground floor and three further stages, each with elegant blind arches.

The tower was built a little later than the body of the church, but both date from the first half of the 13th century.

The south porch of the church itself is flanked by two octagonal pinnacles. Like the tower, these are decorated with elegant blind arches. Both the outer and inner doorways of the porch have superb arches. There is a great deal else to enjoy on the outside of the church, from the big Perpendicular windows to the stonework decoration on the clerestory.

Inside, the outstanding features are the piers of the nave arcades. These are round, with detached shafts made of Purbeck marble. The capitals of the piers have elaborate foliage decoration. Between the arches are painted panels dating from the 17th century, and above these the blank arches of the clerestory have traces of medieval wall painting. Above all of this is the 15th-century roof, complete with angels holding shields.

The tower is in the care of the Churches Conservation Trust.

Wiggenhall
St Mary the Virgin CCT

Why visit: *Outstanding collection of benches and bench-ends*
Where: *At the end of Church Road, PE34 3EJ*

Reached along a lane that gradually leaves the trappings of the 21st century behind, this church is on a spit of land between two fenland 'drains' that enter the Great Ouse about half a mile away. Too big and too remote from any sizeable-enough congregation, it is now in the care of the Churches Conservation Trust.

A building from the 13th century and later, it was heavily restored by the Victorians. It has recently been re-roofed and repaired by the Trust. The tower is handsome, with its lower stages of stone, and the upper part of red brick.

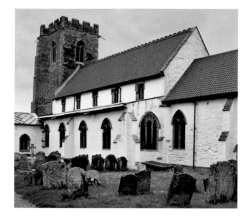

There is much of interest inside the church, but it is its benches and bench-ends that make it not just special, but outstanding. The benches are beautifully preserved and there are many of them. The ranks create a gallery of medieval carpentry and carving. The bench-ends are superb, with little figures on either side of the poppyheads and larger ones in niches on the ends. The little figures are particularly endearing, shown seated in informal and perky attitudes, wearing contemporary medieval dress and with faces that could almost be likenesses of parishioners of the time.

Later woodwork includes a 17th-century font cover, pulpit and alms box. There is also a painted rood screen, with figures of saints, and with the name of Humphrey Kerville, who donated it. The Kervilles are commemorated elsewhere in the church, with a brass in the form of a heart to Sir Robert, who died in 1450, and a monument to Sir Henry and his wife from the 1620s. With them are shown tiny figures of two children, who died before they did.

Wiggenhall Magdalen
St Mary Magdalen

Why visit: *Architecture; woodwork; stained glass*
Where: *Church Close, PE34 3DG*

This Wiggenhall church is situated on the banks of the Great Ouse. While there, visitors can take in the beautiful fenland landscape and huge skies from the bridges over the river and the parallel 'drain'.

The church is on the village's main street. It has enormous aisle windows and a pretty clerestory, and at the east end of the nave are two turrets flanking a small housing for a Sanctus bell. The church is entered through an elegant red-brick south porch with a room above.

The interior is dominated by woodwork from the 15th to the 19th centuries. Over the nave is a 15th-century hammerbeam roof, with angels. It looks down on rows of benches from medieval times and from the early 19th century. At the west end of the church are the panels from the rood screen, painted with the Four Evangelists.

In the north aisle windows is an important collection of stained glass, dating from the 14th and 15th centuries. Forty or so figures are depicted. The colours are bright reds, blues and yellows, and some of the figures have scrollwork names worked around them to identify them. Most are unusual or little-known bishops and saints and this makes the glass all the more special.

This page: St Mary the Virgin church at, Wiggenhall (top left) and its font and bench-ends (below left); St Germain at Wiggenhall St Germans (right).

Wiggenhall St Germans
St Germain

Why visit: *Superb carved benches*
Where: *Just south of the river bridge, PE34 3DW*

A good vantage point from which to enjoy the setting of this church is the bridge over the Great Ouse. The wide view of church, river and fens stretches away to the tower of the ruined shell of Wiggenhall St Peter, which can be seen about a mile upstream.

The church itself is full of character, both outside and in. The exterior reflects the varying ages of the building, with a 13th-century tower, while most of the body of the church is from the 15th century, and there are brick buttresses and a disused brick south porch from the 16th century.

The inside is famous for its ranks of carved benches. These date from the 15th century and have beautifully carved traceried backs. This detailing alone would make them a treat, but the bench-ends put them in the top league of their kind. There are marvellous carved figures on either side of the poppyheads, and the Apostles in niches on the ends of the benches. Among the scenes depicted are vices, such as Lust and Gluttony, literally in the jaws of hell. Less vivid, but equally interesting scenes include a priest blessing a man, and a group of four praying together. There are also animals, some real and some imagined.

ALSO IN THE AREA

Outwell St Clements
Why visit: *Lovely church; beautiful windows; medieval roofs*

FENLAND BORDER COUNTRY

Huge skies, flat landscapes and waterways characterise this area, which includes parts of Cambridgeshire, Lincolnshire, the old county of Huntingdonshire, and even a scrap of Norfolk. The landscape has changed: for example, once Wisbech was on an estuary made by the combined waters of the Nene and the Ouse, but the Ouse was re-routed to King's Lynn. Roads make their way along banks that were once on the edge of the sea. The churches here reflect the wealth of the area from the time of the Normans until the 15th century and beyond.

Castor St Kyneburgha

Why visit: *Outstanding Norman carvings*
Where: *Church Hill, PE5 7AY*

In Roman times Castor was part of a large industrial and residential complex centred around Durobrivae, a little to the south-west at Water Newton. Pottery was one of the main industries, and Castor Ware is a well-known Roman product. In the 1970s a hoard of Roman silver was discovered near Water Newton. Dating from the 4th century, it included items with Christian symbols on, making it the earliest Christian silver yet found in the Roman Empire.

Castor's church stands within Roman foundations, and Roman materials were re-used in its walls. It seems a fair assumption that there was a Christian congregation in this area as early as the 4th century. Three hundred years later,

in 650, St Kyneburgha, a daughter of King Penda of Mercia, founded a Saxon convent within the Roman ruins.

Vikings probably sacked that building, and the present church was begun around 1100. It incorporates several late Saxon items, including a carving of Christ in Majesty over the south porch. He is flanked by the sun and the moon. In the church is an 8th- or 9th-century carving of an Apostle, which may have formed part of the shrine of St Kyneburgha that once stood here. St Kyneswitha, St Kyneburgha's sister, was also buried here. The remains of both were moved to Peterborough in the 11th century.

The church itself is one of the finest in East Anglia, and is famous for its amazing tower. This has some of the most detailed decorative carving seen on any Norman church. Every surface of the top two stages is covered in carving: round-headed windows, blind arcades, balusters

with varying designs, fish-scale patterning, some of it rounded and some triangular, and corbel stones featuring weathered faces. This structure is topped by a spire dating from about 1350.

There is more Norman carving inside the church, especially on the capitals of the piers. These are fascinating and include a bird attacking a serpent, stylised faces with foliage growing out of them, a boar hunt, men fighting, assorted dragons, and much more besides. All of this astonishing work dates from about 1100.

Brightly painted angels, with gowns of different colours and outstretched wings, can be seen on the 15th-century roof. The modern kneelers are just as bright with some showing local scenes.

Barnack St John the Baptist

Why visit: *Saxon tower and Saxon figure of Christ in Majesty*
Where: *Main Street, PE9 3DL*

The name Barnack is synonymous with a particularly fine building stone. It was used for hundreds of buildings in this area and much farther afield, transported by boat on the Welland, Nene and other rivers. By the 1500s the quarry was almost worked out, and today the grown-over remains, called the 'Hills and Holes', are an important nature reserve.

This page: The imposing church of St Kyneburgha at Castor has its roots in Roman times (left); beautiful angels watch over the congregation from the roof (above).

The church is close to the old quarry and is built almost entirely of Barnack stone. Its most famous feature is its Saxon tower, with all of the hallmarks of this type of architecture: long-and-short work, pilaster strips and triangular-headed windows. Also set into it are tantalising pieces of highly decorative patterned stonework. Surmounting the tower is an octagonal belfry and short cap or spire flanked by four little turrets. Dating from about 1200, it is one of the earliest spires in the country.

The body of the church has Norman features, but a great deal of it dates from the later 12th and early 13th centuries. There is also 14th-century work, seen at its best in the lovely east window, while the south chapel is early 16th-century.

There is much of interest inside the church, including a 13th-century font. It is circular, delicately carved and, standing on ornate little pillars, looks rather like a beautifully iced cake. Perhaps the greatest treasure here is a wonderfully well-preserved Saxon carving of Christ, found under the floor in the 1930s, and presumably belonging to the original Saxon church.

Crowland Croyland Abbey

Why visit: *Ruined west front*
Where: *Abbey Walk, PE6 0EP*

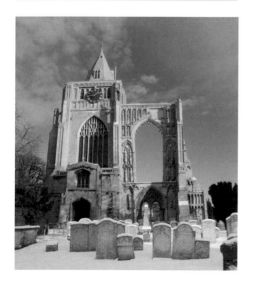

A giant splinter of masonry clings to the side of the church here. Apart from the north aisle, which has been the parish church since the 15th century, it is all that remains of the great abbey church and

the buildings that once stood here. The abbey had an eventful history: sacked by the Danes, burned down twice, then demolished at the Dissolution. The north aisle did not escape upheaval after that, being abused by both sides during the 17th-century civil war.

The ruined masonry that still stands was the west front of the abbey church; there are still saints in the niches on it. The tower and its porch are from the 15th century.

Gedney St Mary Magdalene

Why visit: *Excellent Perpendicular church*
Where: *Churchgate, off the A17, PE12 0BZ*

The elegant and beautifully decorated tower at Gedney is crowned by an unobtrusive spire. The body of the church has the hallmark of a great Perpendicular building: huge windows that fill it with light. It has a two-storey porch within which is one of the best medieval doors in England, its woodwork faded to a silvery-brown. It is carved with shields, ballflower decoration and a Latin inscription. Inside, the clerestory windows light the huge roof above, which has been over-restored but still retains its bosses.

This page: The majestic Croyland church with its accompanying ruined abbey at Crowland (left); a fine example of a Perpendicular building at St Mary Magdalene church, Gedney (above); the two circular, battlemented turrets of All Saints' church, Holbeach (right).

Guyhirn Chapel CCT

Why visit: *Simple 17th-century chapel of ease*
Where: *Off the High Road, north of Guyhirn village, PE13 4ED; the chapel is locked, but named keyholders are nearby*

This little chapel is on the north side of the River Nene, which is embanked along most of its length. In the care of the Churches Conservation Trust, the chapel stands in a large churchyard, but is itself very small. It is simplicity itself on the outside; a stone-faced oblong box with clear glass windows and a tiny bellcote. It is just as simple inside. It was built in 1660 for Nonconformist worship and has its original pews – narrow and close together to be uncomfortable (so you won't nod off in long services) and to discourage kneeling (which would be 'popish'). The pulpit is also original.

Holbeach All Saints

Why visit: *Unusual north porch, 14th-century effigy*
Where: *Church Street, PE12 7LL*

Built in the mid–14th century, All Saints is a handsome building with a sturdy tower and tall spire. The large windows and elegant clerestory add to the architectural harmony. The north porch has two circular flanking turrets, complete with battlements, which make it look exactly like a castle gateway.

The large tomb of Sir Humphrey Littlebury is the most notable feature of the interior – he died in 1365. The table tomb on which his effigy lies has complex carved niches. The effigy itself shows Sir Humphrey in full armour, with a lion at his feet, and his head resting on a macabre head wearing a netted headdress.

Leverington St Leonard

Why visit: *One of Cambridgeshire's best churches*
Where: *Church End, PE13 5DB; the church may be locked; keyholder and church-warden details available on the noticeboard*

Ghosts of old landscapes can be detected here: to the north of Leverington is a track called 'Roman Bank'. It is not actually Roman, but it does follow the line of what was once the shoreline of the River Nene. It had a wide estuary stretching deep into what is now flat fenland. It is a reminder that this landscape has been completely transformed by drainage, and that this area was once very rich through trade by sea and river.

Leverington's church is splendid and reflects the wealth this area once enjoyed. Its roots are in the 12th century but it was rebuilt, beginning in the 13th century. The magnificent tower is crowned by a tall spire clasped at its foot by four small castle-like turrets.

Some of the best elements of the church can be appreciated from the road. The chancel window and the south aisle window have beautiful flowing tracery, while the porch is almost a building in its own right. Built in the 14th century, it is a two-storeyed feast of ogee-headed doorways and windows, with buttresses, niches, pinnacles and other decoration.

The interior of the church takes much of its appearance from the 15th century, but the restoration of 1901 added great wooden tie-beams across the nave. Above these is the original roof. The greatest treasure inside the church is its 15th-century Jesse window, situated in the north aisle. About half of the figures depicted are original or restored; the rest

are from the 19th and 20th centuries. Also of interest are the sandstone font, with carved figures in niches, the 15th-century eagle lectern, and marble monuments of the late 18th and early 19th centuries.

Long Sutton St Mary

Why visit: *Famous spire*
Where: *Market Place, PE12 9JJ*

Long Sutton's tower stands to one side of the church. It was built in the 13th century, and until the 18th century had open arches at its base. It rises through three elegant stages of differing heights to the spire, which has four spirelets at its corners. Built of timber and covered in lead, it is said to be the oldest of its kind in Britain.

The church itself has a Norman nave, with later additions and enhancements that include a south porch, heightened aisles and a clerestory.

March St Wendreda

Why visit: *Angels; hammerbeam roof*
Where: *Church Street, south of March centre, off the B1101, PE15 0QS*

The base of St Wendreda's tower stands right on the edge of the street; there is a walkway under the tower so that you do not have to step into the road to walk around the building. The tower, spire and church are built of a pleasing mixture of

stone, flint and brick, with much of it dating from the early 16th century. However, some elements still remain from the mid-14th century. The flint flushwork of the battlemented clerestory is particularly handsome. The chancel was built in 1872.

Most visitors come here for the angels. These are in the wonderful hammerbeam roof and, like much of the church, they date from the early 16th century. All of them have outstretched wings and they are in three tiers, with more in the apex of the roof. The lowest tier is on the corbels supporting the roof, then there are two tiers at the ends of the hammerbeams. There are yet more on the wallplate between the beams.

Some of the angels carry symbols of the Passion, while others carry musical instruments. There are more than 100 of them and together they create a truly memorable and remarkable sight.

Spalding
St Mary and St Nicolas

Why visit: *Handsome church in a green setting*
Where: *Corner of Church Street and Love Lane, PE11 2PB*

Set in a leafy churchyard in a quiet part of Spalding, this handsome stone church has a fascinatingly complex exterior with numerous elements added at different times. As so often in the Fens, the imposing tower and spire are set apart from the body of the church.

The church has a 13th-century core, but was added to in the 14th and 15th centuries, and yet more was added during the Victorian restoration of the 1860s. The chancel has a very pretty ceiling, designed by architect Stephen Dykes Bower in 1959. For more than 20 years he was 'Surveyor of the Fabric' for Westminster Abbey.

Walsoken All Saints

Why visit: *Carvings of Solomon, Noah and his ark; seven-sacrament font*
Where: *Church Road, PE13 3RA*

The county boundary makes several peculiar changes of direction in this area, with the result that the church and its yard are in Norfolk, while most of the rest of Walsoken is in Cambridgeshire. The boundary made more sense fewer than 50 years ago, when the housing that now surrounds the church did not exist, and the church was virtually in open country.

From the outside the church looks Early English and later, as indeed are the tower and spire, but inside it is dominated by its outstanding Norman nave, with round-headed arches and sturdy piers. One of the treasures here is a very well preserved 16th-century seven-sacrament font. It is one of the best in East Anglia, with clear carved scenes.

There are vivid surprises in the church: at the west end over the tower arch is a carving of King Solomon. On either side of him are paintings showing part of the Judgement of Solomon – on the left is one of the women begging Solomon not to cut the baby in half, while to the right a soldier stands dangling the baby in one hand, with a raised sword in the other.

Over the chancel arch is a carving of Solomon's father, King David, playing a harp. Above is a lovely 15th-century roof decorated with painted angels. There are niches in the wallposts containing brightly painted biblical figures, including Noah holding the ark.

There is much more old woodwork in the church including a screen in the south aisle, carved choir stalls and bench-ends with little carved figures.

Whaplode St Mary

Why visit: *Norman features; 17th-century monument*
Where: *Church Gate, PE12 6TA*

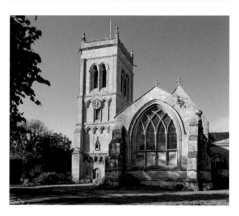

As at Long Sutton, the tower here almost stands aside from the main body of the church. Like the rest of the church, the tower has a somewhat complex building history, having been started in the 12th century and completed in the 14th. The differing styles of architecture from the different phases can be seen rising up through the tower's stages.

There was a church here in Saxon times, and fragments of that have been found, but the core of the church as it stands today is Norman, with massive piers in the nave and a splendid Norman chancel arch. There are additional Norman features, but these have been changed and adapted through the centuries. The hammerbeam roof dates from the late 15th or early 16th century. It has also seen many changes, with only three of its original angels now surviving.

There is a sumptuous 17th-century monument in the church, with effigies of Sir Anthony Irby and his wife Elizabeth surrounded by columns.

Wisbech
St Peter and St Paul

Why visit: *Large church with two naves*
Where: *Church Terrace, PE13 1BW*

In the centre of the town, just to the east of the site of what was once an important castle and close to the River Nene, this church has a long and complex history. This is reflected in its unusual internal arrangements. The outside gives some

of this away, with a variety of roofs over different parts of the building, and a large, grand more-or-less detached bell-tower. This was the last significant part of the church to be built, in the 1530s after the previous tower had collapsed in a storm nearly a century earlier.

The interior is most unusual in that it has two naves and two chancels. This came about because in medieval times the mouth of the River Ouse was just to the east of the church (before the Ouse was completely re-routed), while immediately to the west was the castle moat and mound. So when an expanding population required a bigger church, the often adopted solution of making a longer nave was not an option, and the church was made wider instead.

Features of the different ages and phases of this building and rebuilding can most clearly be seen in the piers and arcades of the two naves. Some are from the original Norman church, while others are from the 13th and 15th centuries. The work was not at all straightforward, which can be seen at the north-east end, where the medieval masons were obliged to 'bodge' the join between chancel and nave.

When the old tower blew down in the 1400s, it fell into the body of the church, making further rebuilding necessary. At this point the two naves were given a shared roof, supported by a central arcade of columns. This makes it one of only two such arrangements in England.

Opposite page: St Mary's, Long Sutton (centre); ceiling angels at St Wendreda's, March (right).
This page: St Mary's, Whaplode.

ALSO IN THE AREA

Stamford All Saints
Why visit: *Early English details*

Stamford St George
Why visit: *18th-century heraldic glass*

Stamford St Martin
Why visit: *Memorials; medieval glass*

Stamford St Mary
Why visit: *13th-century tower*

BOSTON AND THE LINCOLNSHIRE FENS

Far-reaching, flat landscapes and church towers complement each other brilliantly. The partnership is nowhere more exciting than in the Lincolnshire fens, where just the generous distribution and astonishing dimensions of the stone spires often defy superlatives – to say nothing of the sheer magnificence of so many individual examples, all with a backdrop of wide, limitless skies.

Boston St Botolph

Why visit: *Huge 14th-century church with iconic Perpendicular lantern tower*
Where: *Off Church Lane, north of the Market Place in the centre of Boston, PE22 9EP*

It is unfortunate that the ungainly name of 'Boston Stump' has been forever linked with the majestically proportioned tower of this vast parish church. The building harks back to Boston's glory days as England's second most important port, the gateway to European markets for wool and other medieval merchandise. In fact, the town's prosperity had already passed its peak by the time of the tower's completion in about 1520. However, by then a project to enlarge the chancel of the 14th-century Decorated building had already made this the largest parish church in England.

Externally, the church has changed little since that time. Today its glorious Perpendicular tower is still the tallest parish church tower in England, dominating town, country and even inshore waters. In 2009 St Botolph's celebrated the 700th anniversary of the founding of the present church.

Later work inside the church included rebuilding the chancel vault in the 18th century and installing an east window in the 19th. A Victorian restoration opened up the inside of the tower: a remarkable sight if you look up at the soaring vault above. The ornate font was designed and donated by E.W. Pugin, son of the eminent architect A.W.N. Pugin, in 1853.

Other treasures of the church include fine 14th-century carvings, including an amazing collection of 62 late 14th-century misericords with vivid and (as is often the case) sometimes positively unholy scenes. These include one of a choirboy being birched and using a book to shield himself, and another of an ox dressed as a bishop. A more recent quirky

detail is a 20th-century roof boss depicting a white elephant, in recognition of the bric-a-brac stall held to help raise money for restoring the roof.

The church has a famous library of 1,600 historic books, most of which date from the 16th and 17th centuries but also includes a 12th-century manuscript. Open days are held a few times each year, but the library is not normally accessible.

Algarkirk St Peter and St Paul

Why visit: *Imposing medieval church with colourful Victorianised interior*
Where: *Church Lane, PE20 2HH*

Looking like a cathedral in miniature, St Peter and St Paul's sits very grandly in the flat landscape, with its battlements and a row of great Perpendicular clerestory windows. These extend to the transepts, which have aisles as in the nave. Evidence of a Saxon church has been found here, and some Norman work survives. The present building dates from the 13th to the 15th centuries and was sensitively restored in 1854 so that medieval and Victorian work are not

always easy to tell apart. The glass and most of the furnishings and fittings, however, are unmistakably Victorian or later. The tower is 13th-century, with a short leadwork-covered spire of 1850. There are medieval stone effigies, including one of a priest. A stone in the churchyard is reputed to mark the grave of the Mercian earl, Algar, after who the village is named. He is said to have died in battle in 870.

Brant Broughton St Helen

Why visit: *Steeple; medieval porch carvings; Victorian chancel*
Where: *Church Walk, at the southern end of the village, north of the A17 between Newark and Sleaford, LN5 0SN*

Generally agreed to be one of the finest churches in Lincolnshire, St Helen's was already in the front rank before the Victorian architect G.F. Bodley added a sumptuous chancel (with painted vault and lavishly gilded reredos), in his late 19th-century restoration. Bodley worked closely with the rector of the time, Canon F. Sutton, who was sufficiently hands-on to have made the stained glass himself. His nephew, who followed him as rector, installed the beautifully painted font cover in his memory, in 1889.

The two richly embellished, stone-vaulted porches of the 14th century are among the best medieval features of the church, each one a gallery of spirited carvings that range from daily life (including its seamier side) to the pious and the fantastical. In this remarkable area of Lincolnshire, it almost goes without saying that the lofty 14th-century spire is also magnificent, with spire and spirelets alike generously crocketed at every angle.

Grantham St Wulfram

Why visit: *Elegant steeple*
Where: *Church Street, NG31 6RR*

St Wulfram's slender and graceful spire, distinctively flanked by its four spirelets, would very likely have been the tallest in England when it was built in 1280–1300, and it is still one of the most elegant. This was clearly a church of importance by that time, and the pillars in the eastern part of the nave survive from a Norman cruciform church. Successive centuries, with their differing styles of Gothic, have left their imprint. These include 13th-century windows and doorway in the north aisle, fluid tracery of the 14th century in the windows of the Lady Chapel and a crypt of the same period. There is Perpendicular work of the 1480s in the 15th-century Corpus Christi Chapel and a lovely 15th-century font. The church has essentially changed little since that time. Don't miss the gargoyles and corbels on the exterior – a gallery of

medieval face-pulling. The chained library of 1598 is still in its original room above the south porch. Founded by Francis Trigge, a far-sighted clergyman of the time, it was the first public reference library in the country.

Heckington St Andrew

Why visit: *Exceptional stonecarving*
Where: *Jermyn Street, in the centre of the village, off the A17 east of Sleaford, NG34 9JU*

A visit to see this masterpiece of the Decorated style is an exceptional experience. There is much to enjoy, from the window tracery (note especially the seven-light east window and that of the south transept) to the crocketed pinnacles, niches and parapets.

Outstanding carvings are everywhere, including a collection of 14th-century figurative work. It adorns the south front and porch, inside and out, and even the tower, with dozens of statues. Inside the church the chief treasures are in the chancel, where yet more carving demands careful attention: this time in the form of a piscina, three-seat sedilia and a rare Easter sepulchre. The tomb recess is of Richard de Potesgrave, the 14th-century rector of Heckington, who was responsible for all this amazing work.

Sleaford St Denys

Why visit: *Rood screen, window tracery*
Where: *Market Place, NG34 7SH*

On the east side of the market place, St Denys is surrounded by fine old buildings from many periods, including the 16th-century half-timbered vicarage.

The church's west front is magnificent, with delicately traceried windows and crocketed pinnacles framing the tower and its broach spire. The spire is one of the earliest of its type, dating from the early 13th century. The window tracery throughout the church is superb.

The interior of the church is dominated by its rood screen. The base of this is original medieval work, but the rest, with angels, saints and Christ on the Cross is by Sir Ninian Comper and dates from the early 20th century. It is flanked by two monuments, one from the late 16th century and one from about 1618.

Tattershall Holy Trinity

Why visit: *Fine Perpendicular church*
Where: *Sleaford Road (A153), LN4 4LR*

Sharing the limelight with Tattershall Castle is Lincolnshire's grandest Perpendicular church, a collegiate foundation of the mid-15th century. Church and castle are all of a piece, along with the remains of what was once the college – a trio of buildings that were the brainchild of Ralph (Lord) Cromwell, who was Chancellor to Henry VI. He died before the church was completed, so the rest of the work was supervised by the Bishop of Winchester.

The church is very large, and all in the Perpendicular style, and so flooded with light from enormous windows. The original conception for the church was that all the windows should be filled with brightly coloured stained glass, and so they were until the 18th century, when a vicar suggested that the stained glass be removed and replaced with clear. By 1754 all the stained glass was gone. At this point there was a misunderstanding or dispute over how much the new, clear glass would cost, with the result that the chancel windows were left with no glass and other windows were bricked up.

Today, some of the original stained glass can still be seen in the east window and consists of tantalising fragments.

Opposite page: Inside the tallest parish church tower in England at Boston.
This page: St Wulfram's steeple, Grantham (left); intricate stonework decorating St Andrew's, Heckington (centre).

NORTHERN ENGLAND

The North of England ranges from old sprawling industrial cities to the sparsely populated country along the Scottish Borders, some of which is nearly as wild as it was a millennium ago. In every corner of this vast area lie fascinating churches that will repay your interest.

Once you leave the conurbations of Manchester, Leeds and Liverpool and the old city of York, the exploration of the North's churches and chapels takes on new delights. As you travel northwards towards Scotland, your tour is as much about the beauty and history of some of England's most inspiring countryside as it is about the churches themselves.

The Lake District was justly celebrated by the Romantic poets, and the names Ambleside and Grasmere are synonymous with its picture-postcard villages and their equally charming churches, many of which are notable for the loveliness of the stained glass created for them by important Pre-Raphaelite artists. St Bees to the west has another kind of allure, more stark and windswept as it perches above the Irish Sea.

The moors and wolds of Yorkshire are home to many fine Saxon, Norman and medieval churches, nestling in atmospheric villages that stretch all the way to the sea at Holderness and Bridlington. They often still retain the early stone and wooden features that were first used in the early churches built here.

In Cumbria, Durham and Northumberland, you are never far from the sea or the Scottish Borders, both once posing the threat of invasion by Scots and Vikings, who left their mark on the churches here. This area also bears the legacy of Roman settlers, who established the earliest Christian sites in England. Being so far from the central control of London, it has always been a land of dissenters too, so it is no surprise to find important Quaker meeting houses and Methodist chapels hereabouts.

At the northernmost frontier of England, in the strange and ancient lands of Northumberland, this exploration of English churches and chapels ends at Berwick-upon-Tweed, with England's most northerly parish church.

This page: St Gregory, Kirkdale, is an ancient Saxon church with a rare and well-preserved Anglo-Saxon sundial protected by its 18th-century porch.

AROUND GREATER MANCHESTER

It is difficult to imagine what Manchester must have been like when its great churches were being established and bustling communities began to spring up around them, whether this took place in the 13th century or the 19th. Some, such as St Michael's in Mottram, still enjoy a commanding position in the landscape, while others have grown close to their city neighbours. Manchester churches have seen another interesting change – many retain remnants of the 18th- and 19th-century move away from ritual at the altar to preaching at the pulpit, one of the 'modernising' tendencies that cities often foster.

Why visit: *Outstanding 15th-century stained glass*
Where: *Church Street, OL6 6XJ*

It is thought that there was a church on this site before the Norman Conquest as the Domesday Book mentions a St Michael's Church in the east of the ancient parish of Manchester. The present building dates from the 15th century, although much of the church was reconstructed in Victorian times.

St Michael's was built in the Perpendicular style with large windows and the church boasts some of the best examples of 15th-century stained glass left in Britain, with 18 panels illustrating the life of St Helena. Buttresses were required with this type of building as the large window area reduced the strength of the walls.

The nave of the church is dominated by a 19th-century three-tiered pulpit, which is placed halfway along the north side. The pews face towards it rather than the altar, which shows that more emphasis was placed on the sermon rather than on the ceremonial part of the service.

The pews themselves are boxed with small doors for access. They are of different sizes and would have been reserved for particular families, with the better-off families nearer the front.

Manchester St Ann

Why visit: *Beautiful Classical Wren-inspired design*
Where: *St Ann Street, St Ann's Square, M2 7LF*

Dedicated to the mother of the Virgin Mary but paying tribute to its patron, Lady Ann Bland, St Ann's was first consecrated in 1712. The tower marks the centre of the city, and surveyors used to measure distances to other locations from a benchmark that is still visible at the tower door.

The church is the third oldest building in Manchester and was designed by Derbyshire architect John Barker in the Classical style. Its original simple interior, with plain glass windows and the altar placed behind the three-tiered pulpit, was a reaction against the High Church worship practised at the Collegiate Church (now Manchester Cathedral), the centre of the Jacobite cause.

Lady Bland was a staunch supporter of the Low Church and the Whigs, and so she provided most of the money for building a new church – St Ann's – to rival the Collegiate Church.

By the time renovations were carried out in the 19th century, Jacobite-Whig tensions had ceased, so the altar again took centre stage and fine stained glass was installed.

Incendiary bombs in World War II were followed by general decay in the church fabric. In 1996, the windows, especially at gallery level, were caught in the blast of an IRA bomb and were badly damaged. Now recent renovations have restored the church to its former magnificence and many find it more impressive than Manchester Cathedral.

This page: *The sumptuous interior of St Ann's, with its handsome polished-wood galleries (left); some of the precious St Helena glass at St Michael's (above).*

Chorlton on Medlock
The Holy Name of Jesus

Why visit: *Impressive size and soaring medieval-style interior*
Where: *Oxford Road, M13 9PG*

This Catholic church – it is the largest church in Manchester, dominating the surrounding area – was opened in 1871 to reinforce the power of the reforming Jesuit movement. Its architect was a favourite of the Jesuits, Joseph Aloysius Hansom (the inventor of the cab that bears his name), and he designed it in the 14th-century French Gothic style, with impressive dimensions and proportions.

The plan is typical of a Jesuit city church – a broad nave and a short sanctuary with the raised altar in full view (there is no rood screen). The prominent pulpit places the preacher in intimate contact with the congregation, all the better to spread the reformers' beliefs.

Denton St Lawrence

Why visit: *Tudor timber-framed structure*
Where: *Town Lane, M34 6AD*

St Lawrence's is a timber-framed church that at the most conservative estimate dates from 1531. Only 29 examples of this once common medieval building style remain in England and Wales. The beams are held together with wooden pegs, giving the church its original nickname, Th'owd Peg ('the old peg').

Originally it was not a parish church but a chapel of ease. It became a parish church dedicated to St Lawrence in 1839 after some fragments of glass depicting his martyrdom were found within the structure of the building. These fragments are now incorporated into a window on the south side of the sanctuary.

The church was expanded in 1872 when two transepts and the chancel were added. The ornate screen was installed in 1926. At the west end of the nave is an 18th-century minstrel gallery where the musicians and choir were located.

The church stands in one of the few open green spaces in urban Denton; the yew was planted in 1801 and is protected by a Tree Preservation Order, as are many in the churchyard.

Eccles St Mary the Virgin

Why visit: *Medieval carved timber roof*
Where: *The junction of Church Road and Church Street, M30 0DF*

St Mary's has stood here for at least 800 years – the name Eccles is derived from the Welsh 'eglwys', itself borrowed from the Latin meaning 'a church'. By the early 15th century, the nave had been completely rebuilt when the side aisles were possibly widened and the magnificent carved timber roof was constructed. The carved bosses show the Sun in Splendour, the badge of the Yorkist King Edward IV during the Wars of the Roses (1455–85).

Over the centuries, many masons who carried out alterations and extensions left their signatures on their work. There are 16 different masons' marks in this church, to be found especially in the nave and the tower. In the 20th century, the galleries were removed to open the church to its full beauty; in 1929 two stained glass windows were installed at the west end. The one on the south side is the Palm Sunday window, made of 16th-century glass. It is said to have been brought to England at the time of the French Revolution from a convent in Rouen and placed in the now-demolished St John's Church, off Deansgate. When it closed, the window came to Eccles.

Mottram-in-Longdendale
St Michael and All Angels

Why visit: *Life-size stone effigies; 12th-century font*
Where: *Broadbottom Road, SK14 6JB*

This impressive stone-built church perches atop War Hill, the site of a battle between invading Normans and the local

Saxons. It is believed that those killed were buried here and a place of worship established. The first church was probably made of wood, though the present church dates mainly from the 15th century and was built in the Perpendicular style.

Little remains of early buildings: the Norman barrel font, the effigy of a knight and his lady in the Staveley Chapel and possibly the chancel arch. The chancel roof is of a great age, though the beams have Victorian pegs.

The carved screens and much of the furniture date from 1868, though the altar rail was made later by Robert Thompson of Kilburn in Yorkshire, whose mouse trademark is carved into the base of the first right-hand newel post. The church mouse still proves to be a popular attraction for young visitors to the church.

This page: *A view of Eccles, St Mary from the east end, showing the side chapels (centre); interior at Mottram-in-Longdendale (above).*

ALSO IN THE AREA

Burnage St Nicholas
Why visit: *A milestone in modern church design*

Haughton St Anne
Why visit: *A lovely church in the Gothic style but using timber framing*

Middleton Parish Church
Why visit: *A 16th-century church with a fine collection of brasses*

Reddish St Elisabeth
Why visit: *Magnificent chancel with groined and moulded stone-ribbed ceiling*

WITHIN YORK CITY

York's parish churches are notable for the quality of their wood and stone carving and for the beauty of their stained glass. Happily, much of this fine craftsmanship survives intact from the Middle Ages, as it does so gloriously at North Street All Saints and at St Denys. Even Victorian or later additions – at St Martin le Grand or Pavement All Saints, for example – seem to capture the mystery of a distant past.

North Street All Saints

Why visit: *15th-century ceiling; interesting stained glass*
Where: *North Street, YO1 6JD*

Tucked away from York's city centre, near the River Ouse and next to a row of 15th-century timber-framed houses, lies this fine medieval Anglo-Catholic church. From the outside, its main feature is an impressive tower with an octagonal spire. It also has a small hermitage, attached to the west end, where a female hermit lived in the early 15th century.

All Saints took its current form in the 14th century, and by the 1470s the roof and beautifully decorated ceiling – with brightly painted angels bearing emblems and musical instruments – were in place. There is a 15th-century oak stall with a fine carving of a pelican, a Christian symbol of atonement, feeding her young with her own blood.

Worth the visit alone is the fine 15th-century stained glass, which gives remarkable insight into the clothing and customs of the day. In one of the windows a man can be seen wearing a pair of medieval spectacles.

The north aisle contains two famous windows. Corporal Acts of Mercy shows a wealthy man (possibly the merchant Nicholas Blackburn, a mayor of York) visiting the sick, clothing the naked and feeding the hungry. The other, dating from 1410, is the Pricke of Conscience window, an apocalyptic vision of Doom, the last 15 days of the world. Based on a popular contemporary poem, it shows rising seas and monsters, the earth on fire, men hiding in holes – and the dreadful spectacle of a couple lying on a bed with a spear-wielding, skeletal figure of Death standing beside them as horrified figures look on. It is a distressing scene of medieval guilt and the fear of everlasting punishment. But the windows are also an aesthetic marvel, with clear, vibrant colours and detailed rendering of very expressive faces, making them a moving and uplifting sight to behold.

Coney Street
St Martin le Grand

Why visit: *Ancient and modern existing side by side*
Where: *Coney Street near the junction with New Street, YO1 9QL*

St Martin calls itself 'an old church in a modern guise'. Others have called it a phoenix risen from the ashes. Regarded by the Victorians as one of the most beautiful churches in the city, St Martin's was burnt out in World War II, in bombing known as the 'Baedeker raids' for targeting historic cities. Only the tower and the south aisle survived. After extensive rebuilding, the church was re-hallowed as a chapel of peace and reconciliation, and a walled garden was created from the remaining shell.

Some strikingly modern elements have taken their place alongside the old. A suitably fiery east window depicting the burning of the church soars above a gold-painted aluminium sculpture of The Last Supper, the figures angular and twisted. However, the old west window remains. Dating from about 1440 and the

This page: *The 15th-century roof of All Saints, with its early 20th-century rood.*

largest of any parish church in York, it was fortunately removed into storage in 1940 for protection. It was reinstated in the new north wall in 1967 as part of the triumphant restoration.

Duncombe Place St Wilfrid

Why visit: *Detailed Victorian carving*
Where: *Duncombe Place, in view of York Minster, YO1 7ED*

St Wilfrid's Catholic Church is known as the Mother Church of the city of York. It is also the first Catholic church to have been constructed there, built in the Gothic Revival style in 1862–4 near a former Catholic chapel, established 1742.

The arch over the main door has the most detailed Victorian carving in the city. The tower, visible around much of York, is designed to appear taller than the Minster in the background, even though it is not. The church is also rich in sculpture, paintings and stained glass.

Goodramgate
Holy Trinity CCT

Why visit: *Untouched by Victorian restoration and housing fine box pews*
Where: *Goodramgate, YO1 7LF*

You might easily miss the gateway to Holy Trinity, at the end of Lady Row cottages, the most ancient row of humble domestic buildings in York, built in 1316. The church nestles in a secluded, leafy churchyard, with York Minster towering in the background. After St Mary Bishophill Junior, it is the oldest medieval church within the city walls of York.

Dating from the 13th–15th century, this at first seems a humble structure, with uneven floors and listing arcades. But the stone is warm and inviting, and the precious stained glass is rich and dignified. Exceptionally fine box pews, added in the 17th and 18th centuries, crowd round the nave arcades. Holy Trinity has not been rebuilt in modern times and so is a faithful embodiment of the post-Reformation church.

Micklegate Holy Trinity

Why visit: *Based on the ruins of a Benedictine abbey*
Where: *Micklegate at Priory Street, YO1 6EN*

The walls of the nave and the central tower is all that remain of the substantial Benedictine priory church founded in 1089, itself on the site of a pre-Conquest church. Most of the surviving older stonework is 13th-century, but the church decayed after the Dissolution and had to be rebuilt in the 19th century.

As if to make up for its lost heritage, the church now has a fascinating display on the Monks of Micklegate, focusing on the beautiful 13th-century illuminated Book of Beasts they created (currently in St John's College, Oxford).

In the Middle Ages, Holy Trinity was the starting point for the celebrated York Mystery Plays; there is also a set of stocks in the churchyard.

Pavement All Saints

Why visit: *Impressive golden woodwork and Charles Kempe stained glass*
Where: *Coppergate, near the junction with Piccadilly, YO1 8RZ*

The original All Saints was probably destroyed when the current building was constructed in the 11th century, though most of it is 14th- and 15th-century, with the exterior's most striking feature – the octagonal lantern tower used as a beacon for travellers – added in around 1400.

The stained glass is from three different periods. The passion window at the west end dates from the 14th century and is unique. There are four 19th-century windows by the Victorian designer

Charles Kempe and one modern window was installed in 2002 for the Royal Dragoon Guards.

Also not to be missed are the hexagonal pulpit of 1634 (used by John Wesley, co-founder of Methodism), with its biblical texts; the door knocker of a lion swallowing a bearded head (a replica of the 12th- or 13th-century original); and the showy gilded woodwork.

Walmgate St Denys

Why visit: *Earliest stained glass in York*
Where: *St Denys Road, YO1 9QD*

This small medieval church, built on the site of a Saxon church and possibly a Roman temple, conceals a fine collection of stained glass, including the earliest in York – and much else besides. Look for the sculpted Norman doorway, a 15th-century timbered roof and, almost hidden high above the south aisle arcade, four carved 12th-century Norman heads.

St Denys was once a lot larger than it is now, but parts of it subsided after the king's fish pool was drained and a sewer was built nearby, resulting in an unusual square-shaped church made up of just the east end with its flanking chapels. Further mishaps followed: the original spire was hit by cannon shot, struck by lightning and then partially blown down during the 17th and 18th centuries, and was only replaced in the Victorian age.

***This page:** The warm stone of Holy Trinity (left); All Saints' door knocker (above).*

NORTH AND WEST YORKSHIRE

From the moors of Bolton Abbey and Ilkley, proceeding over to the east through Harrogate and Knaresborough, then rounding down just north of Leeds, there lies a trail of wonderful churches, many in idyllic settings. Some – at Bolton Abbey, Adel and Bardsey – retain their essential Saxon or Norman structure. Others are showcases for the fine stained glass that is so often a feature of Yorkshire churches: see superb 18th-century glass at Denton St Helen, and work of the 19th-century masters William Morris, Sir Edward Burne-Jones and Charles Kempe at Knaresborough, Ilkley and Harewood.

Bolton Abbey
St Mary and St Cuthbert

Why visit: *Set in the hauntingly beautiful ruins of Bolton Priory*
Where: *Off the B6160, Bolton Abbey, BD23 6AL; open daily in the summer, weekends only in the winter*

The Priory Church of St Mary and St Cuthbert stands above a wide curve in the River Wharfe amid the ruins of Bolton Priory. The original priory was established in 1154 by a group of black-robed Augustinian priests in a sheltered spot protected from the cruel winter weather by the surrounding hills.

Over the next four centuries, it thrived and grew, and the site became more magnificent. Then, suddenly, in 1539 it was faced with obliteration as Henry VIII undertook his campaign to destroy the monastic houses of England. Work to create the west tower was halted, lead was torn from the roofs, furnishings removed and valuables taken to the king's treasury.

All but the 13th-century nave now lies in ruins. It was left intact and still serves as an atmospheric parish church of great beauty – the Priory Church of St Mary and St Cuthbert.

Its Tudor roof is embellished with gilded bosses, including the face of a Green Man, whose visage is framed by a leaf twisting from an eye and another from one side of the mouth.

Most of the remaining church is in the Gothic style, but more work was done in the Victorian era. The unfinished west tower, begun in 1520 and now roofed in, forms a magnificent entrance, behind which is hidden a fine Early English west front. There are pleasing Early Gothic lancets on the south wall, with six Victorian stained glass windows by A.W.N. Pugin, telling the life of Christ in 36 scenes. Set in the west wall is a tiny stained glass window of St Cuthbert, who the church is named after.

The current east wall, rebuilt in 1877 to replace the old wall erected in 1539 following the Dissolution, was decorated in 1890 by local artists. Pre-Raphaelite paintings of flowers and symbols from the Bible, including the priory cross, lily, rose, passionflower, palm, lion and angel, are set in tall arches that rise behind the pre-Reformation sealed stone altar. Beyond the east wall lie ruins of the original church, an area of great beauty and serenity. The high altar, topped by the imposing east window once resplendent with stained glass, was raised on a step that spanned the entire width of the building. Now this step is covered in grass, a mute witness to the majestic church that once stood on this site.

This page: The ruins of Bolton Priory, in which the church of St Mary and St Cuthbert still stands intact.

Adel St John the Baptist

Why visit: *One of Yorkshire's best Norman churches*
Where: *Church Lane, LS16 8DW; open Wed 10.30am–12noon, Thu 1–5pm*

Adel church is one of the finest examples of Norman architecture in Britain. It has been in existence in its current form since 1150 – making it the oldest church in Leeds – and there is evidence of a Saxon place of worship in the foundations of the current building.

The church is also notable for its remarkable 800-year-old carvings, most of them still very sharp. The south doorway has elaborately carved arches, and there are 37 grotesque beakheads carved into the chancel arch, with more human heads and beasts on a corbel table.

Other treasures include a three-light armorial east window dated 1681, and a medieval octagonal stone font at the west end of the nave, with an amazing oak canopy carved by the Arts and Crafts sculptor and stonecutter Eric Gill. As in all churches dedicated to St John, the font has two steps leading down to it, like stepping down into the River Jordan.

A replica of the recently stolen 13th-century bronze-cast Sanctuary Ring door knocker – showing a man's head protruding from the mouth of a lion, with a decorated ring passing through the lion's mouth – has been made by local craftsmen, employing techniques that would have been used 800 years ago; it now replaces the stolen original on the great south door.

Bardsey All Hallows

Why visit: *Anglo-Saxon buildings*
Where: *Church Lane, LS17 9DN*

The core of the present church – one of the best-surviving Anglo-Saxon buildings in West Yorkshire – was built about 1,200 years ago, and much remains of the tall narrow Saxon nave and tower. At this time the church consisted of just a west porch, a narrow nave and a tiny chancel.

Between 1100 and 1400, north and south aisles were added and then widened, forming fine Norman arcades. An elaborate Norman doorway was moved to its present position at the west end of the south aisle, though it is now partly obscured by the much later addition of a porch. Yet it remains the principal entrance to the church and clearly shows the architectural features typical of early Norman construction.

In the last century, efforts have been made to undo Victorian 'improvements' and try to recapture the medieval character of the interior – wall plaster was removed, floors raised and ancient architecture uncovered. Recently, pews were removed as well.

The church is now home to the Bardsey Millennium Tapestry. Created by people from the village, the four panels of the tapestry, each showing one of the four seasons, portray village life at the turn of the millennium.

Clifford St Edward the Confessor

Why visit: *Its tall tower, the most prominent structure in the area*
Where: *Chapel Lane, LS23 6HU*

The largest church in Clifford, St Edward's was built between 1845 and 1848 in the Romanesque style. It was constructed of ashlar limestone with a green slate roof; this Catholic church was established to serve the growing population of Irish workers who came to work in the local flax mill, beginning in about 1831.

The imposing five-stage west tower – complete with buttresses – was finished in 1866–7 and culminates in a pyramid-shaped ashlar roof and a finial. The base of the tower is open and has massive round arches open on three sides, making a very grand entrance to the church.

A mysterious-looking ground-level door in one of the pillars supporting the tower reveals a square stair turret (becoming cylindrical) that goes all the way up to the fifth stage and is topped with a rather graceful conical roof.

This page: *South door at Adel (left); the partly Norman exterior of All Hallows, with its late Saxon tower (centre); soaring above Clifford, the Romanesque-style tower of St Edward's (above).*

Denton St Helen

Why visit: *Superb Musicians' Window*
Where: *Main Street, LS29 0HH*

St Helen's was designed by John Carr – an 18th-century architect, associate of the great Robert Adam and sometime Lord Mayor of York – as a private chapel to Denton Hall, a grand country estate set in the moors just a few miles from the historic spa town of Ilkley.

This elegant little church, built in the Georgian style in 1776, stands in a peaceful hamlet surrounded by parkland, near Denton Hall itself.

The colourful and painterly east window, known as the Musicians' Window, is signed by Giles of York and dated 1700; it was moved from Denton Hall when the chapel was built. The scene depicts St Cecilia – the patron saint of musicians and church music – playing the organ, surrounded by angels playing the lute, cornetto, violin, cello and trombone. Clearly, the chapel was intended to meet the aesthetic as well as the spiritual needs of its users.

There is other glass by William Peckitt, a leading Georgian glass painter and stained glass maker based in York. He did much to revive the medieval art of stained glass making and keep it alive during the 18th century.

There are also some examples from the famous Whitefriars Glass workshop, English makers of stained glass since 1680, when a small glassworks was established off Fleet Street in London. Armorial detail and fine inscriptions are also of interest.

Farfield
Friends Meeting House HCT

Why visit: *One of the earliest Quaker Meeting Houses*
Where: *Bolton Road (B6160), near Addingham, LS29 0RQ*

The date carved in the stone above the door of this simple meeting house shows that it was built in the same year as the Toleration Act of 1689. In fact, the plot for the building was given to the Quakers in 1669 by a sympathetic local landowner. Land for the adjoining burial ground was given three years earlier, at a time when Quakers were denied burial in parish churchyards.

It is a simple single-cell building with stone walls and mullioned windows. The roof is of stone and supported by a single king post truss; the floor is stone flagged. Apart from some loose benches, the only fitting is the oak minister's stand – where visiting ministers would speak to the meeting – of an unusual panelled design with turned balusters.

In the burial ground there is a row of five table tombs honouring the Myers family, who were the givers of the ground. Most Quaker headstones were of a uniform plain design, so these rare features provide evidence of a commemorative practice that the Quakers subsequently discouraged.

The meeting house has not been in use by the Society of Friends for 150 years and is a remarkable survivor of another age. It is left unlocked and can be visited at any reasonable time; a sign invites visitors to picnic in the grounds.

Harewood All Saints CCT

Why visit: *Largest and finest collection of medieval alabaster tomb effigies in any English parish church*
Where: *Harewood Park (follow signs for Harewood House), LS17 9LG*

All Saints stands in isolation within the park of Harewood House. Built in about 1410 in the Perpendicular style, this imposing long, low church, with its squat west tower, predates the house by 350 years. Around the pale sandstone exterior walls range diagonal buttresses,

and a five-light window looms over the arched west doorway. Early medieval artefacts, including a pre-Conquest carved panel, 12th-century column shafts and fragments of 14th-century stained glass, have been excavated from the site.

Its rather severe interior houses a spectacular collection of alabaster tombs, dating from 1419 to 1510, which commemorate illustrious members of families connected with the Harewood estate. Six pairs of effigies, intricately carved and virtually without rival in England, provide a unique record of the fashions of the late medieval and early Tudor period – armour, official robes, female costume and jewellery. The monuments were once brightly coloured, but this has worn away, leaving ghostly white alabaster.

The church was much restored in 1862–3 by Sir George Gilbert Scott, who replaced the ceiling, the pews and some stained glass; he also added a new altar, lectern and pulpit. There are two fonts, one Norman and another from the Victorian era. The fine stained glass in the west window (1894) is by C.E. Kempe, a well-known Victorian stained glass designer whose studio made windows for many Yorkshire churches. All Saints is no longer in use for regular worship.

This page: *The beautiful early 18th-century Musicians' Window at Denton St Helen (left); two of All Saints' unrivalled alabaster effigies on carved tombs (above).*

Harrogate St Wilfrid

Why visit: *Impressive 20th-century church in the Gothic Revival style*
Where: *Duchy Road, HG1 2EY*

This beautiful church is Gothic Revival at its best and is true to the reforms of the Anglo-Catholic Oxford Movement, which sought to reinstate lost traditions into the Anglican church.

It is also probably the finest building of the distinguished architect Temple Moore, with its lovely exterior stonework in honey-coloured Tadcaster limestone. Work on the church began in 1904, but unfortunately Moore died suddenly in 1920, leaving his son-in-law to complete it in 1935.

Inside, the church is surprisingly spacious and light, the building seeming vast in every direction and enhanced by what Sir John Betjeman described as 'Edwardian vistas'.

Coming into the chancel, you pass beneath the great rood screen, a fine piece of wood carving that adds an air of dignity and reverence to the whole interior, which it dominates. One of the best views is looking east over the high altar, through the open arches to the exquisite Lady Chapel.

There is fine stained glass by Victor Milner, a contemporary of Moore who he often worked with. Bas-relief panels from the 1920s, by local sculptor Frances Darlington, depict the life of Christ and portray members of the congregation.

This page: The spacious nave and rood screen of St Wilfrid's (above); the fine stonework and medieval tower of St John the Baptist (centre); exposed stone walls that give St Mary's, Lead a rustic air (right).

Ilkley St Margaret

Why visit: *The beautiful east window and ornately carved reredos*
Where: *Queens Road, LS29 9QL*

Built in 1879 in the late Neo-Gothic, or Perpendicular, style St Margaret's is constructed in ashlar limestone and has broad east and west windows. The nave has a handsome open-beam wooden roof, and a low arch with a wooden screen to the chancel.

Although Sir John Betjeman rather dismissively described it in his guide as 'spa suburban', the church possesses many fine points, including a sumptuous carved reredos, a Burne-Jones stained glass window and a baptistry painting of the Madonna and Child with St Margaret and St John, by the well-known local artist Graeme Willson, dating from 2004.

Knaresborough St John the Baptist

Why visit: *An early church with good historical features*
Where: *End of Church Lane, HG5 9AR*

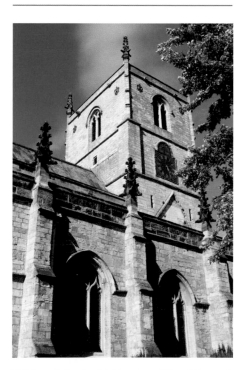

With origins in 1114 when King Henry I gave the church to the Augustinian Priory at Nostell, St John the Baptist was originally a cruciform church with a central tower. It was built in the 13th to 15th centuries. Evidence of the early church can be seen in the string course of brickwork and in the blocked-up windows in the chancel, which is flanked on either side by 13th-century chapels.

St John's is a treasure house at the heart of this historic market town. It has good Early English features in the chancel, a Jacobean parclose screen, a Perpendicular font with a late 17th-century cover, magnificent 17th-century memorials in the Slingsby family chapel and some stained glass by the William Morris studio.

Lead St Mary CCT

Why visit: *Secluded private chapel with a rustic interior*
Where: *5 miles south of Tadcaster, opposite the Crooked Billet pub, LS24 9QW*

This tiny 14th-century chapel stands alone in the middle of a field, close to the site of the 1461 Wars of the Roses' Battle of Towton. Now redundant and cared for by the Churches Conservation Trust, it is known locally as the Ramblers' Church, thanks to the rambler enthusiasts who helped to save it from neglect in the 1930s. The repairs made at that time are recorded on the back of the church door.

Just 5.5m (18ft) long, the simple rectangular building has exposed stone walls inside and out. Massive 13th-century grave slabs, carved with heraldic symbols and inscriptions, are set into the stone floor. They commemorate the Tyas family, who probably built the church.

Otherwise, the furnishings are very spare. Benches thought to be medieval are arranged in rows and act as pews. Later additions dating from the 18th century include oblong boards decorated with painted sentences from the Holy Communion, a clerk's pew, a reading desk and a rustic pulpit.

NORTH AND EAST YORKSHIRE

Nestling in picturesque villages in moorland and wold to the north and east of York, these ancient churches are exceptional finds. Many – in Kirkburn, Sledmere, Cowlam and Bishop Wilton – are part of what is known as the Sykes Church Trail, named after Sir Tatton Sykes, baronet of Sledmere Hall. He financed the restoration of 17 rural churches in Yorkshire between 1866 and 1913.

Pickering
St Peter and St Paul

Why visit: *World-famous 15th-century wall paintings*
Where: *Market Place, (A170), YO18 7AW*

From the outside, St Peter and St Paul's looks no different to other medieval English churches. Hidden in a cluster of cottages at the heart of a picturesque market town, its tower and spire have been beacons of faith and cultural stability for half a millennium.

Not until you enter do you realise what a special church this is, and that is because of the wonderful paintings that adorn the plastered walls of the nave. Almost all medieval English churches had such paintings, albeit with fewer figures. In the absence of printed Bibles, these illustrations – of saints' lives, moral tales and Christian teachings in general – were used to instruct the congregation. In fact, they were referred to as the *Biblia Pauperum*, or the Poor Man's Bible.

One narrative sequence shows the martyrdom of St John the Baptist, another the martyrdom of St Edmund. St George, slaying the Dragon, is one of the largest figures on the walls, and the Passion of Christ is vividly depicted. The whole effect is almost overwhelming to the senses. Scenes are jammed together, comic-book fashion, and colours are remarkably clear. Above all, the stories are very explicitly told, with exaggerated character types and facial expressions, contemporary costumes and larger-than-life actions that the congregation would readily understand.

The paintings were probably commissioned in the mid-to-late 1400s, but were whitewashed over at the time of the Reformation. When they were accidentally discovered in 1852, they

were covered over again a fortnight later, at the insistence of the vicar. 'As a work of art,' he wrote to his archbishop, they are 'fairly ridiculous, would excite feelings of curiosity. And distract the congregation… The paintings are out of place in a Protestant church, especially in these dangerous times.'

Fortunately, a generation later, the more open-minded Reverend Lightfoot decided to restore the paintings and the whole project was finished by 1895, immeasurably enhancing this remarkable place of worship.

Appleton-le-Moors
Christ Church

Why visit: *Beautifully decorated Gothic-style church in a village setting*
Where: *Main Street, YO62 6TN*

The village of Appleton-le-Moors is in the North York Moors National Park, and Christ Church certainly lives up to its description as 'the little gem of moorland churches'. Built in 1863–6 in local limestone in the Early French

Gothic style, this rather low, broad church has a satisfying exterior with an apsidal (semi-circular) chancel, a tall bell tower and a pyramid spire that is a prominent feature in the landscape.

The splendid hammerbeam roof soars above an elaborate High Victorian Gothic interior. Magnificent pink classical sgraffito decorations adorn the walls in the Lady Chapel and apse, the reredos and the pulpit. The beautiful west-facing rose window has a 10-part 'botanical' design and depicts in stained glass panels Christian virtues such as faith, hope and charity. Both sgraffiti and stained glass were carried out by Clayton and Bell of London. An unusual feature is a west porch opening into the church by two doors, between which stands the Caen stone font. On either side of the doors are miniature pews for children.

Flamborough St Oswald

Why visit: *Carved rood screen and loft*
Where: *Church Street, YO15 1PE*

Essentially a 12th-century church, St Oswald's was extensively rebuilt and restored in Victorian times. The chancel arch and font remain from the original Norman church, and the Early English nave arcading dates from the 13th to 14th century. It is the magnificent rood screen and loft – one of only two in Yorkshire, and dating from the 15th to 16th century – that make this church outstanding. The screen is carved with delicate tracery, and the substantial rood loft over it has 15 canopied niches for statues. The statues are gone now, but the wood retains some applied colouring and has a lovely burnished glow.

To the left of the altar is the curious tomb of Sir Marmaduke Constable who died in 1530. He was commended for bravery by Henry VIII. On the tomb is a fragment of a carved skeleton with a lump on its chest – according to legend, this represents a toad Sir Marmaduke accidentally swallowed, which ate at his

This page: *The martyrdom of St Edmund, one of the remarkable 15th-century wall paintings at Pickering.*

heart until he died. Another historic curiosity relates to the local custom of having a young girl lead the funeral procession of a maiden while wearing white paper gloves. A framed pair in the vestry were worn in 1761 at the funeral of a Miss Major.

And to top it all, because St Oswald is the patron saint of fishermen, the weathervane on the tower is of a fish.

Kirkburn St Mary

Why visit: *A fine Norman village church*
Where: *Main Street, YO25 9DU*

Thought to have been built around 1130, St Mary's still has many Norman elements: a spectacular south doorway with carvings of strange beasts and human figures and a delightful font with rustic carvings including Christ in Glory and a cat with a mouse. The nave is original Norman with flat buttresses, windows and a corbel table. A deep, rather coarse, typically Norman carved zigzag motif appears here and there.

The church and its tower have Early English and Perpendicular influences, with the tower housing an outstanding and unusual tower staircase, a very ancient feature. The 19th century saw the addition of a richly carved and painted wooden screen, probably by the Victorian architect G.E. Street (who designed the Royal Courts of Justice), and a reredos in

marble, with relief scenes by James Redfern, known for his works in Gothic churches, including Salisbury Cathedral.

Kirkdale St Gregory's Minster

Why visit: *Outstanding Anglo-Saxon church in peaceful countryside*
Where: *Off Kirkdale Lane, by the river, YO62 7TZ*

Standing alone in a valley, surrounded by its quiet churchyard with a backdrop of woodland, St Gregory's looks ancient – and it is. Basically a late Saxon church, it was built in 1065 and probably included a chancel (not all Anglo-Saxon parish churches did). Saxon stone crosses are built into the remaining original walls.

The church is most famous for its fine and very rare Anglo-Saxon sundial, set in the wall above the south doorway and under cover of the 18th-century porch. Because it was covered by a coating of plaster for several centuries before 1771 and then protected by the porch, it is very well preserved. The Old English inscriptions on the sundial tell us a great deal about when, why and who built it, and recent excavations date the site back to at least 750.

Major restoration and rebuilding took place in the 19th century, but the essential Anglo-Saxon character of the church has been preserved.

Lastingham St Mary

Why visit: *Unique Norman crypt and a picturesque setting among the north Yorkshire moors*
Where: *Off Anserdale Lane, YO62 6TN*

One of the cradles of English Christianity, St Mary's was built on the site of a wooden Saxon monastery

founded in 654 by St Cedd of Lindisfarne (who is buried here) and associated with his brother, St Chad; these Celtic monks were founders respectively of Christianity in Essex and Mercia. After centuries of disruption, St Stephen of Whitby and his Benedictine monks built the basis of the present structure around 1080, and in 1288 it was established as a parish church.

The double-aisled Norman crypt is unique. It has massive, solid pillars, some quite richly carved, and parts of their stonework probably date from an earlier structure. There is also a 12th-century Norman font in the church.

The fine rounded apse at the east end and the square west tower – the basic outline you see today – was set out from the 11th to the 13th century, though the wonderful vaulted stone roof was created during an extensive restoration in 1879.

This page: The carved Norman font at St Mary, Kirkburn (left); the south doorway, at Kirkdale, that houses the famous sundial in the porch (centre).

ALSO IN THE AREA

Bishop Wilton St Edith
Why visit: *Part-Norman church in a handsome Wolds village*

Bridlington St Mary
Why visit: *Large, ancient church, part of a former Augustinian priory*

Cowlam St Mary
Why visit: *Exceptional Norman tub-shaped font*

Old Malton St Mary
Why visit: *Medieval misericords*

North Grimston St Nicholas
Why visit: *A 12th-century church, noted for its Norman carved font*

Sledmere St Mary
Why visit: *Lavish red sandstone interior and lovely woodwork*

Weaverthorpe St Andrew
Why visit: *Norman church in a peaceful hilltop setting*

EAST YORKSHIRE

While Kingston-upon-Hull is home to two remarkable churches, and Beverley Minster is lovely almost beyond compare, it is the Holderness region, towards the sea, that brims with architectural treasures in out-of-the-way places. In the medieval period, the area prospered due to its fertile soil and trade links with Northern Europe, and this is evident in the scale and quality of its parish churches.

architectural styles: Early English, Decorated and Perpendicular. The choir and double-aisled transepts are Early English, the nave of 10 bays is Decorated, and the west front Perpendicular.

Remarkable remnants include a 13th-century double staircase to a lost chapter house in the north choir aisle, a 14th-century altar screen and the huge Perpendicular east window. This is the only surviving medieval window in the minster, built in 1416 to replace a group of Early English lancets.

The interior holds many more delights. Near the superb 14th-century Decorated shrine to the Percy family is an Anglo-Saxon Frid Stool (or peace stool), which offered sanctuary to criminals.

There are also more than 70 carvings of medieval musical instruments, for which the minster is famous. They depict both the familiar and unfamiliar: bagpipes, flutes, tambourines, shawms (early oboes), trumpets, lutes and many more besides.

The 68 misericords delight visitors with their whimsical humour, incorporating bizarre beasts, animal musicians, domestic discord and dancing fools; one delightful seat shows a fox preaching to geese and the geese then hanging the fox.

However individually striking, all these details merely serve to glorify a magnificent edifice, renowned for the grace and harmony of its Gothic style.

Beverley
Beverley Minster, St John

Why visit: *One of the most beautiful churches – and perhaps the most lovely Gothic building – in all of England*
Where: *Minster Yard North, HU17 0DP*

One of the finest Gothic churches in Europe, Beverley Minster is equal to the greatest of British cathedrals. After Westminster Abbey (the twin towers of which it may have inspired), it is regarded as the most impressive 'non-cathedral' church in England.

It is named after John, Bishop of York, who founded a monastery on the site and was buried in the chapel of his Saxon church in 721. He was canonised in 1037 and a Norman church was built around his tomb – his bones still lie beneath a plaque in the nave of the present church.

After a fire, a new church was built between 1220 and 1425, embracing – and blending – the elements of three

Hedon St Augustine

Why visit: *One of the grandest parish churches of the East Riding*
Where: *Junction of Church Lane and Church Gate, HU12 8EH*

The only one of Hedon's three medieval churches to survive, the oldest part of St Augustine dates from 1190. Its rugged 15th-century Perpendicular central tower gives it the name King of Holderness, in contrast to Patrington's fine spire (see

This page: *The magnificent Gothic facade of St John of Beverley, with its slender twin west towers (top); St John's vaulted ceiling and the great west window (below).*

right), known as the Queen. The chancel and transepts are Early English and the nave early Decorated, as is the notable octagonal font.

The church was restored in 1866–77 by G.E. Street, an important architect closely associated with the Victorian renovation of medieval parish churches. The impressive stained glass window depicting Christ in Majesty and St Augustine of Hippo dates from this period, and recent repairs to the church's structural masonry and carvings have brought back an air of respectability to this proud old patriarch.

Hull Holy Trinity

Why visit: *According to the* Guinness Book of Records, *this is England's largest parish church (by area)*
Where: *South Church Side, HU1 1RR*

This awe-inspiring building is over 700 years old, and its 14th-century brickwork is among the most magnificent in England. The beautifully carved 14th-century marble font is where William Wilberforce, MP for Hull and a leader of the movement to abolish the slave trade, was baptised, and the 18th-century rococo altar and reredos are exceptional.

What Holy Trinity lacks in medieval stained glass, it more than compensates for in Victorian and 20th-century glass of the highest quality. The fine oak medieval-style carvings on the nave pew ends date from the 1840s and are the work of a local craftsman. They depict mythical creatures including a Green Man and a Lincoln Imp. The pew ends in the chancel are medieval.

Hull St Charles Borromeo

Why visit: *A very colourful and dramatic 19th-century interior*
Where: *12 Jarratt Street, HU1 3HB*

This Catholic church began life as a chapel, paid for by a priest (possibly an aristocrat) fleeing the French Revolution. Its wonderfully colourful and decorative interior, inspired by the Austrian Rococo and the Italian Baroque, developed over most of the 19th century with an increasingly flamboyant vigour. It could not be guessed at from the rather sober and restrained façade that greets visitors on Jarratt Street.

Almost every surface is exuberantly embellished, dramatically lit by shafts of light from the upper windows and dome. The altar depicts scenes from the life of St Charles Borromeo, the 16th-century Archbishop of Milan; and a stunning painted and sculpted set piece above it – created by Heinrich Immenkamp, an Austrian craftsman living in Hull – shows the then parish priest on his way to heaven at the Last Judgement.

Patrington St Patrick

Why visit: *One of England's finest Decorated churches*
Where: *Church Lane, HU12 0RE*

The doyen of architectural historians, Nikolaus Pevsner, was much taken with St Patrick's. 'For sheer architectural beauty,' he wrote, 'few parish churches in England can vie with Patrington.' Completed in 1410, it is distinguished by the quality of its stonework and a 55m (180ft) spire known locally as the Queen of Holderness (twinned with the King, its neighbour at Hedon, see opposite).

Ornamenting the walls and columns there are more than 200 carved faces of humans and animals, ranging from grotesque creatures to village parishioners. So skilled were they, the masons of this church went on to work at York Minster and Westminster Abbey.

There is also a delicately carved medieval screen, an Easter sepulchre and a reredos of 1936 in memory of George V, who was lord of the Manor.

Swine
Priory Church of St Mary

Why visit: *The finest collection of medieval monuments in East Yorkshire*
Where: *Main Street, HU1 1UU*

St Mary's is a fragment of a priory of Cistercian nuns built in the late 12th century. The church consists of the original aisled chancel, with large Perpendicular windows, and a later west tower, rebuilt in 1787.

There are eight choir stalls with misericords (one depicting a man looking through his legs) two screens partly dating from 1531, a 17th-century pulpit with decorative panels and a late 18th-century font.

But most remarkable of all are the medieval alabaster effigies located in the aisles and chapels. Finely carved with life-like faces, detailed armour and the dignified costumes of the late 14th century, these knights of the Hilton family and their ladies lie on tomb chests decorated with shields and angels. They have a very powerful, majestic presence and are surprisingly well preserved.

This page: St Augustine's nave (left); the Queen of Holderness spire at Patrington (centre); carved effigies at Swine (above).

LIVERPOOL AND LANCASHIRE

Any tour of Lancashire parish churches must begin with Liverpool, where the city's links with shipping are evident, not only in the riches that endowed these proud places of worship but also in the seafaring associations of Our Lady and St Nicholas. Smaller neighbouring towns are not to be outdone, however – some fine early churches can be found at Ormskirk, Sefton, Warrington and Winwick.

Liverpool
Our Lady and St Nicholas (Liverpool Parish Church)

Why visit: *Links to Liverpool and the River Mersey*
Where: *Old Church Yard, Chapel Street, L2 8TZ; open 9–5pm weekdays, mornings only at the weekend*

Lying close to the River Mersey near the Royal Liver Building, the so-called Sailors' Church was originally two medieval chapels, one dedicated to Our Lady of the Quay and one to St Nicholas, the patron saint of sailors. Its distinctive lantern spire – added in 1746 as a landmark for shipping – can easily be spotted from the river. The spire collapsed in 1810, killing 25 people, and was rebuilt in 1815.

The history of Liverpool Parish Church is inseparably linked with the Mersey. Before the tall buildings of the 20th century, the parish church was the first and last thing that sailors saw as their ships approached or departed the city. In fact, until the building of George's Dock (opened 1771), the seaward wall of the churchyard was the waterfront and the river reached the churchyard wall at high tide. A wooden crucifix on the 'east' wall of the church has become known as the Dockers' Cross. As they came into work on the railway line that ran close to the churchyard, the men would see the crucifix and cross themselves.

Nearby is the Blitz Memorial to civilians who lost their lives during the Blitz, which targeted the docks and their vital part in Britain's war effort. The church suffered too – hit by incendiary bombs in 1940, it burned to the ground leaving only the tower standing. Work started on the new church in 1949, and it was consecrated in 1952.

Liverpool Toxteth Park
St Agnes

Why visit: *Exceptional, stunning Victorian design*
Where: *Ullet Road at Buckingham Avenue, L17 3BA*

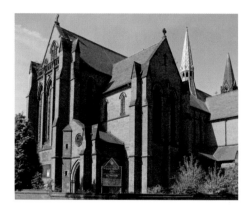

Often referred to as a 'mini cathedral', St Agnes has been described as '...by far the most beautiful Victorian church of Liverpool...'. It is constructed of pressed red brick in a simple form of Gothic known as Early English or Lancet. The interior is of mellow Bath stone, and the effect is breathtaking. The nave has soaring arcades with round piers and balconies above them.

Behind the altar, an ambulatory runs round the apse and is divided from the sanctuary by an arcade with statues of angel musicians in the spandrels. Above this is a frieze of exceptionally fine workmanship depicting the Adoration of the Lamb, after Van Eyck, surmounted by statues of angels under canopies.

The church contains many interesting medieval-style carvings of grotesques that peep out from unexpected corners.

This page: The red brick Victorian Gothic exterior of St Agnes (above); St John's high altar, tabernacle and reredos, with panels painted by C.E. Kempe (right).

Liverpool Tuebrook
St John

Why visit: *Fine example of English Decorated Gothic style*
Where: *West Derby Road, L13 7EA*

The Parish Church of St John the Baptist is one of the most impressive of Liverpool's suburban churches. It was built between 1868 and 1870 in an unusual mixture of styles but with a decidedly florid twist. The exterior is in pale sandstone, which is irregularly banded in red sandstone, while the richly coloured interior has been described by architecture historian Nikolaus Pevsner as '...one of the finest examples of Victorian polychromy.'

Most striking are the walls and beautiful arched Gothic roofs, which are all ornately stencilled, and there are colourfully painted panels and screens by C.E. Kempe, a Victorian artist best known for his stained glass designs in jewel tones. Here, some of the windows are by the Pre-Raphaelites William Morris and Edward Burne-Jones.

St John's is one of Liverpool's leading churches in the Anglo-Catholic movement, with its emphasis on the Catholic heritage of decorative embellishment, faith and liturgical practice. That said, the intended use of an early 16th-century altarpiece from Antwerp was rejected by the Bishop of Chester for being too 'Popish.'

Ormskirk
St Peter and St Paul

Why visit: *Unique placement of tower and steeple at one end of the building*
Where: *Just off Church Street, L39 3AJ; open Thu 10.30am–2.30pm*

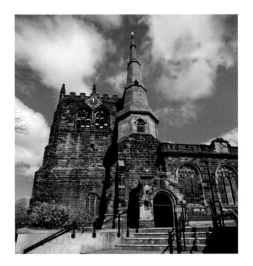

It is unusual enough to see a church with both a tower and a steeple – there are only three in England – but this church is unique in having them placed at the same end. In keeping with this oddity, the church is a mixture of styles, spanning many centuries.

Despite extensive renovations, there are many interesting features, including a Norman window (the oldest part of the building), a 17th-century font and many references to the Derby family, who are patrons of the church. The Derby Chapel contains 15th- and 16th-century effigies, one being of Margaret Beaufort, mother of King Henry VII, who died in 1509.

Sefton St Helen

Why visit: *Carved Tudor woodwork*
Where: *Sefton Mill Lane, L29 6YB*

Described as the 'Cathedral of the Fields' and the 'Jewel of South West Lancashire', St Helen's is probably the oldest building in the whole of Merseyside and is prized for its extensive carved Tudor woodwork. No part of the original 13th-century chapel exists today, though during recent building works substantial Norman floor tiles were discovered.

It was during the reign of Henry VIII that the church was extensively rebuilt, in a traditional Tudor style. The great glory of the interior is the complex of seven screens, richly carved with Gothic and Renaissance motifs. Oak stalls in the chancel and 26 rows of pews in the nave are richly carved with secular motifs, including the then-fashionable poppyhead and Gaelic letters.

Warrington St Elphin

Why visit: *Oldest church in Warrington*
Where: *Church Street, WA1 2TL*

The very tall spire, at 281ft (86m), is the most arresting feature of St Elphin's. Among parish churches, it is the third tallest in England. But nothing survives above ground of the original building (a Saxon wooden church), and only the chancel and crypt – though restored and altered over the centuries – remain from its successor, the first stone building, which was built in 1354.

Shelled and badly damaged by the Parliamentary forces in the Civil War of the 17th century, the tower of that church had to be rebuilt in 1696, and the nave was rebuilt in 1770. The south aisle was added in the early 19th century, and the whole building was restored between 1859 and 1867, when the present distinctive spire was added.

Inside, galleries in the aisles contain pews with doors, and the 19th-century east windows, designed by A.W.N. Pugin.

Winwick St Oswald

Why visit: *The Pugin chancel*
Where: *Golborne Road, WA2 8SZ*

There is a tradition that this impressive church occupies the site of an ancient Druidical altar. Its earliest Christian associations are with St Oswald, King of Northumbria from 634–42, who was killed in battle possibly near the site of the church; a nearby well also commemorates his name. Saxon stone carvings and other remnants survive from around this time, as does the intriguing Winwick Pig on the tower's west wall.

The present building is said to date from 1358; after the Civil War Cromwell stationed his troops in the church following the Battle of Winwick Pass in 1648. It was much restored in the 18th century. From then onwards the medieval chancel decayed and it was not reconstructed until 1849 by the famous architect A.W.N. Pugin. He designed every detail – modelling his work on the old chancel – from floor tiles to ceiling, and from stained glass to vestry cupboards. Restored to Pugin's original design in 1970, it is one of the absolute glories of the church.

This page: *The unusual tower and steeple combination at Ormskirk (left); St Elphin's very tall spire (centre); the famous Winwick Pig, next to St Oswald on the tower's west wall at Winwick (above).*

WINDOWS, DOORS AND DOORWAYS

Doors and windows are obviously key elements in the structure of a church, but they also tell the story of building design and fashion through the centuries. Many of us go into churches without taking a good look at the outside first, but the outside is often as full of interest and beauty as the inside. Once inside, stained glass can have a breathtaking impact.

Windows

The earliest surviving windows are in Saxon churches, such as the little Saxon chapel at Boarhunt, Hampshire. Here, high up on the north wall, is a small opening (blocked on the inside now) with the characteristic narrow, round-headed shape and rope-pattern decoration of a Saxon window. Such windows did not have glass, but may have had wooden shutters.

Early Norman windows are similar, and both Saxon and Norman churches must have been very dark inside, with very little natural light entering.

Glass began to be used in the 12th century, but windows remained small in many cases until the pointed arches of the Early English period developed. Early single, tall, narrow lancet windows first developed into groups of lancets that eventually merged to become the large windows of the Decorated period in the late 13th century. Window design became ever more complex, with styles that were given names such as Reticulated and Curvilinear, with flowing, interweaving stone tracery. In the Perpendicular period, from the mid-1300s to the mid-1500s,

window design reached its apogee, with larger and larger windows and more and more variety in shapes, including flattened and flat tops.

Stained glass

The earliest English stained glass dates from the 12th century, though very little remains in parish churches. Biblical characters portrayed from that time show a fluidity and pleasure in line work that permeates English art through to today.

There is more stained glass surviving from the 13th century, and the colours are often extraordinarily rich, with differing colours used together to create jewel-like effects. Some of the earliest can be seen at Dorchester, Oxfordshire. A different kind of glasswork called grisaille was introduced in the 13th century. This used white or plain glass painted with black lines that in conjunction with the leadwork made complex patterns. The grisaille glasswork was sometimes brightened with the use of areas of coloured glass. Being clear, grisaille glass lets in more light than large areas of coloured glass.

Porches

A church doorway can be enhanced, framed and even outshone by a porch. Examples are the three-storey porch at Cirencester, Gloucestershire, built in 1490, and the twin north and south porches at North Cadbury, Somerset. From the Early Gothic period is the mighty porch at Christchurch Priory, Dorset, virtually a building in its own right. These contrast with humble rural porches such as that at Great Durnford (*right*), Wiltshire, which protects an excellent Norman doorway.

As windows became bigger, so the stained glass artist had to create more and more dazzling effects, but also had to create work that was practicable and affordable. So, lancet windows might have a figure in them (elongated to fit the lancet shape) with a background of semi-abstract designs based on architecture or foliage. A wider range of colours and techniques was developed to give greater effects, often with the aim of letting even more light into the church.

In the 15th century, the larger and squarer windows of the Perpendicular period gave more scope for design, and an increasingly wealthy population lavished money on stained glass for their churches.

In later centuries stained glass became increasingly like painting, and the subject matter became less to do with God and the Bible, and more to do with the world of man. Many 17th- and 18th-century churches dispensed with stained glass altogether, instead opting for clear glass and as much natural light as possible.

Victorian stained glass has a poor reputation, but some of it is superb, and with the Arts and Craft movement spearheaded by William Morris, outstanding stained glass was produced. Excellent glass is still installed in churches, an example

being at Aldeburgh, Suffolk, where in the 1970s John Piper designed work to commemorate composer Benjamin Britten.

Doorways

Church doorways can be theatrical set-pieces for entering the building, and the Normans excelled at them. Outstanding examples are at Iffley, Oxfordshire; St Germans, Cornwall, with seven orders of receding arches; and Adel, Yorkshire, with a striking mass of Norman decoration.

With the pointed arches of the Early English period a different look is enhanced by dog-tooth ornamentation and stiff-leaved foliage, as at Skelton, Yorkshire. The Decorated period brought in broader, elegant arches, while the Perpendicular style might combine a pointed arch with a square hood-mould and rich decoration, as at Hilborough, Norfolk, where there is a complex mix of stonework, flintwork, sculpture and heraldic symbols.

Doors

There are a surprising number of very old doors still in use in churches. Some have outlived their original doorways and been re-used. At Stillingfleet, Yorkshire, the door is 12th-century, with huge C-shaped hinge straps and a representation of a Viking boat in ironwork. In Bedfordshire, at Leighton Buzzard and at Eaton Bray, are 13th-century doors with ornate ironwork patterns, possibly made by the same craftsman. Ancient doors were sometimes restored, and the names of the churchwardens responsible were inscribed on the woodwork.

Opposite page: Christ in Glory, 16th-century stained glass at Fairford, Gloucestershire.
This page: *The Norman doorway at St Germans, Cornwall (top); stained glass by John Piper at Aldeburgh, Suffolk (below).*

IN THE SOUTH OF CUMBRIA

The history of South Cumbria is written in its places of worship. Viking invasions were a threat for hundreds of years, and the 17th-century Civil War made its mark as well. The Lake District has a more poetic heritage, with Wordsworth forever associated with Grasmere, and Pre-Raphaelite artists designing many fine stained glass windows.

Cartmel The Priory Church of St Mary and St Michael

Why visit: *Uniquely aligned belfry tower and wonderful carving*
Where: *Priest Lane, LA11 6PU*

This priory church makes a lasting impression on the visitor, overshadowing the village as it does and giving an idea of the way early priories – especially with all their attached buildings – must have dominated their surroundings.

It was founded as a priory for Augustinian canons in around 1189 and also served as a parish church, which saved it from outright destruction during the Dissolution of the Monasteries in the 1530s. The priory was dissolved, and four of the monks were hanged along with 10 villagers who had supported them, but the church survived as did the precinct gatehouse, though other domestic structures were destroyed.

The church was built during changing times in monastic architecture, and three distinct periods of architecture can be seen: Transitional Norman (1190–1250), Decorated (1320–50) and Perpendicular

(1400–50). The oldest parts of the priory are the chancel, transepts, the south doorway and part of the north wall of the nave, where you can see the plain and massive arches that are characteristic of the period.

The transepts also contain two blocked-up doorways, one of which once connected with the monks' dormitory.

The huge east window, nearly filling the east wall, is from the Perpendicular period, and some sections hold fragments of medieval glass rescued from earlier works. The south porch has the oldest glass, which dates from the 14th century and depicts angels. There is also some stunning Victorian glass, with rich colours and beautifully detailed drawing.

From the mid-15th century, the priory also possesses an excellent set of 26 choir stalls, each with a delightful misericord. They are of exceptional quality and bear many carvings of animals, including a unicorn, mermaid, ape and peacock, as well as a Green Man. In 1618–22, new stall backs were erected, boasting very fine openwork panels and slender columns topped with ornate capitals and covered in twining vines.

On entering the priory, you may be struck by the unusual formation of the tower that rises above the transept. The so-called crossing of Cartmel – a 15th-century extension to the tower – is believed to be unique in England. A new square belfry tower was constructed across the original low lantern tower at a 45-degree angle. Unusually it allowed the weight to be supported not by the walls below but by arches set diagonally in the top of the lower tower.

Other features to note include the Piper Choir, with its early English pointed arch and groined roof, and the Town Choir, which is dedicated to St Michael and was set aside by the canons for the lay people of Cartmel.

Then there are the bullet holes still visible in the southwest door of the nave. These are leftovers from the 1640s, when Roundhead troops stayed in the village, stabling their horses in the church. The priory was put to yet more unholy uses: after the Dissolution it served as a prison and, between 1624 and 1790, as a grammar school.

With such a rich history, it is not difficult to imagine what a significant role the priory played in the lives of ordinary village folk. It dominated not only the skyline but their very way of life.

Ambleside
St Mary the Virgin

Why visit: *The striking Rushbearing Mural, and the Rushbearing Ceremony in June*
Where: *Vicarage Road, LA22 9DH*

Designed by the great Victorian architect Sir George Gilbert Scott in the revival of the Early Gothic style, and built between 1850 and 1854, St Mary's is a large and striking building. Its tall tower and spire is a landmark in the town. The interior is dominated by an arcade of piers and arches, which rise up to the hammer-beam roof and emphasise the height of this spacious interior.

On the west wall is one of the most notable features, the Rushbearing Mural. This was created by Gordon Ransom, a lecturer at the Royal College of Art, while he was evacuated to Ambleside during World War II. The Rushbearing Ceremony takes place on the first Saturday in June and dates back to a time when the old rushes on the church floor were thrown out and replaced with new ones. There are also some fine stained glass windows.

Barrow-in-Furness
St Mary

Why visit: *An impressive structure in the Gothic Revival style*
Where: *Duke Street, LA14 3QU*

St Mary's was the first – and is arguably the finest – Catholic church to be built in Barrow. It was designed by Edward Welby Pugin in 1866 and completed in 1888 with its landmark tower and spire. Edward's father, A.W.N. Pugin, who

designed parts of the Houses of Parliament, was a leading figure in the Gothic Revival, a style that Edward employed here at St Mary's. The arcaded interior is richly decorated with carvings, including the magnificent altar and reredos. Different-coloured marbles – red, Galway green and white – are also used to striking decorative effect.

Bowness-on-Windermere
St Martin

Why visit: *Beautiful interior decorations and skilfully renovated stained glass*
Where: *Junction of Church Street and St Martin's Parade, LA23 3DG; open Tue 10.30am–12 noon, Sat 11.30am–3pm, 10.30am–3pm rest of week*

The remains of a church dating from 1203 are incorporated into the present building – what's left of the original pattern of decoration is to be found above a window in the south aisle.

Most of what you can see today, however, dates from the 1870 restoration, when the chancel was extended to the east (note the differing roof beams), the tower was heightened and all the seating renewed. Most of the fine murals, including two large wall paintings in the chancel, date from this time as well.

Opposite page: Cartmel Priory Church (top) and its stunning stained glass (right).
This page: St Mary Ambleside's Rush-bearing mural (left); stained glass at Bowness-on-Windermere (above); the historic Gosforth Cross (right).

The 1870 restoration also preserved the 15th-century stained glass east window – perhaps containing some glass from 1260 – which managed to survive the vandalism of Cromwell's soldiers. Looking towards this great window from the font is another stunning feature: eight black-letter inscriptions from the 16th century, high up on the beams between the arches – literally an uplifting sight.

Gosforth St Mary

Why visit: *Renowned collection of Saxon and Anglo-Danish monuments*
Where: *Wasdale Road, north-east of village, CA20 1AU*

St Mary's has been an important religious site since the 8th century. It has both Anglo-Saxon and Anglo-Danish work and in the churchyard the Gosforth Cross. This Norse cross – from around 940 – depicts the victory of Christ over the heathen gods, showing the transition from pagan to Christian beliefs. Standing 4.3m (14ft) tall in the churchyard and notable for its slenderness, it is unique among English Viking crosses, not only in size and complete survival but in the quality and detail of its carving.

Inside the church are two 10th-century Viking hogback tombstones. Designed as houses of the dead, they are carved with battle scenes. You can also see early stonework on the walls, including carved faces on the chancel arch and a Viking stone carved with a fishing scene.

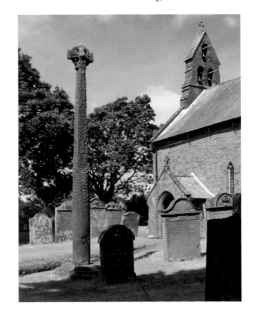

Grasmere St Oswald

Why visit: *Burial place of poet
William Wordsworth*
Where: *Church Stile, LA22 9SN*

This church is well known because of its
associations with the great Romantic
poet William Wordsworth, who lived in
nearby Dove Cottage and is buried in
the churchyard. It is named after
St Oswald, a 7th-century Christian king
of Northumberland, who is said to have
preached on this site.

The tower, porch and south wall are all
that remain of the 14th-century church.
In around 1500, the north wall was
punctuated with a striking arcade to
create an aisle and enlarge the church. It
was not until 1841 that the church floor
was flagged – prior to that it was earthen
and parishioners were simply buried
beneath it. The baptistry window depicts
St Oswald, and two of the south windows
are by the famous Pre-Raphaelite artist
Henry Holiday. Every year, Grasmere
celebrates its Rushbearing Festival, a
custom dating back to the days when the
earthen floor was strewn with rushes,
both for warmth and cleanliness.

*This page: Wordsworth's memorial at
Grasmere (above); St Mary's thick-walled
tower at Great Urswick (centre).*

Great Urswick St Mary the Virgin and St Michael

Why visit: *Reputedly the most ancient
church in Furness peninsula*
Where: *Church Road, LA12 0TA*

St Mary and St Michael's church is said
to have very early origins, as 9th- and
10th-century richly carved crosses were
found on the site and are now on display
in the church. Clues to the building's
development can be found in the changes
in its stonework including evidence of a
Georgian ceiling, which was removed in
the early 1900s to reveal the roof
structure. The tower has very thick walls
and was perhaps used as a place of refuge.

Timber is a key feature of the inside,
including the pews, a rare 18th-century
three-decker pulpit, the roof timbers
(which are dated 1598) and the richly
decorated timber work of 1910. There are
also interesting stained glass windows,
including fragments of medieval armorial
stained glass in the chancel, and a gallery
at the west end dating from 1828.

Hawkshead Methodist Chapel

Why visit: *Small, unusual chapel in an
attractive 17th-century market town*
Where: *The Square, LA22 0PG*

This simple whitewashed building
stands in the corner of The Square
and was converted in 1862 into a
Nonconformist chapel from two cottages,

both possibly dating from the 17th
century. The first floor jetties out over
Flag Street and is likely to be a remnant
from the early cottages. From the outside,
you can see a graceful round-headed
window and a handsome porch.

The chapel is small and seats around
40 people. The building became a
Methodist chapel in the early 20th
century. The Methodist founder, John
Wesley, had been a priest in the Church
of England but started a new movement
that became a separate and rapidly
increasing church. He visited Cumbria
26 times – his last visit to Kendal was in
1788, when he was 85 years old.

Millom Holy Trinity

Why visit: *Beautiful alabaster tomb and
peaceful location*
Where: *Salthouse Road, LA18 5EY*

Surrounded by farmland, Holy Trinity
lies close to the ruined 12th-century
Millom Castle, once home to the
venerable Huddleston family, royalists
whose property Cromwell's troops
damaged during the Civil War.

The church was built in the 12th
century, extended in the 13th century
with a south aisle and enlarged again in
the 14th century. Located within are
monuments to the Huddleston family,
including a fine 15th-century carved
alabaster tomb chest of rare beauty and
workmanship. It consists of the reclining
effigies of a man and a woman, with the
representation of six angels on either side,
each bearing a scroll.

Although the communion rail contains
work from the 1630s and the box pews
remain, many of its interior features are
Victorian. There are several interesting
stained glass windows, one called the
'fish' window due to its shape. In the
churchyard are further monuments to
the Huddlestons, including a sundial.

Muncaster St Michael

Why visit: *Exceptional stained glass*
Where: *Muncaster Castle, CA18 1RJ*

Set within the wooded grounds of
Muncaster Castle, St Michael's dates from
the 15th or 16th century. However, it

may have earlier origins as in the nave there is evidence of a 12th-century stone.

The church contains excellent stained glass windows by Henry Holiday, a Pre-Raphaelite artist who had a home in Ambleside. The west window is one of the few 'Doom' windows in the country, so called because it represents the Day of Judgement, showing Christ in Glory with Archangel Michael, and groups of the 'saved' and the 'damned'.

In the churchyard stands a cross-shaft and a wheel-head believed to date from the 10th century, a reminder of the times when Norse Vikings settled here.

St Bees Priory Church of St Mary and St Bega

Why visit: *Pre-Norman remains*
Where: *Abbey Road, off the B5345, CA27 0DR*

The splendid 12th-century Priory Church of St Mary and St Bega has a magnificent tower, a significant landmark in the village. Elements of the 12th-century building remain, including the south transept, the base of the tower and the west door. This entrance is one of the priory's outstanding features, with its five semi-circular arches decorated with beaked heads of men and serpents. In the wall opposite the door is the Dragon Stone, which has a carving of St Michael killing a dragon. A new chancel was built some time before 1190.

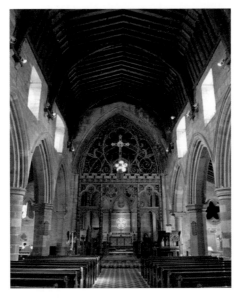

The priory has had a number of restorations. In 1855–68, the outstanding decorative chancel screen was installed, along with bright tiles and patterns designed to take the place of an east window. Before the restoration, the priory had a flat ceiling with box pews in the nave; in the 1960s, a central aisle was created. Within the church there are a number of carved stones, medieval slabs and effigies dating from the 10th century onwards, as well as part of the shroud of St Bees Man, one of England's best-preserved medieval bodies. A 9th-century carved Celtic cross stands in the graveyard, a reminder of the pre-Norman church that once stood on this site.

Troutbeck Jesus Church

Why visit: *Wonderful east window by Edward Burne-Jones, and an idyllic setting*
Where: *On the A592, LA23 1PE*

Little is known about the origin of this church, but traces of it exist from 1506. In 1736, the entire church was dismantled and rebuilt; remnants of this structure include the massive beams, the tiny three-light window in the tower and the coat of arms of George II, painted on wood in 1737, in the gallery. Dating from the time of its 1861 restoration, the light and colourful east window dominates the relatively small building. It was designed mainly by Sir Edward Burne-Jones, an artist involved in the rejuvenation of stained glass in England, in collaboration with fellow Pre-Raphaelite artists

William Morris (whose company manufactured it) and Ford Madox Brown. According to local tradition, Morris and Madox Brown came to Troutbeck on a fishing holiday while Burne-Jones was working on the window, and they stayed to assist him.

Whitehaven St James

Why visit: *Magnificent Georgian interior*
Where: *High Street, opposite Queen Street, CA28 7PZ*

Built in 1752, St James' is noted for its outstanding interior and fittings. It was described by architectural historian Nikolaus Pevsner as having the finest Georgian church interior in the county. The three-sided gallery is supported on columns, and the ceiling is decorated with roundels of decorative plasterwork depicting the Annunciation and the Ascension. The apse has a top-lit dome and a striking central painting of the Transfiguration by Giulio Cesare Procaccini (1548–1626).

In the west end porch are fine Georgian staircases leading to the gallery. All of the ground-floor windows are stained glass and include work by the renowned Victorian firms Shrigley and Hunt and William Wailes, as well as a modern (1976) window by L.C. Evetts.

This page: St Michael's Pre-Raphaelite glass (left); the chancel screen at St Bees (centre); Troutbeck's idyllic scenery (above).

EAST AND CENTRAL CUMBRIA

A millennium ago, Vikings were early settlers in Cumbria, where their strange and mysterious relics cast an otherworldly spell over parish churches at Penrith, Dacre and Kirkby Stephen. Elsewhere, churches bear distinct Norman influences, as well as boasting stained glass, stonework and woodcarvings of great power and beauty.

were stationed at Carlisle at the end of World War II. Another, of the crucified Christ on the west wall, is by the sculptor Josefina de Vasconcellos, who lived in Cumbria.

But the past is ever-present. A stone by the path leading from the church to Thorpe is still known as the Plague Stone. Its hollowed top, which fills with rainwater, may have once held vinegar in which coins were purified when plague sufferers paid their dues.

Greystoke St Andrew

Why visit: *Fine carvings and stained glass*
Where: *Church Road, past the post office, CA11 0TL*

An area of ancient sacred wells, Greystoke attracted pilgrims from pagan times. In St Andrew's, the strange fact that the base of the chantry altar is never dry could be the reason for the earliest wooden-built church on this site.

The church grew to its present great size in the 14th century, when chantries for saying masses for victims of the Black Death were added on either side of the central arcade. When the oak screens that divided the church were removed during the Reformation, they left a large nave.

Various items in the church remain from the medieval church, the oldest being the rood beam that bridges the chancel arch and carries floral symbols representing the wounds of Christ. The church is famous for its ancient choir stalls in the chancel with an array of

carved misericords with Christian symbols such as a pelican and a dragon.

And in the great east window is a fine collection of medieval glass. According to village lore, the glass was removed in haste and buried as Cromwell and his army approached, and then finally restored in 1848. But the restorers had difficulty in re-assembling the pieces in the original order and substituted fragments from other, destroyed, windows. Look at the extreme left, middle height, and you will see a curious sight – a red devil beneath the feet of a bishop. But the devil was originally in another window, whispering to Eve in the Garden of Eden.

The bestiary window on the north side of the chancel is the oldest glass; other ancient glass is behind the organ and in the clear window above the Lady Chapel altar. Because of the value of this clear glass, fragments have been joined by lead.

Modern times have left their mark on St Andrew's too. A sculpture of the Madonna and Child was carved by two German prisoners of war who

Appleby-in-Westmorland
St Lawrence

Why visit: *Attractive setting in historic market town*
Where: *Low Wiend, CA16 6XG*

The town of Appleby has a typical medieval layout, with the castle at the top of the hill and the church at the bottom in a pleasant riverside location. Enter the churchyard through the imposing arch of the Gothic-style cloisters.

The church itself is eclectic in style, the exterior being Perpendicular, the interior Early English and Gothic Revival. The lower part of the tower, the oldest surviving part of the building, dates to the 12th century, although only one of its windows is original. The porch is early 14th century, but the arch with its impressive dog-tooth moulding was constructed 100 years earlier.

This page: *The south façade of St Andrew's (left); St Andrew's east window, with the devil lying at a bishop's feet (above).*

Barton St Michael

Why visit: *Original Norman structure and attractive stained glass*
Where: *Finkle Street, Pooley Bridge, off the B5320, CA10 2LR*

Situated in open countryside with views to the Lakeland fells, St Michael's church lies on a mound in the centre of a circular graveyard, perhaps a pre-Christian site. The church's plan is dominated by a squat 12th-century central tower, whose narrow windows show that it may have been used for defence during the border raids.

Although it has been extended, the plan of the 12th-century church is discernible: the recently exposed stonework allows you to trace the building's development. All four corners of the Norman nave survive, and the north and south aisles were added in the 13th and early 14th centuries. The nave and chancel have striking waggon roofs. The west window, dated 1912, is by Victorian designer Charles Kempe.

Dacre St Andrew

Why visit: *The Dacre Bears and other Viking remnants*
Where: *Unnamed road north of Dacre centre, CA11 0HL*

Built in the local red sandstone, the church of St Andrew is on a monastic site referred to by the Venerable Bede in 731. The existing building is Norman, with additions of the 13th and 14th centuries and then extensive alterations in the 18th and 19th centuries, but there are intriguing remnants of an earlier age.

The stone on the floor belongs to the 10th-century Viking period, and two ancient stone cross-shafts, carved with people and fantastical creatures, date from the 9th to the 11th century. Then there are the famous and intriguing stone-carved Dacre Bears. Set in the four corners of the graveyard, the bears appear to tell a story. The first shows the bear asleep with its head resting on a pillar. The bear then wakes to find to find a cat or a lynx on its back, which it tries to remove in the third carving. In the fourth the bear appears to have eaten the animal.

Keswick Crosthwaite St Kentigern

Why visit: *A fine set of consecration crosses*
Where: *On the roundabout at the end of Church Lane, CA12 5RA*

This enormous church is dedicated to St Kentigern (St Mungo), who came to Keswick in 553. The present church was built in 1181, with many interesting elements dating from the 12th to the 16th century. The elaborately carved font is one of the most remarkable objects, the base dating from 1395 and the bowl 16th-century. Look too for the uniquely English consecration crosses of 1523 (nine inside the church, and three outside near the window openings), marking the spots where holy water was sprinkled.

Kirkby Stephen St Stephen

Why visit: *Picturesque cloisters, impressive nave and ancient relics*
Where: *Off North Road (A685), CA17 4QT*

Entered from the Market Square through handsome cloisters built in 1810, St Stephen's stands on the site of a Saxon church and contains many ancient relics.

At the west end is the Viking Loki Stone, decorated with a carved horned figure of the Norse god Loki. There is also a hogback stone, a Viking grave marker with a curved ridge that is thought to represent the shingled roofs of these 'houses of the dead'. The tower was built in the early 16th century, and the nave, with its tall piers, still displays fragments of a painted weave pattern.

Penrith St Andrew

Why visit: *Handsome Georgian interior, and a Viking grave*
Where: *Kings Street (A6), CA11 7XX*

Rebuilt in 1720 on an ancient site, St Andrew's is said to have been modelled on Wren's St Andrew's Church in Holborn. The original 13th-century tower still stands, while the nave and chancel is built of regular sandstone blocks. The splendid and spacious Georgian internal layout remains intact, with its galleries on three sides supported by two tiers of columns, and a richly decorated box-panelled ceiling. The large, vibrant stained glass east window is surrounded by colourful Victorian murals.

In the graveyard is the Giant's Thumb, a grave consisting of two tall Norse crosses between which lie four hogback stones or gravemarkers. Legend has it that this is either the grave of Owen Caesarius, King of Cumbria 920–37 or his son.

This page: *One of the four famous Dacre Bears in corners of the graveyard at St Andrew's. This one appears to have its eyes closed and to be resting its head on a pillar.*

ALSO IN THE AREA

Bassenthwaite St Bega's
Why visit: *Fine setting; look for the 17th-century hourglass used for sermons*

Long Marton
St Margaret and St James
Why visit: *Saxon stone carvings above entrance and tower doors*

Martindale St Martin
Why visit: *Good example of a Lakeland vernacular church*

Matterdale
Matterdale Church
Why visit: *Spectacular views; beautiful oak truss roof*

Morland St Lawrence
Why visit: *Wonderful mix of styles spanning 1,000 years*

NORTH OF CUMBRIA

That such marvellous churches could still exist along the bloody Anglo-Scottish border is remarkable. Originally established as peaceful monasteries in the 12th century, Lanercost and Abbeytown were destroyed by marauders – and at Bewcastle, the clergymen seem to have joined the cross-border raiders themselves. Later centuries brought more peaceful times, which saw the creation of two of the most exquisite and unusual church interiors in Cumbria. Pre-Raphaelite use of colour at Brampton is breathtaking, and nothing surpasses Wreay's St Mary for sheer idiosyncratic drama.

Lanercost The Priory Church of St Mary Magdalene

Why visit: *Wonderful medieval complex in the shadow of Hadrian's Wall*
Where: *To the west of Nawath Castle, CA8 2HQ; open 1 Apr–30 Sep 10–4pm*

St Mary's Church sits within the former nave of Lanercost Priory, an Augustinian monastery founded in 1169. Part of the medieval settlement is in use as the village hall, part is cared for by English Heritage and can be visited, and part has been converted to private dwellings.

Set in a tranquil rural landscape, surrounded by fields and close to Hadrian's Wall, Lanercost forms a magnificent and fascinating complex of historic buildings. It has been a place of worship for almost 850 years. But these have not always been peaceful

years. Because it is so close to Scotland, the priory suffered during the Anglo-Scottish wars of the 14th century – in 1311 Robert Bruce himself raided it. The thick walls of the tower may well have been used for defence.

Then with the Dissolution of the Monasteries, the priory church began to fall into disrepair. The ruins at the east end of the church – some standing almost to their full height and forming a dramatic silhouette – are a silent witness to this story of destruction and decay.

Despite everything, worship continued in the north aisle, which was walled off and re-roofed in about 1740 and became the parish church while the remainder of the original church was left roofless.

The church houses interesting artefacts, both ancient and modern. An inscribed Roman centurial stone in the priory's fabric shows that stone to build the

original structure came from Hadrian's Wall. This stone is clearly visible, but it was incorporated into the stonework upside down.

In relatively recent times, stained glass windows from the late 19th century were designed by the Pre-Raphaelite artist Edward Burne-Jones and made by the company belonging to William Morris. They add a welcome burst of colour to the otherwise muted church, where time casts a very long shadow.

Abbeytown Holm Cultram Abbey/St Mary

Why visit: *Inspiring restoration of an historic abbey church*
Where: *Abbey Road, (also known as Holme Abbey), CA7 4SY*

Following a fire, set by arsonists in 2006, the repairs to one of Cumbria's largest parish churches continues and the building is once again open to visitors, who can enjoy its remarkable space.

This is not the first time this Cistercian monastery, founded in 1150 by David I of Scotland, has suffered. In more turbulent times it was caught in the Anglo-Scottish wars of the 14th century. But a good bit of luck followed the Dissolution of the Monasteries, when the local people successfully petitioned Thomas Cromwell to allow them to continue to use the church, partially as a refuge and defence against the Scots.

The rest of the abbey, however, fell into disrepair; bumps in the nearby field indicate the precinct remains, and regular archaeological excavations uncover fragments from the abbey's past.

This page: *The surviving inner archway in the original gateway of the monastery of Lanercost Priory, forming an excellent entrance to the site.*

Bewcastle St Cuthbert

Why visit: *Peaceful interior and the 7th-century Bewcastle Cross*
Where: *Unnamed road to the north of Bewcastle village, CA6 6PX*

Though only the east end remains, the earliest recorded church here dates from 1277, building material being taken directly from the remains of the Roman fort previously on the site.

The present church was rebuilt in 1792, and past rectors have included successful reivers, border raiders that operated along the Anglo-Scottish border from the late 13th century through the 16th century. This may account for the local legend that only women were buried in Bewcastle – the local men were all hanged in Carlisle!

The simple building has a west tower and bell-cote; inside there is a tapestry depicting St Cuthbert. The interior conveys an atmosphere of peace, enhanced by the simple windows.

Most people come here to see the cross, which is made of sandstone and stands in its original position. The cross head is missing, but the shaft is exceptionally well preserved.

Unfortunately, the runic inscriptions have been worn and damaged over time and their meaning is unclear. Figures on the cross, however, point to a possible intriguing connection with Syria, from where the stonemasons might have come, nearly 1,500 years ago.

Brampton
St Martin

Why visit: *One of the finest collections of Pre-Raphaelite stained glass in England*
Where: *Front Street, CA8 1SH*

On the outside, St Martin's is stern and dour, with battlements that are a reminder of this area's turbulent past. Inside, it is a Pre-Raphaelite masterpiece. It is famous as the only church designed by Pre-Raphaelite architect Philip Webb.

The church was built in 1877 to replace an earlier church 1½ miles away and is a complete departure from the Gothic style of the time in terms of design, detailing and layout. Webb deployed visual experiences in St Martin's that were typical of Arts and Crafts houses, such as a low, dark entrance that opens into a volume of light and, in St Martin's case, an explosion of colour.

It contains one of the most exquisite and breathtaking sets of stained glass windows designed by Edward Burne-Jones and executed in William Morris's studio. The east window is a blaze of intense colour depicting Christ the Good Shepherd and a pelican, the traditional symbol of sacrifice. This celebrated Pelican Window is acknowledged as a precursor of the Art Nouveau movement.

This page: The cross at Bewcastle (left); one of Sir Edward Burne-Jones's exquisite windows at Brampton (above); the apse end of St Mary's, inspired by the designer's Grand Tour of Europe (right).

Wreay St Mary

Why visit: *A dramatic and highly imaginative design*
Where: *Chapel Hill Road, CA4 0SA*

Sara Losh (1785–1853), a local landowner, designed St Mary's in 1842, partly in memory of her sister and parents. Influenced by the architecture seen on her Grand Tour of Europe in 1815, she created an original design that was very much at odds with the English Gothic style of the time.

Her choice of materials and the Roman basilica plan are used to dramatic effect. The light stone and white-painted interior walls contrast strongly in colour, shade and texture with the dark timbered roof, pews and decorative details, which are all beautifully lit.

The building is alive with symbols expressing the recurrent themes of life and death, darkness and light. Gargoyles of fantastical creatures guard the exterior, and, on entering, you are nearly overwhelmed by figures including a host of angels, an owl and cockerel, chrysalis and butterfly, an arrow, and acorns and pinecones everywhere. The church is also a memorial to one of Sara's friends, a Major Thain, who died from an arrow wound in battle and is said to have sent her a pinecone before he died.

ALSO IN THE AREA

Carlisle St Cuthbert's
Why visit: *Georgian interior, and connections with Bonnie Prince Charlie*

Warwick Bridge
Our Lady and St Wilfred
Why visit: *Gothic Revival architect A.W.N. Pugin's only church in Cumbria*

DARLINGTON AND DURHAM COUNTY

There are few counties of England where parish churches have been shaped by so many diverse influences. From robust Roman and Saxon remains at Escomb and Gainford to medieval splendour at Staindrop, from Quaker restraint at the Friends Meeting House in Darlington to opulent Victorian restorations at Heighington and elsewhere; a tour of these churches is a 2,000-year history lesson.

Escomb St John

Why visit: *One of the finest Saxon churches in England*
Where: *Saxon Green, DL14 7SY; key available from nearby house*

One of only three complete Saxon churches in Britain, this wonderfully preserved church sits in a sunken circular enclosure bordered by battered walls, an influence from Celtic Ireland. Shut your eyes to the surrounding modern housing and you could be back in the 7th century.

The masonry of large blocks and quoins is partly made up of Roman stones from nearby Binchester fort, but the walls are constructed in the Saxon style of long-and-short work. The church is a simple two-cell structure and is largely as it was originally built in 650–800, though the south porch, with its ancient cross fragments, is a much later 14th-century addition.

As you approach the west end of the church, try to spot the footprint of a former two-storey annex, which was discovered during 1968 excavations. Notice too the curved roof line on the exterior nave wall. Access to the church was once by means of stone steps and included an underground chamber.

The interior of the church is dominated by the re-used Roman arch to the chancel, beneath which can be seen the remains of simple red decorative painting that is believed to be from the 12th century. The nave is lofty, with steeply pitched rough timbers. The north nave windows are of small Saxon style, but the south nave wall is a veritable gallery of historical English styles. It features windows in Saxon,

This page: The large stone blocks in the Saxon church's exterior are clearly visible (above); a view of the modest rear of the Darlington Friends Meeting House (right).

Norman and Gothic traditions, each giving its own light but without detracting from the others.

A Roman inscription reading LEG VI (the Sixth Legion) can be seen on a stone built into the north wall, though it was placed in upside down as simply another piece of masonry. The font (probably 7th century) contains lock holes on the edges dating from the 13th century, when it was covered to prevent baptismal water being taken 'for superstitious use'.

A Saxon sundial – believed to be the oldest in the country still in its original position, and not to be confused with the later 17th-century sundial – is built into the south wall. Besides a beast and a fishtailed serpent, there are only three marks on the dial, showing the early monks' three principal times of worship around which their lives revolved.

Darlington
Friends Meeting House

Why visit: *One of the largest Meeting Houses in the north-east*
Where: *The junction of Skinnergate and Coniscliffe Road, DL3 7LX*

Although The Religious Society of Friends (Quakers) built a Meeting House in Darlington in 1678 (when they bought the plot for £35), the present structure was not completed until about 1846. It comprised two large chambers, one for men and one for women, separated by large sliding shutters that were raised into the roof space by a winding mechanism that still survives.

Elegant wooden steps led up to a gated minister's stand, with a sounding board over the stand added later.

Great north and south windows under brick arches have delicate glazing bars and margin lights, and the Skinnergate front boasts a rather grand single-storey stone porch with Doric columns.

Quakers played a large role in establishing Darlington as a major industrial force from the 18th century onwards. Edward Pease, a devout local Quaker known as the Father of the Railways, is buried under a simply inscribed headstone in the high-walled burial ground behind the Meeting House, which contains trees planted by him.

Darlington St Cuthbert

Why visit: *One of the few churches in the north-east with a complete medieval spire*
Where: *The Market Place, Church Row, DL1 5QG*

With its cathedral-like proportions and presence, St Cuthbert's epitomises late 12th- to early 13th-century Early English style, with extensive use of wall arcading to frame both internal and external windows. In the 14th century, the aisle roofs were raised and new windows inserted, and the belfry and impressive octagonal spire were added over the central tower.

The church – also known as the Lady of the North – is richly decorated at the east end but is quite austere, though well proportioned, in the nave. The masonry is dressed local sandstone, and most of the main roofs have medieval oak supports.

Outstanding features include 15th-century chancel stalls with misericords, a 14th-century font with a 17th-century 'Bishop Cosin' canopy, and a fine collection of 19th-century stained glass.

Gainford St Mary

Why visit: *Beautiful location next to the River Tees*
Where: *Low Green (south side of the village green), DL2 3EN*

Though erected in the 13th century, the present structure is believed to occupy a Saxon site, as it is recorded that Edwine,

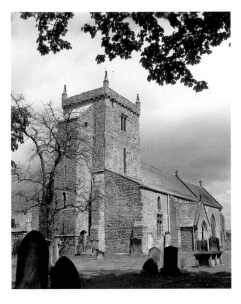

a Northumbrian chief who became a monk, died in 801 and was buried in the monastery of Gainford 'in the church'.

St Mary's consists of a nave, aisles, chancels and a square west tower that is open to the nave and supported by pointed arches, similar to the ones, resting on cylindrical pillars, that separate the nave and aisles. This graceful arch is repeated in the opening to the chancel and in the three lancet stained glass windows at the east end.

During much-needed repairs in 1864, a number of pre-Conquest sculptured stones were found and placed under cover. Several fragments of fine Saxon crosses are also preserved, some of which are beautifully carved. Among the collection of ancient stones there is a Roman altar. Various grave covers, and other stones of a later date, are built into the walls of the north porch. Look also for the 13th-century font with a tall wooden Jacobean-style cover, and three medieval brasses in the chancel.

Heighington St Michael

Why visit: *Rare pre-Reformation pulpit*
Where: *Between East Green and Church View, DL5 6PP*

St Michael's embodies an architectural history typical of the English parish church: Anglo-Saxon foundations; a Norman nave, tower and chancel; aisles of the 13th century; and sensitive reworking at the end of the 19th century. It blends together remarkably well.

Balancing the nave and chancel, the pre-Conquest unbuttressed tower has three stages with an embattled top and gargoyles, and twin louvred openings in the top stage. Carved Tudor poppyheads grace the chancel stalls, the rare pre-Reformation oak pulpit has six linenfold panels and an inscribed prayer, and at the base of the tower are a 14th-century octagonal font, a cross slab (grave cover) with sword and two worn 13th-century female effigies. The church's situation on the green has been much admired and is mentioned in *The Anatomy of the Village*, written in 1946 by Thomas Wilfrid Sharp.

Staindrop St Mary

Why visit: *Resting place of the Neville family and adjacent to Raby Castle, their ancestral home*
Where: *Front Street, between Church Street and Swan Wynd, DL2 3NJ*

Thanks to the powerful Neville family – Ralph Neville was created 1st Earl of Westmorland by Henry IV in 1397 – this once-humble Saxon church was altered and enlarged until it was completed at the end of the 14th century, which is the last time any major work was done on it. By then, it was nearly a square shape because of additions to the aisles.

Memorials to the Lords of Raby have accumulated over the centuries. The ceiling of the choir is decorated with the Neville arms, the 15th-century font carries the arms of Ralph's son Edward, and many effigies lie in state on carved chest tombs. Elaborate stained glass windows by the Victorian master C.E. Kempe, and others, are relatively recent additions, dating from 1893.

This page: St Mary's, Gainford.

ALSO IN THE AREA

Brancepeth St Brandon
Why visit: *Beautiful setting; recently restored after a catastrophic fire*

Norton St Mary the Virgin
Why visit: *Magnificent 1,000-year-old church in a very pretty churchyard*

TYNE AND WEAR VALLEYS

In the Tyne Valley that stretches westwards from Newcastle there are a number of churches with Saxon origins. St Andrew's at Corbridge is one of the most ancient and reflects the Roman settlement there, not far from Hadrian's Wall. Then if you travel south to the Wear Valley in the North Pennines you will find the unpretentious 18th-century High House Methodist Chapel at Ireshopeburn – the beautiful countryside alone is worth the journey.

Corbridge St Andrew

Why visit: *Magnificent Roman arch and Saxon tower*
Where: *Market Place, NE45 5NH*

The history of the parish church of St Andrew combines the solid, civilising influence of a Roman outpost with the unsettling raids of Scottish and Danish marauders. Corbridge was once a Roman garrison town (*Corstopitum*), not far from Hadrian's Wall.

The first church on this site may have been built in 676 by St Wilfrid, at the same time he was building the church at Hexham. Taken together, these two Saxon foundations are among the most important in England.

The walls are filled with Roman stones, and the church still contains an intact Roman archway at the base of its Saxon tower, which dates from the 8th century. The main body of the church is a combination of Gothic and Saxon: one of the gems of St Andrew's is a beautiful Early English archway, while the entrance is of later Norman construction.

In the early 14th century, a vicar's pele – a sort of fortified keep or tower – was built in the churchyard from old Roman stone, probably as a refuge and stronghold defence against attacks from Scottish cattle raiders from across the border. It was used to shelter both villagers and livestock, and also to house the vicar and his family on the upper floor, in times of attack.

Its three storeys are surmounted by a parapet walk – no doubt designed to be a lookout vantage point – and there is a secure barrel-vaulted chamber on the ground floor.

The pele was used as a vicarage until the early 17th century, when it was abandoned and left to ruin, only to be restored and re-roofed in 1910 by the Duke of Northumberland.

Another curiosity is the Kings Oven, built around 1300 and set into the west wall of the churchyard on Watling Street. Here, villagers baked their meat and bread communally, until around 1710. Nowadays, the church is unusual in holding Roman Catholic Sunday Mass (on Saturday evenings) within its magnificent interior.

Bywell St Peter

Why visit: *Some of the finest Saxon architecture in Northumberland*
Where: *No-through-road to Bywell, off B6309, NE43 7AD*

One of two adjoining rival Saxon churches, the other being St Andrew's, St Peter's is beautifully positioned in this private village consisting of a castle, hall and estate cottages. Bywell must certainly be the only village in England with two surviving Saxon churches.

Built around 800 by Benedictines (Black Monks) of Durham – St Andrew's was built by Dominicans (White Monks) – this early church contained Roman stones in its walls, which may indicate that it stood on a Roman site. The north wall of the nave and west parts of the chancel are the oldest existing parts of the church, and some foundations also remain from this early structure.

Discovered in the wall of the tower, and now placed inside the church, is an ancient cross-shaft carved with a Crucifixion scene, which may date from the 7th century.

After being destroyed by fire, the church was rebuilt in the 13th and 14th century and now consists of a nave, south transept, chancel, north vestry and a west tower. The tower is plain and square and, with walls 5m (16ft) thick, it is thought to have been built for defence.

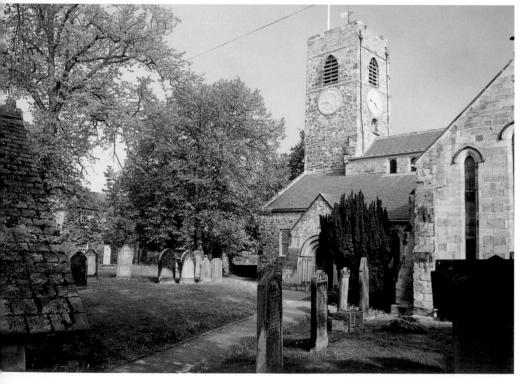

This page: The Saxon tower at Corbridge.

Well-carved medieval grave slabs are inside and out, and although most of the church is 13th-century, there is Victorian remodelling in the vibrantly coloured stained glass, a splendid reredos and a tiled mosaic floor.

Hexham Hexham Abbey (St Andrew)

Why visit: *Original Anglo-Saxon crypt*
Where: *Beaumont Street, NE46 3NB*

There has been a church on this site for over 1,300 years, but the one you see today is based mainly on the Augustinian priory built about 1170–1250 in the Early English style. The choir, north and south transepts and the cloisters, where canons studied and meditated, date from this period. The east end was rebuilt in 1860, and the nave, the walls of which incorporate some of the earlier church, was built in 1908. In 1996, St Wilfrid's Chapel was created at the east end of the north choir aisle, to honour the 7th-century founder.

The greatest treasure of all is the Anglo-Saxon crypt. A steep stone stair descending from the nave takes you down into rooms and passages left intact

from St Wilfrid's original church. Everything he built above ground at Hexham has gone, except for carved fragments set in the walls of the nave – only his crypt is essentially as it was first built.

Other outstanding features include the remains of an 8th-century cross, the 7th-century sandstone Frith Stool in the middle of the choir, the surviving wooden rood screen and 13th-century lancet windows in the south transept, filled with richly coloured Victorian glass.

Ireshopeburn High House Methodist Chapel

Why visit: *The oldest Methodist chapel in continuous use*
Where: *Next to the Weardale Museum, DL13 1HD*

High House Chapel was built in 1760 as 'a preaching house for Divine worship' and is the oldest Methodist Chapel in the world to have been in continuous weekly use since then. Wesley himself preached in the small village in 1752, and a plaque outside the chapel marks the site.

Nestled by the side of the road in rolling countryside, the sandstone building has a Welsh slate roof and 19th-century sash windows. The interior is tall, split by galleries running around the walls, and dominated by the large and imposing pulpit.

The former minister's house is now the Weardale Museum, which depicts life in the Durham Dales in the 19th century, and has a strong Wesleyan connection, with possibly the largest collection of Methodist memorabilia in the region.

Ovingham St Mary the Virgin

Why visit: *Lovely church, with the tallest Saxon tower in the Tyne Valley*
Where: *Before the railway bridge on the way to Prudhoe Castle, NE42 6AJ*

In an attractive village beside the River Tyne lies St Mary the Virgin, graced by a magnificent late Saxon tower. The church was consecrated around 1050, and subsequent years saw the addition

of a Norman doorway and an Early English nave and chancel, with an excellent arcade and lancet windows from that period. There is also a fine 13th-century font inside. Beneath the pulpit is a clue to an even earlier place of worship on this site: a fragment of a stone preaching cross that appears to depict a hunting scene from a Norse saga. It was probably carved in the 9th century.

Thomas Bewick (1753–1828), the renowned engraver and ornithologist, was born in the parish and is buried in the churchyard by the Saxon tower. His wildlife engravings are still considered to be masterpieces.

Forming an equally ancient backdrop to the church, just over the bridge stands the picturesque ruin of the 12th-century Prudhoe Castle. It clings to a steep-sided rocky outcrop and commands a lofty view over the river and the village below.

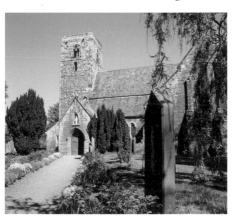

This page: *The 7th-century sandstone Frith Stool at Hexham (left); the tranquil setting of St Mary at Ovingham (above).*

ALSO IN THE AREA

Blanchland St Mary
Why visit: *Parish church built using remnants of the 12th-century Blanchland Abbey*

Hamsterley St James
Why visit: *A haunting 13th-century church, with a Norman doorway*

Minsteracres St Elizabeth
Why visit: *18th-century mansion house, now a Roman Catholic retreat centre*

NEWCASTLE TO THE NORTH SEA

Even in the bustling conurbation of Newcastle, you can still find –
along the River Tyne and north past Whitley Bay – wonderful old
churches and chapels with fascinating stories to tell. Conjure up
Anglo-Saxons at Jarrow, William the Conqueror's nephew at Seaton
Delaval and Civil War Dissenters at North Shields, before indulging
in some Georgian grandeur at Gateshead.

Jarrow St Paul

Why visit: *Home of Bede and an ancient
foundation stone*
Where: *Church Bank, NE32 3DZ*

With a long and distinguished history,
Jarrow was one of the first places to be
invaded by the Vikings, who eventually
colonised the north-east. It was also the
home of the Venerable Bede: scholar,
monk and writer, known as the Father
of English History.

Bede received his education from the
age of seven at St Paul's monastery, which
was founded in 682 by Ceolfrith, an
Anglo-Saxon abbot and saint. Its superb
library, assembled by Benedict Biscop on
his travels to Rome, soon turned it into
the cradle of English art and literature.
Drawing on these resources, Bede's
writings became so celebrated in the 8th
century that they assured the reputation
of the monastery, which sadly now lies in
ruins at the south side of the church that
exists to this day.

The dedication stone of St Paul's
church, set above the chancel arch and
facing you as you enter the west door,
declares the date of 685, making it the
oldest such stone in the country. As you
pass into the chancel, you will see an
Anglo-Saxon window on the south side,
inset with a circular pane holding
fragments of 7th-century stained glass,
the oldest in the world. Sharing this space
are 20th-century windows by the artists
John Piper and Leonard Evetts, which
somehow make the great age of the
chancel, the oldest part of the building,
even more palpable.

In the north aisle you can see the
Saxon Cross, excavated by the Victorians
when digging the foundations for a nave
to replace the Saxon-Norman nave,
which had collapsed. Some fine early
sculptured stones are also to be admired.

Another modern piece, a wonderful
sculpture of the risen Christ, carved from
a single tree, seems to soar above the nave,
with no visible means of support.

Just 7 miles away and founded
13 years earlier, Wearmouth (or
Monkwearmouth) Monastery on the
River Wear in Sunderland is coupled
with Jarrow as a twin-foundation
monastery, with the formal name of
The Abbey Church of St Peter and
St Paul, Wearmouth-Jarrow. Both
monasteries were destroyed by the
Danes in about 860 and it is thought
they were probably abandoned by the
end of the century, ending a golden age
of early Christian scholarship.

Gateshead Gibside Chapel

Why visit: *Strict Georgian classical style*
Where: *Near Rowlands Gill, Burnopfield,
NE16 6BG; owned by the National Trust,
entrance fee*

This impressive Palladian chapel stands
proudly in the grounds of Gibside
House, which was once owned by the
Bowes-Lyon family, relations of the late
Queen Mother. Originally intended as a
mausoleum for George Bowes, the chapel
was built between 1760 and 1812, and he
was eventually buried in the crypt along
with other family members. Protected

by double iron doors at the rear of the chapel, the crypt is usually open to the public only on Heritage Days.

Inspired by the Pantheon in Rome, the chapel combines the form of a Greek cross with a porticoed dome that is raised on a high drum and decorated with festoons. It is constructed of local sandstone, with cherrywood interior furnishings.

The entrance to the chapel is, unusually, on the east side behind the altar. Under the dome visitors will find a rare mahogany three-tiered pulpit, as well as two sets of box pews: one for the Bowes-Lyon family, the other for the chaplain, dignitaries and tenant farmers; servants sat in the stone seats.

North Shields
Christ Church

Why visit: *Presbyterian-style church dating from the Commonwealth period*
Where: *Preston Road, on the junction of Albion Road, NE29 OLW*

Originally attached to the medieval community of Tynemouth Priory, the first parish church of Tynemouth stood within the walls of its castle. During the troubled times of the Civil War, worship there was frequently prevented, and in 1652 Oliver Cromwell's commissioners decided that a new church was needed outside the castle walls.

In the 1650s–60s, Christ Church was built in the plain style of a Presbyterian preaching house, with four arms of equal length and a pulpit in the centre. The church proved popular and soon had to be expanded to accommodate the growing congregation, and by 1793 the four corners had been extended, the walls raised and galleries built above the north and south aisles; in 1869 the chancel was also expanded.

Edward Hodgson, Cordwainer of North Shields and an early founder of this church, had his 1690 burial south of the distinguished tower. The organ is at the west end in the last surviving gallery.

Opposite page: St Paul's at Jarrow.
This page: Seaton Delaval's Norman church (right).

North Shields St Columba
United Reformed Church

Why visit: *Unusual Italian style*
Where: *Northumberland Square, NE30 1PW*

Standing out from the rest of the buildings in the square, St Columba's is the rather grand permanent home to several Presbyterian and Congregational chapels, the first founded in Howard Street in 1662 by early Dissenters.

Built in 1857, the present church – the 'Square Pres' – has a two-storey central block, built of ashlar sandstone under a slate roof in the Palladian style. Above the arcaded first floor is a dentilled cornice and balustrade parapet, and there are sandstone chimneys at both ends. The central door is raised up three steps and recessed under a canopy. The brick wings look very domestic in comparison with the central block, being built slightly later.

Light-filled and quite spacious, the interior has galleries on three sides, standing on iron columns. Their original wooden pews are still in place.

Seaton Delaval
Church of Our Lady

Why visit: *Wonderfully preserved Norman building with many fine monuments*
Where: *Off the Avenue (A190), between Seaton Sluice and Seaton Delaval, NE26 4QS*

Hidden behind Vanbrugh's Seaton Delaval Hall, this tiny, unassuming Norman church can be reached by a short walk down a country path. Built at the end of the 11th century by Guy de Laval, the nephew of William the Conqueror, it was the private chapel of the Delaval family for over 700 years. Above the entrance is an ancient window, carved from one piece of stone for the original 14th-century east window, and now filled with Victorian glass.

Inside, the church is sparse by modern standards, with stone floors, plaster walls and high-backed wooden pews at either side of a central aisle. But closer inspection reveals the magnificent Norman chancel, choir and nave, which are separated from each other by two

beautiful arches, perfectly carved with the zigzag pattern typical of Norman design. On the nave and west walls hang six funeral hatchments (coats of arms), of which there are only 50 in the whole of Northumberland. There is a Norman piscina used for washing the Communion vessels on display, and the two remaining aumbries (wall safes) show off the depth of the walls.

Even more striking, the effigies of a Delaval Crusader knight and his lady lie in the crypt beneath the altar, though he might have been part of a tomb chest that stood where the altar is now. Although they are badly damaged and worn, and retain no traces of the bright colours with which they must once have been adorned, they are powerful reminders of 900 years of history.

ALSO IN THE AREA

Cullercoats St George
Why visit: *19th-century French Gothic-style church with a commanding position above the beach*

Newcastle St Andrew
Why visit: *The oldest church in Newcastle, now hosting both Anglican and Greek Orthodox services*

Newcastle St John the Baptist
Why visit: *Mainly medieval church with fragments of medieval glass*

THE NORTHUMBERLAND COAST

Nowhere in England can parish churches be more romantically located, in coastal country of such strange and ancient beauty. From Berwick-upon-Tweed down to Warkworth at Coquet Island, this land was the northernmost frontier of Christianity in England, and the presence of so many defensive fortifications along the rugged coast gives a clue to the endurance and determination of these early settlers.

Bamburgh St Aidan

Why visit: *Architectural intricacies and an elaborate reredos*
Where: *Radcliffe Road, NE69 7DB*

In 635, St Aidan was called from Iona to Bamburgh by King Oswald to establish Christianity in his newly united kingdom of Northumbria. No trace of this first wooden structure now exists, except supposedly a beam in the baptistry – said to be the beam against which St Aidan was leaning when he died.

The sumptuous chancel of the present church – with its magnificent reredos in Caen stone – was built in about 1230, and is believed to be the second longest in England. It is typical of the aisleless chancels of Northumberland. The church also contains some intriguing medieval 'architectural puzzles' to look out for, in which certain elements of the building are not co-ordinated or explained.

In the north aisle is an effigy of Grace Darling, who in 1838 rowed from the Farne Islands to rescue 13 people from shipwreck. A memorial to her is situated in the churchyard, where it can be seen by passing sailors.

Bamburgh is best approached from Budle Bay, which gives you a spectacular view of the village, with its castle, coastline and the Farne Islands beyond.

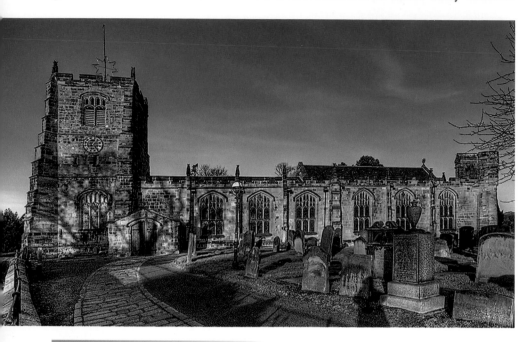

Alnwick St Michael

Why visit: *A regional architectural gem*
Where: *Bailiffgate, just off Canongate, NE66 1ND; open afternoons May–Sep*

Its tower may not be high, but with its buttresses, battlements and small pinnacles St Michael's gives an impression of strength and majesty. From the outside, it presents a unified Perpendicular style that is unusual in Northumberland, as is its size. This grandeur may owe much to the presence of the noble Percy family, whose seat is at nearby Alnwick Castle.

Its date is not certain, though the architecture of the arches and the arms of the Vesci and Percy families indicate that it must have been built around 1300. Other early remains include a small west window and its adjacent masonry in the north aisle, and Norman stonework relocated above the chancel arch.

The church was handsomely rebuilt in the 14th and 15th centuries, and the nave roof is of that period. The arcades to the chapels are unusually ornate late 15th-century work. The capitals are richly carved, with the 'Hotspur' capital on the north carrying a combination of crescent and fetterlocks that was perhaps first used by the fourth Earl of Northumberland (1470–89) in the reign of Henry VI. He also founded a chantry in the church, dedicated to Our Lady, which no longer remains.

Although there are few monuments of any real importance, an early 14th-century Flemish chest, decorated with foliage, dragons and a hunting scene, is impressively large. There are also two 14th-century tombs with effigies. There is a wide range of superb Victorian stained glass; the modern font is late 20th-century.

This church has been frequently repaired – especially in the 19th century – but much of its original character remains. Not far away, Alnwick Castle helps complete the picture of St Michael's early history, and Hulne Priory 2 miles away has associations with both William de Vesci, who founded it in 1240, and the Percy family.

Berwick-upon-Tweed Holy Trinity

Why visit: *Exceptional architectural interest*
Where: *End of Walkergate, TD15 1EB*

The most striking feature of Holy Trinity – England's most northerly parish church – is that, because the main body of the church was built in Cromwellian times, it has neither a tower nor a steeple. And this is not the only fascinating architectural element. Set within the 16th-century Elizabethan walls of Berwick-upon-Tweed and founded on a 12th-century structure, the present 16th-century

This page: *The well-trodden stone path approaching the square tower at Alnwick.*

church was significantly altered in the Victorian restoration of 1855. This saw the first insertion of a chancel and replaced Gothic features with Classical windows and arcading.

The interior still contains many fine elements that are roughly contemporary with the Commonwealth church. These include roundels in the west window of 16th- and 17th-century Flemish or Dutch glass, monuments in the north and south aisles, Jacobean-style woodwork in the west gallery, the pulpit and tester, and 17th-century panels in the 19th-century choir stalls. The 1893 reredos is an early design of Sir Edwin Lutyens.

Holy Island
St Mary the Virgin

Why visit: *Cradle of Christianity in the north-east*
Where: *Church Lane, TD15 2RZ*

The site of a monastery founded by St Aidan in 635, Holy Island, or Lindisfarne, marks the establishment of Christianity in the north east and is still a centre of pilgrimage today.

Dating from between 1180 and 1300, the parish church is the oldest building on the island (older than the ruined Norman priory that stands next to it), though a round-headed arch in the chancel, and a strange high-level doorway above it, are certainly Saxon in style. The long nave could indicate that this is one of the churches of the original monastery, or it could have been built by the Christianised Vikings, who this was an important place for.

Inside, the chancel with its lancet windows is of the 13th century; the priest's door and a lowside window in its south wall remain intact inside a new vestry. Within the church, the round arches of the north arcade are from the late 12th century, and the south arcade, together with the original windows of its aisle (now blocked), is from around 1300. The west end is capped by a typical Northumberland bellcote – perhaps of the same 1754 date as one of the bells – and the little 19th-century north vestry once served as a mortuary for drowned sailors.

A modern sculpture of a party of monks carrying St Cuthbert's coffin is in the south aisle; after Viking raiders first struck in 793, they left Lindisfarne and eventually buried his body at Durham in around 920.

Norham St Cuthbert

Why visit: *Fine monuments and Anglo-Saxon carvings*
Where: *Church Lane, TD15 2LF*

This grand church, closely associated with the Prince-Bishops of Durham, was built in 1165, but its many Anglo-Saxon carvings indicate that there was a 9th-century church here, beneath it or to the east, where a raised section in the graveyard suggests a former building.

The oldest parts of St Cuthbert's are the very fine late Norman chancel arch, the south arcade of the nave, pillars on the north side, and the foundations of the side wall; there are also some later medieval sections. But after a long period of neglect, most of the existing building was reconstructed in the 19th century, in a harmonious neo-Norman style.

The church contains some attractive 19th-century stained glass and late 17th-century 'Bishop Cosin' woodwork brought from Durham Cathedral – note especially the Charles II large carved timber coat of arms in the tower archway.

Old Bewick Holy Trinity

Why visit: *Anglo-Saxon stone cross*
Where: *Just off the B6346, in the south of the village of Eglingham, NE66 3NJ*

Near the Borders in one of the most beautiful parts of Northumberland lies the quiet and isolated hamlet of Old Bewick. Some say the name comes from beau (Norman French for beautiful) and wick (Saxon for village), others that it is Anglo-Saxon for bee farm – either way, the atmosphere of the church is certainly enhanced by its location.

A Celtic cross at the entrance to the lane that leads to Holy Trinity is the only clue to its destination. At the right of the churchyard entrance gate, the first thing you see is a charming pouslinia (gardener's hut), which provides a bed, pen and ink, and a prayer book for the passing pilgrim; then you are arrested by the sight of the small basilica.

The church is 12th- to14th-century, with restorations in 1695 and 1866–7. It has an externally concealed eastern apse containing three windows, and medieval grave slabs built into the fabric of the south porch. On the north side of the chancel, a stone effigy of a lady seems to embody the spirit that resides in this isolated place.

Warkworth St Lawrence

Why visit: *Mainly Norman church*
Where: *11 Dial Place, NE65 0UR*

Although there was an important Saxon church here, the present building dates mainly from the 1130s. This includes the whole north side of the nave and much of the vaulted chancel, which originally had a mysterious high-level chamber, perhaps a treasury or a relic house. The church survived the Sack of Warkworth by the Scots in 1173, when hundreds of villagers were slaughtered inside it.

The west tower dates from around 1200, but the belfry and spire were built around 1350. The rather grand 15th-century south aisle, and its two-storeyed south porch, are a rarity in Northumberland but can be explained by the patronage of the powerful Percy family and the proximity of their castle.

This page: St Mary's on Holy Island.

ALSO IN THE AREA

Edlingham St John the Baptist
Why visit: *12th-century church, next to Edlingham Castle*

SCOTLAND

The churches across Scotland's diverse landscape are often an eclectic mix of the ancient and the lovingly restored – shaped by a strong Celtic heritage and later battles caused by civil and religious upheaval in the Middle Ages.

This page: Intricate carving on the Apprentice Pillar at Rosslyn Chapel (top); Canongate Kirk, Edinburgh, parish church for the Palace of Holyroodhouse (right).
Opposite page: The octagonal Gothic church of Glenorchy, in the picturesque setting at Dalmally.

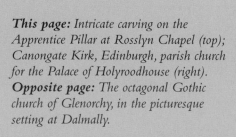

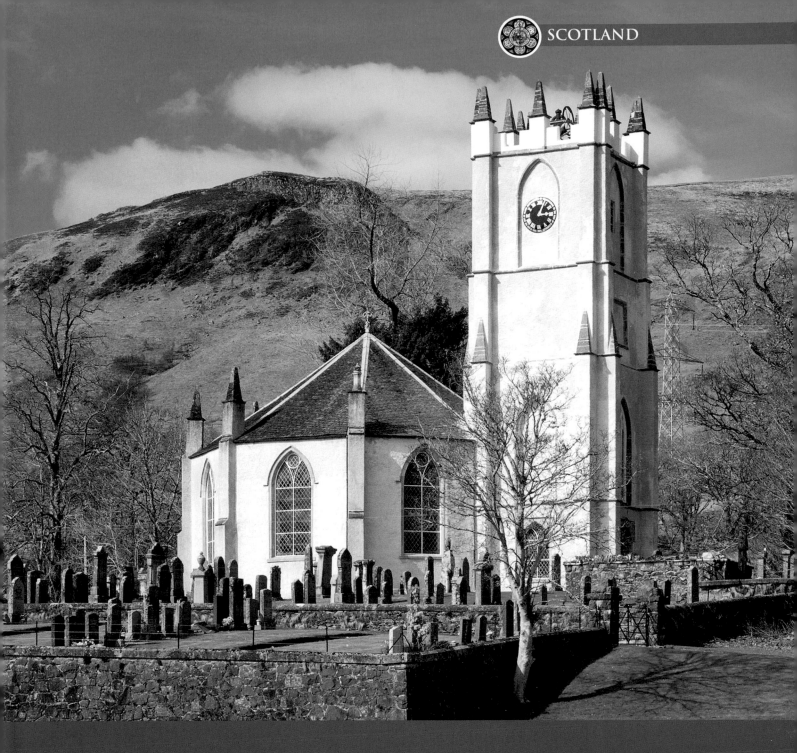

With Scotland's dramatic landscape and craggy coastline, it may be surprising to find churches in even the most remote isles. Even more remarkable, perhaps, is the variety.

Ancient carved hogback monuments – with Scandinavian origins – have been found near the west coast and at Glasgow's Govan Old Parish Church. Irish Celtic influences can be seen in the medieval tower on the east coast at Brechin Cathedral.

The word kirk means church, and can be used to describe an individual building, or to describe the Church, or Kirk, of Scotland. It is also found as an element in place names, where it also means church.

In addition to churches and chapels, you will find cathedrals within this section, namely the Cathedral of the Isles at Millport and Brechin Cathedral in Angus, although not elsewhere in this guide. This is a relic of a previous age, where a church may have

been named a cathedral by the previous order and been an ecclesiastical centre. The Church of Scotland, the official religion from 1690, allows these historic names to remain.

Scotland has a history of 'planned towns' to support a local industry or landowner, who would provide a place of worship for the workers. The Gordon Chapel at Fochabers is one such church. Periods of prosperity in the last 200 years have seen old churches restored to their former glory, such as the Norman Symington Kirk. Wealthy patrons have left legacies, ranging from the grand to the unexpectedly exotic, of which Galston's exotic Byzantine church is a fine example.

To be able to feature some worthy churches that do not fall easily within a tour, but would be worth a visit if in the area, there is a selection of churches in the Farther Afield section at the end of this chapter.

AYRSHIRE'S COAST AND COUNTRYSIDE

With a sheltered coastline along the Firth of Clyde and low-lying hills, this western area of Scotland is a gentle landscape with some unexpected and historic churches. Symington Church with its 12th-century stonework is believed to be one of the oldest in Scotland. Contrast this with the modern St Peter in Chains on the coast at Ardrossan, and you will have a sense of what Ayrshire has to offer.

Millport, Isle of Cumbrae
Cathedral of the Isles

Why visit: *Intriguing combination of small island and handsome cathedral*
Where: *College Street, Isle of Cumbrae, take the ferry from Larg, KA28 0HE*

Consecrated in 1876 as the Cathedral of the Isles, this church is the smallest 'cathedral' in Britain. At first sight it looks very substantial, but the church is in fact attached at its east end to a theological college and cloister. It was commissioned by George Boyle, who was a supporter of the Tractarian Movement, also known as the Oxford Movement, which opposed the new 'liberalism' in the Anglican church.

Boyle chose William Butterfield as his architect, a man renowned as a master of Gothic Revival style. The complex of buildings was finished in 1851. Stone was quarried on site and this accounts for the lower level of some buildings.

At 37.5m (123ft) the proud four-stage tower and spire dwarfs the nave, which is only 12.2m (40ft). Now surrounded by mature trees, it is almost hidden from some aspects.

The interior has magnificent and quite unusual furnishings. Separating the nave and the chancel is a superb carved stone cross that appears almost suspended within the arch. In the chancel itself and behind the choir there are bold tiles of red, yellow and blue creating geometric patterns and designed by Butterfield. These contrast wonderfully with the dark wood of the choir.

The stained glass by master craftsmen William Wailes and John Hardman contributes wonderful colour to the fabulous interior.

Why visit: *Striking modern interpretation of a traditional Roman Catholic church*
Where: *South Crescent, KA22 8DU*

Designed mainly by architect Dr Jack Coia and opened in 1938, St Peter in Chains has distinctly Scandinavian influences, with the tower said to be reminiscent of Stockholm Town Hall. It has a simple, light interior.

The church is built of red brick and has a red tiled roof, making it a bold shape on the landscape. The striking design around the main doorway resembles a bishop's hat, with bricks fanning up to frame a monogrammed stone keystone.

The windows are set at a high level allowing light to pour down into the large nave, with low aisles. A variety of pale-coloured marbles for the simple altar and rails enhance the sense of space. The font in the porch is made of granite.

Decorative panels in the canopies show the keys of St Peter, the bull of St Mark, the eagle of St John, the lion of St Mark and the angel of St Matthew.

This page: The Cathedral of the Isles adjoined to collegiate buildings (left); unusual door of St Peter in Chains (above).
Opposite page: The whitewashed walls at Fenwick (left); Norman lights behind the altar at Symington Church (right).

Fenwick
Fenwick Parish Church

Why visit: *Remarkable church arrangement and furnishings*
Where: *Kirkton Road, KA3 6DH*

This whitewashed church was built in 1643 in the shape of a Greek cross, having four arms of equal length. This 'central planning' occurs frequently in the Presbyterian style of worship in Scotland, although the traditional east/west orientation of churches means that the building does not sit neatly within its square, walled graveyard.

Here are martyrs' graves and monuments from 1685, including the battle-flag of the Fenwick Covenanters. The Covenanters were a powerful Presbyterian group committed to making its doctrine the only religion of Scotland. Inevitably there were casualties of this civil war.

In 1828 small 'sentry boxes' were built at the entrance to the churchyard for the elders of the church to take collections from the congregation as they passed. Walk around the exterior to see the traditional outside stairs giving access to galleries. There are also crowstepped gables, and 'jougs', an iron collar used to detain offenders, set into the south wall.

Galston St Sophia

Why visit: *Byzantine style*
Where: *Bentinck Street, KA4 8HT; open by arrangement*

This distinctive church was created by architect Sir Robert Rowand Anderson and was constructed in 1885-6. The third Marquess of Bute, a wealthy Catholic convert, commissioned Anderson to enhance Galston with a touch of Byzantine exoticism, so St Sophia echoes aspects of the Hagia Sophia in Istanbul.

While the red brick glows when bathed in a sunset, the interior has calming white walls, and elegant arches with lines that swoop within its cruciform structure.

Kilbirnie
Auld Kirk of Kilbirnie

Why visit: *Town church with a magnificent carved timber interior*
Where: *Dalry Road, KA25 6HY; restricted opening times, check in advance*

The Auld Kirk of Kilbirnie combines pre-Reformation design with elaborate post-Reformation craftsmanship. It was built in 1470 on the site of an ancient 6th-century cell, possibly dedicated to St Brendan of Clonfert.

Inside is an amazing collection of Renaissance-style wooden carved pews, aisles and lofts – with the elaborate canopied and bow-fronted Crawford Loft from 1705 taking pride of place among them. Armorial panels grace its canopy and Corinthian columns. Also known as the Lord's Loft, this is considered one of the finest 18th-century pieces in any Scottish church.

Earlier, in 1597, the Glengarnock Aisle was added; the pulpit, with blue and gold canopy, was put in place around 1620; and the Crawford aisle followed in 1642.

Symington
Symington Church

Why visit: *Beautiful Norman church, the oldest in Ayrshire*
Where: *Symington, KA1 5QP*

Symington Church is a fine example of a Norman church and is one of the oldest in Scotland. The church was founded in 1160 by Symon Loccard, a Norman noble whose name is the basis for that of the village 'Symons town'. Believed to stand on the mound of an earlier church, the building, dating from the 12th century, has become the nave of the present church, and was altered and extended extensively in the 18th century. These alterations were followed in 1919 by a restoration

that revealed the walls and ancient oak roof beams that had been plastered over.

The church has been returned to its Norman glory and further enhanced by stained glass windows, many by Douglas Strachan. Look out for two crosses carved into the chancel floor. One marks the grave of the Reverend Gage Boyd, who oversaw the 1919 restoration. The other is over remains found under the chancel during the restoration, and believed to be those of Symon Loccard.

Troon
Our Lady and St Meddan

Why visit: *Early 20th-century church*
Where: *Cessnock Road, KA10 6NJ*

In creating this commanding church, architect Reginald Fairlie was said to have been inspired by the Church of the Holy Rude in Stirling. Here he has produced a handsome church that is a fine example of Gothic Revival style. On the exterior he overlaid bold elements of detailing on a simple design to lead your eye across and around the building.

Buttresses alternate with windows the length of the nave, and the square tower (at the west end) is crowned with finials. A statue of St Meddan, by Hew Lorimer, stands in a recess in the broad façade, high up on the left above the main entrance. She holds a shamrock with a cross; St Patrick used the shamrock as a symbol of the Trinity.

Inside, the stone walls, pale octagonal columns and dark timber roof add to the atmosphere of serenity. In the centre aisle look up to see the brightly painted apostles above. The pulpit is encased with linenfold carving, and the reredos is a medley of stone, marble and mosaic.

GLASGOW AND AROUND

As might be expected from one of Scotland's oldest cities, its churches span history, offering gems such as the ancient Celtic monuments at Govan Old Parish Church and the red brick modernism of St Patrick's Catholic Church at Kilsyth. Several have benefited from renovations, giving them a new lease of life and preserving them for years to come.

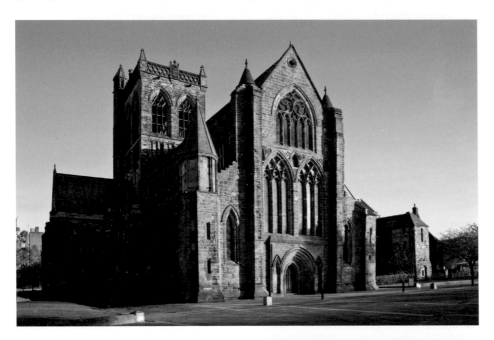

Paisley Paisley Abbey

Why visit: *Medieval architecture; 10th-century Barochan Cross; royal tombs of Marjorie Bruce and Robert III*
Where: *Abbey Close, PA1 1JG*

Originally on the site of a 6th-century Celtic church dedicated to St Mirin, this was one of western Scotland's greatest abbeys when founded in 1163 and it still impresses today. The priory was set up by 13 monks who came from Shropshire. William Wallace was said to have been educated by monks here, but the abbey was destroyed by the English in 1307 during the Scottish War of Independence. In 1533, further misfortune occurred when the tower collapsed, crushing parts of the choir and transept, leaving only the nave for worship.

This sorry state of affairs lasted for a couple of centuries, until sporadic restoration was attempted. Eminent architects and craftsmen returned Paisley Abbey to medieval splendour, with the tower being rebuilt in stages from the late 1800s. Glorious stained glass by Edward

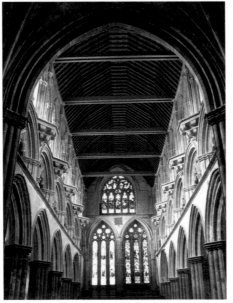

Burne-Jones, among others, has also contributed greatly. The outstanding woodwork, including the choir and organ case by Sir Robert Lorimer, is a delight.

The abbey contains a number of important Scottish monuments: tombs of Marjorie Bruce (Robert the Bruce's daughter) and Robert III, and the stone Barochan Cross from the 10th century.

Why visit: *Attractive rural church*
Where: *At crossroads of Dowan Road and Craigmaddie Road, G62 6HA; open Sun 2–4pm, May–Sep*

The best way to approach this charming 18th-century parish church is to stroll the mile from Milngavie. On a site of worship since the 13th century, this church was erected in 1795, yet contains an ancient panel in the bell-tower that is believed to have come from a nearby Roman wall.

Inside, the church has a wealth of panelling, including the central pulpit with sound board and timber dado. There is also a beautiful gallery along three sides that is supported by wooden columns.

Outside, there are several gravestones of note, including that of Archibald Bulloch, the ancestor of former President Theodore Roosevelt and Roosevelt's niece, the author and activist Eleanor Roosevelt, First Lady from 1933–45.

Glasgow
Govan Old Parish Church

Why visit: *Christian site dating back to Celtic times*
Where: *866 Govan Road, G51 3UU; phone 0141 440 2466 for opening times*

This church was built in 1888 primarily in the Early English style by architect Robert Rowand Anderson, who also brought in elements of Scottish design. This magnificent building has been dubbed 'the people's cathedral', yet it is worth first exploring the much older churchyard for its incredible collection of Celtic monuments, which make this site the oldest place of worship in Glasgow.

Dating from the 9th and 10th centuries, the 31 monuments constitute a unique body of medieval Scottish sculpture. The intricate Celtic carving is relatively well preserved and the site includes flat cross-slabs, free-standing crosses and cross-slabs, a sarcophagus and five low, wide hogback monuments. After the churchyard's ancient stones, the welcoming interior of Govan Old Church is another world. Under the soft lighting and stained glass windows by masters of the day – C.E. Kempe, Burlison & Grylls, Clayton & Bell and Shrigley & Hunt – the red stone and polished wooden pews create a warm and inviting atmosphere.

Glasgow Kelvinside Hillhead

Why visit: *Stained glass by Burne-Jones*
Where: *23 Saltoun Street, G12 9AD; open Sat pm, Sun am*

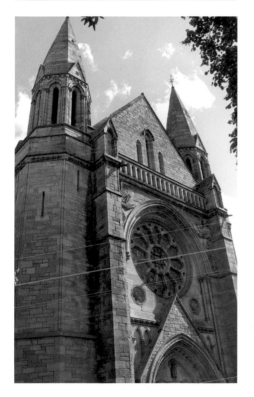

After the grand Gothic exterior of this fine church, opened in 1876, the rich interior does not disappoint. Outstanding are the seven stained glass windows in the apse, illustrating events from the life of Christ. Three, including one to the designs of Edward Burne-Jones, were erected in 1893, while others were added in 1903. All have recently been cleaned and restored. There is further fine stained glass elsewhere in the church, including in the baptistry.

The prolific architect James Sellars designed this tall church with the Sainte-Chapelle of Paris firmly in mind, and was also inspired by the work of another acclaimed Scottish architect,

William Leiper. It was built without pillars as it was deemed these would interfere with the congregation's view and the building's acoustics. The organ was made by H. Willis & Son in 1876 and restored in 1930. In 1921 the chancel was remodelled as a war memorial.

Glasgow St Vincent Street – Milton Free Church

Why visit: *Masterpiece by architect Alexander 'Greek' Thomson*
Where: *265 St Vincent Street, G2 5RL; open by appointment*

Alexander 'Greek' Thomson was a Scottish architect with a penchant for overtly combining classical and oriental architectural styles. He was perhaps an unusual choice for designing a Presbyterian church in central Glasgow, yet in doing so he created one of his enduring masterpieces.

The exterior appears to be influenced by a variety of different styles, including Greek, Classical, Egyptian and Indian. In fact the large base forms the church and the Greek temple is the clerestory and roof, topped by a tall square tower, which is suggestive of Indian design.

The exotic theme continues with colourful Egyptian-style cast-iron columns with stylised capitals supporting the gallery. There is also an impressive pulpit and organ case combination, with unusual sloping door cases. The wooden pews are beautifully carved and shaped to curve towards the central pulpit, a main feature of Presbyterian churches.

Now owned by Glasgow City Council, this extraordinary building has been recognised as Alexander Thomson's last surviving intact church and in recent years has received grants for restoration work to be carried out.

Kilsyth St Patrick

Why visit: *Stunning modern church with dramatic use of light*
Where: *Low Craigends, G65 0PF*

This is one of only four churches by architects Gillespie, Kidd & Coia, with Isi Metzstein and Andy MacMillan being its key designers.

It was built on a sloping site in 1965 in their trademark red brick, inside and out. The building appears almost monolithic with some exterior walls interrupted by full-height vertical glazing of varying widths. From certain angles the bowed roof appears to float above the structure, as it sits above small windows.

The inner space is huge and feels almost minimalist in design – the broad wood-clad ceiling is supported by hidden steel beams, leaving the entire floor space free from obstructions. Angular 'light chimneys' set into the east wall reflect light into the interior from angled surfaces. They contribute greatly to the modern feel of the church, along with arched clerestory windows and a large window in the west wall.

Paisley Thomas Coats Memorial Church

Why visit: *Largest Baptist church in Europe; imposing Gothic style*
Where: *High Street, PA1 2BA*

It is difficult for the eye to take in all the intricate detail when confronted with this amazing Gothic church in rich red sandstone. From the grand steps leading up to the main entrance, to the flying buttresses along the nave, to the magnificent crown steeple, the attention to detail by architect Hippolyte Blanc (Scottish, although born of French immigrant parents) is in evidence at every turn. It was built as a memorial to Thomas Coats, a member of the highly regarded Paisley thread family, and was opened in 1894.

The church is of a cruciform design and, with a capacity to seat 1,000 people, is almost cathedral-like in its proportions. No wonder then that it was seen fit to install a wonderful pipe organ built by William Hill with 3,040 pipes. Further fine detailing can be seen in the various mosaics, stencilled decoration, carved marble and alabaster inside this remarkable Scottish church.

This page: The grand Gothic exterior of Kelvinside Hillhead.
Opposite page: *Paisley Abbey with its restored central square tower (top), and impressive interior (below).*

CHAPELS

There are thousands of Nonconformist places of worship in Britain, many of which are called chapels. They vary from very old buildings that look like cottages to grand 19th-century celebrations of nonconformity. Chapels can also be private places of worship within houses, schools or other institutions, special areas within churches, or buildings that may have started out as a church or abbey but which have declined in status.

Early chapels

The first Nonconformist chapels that can be reliably dated are from the 17th century. There are candidates for earlier dates, including the chapel at Horningsham, Wiltshire, which is dated 1566 on the outside. But that date is probably when the original cottage on which it is based was built, or thought to have been built. It is however, a very early example of its kind, and was probably used by Scottish Presbyterian builders working at nearby Longleat in the 1600s.

Another very old chapel is the Old Baptist Chapel at Tewkesbury, Gloucestershire. It dates from the mid-17th century, but the building itself is timber framed and from the 15th century. Today, it still appears much as it did in 1720.

The Congregational Chapel at Walpole, Suffolk, was originally a cottage, and was converted for use as a chapel in the 17th century. It is no coincidence that these three buildings started life as cottages, for the early days of nonconformity were hazardous, and meetings had to be held in secret for fear of persecution. The roots of nonconformity in Britain can be traced back to the 1500s, a time of religious upheaval and change throughout Europe.

While most of the Nonconformist denominations feared persecution, the Society of Friends, or Quakers, were less prone to controversy as they had no formal creed. Nonetheless, their early chapels are domestic in look and feel. Only the style and size of the windows gives them away. The Friends Meeting House at Dolobran,

Sandham Memorial Chapel

The austere exterior of Sandham Memorial Chapel, Hampshire, shelters some of the most moving pictures about war ever painted. They are by Stanley Spencer, who was commissioned to paint them in 1923. He moved to Sandham and completed the work in 1932, by which time he was emotionally and physically exhausted. There are many scenes, inspired by Spencer's own experience in World War I, culminating in the Resurrection, with soldiers laying their white memorial crosses at the feet of Jesus.

Powys, does not even have that as a clue. Dating from 1700, it is built of brick and looks entirely like a cottage and entirely unlike a chapel.

This page: The Congregational Chapel at Walpole, Suffolk.

Italian Chapel, Orkney

From the front the chapel on the little island of Lambholm could almost be from Italy, but its façade hides the fact that it is in fact two wartime Nissen huts joined end to end. It was begun by Italian prisoners of war during World War II, but not actually finished until the war was over. The inside is highly decorated, with many paintings and decorative details (*right*), some intended to disguise its actual structure. It has been restored several times, twice with the help of Domenico Chiocchetti, who painted much of the original interior.

Later chapels

Generally, 18th-century chapels have a more ecclesiastical appearance, with a typical exterior that consisted of a Classical, oblong shape with two tiers of windows along the sides and an entrance front with a portico and pediment. The absence of towers is very marked, and was a continuing distinction in Nonconformist buildings until the 19th century.

The numerous Nonconformist denominations favoured various kinds of chapels. For example, in the late 18th century a fashion for octagonal chapels among Methodists led to many of that shape being built, such as the one at Heptonstall, Yorkshire. Baptists were especially attached to Classical designs, building stately chapels such as at the Particular Baptist Chapel in Leicester, now an education centre.

Some Nonconformist architecture was positively eccentric, none more so than the Congregational Church at Saltaire, Yorkshire. Built in 1859, it is Italianate in style, circular in shape and has an enormous round tower or turret, making it resemble a giant salt shaker.

The great age of chapel building was undoubtedly the 19th century. The various Nonconformist denominations were quick to realise that the growing, shifting population was looking for different ways to worship. In any case, they needed places of worship in areas where there were none, such as the new cities of the Industrial Revolution. In the countryside, too, Nonconformity took strong roots in those areas where the Church of England was less strong.

Chapels in Wales and Scotland

The picture in Scotland is much more straightforward than in England and Wales, simply because the Church of Scotland is Presbyterian and has been since 1690.

In Wales, the first Nonconformist meeting dates from 1638, when William Wroth began preaching from his church in Llanvaches, Gwent. By 1639 he had built a Congregationalist chapel there.

Most Welsh chapels were rebuilt in the 19th century, a sign of the vigour of the Nonconformist movement and a visible sign of its growth and confidence. The pinnacle of that confidence can be seen in such buildings as the Bethania Baptist Chapel in Maesteg, Glamorgan, of 1906. Here, a wealth of Classical architectural detail creates a memorable building.

Also in Glamorgan, at Morriston, is the Tabernacle, built in 1872. It combines Classical and Gothic features, and is sometimes called the 'Cathedral of Nonconformity', perhaps, in part, because unlike so many of the earlier more modest chapels of all denominations, it has a soaring tower.

This page: The splendid galleried interior of Bethania Baptist Chapel, Maesteg, Glamorgan.

EDINBURGH AND BEYOND

Across the city of Edinburgh there are churches that are surprising in their diversity – from the cool interior of Canongate, with white walls and blue pews, to the staggering majesty within St John the Evangelist. Travel just a few miles out of the city and again you will be impressed – Romanesque architecture at Dalmeny, a Byzantine basilica at Linlithgow and unsurpassed carving at Rosslyn Chapel.

Edinburgh Barclay Church

Why visit: *One of the most dramatic churches in Scotland*
Where: *Bruntsfield Place, 1 mile south-west of Princes Street, EH10 4HW; open by arrangement*

This church is named after Mary Barclay, who left money for its building. The architect was Frederick T. Pilkington and it is considered to be one of his greatest achievements. The exterior stonework is distinctive – large, roughly cut blocks alongside columns with carved capitals in the windows. Finished in 1862, it is a great example of Gothic Revival. The building sits on a small footprint but makes good use of a restricted site, roofs clambering upwards with tiered galleries creating space that is not available at ground level. The soaring spire is a well-known landmark and one of the tallest in the city.

The interior is spectacular – heart-shaped and theatrical with a painted ceiling and two tiers of galleries that originally seated 1,200. The vibrant colours give an overall effect of richness and the eye is drawn upwards to the magnificent beamed roof.

Edinburgh
Canongate Kirk

Why visit: *Beautiful kirk providing a haven of peace in the city centre*
Where: *The Canongate, EH8 8BN*

When stepping up to Canongate Church you may be excused for not quite knowing what the building is. The front is unusual with its flat façade, heavy Doric porch and strange Dutch-style gable, topped by a set of real antlers. Above the porch is a plaque to Thomas Moodie, who left money in his will to build this conundrum. It was opened in 1691, and its layout is unique for its time.

Canongate is the parish church for the Palace of Holyroodhouse, the home of the Queen in Scotland, which explains the Royal pew at the front of the church and the military colours hanging over the

nave. The white interior, with much pale blue painted woodwork, including pews, gives a startling, elegant effect.

Edinburgh Greyfriars Kirk

Why visit: *Church steeped in history, from the signing of the National Covenant to the story of Greyfriars' Bobby*
Where: *Greyfriars Place, EH1 2QQ*

Greyfriars was the first church in Edinburgh built after the Reformation, completed in 1620. However, it has had repeated alterations from the 18th to the 21st century. The church was built in the grounds of a former Franciscan friary that was dissolved in 1559. In the mid-1600s it was used as a barracks by Cromwell's troops. In the 18th century, gunpowder was stored in the tower and perhaps inevitably, this exploded and destroyed the tower and damaged the two west bays. Further disaster struck in

This page: Interior and exterior of the unusual Canongate Kirk.

January 1845 when a fire gutted part of the building. Fire-damaged stones can still be seen. There is fine 19th-century coloured glass by Ballantine, and in 1990 a magnificent organ was built by Peter Collins Ltd, a well-respected firm.

The National Covenant was signed here in 1638; this was a contract with God, signed by the Nobles, Ministers and thousands of ordinary Scots, who pledged themselves to defend Scotland's rights and the Presbyterian religion.

Greyfriars churchyard, with views to Edinburgh Castle, is full of interest. It has exceptional examples of 17th-century monuments, including the Martyrs' Monument and Covenanters' Prison. It was also the setting for the story of Greyfriars' Bobby. When John Gray, a city nightwatchman, died in 1858 his loyal Skye terrier Bobby remained by his master's grave until his death 14 years later. The dog was not allowed to be buried in the churchyard but was laid to rest just outside, as close to his beloved master as possible. A red granite stone now stands in his memory with the words 'Let his loyalty and devotion be a lesson to us all'.

Edinburgh
St Andrew and St George

Why visit: *One of the architectural gems of Edinburgh's New Town*
Where: *13 George Street, in the First New Town, EH2 2PA*

New Town is the term for the central part of Edinburgh, built between 1765 and 1850, and the First New Town was the earliest part of the area. Two churches were originally planned and built, but in 1964 they merged using the original St Andrew's building, forming

the new St Andrew and St George. The church was designed by Captain Andrew Frazer and Robert Kay, and was founded in 1781. In keeping with mid-18th-century interest in the Classical style it has an imposing Corinthian portico. Step inside to see the elliptical design with shaped pews – unique in its time and a delight to this day – then look up to see the plaster ceiling, designed in the style of Robert Adam.

The original Georgian glass no longer exists but there are two interesting modern stained glass windows, one by Alfred Webster (1913) and the other by Douglas Strachan (1934).

Edinburgh
St John the Evangelist

Why visit: *Uplifting architecture and calm atmosphere amid the hurly-burly of Edinburgh's main shopping street*
Where: *West end of Princes Street, EH2 4BJ*

St John's is in the very heart of the city and no visit could be more rewarding than to this church with its excellent interior. It was completed in 1818 and designed by the architect William Burn. Built in the Perpendicular Gothic style, it is one of his finest creations.

There have been various additions to the original structure over the years – the chancel in 1882 and, most recently, a lovely side chapel to the south in 1935. The most dramatic element of the church must be the vaulted plaster ceiling of dark detailing against a light-coloured background, which was inspired by King Henry VII's chapel in Westminster Abbey.

Apart from the ceiling, the church is filled with what many consider to be the most exceptional stained glass in Scotland. The installation began between 1857 and 1861 by the Ballantyne and Allan studio in Edinburgh and was continued until 1930 by several generations of the Ballantyne family. The stained glass in the side chapel is from 1935. The colours of the glass are all the more effective because of careful cleaning and restoration during the decade up to 1995.

Edinburgh
Reid Memorial Church

Why visit: *Superb example of 20th-century church architecture*
Where: *182 West Savile Terrace, EH9 3HY; open by arrangement*

The church was built by William Crambe Reid to fulfil his father's dying wish. It was designed in 1928 by the architect Leslie Grahame Thomson. The soaring tower brings to mind the architect's inspiration – the Ascension. The cathedral-like proportions of the building seem rather incongruous in this Edinburgh suburb. It is in neo-Perpendicular style.

There is a recessed window in the west end illuminating a dramatic entrance. The layout follows the cruciform design, which is clearly seen. There is much beautiful stone carving and stained glass by Arts and Crafts designers. The painting

This page: Greyfriars Kirk (left); interior of St Andrew and St George (top centre); vaulting in St John the Evangelist (below).

on the reredos is by William R. Lawson and the stained glass by James Ballantyne.

At the east end of the church, the architecture is less monumental and there is a lovely, intimate cloister court and a peaceful garden. Look for the carved panel of 'Christ at the well of Samaria' by Alexander Carrick.

Edinburgh
Colinton Parish Church

Why visit: *Interesting church in an idyllic position on the outskirts of Edinburgh*
Where: *Dell Road, EH13 0JR*

A church has stood here for around 1,000 years, although what is seen today is largely the result of an outstanding rebuild in 1907–8 by architect Sydney Mitchell. Mitchell incorporated the tower that was erected by David Bryce in 1837. The interior is in the neo-Byzantine style and includes a semi-circular apse and pink sandstone columns along with new woodwork – see the pulpit, communion table and screen.

In the 1990s architects Page & Park designed an extension to the south side, overlooking the Water of Leith – this contemporary design marries old and new and reaches out into the woodland.

In the churchyard stands an iron mort-safe, probably dating from the 1820s. This one-tonne object was placed over newly buried bodies to keep body-snatchers at bay.

Edinburgh
Duddingston Kirk

Why visit: *Attractive 12th-century church; restored stained glass*
Where: *Old Church Lane, Duddingston Village, EH15 3PX; restricted opening times, see church website before visiting*

This church has its foundation in the early 12th century, although there were additions in the 17th and 18th centuries. In the late 19th century there was restoration work and this has continued to the present day, with stained glass windows being removed, renovated and replaced in recent years. Remarkable Norman stone carving decorates the arch of the original entrance.

At the entrance to the churchyard there is an octagonal gatehouse intended as a deterrent to body-snatchers in the early 19th century. The Edinburgh body-snatchers of the day notoriously acquired cadavers and sold them to the city medical school.

The church has many associations with the literary and artistic world; the much revered 19th-century minister John Thomson, a notable landscape painter, was a friend of Turner. Walter Scott was an elder at Duddingston and is reported to have worked on his novel *Heart of Midlothian* here. The church stands next to Holyrood Park.

Dalmeny
St Cuthbert

Why visit: *The best preserved example of Romanesque architecture in Scotland*
Where: *Main Street, EH30 9TU*

Dalmeny parish church is a gem of Romanesque architecture, certainly the most complete in Scotland. It was probably constructed around 1160 and, surprisingly, withstood destruction over the centuries, even being left unscathed by the Reformation. The only exception is the tower, which collapsed in the early 1400s and had to wait until 1937 to be rebuilt. However, even this new addition works well. The interior follows the original layout of nave, chancel and apse with marvellous carving on the stone of the arches and column heads.

In 1671 the nearby Earl of Rosebery's family built The Rosebery Aisle, on the north side. This includes a lairds' loft above the main church so the family could follow the service in private.

Linlithgow
St Michael

Why visit: *One of the finest examples of a Scottish medieval burgh church*
Where: *Kirkgate, EH49 7AL; open mornings winter, all day summer*

This page: Colinton Parish Church (left); engraved stonework on the arches at Dalmeny (top); the aluminium crown steeple on St Michael's, Linlithgow (below).

Although the history of St Michael's stretches back to medieval times, it is the unusual lightweight aluminium crown that strikes the visitor first. This was installed in 1964 and took the place of an original crown steeple that was removed in the 1820s.

Stepping inside, the parish church is an impressive size. A church has stood on this site since very early times and the first record of a building dates from the early 12th century. Most of the present building is from the 15th century. It has close connections with Scottish royalty as it stands beside Linlithgow Palace where Mary Queen of Scots was born in 1542; she was baptised in the church. In the mid-1600s Cromwellian soldiers – and their horses – resided in the church and much repair was needed thereafter.

In 1992 a dramatic new window was installed in St Katharine's aisle to commemorate the 750th anniversary of the church. It was designed by the Scottish stained glass expert Crear McCartney on the theme of Pentecost.

Linlithgow St Peter

Why visit. *A miniature Byzantine basilica in a charming Scottish burgh*
Where: *High Street, EH49 7EJ*

St Peter's is very much a church of the people, sitting on the High Street and tucked between a fish-and-chip shop and a hairdresser's. It is a surprise to find this tiny Episcopal church, built in a Byzantine basilica design, looking down towards Linlithgow Loch.

It was built in 1928 as a memorial to George Walpole, Bishop of Edinburgh, and his wife Mildred. Typical of the basilica design, it has a high central dome and a half dome over the apse. The interior is light and cool, with a three-light window over the altar.

The stained glass shows the work of women in the Church, with images of St Margaret of Hungary and St Mildred. Originally, the congregation had been known as St Peter's, but Bishop Walpole dictated that the new church be dedicated to St Mildred. At the church's 50th anniversary, long after the death of the bishop and his wife, the church was renamed St Peter's.

Roslin Rosslyn Chapel

Why visit: *Stunning building, dramatic setting, unsurpassed stone carving*
Where: *Roslin, 6 miles south of the centre of Edinburgh, EH25 9PU*

Work started on this amazing building in the mid-15th century. It was to be a cruciform church with a central tower, part of the college set up by William Sinclair, 3rd Earl of Orkney. From the first it was a very complex conception and so intricate that by the earl's death only part of the building was completed. Little has been added since, with the result that we now see a small chapel rather than a full-scale church.

The interior is spellbinding in its dramatic carving with cascading foliage and flowers, soaring vaulting, angels, knights, gargoyles and Green Men. One of the most famous carvings is that of the Apprentice Pillar. The story goes that the master mason was charged to carve a beautiful pillar based on an actual Italian design; to make sure it was right, he travelled to Italy to see the original. However, in his absence his apprentice completed the work. When the master returned he was amazed, and so furious that he killed the apprentice outright.

The chapel fell into disrepair in the 16th century; in the 1700s it returned to use and restoration continues to this day.

Torphichen
Kirk and Preceptory

Why visit: *Parish kirk alongside ancient Preceptory*
Where: *The Bowyett, EH48 4LT; Preceptory open summer weekends, charges apply; see kirk website for information on opening times*

The history of this unusual site with its two buildings begins in the 12th century when the order of St John of Jerusalem was charged with building a preceptory. Over the years the ownership was transferred to the Knights Hospitaller and the Preceptory is the tower and two transepts of their church. Foundations of other domestic buildings and a cloister used by the order can be seen nearby.

The nave of the Preceptory became the parish church but was demolished in 1756 when the new church was built. The original tower still stands and was re-roofed in 1947.

In the churchyard is an interesting collection of headstones and also a sanctuary stone. This marked the centre of an area of sanctuary of about a square mile – the east and west marker stones can still be seen.

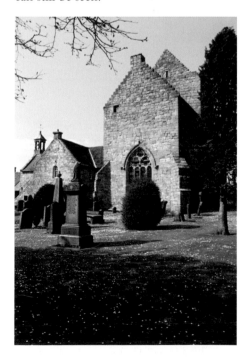

This page: *Intricate carving on the Apprentice Pillar at Rosslyn Chapel (centre); exterior of Torphichen Kirk and Preceptory (above).*

FIFE AND ANGUS

Between the Grampian mountains and the Firth of Forth, Angus and the ancient Kingdom of Fife belong to the gentler lowlands of eastern central Scotland, with their strong maritime links. With its rare Celtic tower, medieval Brechin affords an insight into the time of marauding invaders. Meanwhile, Holy Trinity at St Andrews offers a later segment of history, from the Reformation to the 20th century.

Brechin Brechin Cathedral

Why visit: *Ancient round tower; medieval architecture; 20th-century stained glass*
Where: *Church Lane, DD9 6JS*

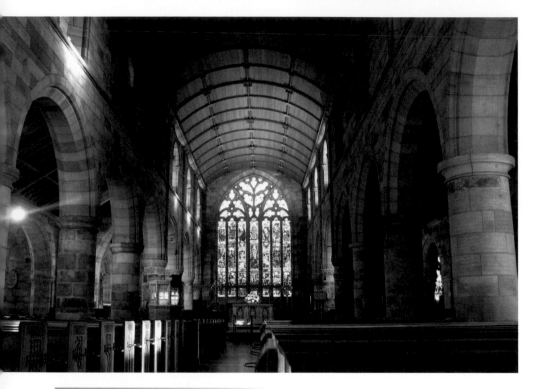

St Andrews Holy Trinity

Why visit: *The town kirk of St Andrews; splendid furnishings*
Where: *South Street, KY16 9UH; open Jun–Sep Mon–Fri 10–4pm, and Oct–May Tue–Fri 10–12pm*

References to Holy Trinity at St Andrews can be traced back over 1,000 years. The oldest parts of the current building are the tower and some of the pillars, which date back to the church built here in 1412. In the 1800s it was considerably altered, but a major restoration in 1909 restored the church to its original floor plan. The architect responsible was Peter MacGregor Chalmers, who was known for his sympathetic historical work.

John Knox, often called the father of Presbyterianism, preached here when the church was 'reformed' from Catholic to Protestant. He is commemorated in the south porch. There is also a grand black-and-white marble monument depicting Archbishop Sharp receiving a crown from heaven. He was assassinated in 1679. The elaborately carved font of Caen stone with figures in the pedestal, and the memorial pulpit carved from Iona marble, alabaster and onyx, are also worthy of note.

The real splendour, however, is in the Arts and Crafts wooden furnishings, with many pieces in the Hunter Memorial Aisle, and the variety of finely executed stained glass by leading artists. Contributors include Douglas Strachan, Herbert Hendrie and William Wilson. The badges of all the Scottish regiments of World War I are set into the clerestory windows.

Further admirable features include the oak barrel roof, a Harrison & Harrison organ, and a 27-bell carillon by Taylor of Loughborough. The operator of this contraption manipulates levers that move the bell hammers to play music.

This ancient church (a cathedral only in name) has many unusual features. Perhaps most intriguing is the rare 11th-century conical tower. It reaches 28m (86ft) and is said to echo aspects of early Irish Celtic design. The tower is 5m (15ft) in diameter and tapers towards the top, yet the interior measures a fairly constant 2.6m (8ft). There are several storeys inside yet few windows. Curiously, the highly decorated doorway is 2m (6ft) above ground level – thought to be a precaution against raids. However, the design may have worked against the occupants if attackers had lit a fire at the base, transforming the tower into a chimney.

The church underwent a major restoration at the turn of the 20th century. It is now an outstanding example of medieval architecture, with a 12th-century font and Pictish sculptures. It is also much visited for its lavish 20th-century stained glass. See Henry Holiday's work in the chancel, and William Wilson's in the clerestory – it is Scotland's largest collection of his glass.

This page: *St Andrews' restored interior (left); Brechin's two towers (above).*

Cortachy Cortachy Church

Why visit: *Attractive church set in the grounds of Cortachy Castle*
Where: *Off the B955, 5 miles north of Kirriemuir, DD8 4QF; open by arrangement*

In a tranquil setting in a green glen and close to the rushing River Esk, Cortachy Church is close to the gates of the castle, to which it belongs. It was designed by David Patterson and built in 1828 by the 7th Earl of Airlie on the site of an older church. Its red sandstone exterior has been worked in Gothic Revival style, with castellations and finials. Although relatively compact, the church can seat 300 people. Inside there are various memorials to Cortachy earls. The burial aisle of the Airlie family is situated against the east gable.

Dundee St Salvador

Why visit: *Colourful interior decoration*
Where: *St Salvador Street, entrance off Carnegie Street, DD3 7EW*

St Salvador's was an early work by the Gothic Revival architect G.F. Bodley. It is constructed of red sandstone and was finished in 1868. The exterior shows its Gothic design, yet inside is where Bodley explored past traditions of stencilling walls and ceilings in vibrant colours, especially in the chancel and apse, where little is not richly decorated in some way. The London firm of Burlison & Grylls painted the chancel arch and created much of the church's stained glass.

Soft greens, warm reds, cream and gold dominate in simple, abstract or naturalistic patterns. The varying harmonious shades and combinations emphasise and link separate areas of the interior. The panelled and gilded reredos that fills the entire east wall cannot be missed. Here is a painted Crucifixion, flanked by 18 further images of apostles, angels, the Virgin and St John, with a detailed scene of the Annunciation depicted above.

The Wordsworth & Maskell organ dates from 1882 and is encased in an ornately gilded and painted frame, in keeping with the rest of the magnificent interior.

Kirriemuir St Mary

Why visit: *Sir Ninian Comper's most accomplished and celebrated Scottish church*
Where: *West Hillbank, north of the centre of Kirriemuir, DD8 4HX*

This church is Scotland's only complete church by the architect Sir Ninian Comper. In St Mary's he delicately combines elements of Gothic, Arts and Crafts, and Scottish Revival style. The church's reddish exterior initially looks somewhat squat, with a relatively short bell tower, but closer inspection reveals a light touch.

The simple interior contains plain pews and a handsome red sandstone font. Apart from one window by William Wilson, all the stained glass is by Comper. His signature strawberry can be found within the panels he designed. This was a tribute to his father, a reverend who died suddenly in Duthie Park, Aberdeen, after buying some fresh strawberries.

J.M. Barrie, the author of *Peter Pan*, was born in the town and one of the windows is dedicated to his family.

Leuchars St Athernase

Why visit: *12th-century Norman church with striking apse and bell tower*
Where: *Main Street, KY16 0HD*

St Athernase has a commanding hilltop position over the town. Thankfully, since its construction in the 12th century, alternating periods of neglect and 'improvement' have not harmed its most distinctive Norman feature: the elaborate 12th-century chancel and apse at the east end. On the exterior the stonemasons created two tiers of blind round-headed arcading and fine wallhead corbels; their

working marks can still be seen. Inside, the chancel arch is beautifully carved with typical Norman patterns enhancing the simple interior. The 18th century saw the addition of the octagonal bell tower, and in 1858 the dilapidated nave was rebuilt for £200. The furnishings are of the early 20th century.

Lochee
The Immaculate Conception (St Mary's)

Why visit: *A Gothic Revival church with a new slant on an old style*
Where: *High Street, DD2 3AP; open by arrangement*

Joseph A. Hansom, also known for designing the taxi-cab, was the architect of this unusual Gothic Revival church with a large octagonal tower and offset presbytery. The interior is of most interest, with grey stone, yellow brick and red sandstone used to create bands of colour within the fabric of the building.

Light is used to great effect. The nave is dark in comparison to the polygonal chancel, which is illuminated by the windows of the tower. The stained glass was commissioned from Franz Mayer & Co of Munich, while A.B. Wall of Cheltenham created the flamboyant altar. The deep floodlit well is an unexpected feature.

This page: The handsome exterior of St Mary's Kirriemuir (centre); the apse and octagonal tower at St Athernase, Leuchars (above).

FARTHER AFIELD

Scotland is such a huge and diverse country that some churches are well off the beaten track, but those included on these two pages are definitely worth a detour. You may need to take a ferry or head down a remote road, but these buildings will be a sure reward.

ABERDEENSHIRE

Arbuthnott St Ternan

Why visit: *Ancient church; peaceful setting*
Where: *On the B967, 3 miles from Inverbervie, AB31 5TB*

A church has stood on this site for centuries, with St Ternan's being designated a parish church by the late 12th century. The exterior appears severe and imposing, and many of the inside walls around the windows are cut at angles to spread the light that enters.

The chancel is the oldest part of the church, dating from the early 13th century. Inside, the mood is softened by plain light walls illuminated by the small lancet windows set with stained glass. The nave is also medieval, or even earlier, but has been much altered over time. The Arbuthnott family aisle and the bell-tower, added in the late 15th century, enhance the church's medieval feel. There are other interesting elements, such as the piscina and stoup, and the fine 19th-century pedal organ.

Kildrummy Kildrummy Church SRCT

Why visit: *Remarkable early 19th-century kirk; historic burial ground.*
Where: *Off the A9, off a single-track road, AB33 8PH; open weekends Apr–Oct*

Kildrummy Church stands within an ancient walled graveyard, shared with the ruins of St Brides, the previous church on this site, and its medieval tombstones date from the 16th century. It may seem strange that these slabs have been arranged in lines and appear to be used as paths around parts of the hillside.

The church was built in 1805 and is a sturdy rectangular building. Its bow front contains a staircase to the centre bellcote. The two intricate Gothic windows are set into the east wall and draw the eye from the exterior. From the interior they frame the pulpit and flood the church with light. The furnishings include a horseshoe gallery set on square columns and plain wooden pews that probably date from the mid-19th century.

ARGYLL AND BUTE

Bowmore, Isle of Islay Kilarrow Parish Church

Why visit: *Rare circular church*
Where: *At the top of the main street, PA43 7JD*

This is one of only two such churches in Scotland. Also known as 'The Round Church', this 18th-century building was commissioned in 1767 by the laird, Daniel Campbell of Shawfield and Islay, with a bow-fronted pew for his family. According to local lore, the circular form of the church was meant to allow 'no corner for the Devil to hide'. Inside, the fascinating supporting structure is left exposed: a sturdy central beam measuring 48cm (19in), with eight principal spokes jointed into it.

Dunoon St John

Why visit: *Gothic church in a resort town*
Where: *Argyll Street, PA23 7AB*

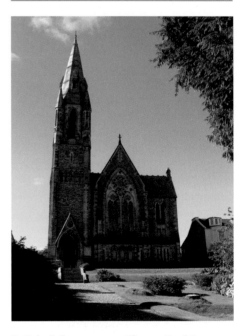

St John's boasts magnificent Gothic Revival architecture, with its impressive tower and spire, and replaced the previous church on the site. Designed by Scottish architect R.A. Bryden, it has stained glass windows by renowned artists Stephen Adam and Gordon Webster. The interior layout resembles a concert hall, with the choir behind the central pulpit in a raised and raked gallery and a horseshoe-shaped gallery for the congregation.

This page: St Ternan's tranquil interior and pedal organ (left); Bowmore's unusual Round Church (centre); Dunoon's Gothic Revival landmark (above).

Dalmally Glenorchy Church

Why visit: *Unusual octagonal church; 16th-century graveyard; idyllic setting*
Where: *On the A85, near the head of Loch Awe, PA33 1AS*

With its whitewashed walls shining brightly against the green hillside behind, this rare octagonal church is particularly striking.

Gothic in design with a four-stage square tower, Glenorchy Church dates from 1811, yet its graveyard contains slabs from the 16th century – relics from a previous church. Members of various Scottish clans lie here, including Campbells, Macgregors, MacIntyres and Macnabs. A U-plan gallery occupies the interior and there is a fine stained glass window from 1898.

DUMFRIES AND GALLOWAY

Dumfries
Crichton Memorial Church

Why visit: *Grand church in parkland*
Where: *The Crichton, Bankend Road, DG1 4UQ; open by arrangement*

This cathedral-style church was completed in 1897 for the patients and staff of Crichton Royal Hospital. Its detailed red sandstone exterior is a match for the elegant interior that is sculpted from pink sandstone. Marble from Ireland and Sicily graces the floors, and other rich furnishings include an oak roof, stone carving by William Vickers of Glasgow, richly carved wood screens and a magnificent organ installed in 1902.

Durisdeer
Durisdeer Church

Why visit: *Elaborate marble monument*
Where: *1 mile east of the A702, 6 miles north of Thornhill, DG3 5BJ*

This sleepy 17th-century parish church, which also served nearby Drumlanrig Castle, houses the baroque white-marble Queensberry Aisle to the second Duke of Queensberry and his wife. By the prolific Flemish sculptor Jan van Nost to a design by the church's architect James Smith, it includes a free-standing baldacchino (canopy) on four barley-twist columns over the reposing couple, against a backdrop of flowers and cherubs.

MORAY

Fochabers Gordon Chapel

Why visit: *Beautiful chapel with stunning stained glass by Arts and Crafts masters; note that at the time of writing the glass is undergoing restoration*
Where: *Castle Street, IV32 7DW*

The Gordon Chapel, named after the Gordon Lennox family who had it built, was erected in 1834. The church itself is above the rectory (a former school). Between 1874 and 1919 the breathtaking stained glass windows were added showing beautiful images of Christ and saints against masses of foliage. Designed by Edward Burne-Jones they were made by Morris & Co.

This page: *Glenorchy's octagonal church (left); stained glass at the Gordon Chapel (above); Sandwick's exposed site (right).*

ORKNEY

Lambholm
The Italian Chapel

Why visit: *Poignant World War II relic*
Where: *Lambholm Island, KW17 2RT; avoid visiting in poor weather as the causeway across to the uninhabited island of Lambholm may be closed*

This chapel was ingeniously created by artist, sculptor and POW Domenico Chiocchetti, and his fellow prisoners, stationed on Lambholm during World War II. They lined two linked Nissen huts with plasterboard and used trompe l'oeil decoration to create incredible stained glass windows, stonework and a ribbed ceiling. The inventiveness and passion of the men also resulted in a beautifully designed concrete altar, brass candlesticks made from stair rods from a wreck, and, outside, a statue of St George fighting a dragon. This was created by covering a barbed wire frame with concrete.

Sandwick
St Peter SRCT

Why visit: *Traditional Presbyterian church in a wild setting*
Where: *Mainland, KW16 3LS; open Apr–Oct 10–6pm*

St Peter's is an exceptional example of an untouched Scottish parish church dating from the early 19th century. It sits on an exposed site and overlooks Skaill Bay. The simple whitewashed building conceals a towering pulpit that faces the pews and galleries. From here the preacher could easily preside over the whole congregation. Two tall round-headed windows face south and flank the pulpit.

GLOSSARY

Here you will find explanations of terminology used to describe church buildings and their history. The illustrations label the main areas and principal features of many churches. For a general overview of church building in Britain through the ages, and descriptions of terms such as Gothic and Perpendicular, see pages 10–17. Refer to the Feature article within each region for explanations and examples of various aspects of church architecture, furniture and churchyards (see Contents).

Typical church plan

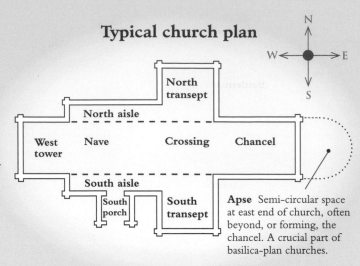

Apse Semi-circular space at east end of church, often beyond, or forming, the chancel. A crucial part of basilica-plan churches.

Ambulatory An aisle around the east end of a church, often the apse.

Anchorite cell Tiny, walled-in space where a recluse would spend his or her life in prayer – they were not allowed out.

Anglo-Catholic Anglican church with Roman Catholic leanings; the building may have more statuary and be more ornate.

Apse Semi-circular space at east end of church, often beyond, or forming, the chancel. A crucial part of basilica-plan churches.

Arcade A series of pillars, columns or piers, often forming a division between nave and aisles.

Ashlar Worked masonry – smoothed and squared.

Aumbrey A niche near the altar for keeping vessels used in worship.

Ball-flower Decorative device of the Decorated period. Similar in shape to the bell on a cat's collar.

Baluster Short, stubby column, very often seen in Saxon windows.

Baroque Late 16th- to 18th-century ornate style of decoration.

Barrel roof or ceiling Wooden roof semi-circular in section rather than flat or triangular.

Basilica A term adopted from Roman architecture and usually used to describe a church plan with a nave and apse.

Battlement Decorative device borrowed from castles. Takes the form of regular square indentations in a parapet.

Beakhead Decorative device used in Norman architecture, most often round doorways. Takes the form of stylised heads of birds, animals, monsters, for example.

Blind arcade A row of arches built directly against a wall and that serve a decorative or strengthening function, unlike arches that can be walked through.

Boss Often highly-decorated wooden or stone device at the intersection of ribs or beams.

Broach spire A spire arising directly from the top of a tower, with no parapet.

Buttress Masonry mass used to support and strengthen walls; can be large or slim.

Byzantine A style echoing that of the (Greek) Orthodox church and characterised by certain features, especially large domes.

Capital Stonework at the top of a pier or column that supports the arch; often highly decorated.

Carillon A set of bells hung for ringing by one person using a keyboard or striking mechanism.

Castellation See Battlement.

Chantry chapel Part of or within a church. A place for prayers for the souls of those who endowed it, who are often buried there.

Chapel A Nonconformist building for worship, or an area within a church or institution with its own separate altar.

Christ's Passion The sufferings of Jesus from the Last Supper to the Crucifixion.

Clerestory Upper storey of nave and occasionally chancel, with many windows (sometimes round) to let in more light.

Clunch Rough and relatively soft stone of chalk or clay used as a building material.

Collegiate church Church created for the support of a college of priests.

Columbarium In churches, a dovecote, often integrated in the tower.

Commonwealth The system and rule of Oliver Cromwell's government, from 1649–1660.

Communion The partaking of the Eucharist by members of the congregation.

Corbel Structural support on a wall for a vault or arch, often treated decoratively. A corbel table is a row of connected corbels – exterior or interior – and at roofline or ceiling height to support the roof.

Crocket Decorative stonework, often in the form of foliage, buds or flowers, protruding from sloping arches, pinnacles, spires and so on.

Crozier A hooked staff carried by a bishop.

Cruciform Church plan in the shape of a cross.

Crypt Chamber below ground level, usually beneath the chancel.

Cupola Domed turret on top of a tower or roof; often a primarily decorative feature.

Dissolution of the Monasteries The disbanding and subsequent selling-off and destruction of monastic buildings and property ordered by Henry VIII.

Doom Painting showing the Day of Judgement. Often above the chancel arch and with graphic scenes of the damned going down to hell, while the souls of the blessed climb up to Heaven.

Early English period The first major period and style of Gothic architecture.

Flushwork Flint 'knapped' (chipped to create flat shiny surfaces) and set into stonework, often in complex patterns.

Flying buttresses Half-arches that link inner and outer walls so as to spread the load of the inner wall to the outer.

Gallery Additional seating space, or area for musicians if at the west end, created by building wooden platforms within the church. Many were inserted in the 18th and early 19th centuries, but later removed in Victorian times.

Gargoyle A water spout, often a carved face or creature, designed to throw water away from the base of the wall.

Golgotha The place where Jesus was crucified; believed to be a small hill outside Jerusalem.

Gothic Architectural period and style, encompassing the Early English, Decorated and Perpendicular periods and styles.

Gothick Usually used to describe an 18th- and early 19th-century blending of Gothic with an English version of Baroque styles.

Gothic Revival Usually used to describe the emulation of original Gothic styles in the 19th century.

Green Man A face among foliage or from which foliage protrudes from the mouth, eyes, ears, etc., usually a carving. Said by some to be a harking-back to pagan times and the worship of nature gods; said by others to be an entirely Christian warning against worldliness.

Hammerbeam A wooden beam projecting from a wall at right angles to support the timbers of the roof. A double hammerbeam is one hammerbeam above another.

Hagioscope See Squint.

Hunky-punks Somerset word for carved faces, monsters and creatures on the exterior of church walls. Also known as grotesques.

Jacobean A period and style of the early 17th century, often typified by ornate woodwork.

King post truss Single vertical post that sits on a roof crossbeam and supports the apex of a triangular construction.

Lady Chapel Dedicated to the Virgin Mary. Often desecrated at the Reformation and after as being 'popish' (Roman Catholic).

Lancet A narrow window, pointed at the top, and usually indicative of the Early English period. Seen in ones, threes, fives and even sevens.

Lantern tower Central tower, often of wood, pierced with openings or windows to allow light down into the space beneath.

Light Window or opening to allow light in; can also be the individual elements contained within a window.

Linenfold panelling Wooden panels emulating the patterns created by hanging fabric.

Long-and-short work Alternating vertical and horizontal masonry pieces at the corner of the church. Typical of Saxon work.

Common church features

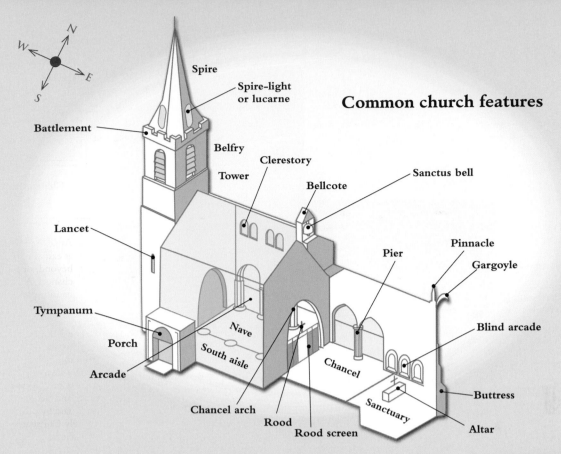

Spire

Spire-light or lucarne

Battlement

Belfry

Tower

Clerestory

Bellcote

Sanctus bell

Lancet

Pinnacle

Gargoyle

Tympanum

Pier

Blind arcade

Porch

Nave

Arcade

South aisle

Chancel

Chancel arch

Rood

Rood screen

Sanctuary

Buttress

Altar

Lychgate Covered gateway at entrance to churchyard; traditionally used to rest the body or coffin on its way to the burial or funeral.

Minster Large church, originally that of a monastery.

Misericord Hinged half-seat, often decorated or with carved scenes, which enabled priests and others to stand supported during long services.

Mitre A bishop's hat.

Mullions Narrow uprights in windows.

Narthex Enclosed porch or vestibule.

Nonconformist Protestant but not within Church of England.

Norman period From 1066 to about 1200.

Ogee-headed The top of an arch that is pointed and with an S-shaped curve on each side.

Parapet Decorative section of walling continuing above the level of the roof line, often battlemented.

Parclose screen A screen dividing a chapel from the rest of the church.

Perpendicular period The last great period of Gothic architecture, ending in the 1530s. Often thought of as the greatest flowering of creativity in church architecture.

Pier Free-standing masonry support for arches or vaulting.

Pillars A less robust type of pier; can be more elegant.

Pilaster strip Typical decorative Saxon stonework in the form of a shallow rectangular column attached to a wall.

Pinnacle Decorative flourish used to top a gable, tower or buttress.

Piscina Stone basin within a niche, nearly always in the chancel. Sometimes with a sedilia.

Poppyhead Decorative top of a bench-end or choir stall in the shape of exuberant foliage.

Pyx The receptacle that is used to store the Eucharist.

Quatrefoil A carved ornament showing four arcs around a centre.

Queen post truss One of a set of vertical posts that sit on a roof crossbeam and supports the roof construction.

Quoins Dressed stones at corner of a church.

Reformation, the The religious revolution begun by Henry VIII in the 16th century. Simplistically, Roman Catholicism was replaced by Protestantism.

Reredos Decorative device behind the altar. Can be of wood, stone or cloth and be very grand indeed, especially in some Victorian churches.

Restoration and restored Two church architectural terms that often mean the building was 'restored' to its supposed Gothic or medieval appearance, with varying sympathy and success.

Retable Structure forming the backdrop to the altar, often with areas for religious and other items.

Rococo An elaborate style of decoration using scrolls and curves.

Romanesque Architectural and decorative style most associated with Norman work.

Rood Christ on the Cross, flanked by the Virgin Mary and St John the Evangelist. All of the original medieval roods were destroyed at the Dissolution. Some were replaced during and after the Victorian era.

Rood screen Carved or painted screen below the rood, dividing nave from chancel. The rood loft supported the rood itself. Sometimes of stone, more often of wood. Their images may have been defaced at the Reformation and/or later.

Rose window Round window often divided into segments by tracery.

Rotunda Circular, often domed, building or room.

Sanctus bell Bell often contained in a small structure at the external junction of nave and chancel. Rung during (Roman Catholic) Mass.

Saxon In church architectural terms the style and buildings before the Norman Conquest of 1066.

Sedilia Decorated, recessed seats for priests, usually three in the chancel and in a line with a piscina.

See Geographical area of authority of a bishop.

Sgraffito A way of producing a decoration by scratching through a surface layer to reveal another colour underneath.

Spandrel Triangular area formed between a pier or column and an arch.

Squint Oblique opening to give a view of the altar from side aisle or exterior of church.

Steeple Tower and spire combined and described as one structure.

Stoup A basin for holy water near the entrance to a church.

Tester A board over the top of a pulpit, designed to amplify the speaker's voice.

Tie-beam roof An open construction of beams supporting diagonal roof rafters.

Tracery Decorative stone- or woodwork, often in the upper parts of windows or in screens.

Trefoil A carved ornament showing three arcs around a centre.

Vault(ing) Arched roof or ceiling built of stone, brick or timber. Fan vaults are the most complex and decorative.

Tympanum The area between a door lintel and the shaped arch above it.

Vesica A shape created by interlocking circles to create an almond-shaped halo.

Wagon roof or ceiling See Barrel roof or ceiling.

251

NATIONAL CHURCHES TRUST CONTACTS

This guide has been made possible with the help and guidance of a number of the Trusts detailed below. Their intimate knowledge of the churches, chapels and meeting houses in the regions they care for, coordinated by the National Churches Trust, forms the basis of the tours featured in the guide.

All of the Trusts listed on this page work tirelessly to support both our nation's church buildings and those charged with their care. The majority of the Trusts listed here provide grants to eligible church buildings in their area. For details of how they can help you and their own grants eligibility, visit their websites as indicated.

Most of the Trusts also participate in the annual sponsored *Ride & Stride* event, which offers a fun-filled day to people of all ages and abilities. It is a fund-raising event, providing much-needed money to restore and protect historic churches. Visit www.rideandstride.org for more details about this event.

Caring for churches across England

Bedfordshire and Hertfordshire Historic Churches Trust www.bedshertshct.org.uk or email general.enquiry@bedshertshct.org.uk

Royal County of Berkshire Churches Trust www.berkschurchestrust.org.uk or email secretary@berkschurchestrust.org.uk

Buckinghamshire Historic Churches Trust www.bucks-historic-churches.org or email info@bucks-historic-churches.org

Cambridgeshire Historic Churches Trust www.cambshistoricchurchestrust.co.uk or email secretary@cambshistoricchurchestrust.co.uk

Historic Cheshire Churches Preservation Trust www.hccpt.org

Cornwall Historic Churches Trust www.chct.org.uk or email mail@chct.info

Churches Trust for Cumbria www.ctfc.org.uk, email info@ctfc.org.uk or write to Enterprise House, Gillan Way, Penrith, CA11 9BP

Derbyshire Churches and Chapels Preservation Trust www.derbyshirehistoricbuildings.org.uk or email dccpt@dhbt.clara.net

Devon Historic Churches Trust www.devonhistoricchurches.co.uk

Dorset Historic Churches Trust www.dorsethistoricchurchestrust.org.uk

Friends of Essex Churches Trust www.foect.org.uk

Gloucestershire Historic Churches Trust www.ghct.org.uk or email news@ghct.org.uk

Hampshire and the Islands Historic Churches Trust www.hampshirehistoricchurches.org.uk or email sec@hihct.org.uk

Herefordshire Historic Churches Trust www.herefordhistoricchurchestrust.org.uk

Friends of Kent Churches www.friendsofkentchurches.co.uk

Leicestershire Historic Churches Trust www.lhct.org.uk or email chairman@lhct.org.uk

Lincolnshire Churches Trust www.easishop.com/lct email secloct@btinternet.com or write to: Lincolnshire Churches Trust, PO Box 195, Lincoln, LN6 9XR

Greater Manchester Churches Preservation Trust www.manchesterchurches.btck.co.uk

Norfolk Churches Trust www.norfolkchurchestrust.co.uk or email secretary@norfolkchurchestrust.org.uk

Northamptonshire Historic Churches Trust www.nhct.org.uk

Northumbria Historic Churches Trust www.northumbriahct.org.uk or email Secretary@NorthumbriaHCT.org.uk

Nottinghamshire Historic Churches Trust www.nottshistoricchurchestrust.org.uk or email nhct@hotmail.co.uk

Oxfordshire Historic Churches Trust www.ohct.org.uk

Romney Marsh Historic Churches Trust www.cantab.net/user/n.p.hudd.64/romneyma.htm or email sec@romneychurches.net

Rutland Historic Churches Preservation Trust www.rhcpt.co.uk or email rhcptrust@googlemail.com

Shropshire Historic Churches Trust www.shropshirehct.org.uk

Friends of Somerset Churches and Chapels www.fscandc.org.uk

Staffordshire Historic Churches Trust www.staffordshirehistoricchurchestrust.org

Suffolk Historic Churches Trust www.shct.org.uk

Surrey Churches Preservation Trust www.surreychurchespreservationtrust.org

Sussex Historic Churches Trust www.sussexhistoricchurches.org.uk

Warwickshire and Coventry Historic Churches Trust www.warwickshirechurches.org.uk

Wiltshire Historic Churches Trust www.wiltshirehistoricchurches.org.uk

Worcestershire and Dudley Historic Churches Trust www.worcestershirechurches.blogspot.com

Yorkshire Historic Churches Trust www.yhct.org.uk or email YHCT@ferreyandmennim.co.uk

Caring for churches in London

Heritage of London Trust www.heritageoflondon.com or email info@heritageoflondon.com Alternatively, you can telephone 01981 550 747 or write to: Heritage of London Trust, 34 Grosvenor Gardens, London, SW1W 0DH

Friends of City Churches www.london-city-churches.org.uk or email contact_us@london-city-churches.org.uk Alternatively, you can telephone 020 7626 1555 or write to: The Friends of the City Churches, The Church of St Magnus the Martyr, Lower Thames Street, London, EC3R 6DN

Caring for churches in Scotland and Wales

Scottish Churches Architectural Heritage Trust www.scaht.org.uk or email info@scaht.org.uk Alternatively, you can telephone 0131 225 8644 or write to: Scottish Churches Architectural Heritage Trust, 15 North Bank Street, Edinburgh, EH1 2LP

Scotland's Churches Scheme www.sacredscotland.org.uk Alternatively, you can telephone 01355 302416 or write to: The Director, Scotland's Churches Scheme, Dunedin, Holehouse Road, Eaglesham, Glasgow, G76 0FJ

For information about organisations caring for church buildings in Wales, please visit www.nationalchurchestrust.org

Caring for churches no longer open for regular worship in England and Wales

Churches Conservation Trust www.visitchurches.org.uk or email central@tcct.org.uk Alternatively, you can telephone 020 7213 0660 or write to: 1 West Smithfield, London, EC1A 9EE

Friends of Friendless Churches www.friendsoffrienndlesschurches.org.uk or email office@friendsoffriendlesschurches.org.uk Alternatively, you can telephone 020 7236 3934 or write to: St Ann's Vestry Hall, 2 Church Entry, London, EC4V 5HB

Historic Chapels Trust www.hct.org.uk or email chapels@hct.org.uk Alternatively, you can telephone 020 7481 0533 or write to: St George's German Lutheran Church, 55 Alie Street, London, E1 8EB

Many of these organisations are managed by volunteers and are reliant on donations and your participation in their events to continue their valuable work. For more details on how to help these Trusts, and how they may be able to help church buildings in your area, please visit the websites provided above.

For further details of other organisations helping these buildings across the UK please visit the National Churches Trust website: www.nationalchurchestrust.org

---

Church opening times

The Churches Conservation Trust, Friends of Friendless Churches, and Historic Chapels Trust all have opening times on their websites – see above for contact details. As well as official websites of church and chapel organisations, there are a number of excellent websites run by enthusiasts. Often, these cover specific counties and/or are dedicated to aspects of church architecture, and they can be a great source of detailed information.

www.achurchnearyou.com Church of England website
www.churchmonumentssociety.org searchable site covering UK
www.findachurch.co.uk UK wide
www.openchurchestrust.org.uk provides opening times and contact details for about 300 member churches across England and Wales

INDEX

Page numbers shown in italic indicate a key church in a tour.

PICTURE CREDITS

The Autombile Association would like to thank the following photographers and picture libraries for their assistance in the preparation of this book. Every effort has been made to contact the copyright holders, and we apologise in advance for any accidental errors. We would be happy to apply the corrections in the following edition of this book. Abbreviations for the picture credits are as follows – (t) top; (b) bottom; (c) centre; (l) left; (r) right.